INSTITUTE OF ADVANCED LEGAL STUDIES | SCHOOL OF ADVANCED STUDY UNIVERSITY OF LONDON



**THE LEGAL RECORDS AT RISK PROJECT**

Project patrons: William Twining, Professor of Jurisprudence Emeritus, UCL and Avrom Sherr, Emeritus Professor, IALS

# Legal Records at Risk

## A strategy for safeguarding our legal heritage

Clare Cowling

Associate Research Fellow, IALS and Director, Legal Records at Risk project

2019

First published 2019


ISBN 978-1-911507-14-7 (paperback edition)

ISBN 978-1-911507-15-4 (PDF edition)

DOI: 10.14296/919.9781911507154

University of London Press

Institute of Advanced Legal Studies
Charles Clore House
17 Russell Square
London
WC1B 5DR

Email: ials@sas.ac.uk



Cover image: Official/shutterstock.com

# Contents

# Foreword

William Twining[1]

This report is the culmination of a three year project on private sector legal records at risk in England at Wales. It summarises the work of this project and its predecessors, diagnoses the problems of preservation of archives in the legal sector in England and Wales and outlines a national strategy for such records, which we hope will form part of a national strategy for private sector records generally to be developed by The National Archives (TNA). The appendices, together with the project website (http://ials.sas.ac.uk/research/areas-research/legal-records-risk-lrar-project) bring together a unique collection of detailed information about legal institutions and their records.

Clare Cowling is the sole author of this report. An experienced archivist and records manager who has worked in several parts of the legal sector over many years, Clare has been the part-time Director of the LRAR project for three years, working with minimal assistance, but consulting widely. The report is evidence of her energy, enthusiasm, efficiency and deep understanding of the issues. 'Legal records' sounds like a dry, esoteric, fustian subject concerned with ancient deeds and dead disputes, but she manages to show that its fascination, complexity and practical importance are of critical concern in the digital age. Although pragmatic and sensible, she works more in the spirit of Arlette Farge's *The Allure of the Archives*[2] than of Dickens.

There were three original concerns behind the LRAR project. First, that many potentially valuable private sector records of legal institutions have been destroyed or otherwise lost or are now at risk, without anyone other than the holders being responsible and with many holders of such records being unaware of, apathetic about or lacking the capacity to preserve them. With a few exceptions, survival has so far been a matter of inconsequential serendipity. Second, in ordinary usage the concept of 'legal records' has been largely restricted to court records, land records and formal legal documents such as deeds; similarly the concept of 'lawyers' has been confined almost entirely to barristers, solicitors and judges, leaving records of several kinds of providers of legal services (e.g. legal executives, licensed conveyancers) and many other law-related institutions only very rarely preserved. Third, in a period of radical, possibly revolutionary change, including especially the creation of digital records, the amount of public funding available for preservation has seriously eroded.

The LRAR project represents an attempt to respond to these concerns by laying the ground for a more systematic approach by using 'institutions specialised to law (ISLs)' as a broader organising concept with a focus of attention that goes beyond official records and state-centric perspectives to include, for example, arbitration, law publishers and the business records of solicitors; and by focusing the project more on modern and contemporary records (including 'born-digital' ones) since 1900.

Several themes run through the report: perhaps the most important is that archives are one aspect of records management, which in turn is one aspect of information management; that records management is a process that should start with the initial creation of a record (e.g. minutes, emails), that this 'cradle to grave' (or archival 'heaven') approach requires the services of trained professionals (archivists/records managers); that these services are cost-effective and different from 'archiving' by IT specialists; and that within the legal sector there is a general lack of awareness of and indifference to these points.

We found it startling that so few institutions in the legal sector have professional records managers or archivists on their staff or at least employ them as consultants to help set up efficient systems and retention schedules, as we did in the case of one law publisher. One of the by-products of LRAR was to produce seven guidelines for legal institutions summarising current recordkeeping advice and making further recommendations on how to achieve maximum business benefit from managing and archiving records appropriately. The long-term preservation of records (archiving) is just one aspect of records management. It is not merely of academic interest to historians and other scholars. It is of practical importance to the institutions themselves in terms of efficiency, ethos, brand image and the occasional valuable treasure trove. It is in the public interest.

There are some potential areas of controversy in this report. For example, it highlights a great divide between the perceptions of the legal community and archivists about confidentiality, data protection and transparency in relation to archives. Early on we encountered the view that an archive of records of arbitration is unthinkable: a main function of arbitration is to avoid publicity; all participants are bound in perpetuity by confidentiality clauses; often even the very occurrence of an arbitration is meant to be secret. Yet Derek Roebuck's extensive work on the history of arbitration relies heavily on archival sources; the catalogue of Transport for London's (TfL) Corporate Archives lists over 291 'arbitration' entries, mainly cases to which TfL was a party, with further arbitration material catalogued under 'disputes' or 'contracts'.

1 FBA, QC, FASS, Quain Professor of Jurisprudence Emeritus, University College London; member of Executive Committee of LRAR

2 Arlette Farge, *The Allure of the Archives*, Yale University Press, 1989.

Subject to normal safeguards, such as Data Protection, nearly of these are, or will be, accessible to the public after twenty years. A recent search of *Discovery*, the wonderful TNA search engine that covers over 2,500 repositories, revealed over 25,000 hits just for 'arbitration', even though the catalogues of many non-government archives, such as those of TFL, have not yet been included in *Discovery*.

There is a puzzle here: maybe part of it can be dissolved by making a clear distinction between individual and family records, where privacy is an important concern, and most business and administrative records for which confidentiality concerns can usually be satisfied by short-term restrictions, like the archival practice of initially limiting access for 20 years or more. This is a complex area. One priority for the future is a project on confidentiality, data protection and transparency in relation to archives.

Another controversial area concerns records seized under the disciplinary powers of the Solicitors Regulation Authority (SRA) ('interventions'). It has been reported that very large quantities of solicitors' records have been stored in the SRA's Intervention Archives warehouse[3]. Many have been destroyed, but the accumulation is continually renewed. Intervention is a highly controversial, sensitive, and costly process and it is hardly surprising that preserving records of historical value is not a high priority for the SRA. Despite the cost, it has made attempts to deposit some records with local authority archives, yet there is still a major problem. The crux of the matter is that this a heritage issue rather than a regulatory one and only a major project requiring substantial funding, probably with major contributions from private sector sources, could clear the backlog and rescue records of real historical value.

To end with some good news: the LRAR project has sufficient funding to continue until the summer of 2019; a pilot project designed to assist those concerned with facilitating proactive approaches to identifying and preserving private sector records has been supported by a grant from UCL Laws; a special interdisciplinary project of confidentiality and data protection in relation to records of institutions specialised to law is under consideration, and some additional funding may be available to continue LRAR on a modest scale indefinitely. We are still in business. But more will be needed to sustain LRAR in the future. This is a long-term problem which needs sustainable solutions, perhaps assisted by a Legal Records Trust.

3 'Based on interventions over the last 20 years, the historic average number of archive files was 4,000/5,000 files. With interventions into larger firms, we are seeing unprecedented numbers of archived files – on one intervention this year, we took possession of some 450,000 files.' (SRA consultation paper, *File retention following an intervention into a firm*, 14 October 2013 http://www.sra.org.uk/sra/consultations/file-retention-post-intervention.page)

# Acknowledgements

The Legal Records at Risk project Director and Executive Committee wish to express our thanks to the following organisations and individuals who generously gave their time to assist and inform the project:

- Providers of financial support for associated studies into legal records at risk: the UCL Laws Emeritus Fund for financing two small scale projects on legal records in Oxfordshire and the Chartered Institute of Arbitrators for funding a feasibility study on records of international commercial arbitration.
- The members of the LRAR Advisory Panel, who generously gave of their time and expertise to assist the project: Penny Baker, Sir Ross Cranston, Clive Freedman, Philip Gale, Michael Lobban, Julie McLeod, Michael Maher, Antonia Moon, Linda Mulcahy, Juliet Oliver, Martin Partington, Murray Rosen, Judith Slinn, Richard Wiltshire, Jane Winters and Philip Wood.
- National archive bodies: AIM25 (Archives in London and the M25 area), especially Sarah Aitchison; the British Records Association, especially Penny Baker and Nat Alcock; the Chief Archivists in Local Government Group, especially Sarah Chubb; the Information and Records Management Society, especially Fiona Kearney; The National Archives, especially Philip Gale, Alex Ritchie and Fleur Soper; the Pensions Archive Trust, especially Alan Herbert and Jane Marshall.
- Local/specialist archives: the Archives and Libraries of the Inns of Court, especially Celia Pilkington and Margaret Clay; Derbyshire Record Office, especially Sarah Chubb (again); Devon Archives and Local Studies Service, especially Stuart Tyler; Gloucestershire Archives, especially Julie Courtenay; the London Metropolitan Archives, especially Richard Wiltshire; the Oxfordshire History Centre, especially Mark Priddey; the Records of Legal Education Archives, especially Sian Astill; the London School of Economics Archives, especially Anna Towlson; the Surrey History Centre, especially Mike Page; the Transport for London Corporate Archives and Legal department, especially Melissa McGreechan and Jonathan Morris.
- Legal institutions: the Centre for Effective Dispute Resolution, especially Karl Mackie; Chadwick Lawrence Solicitors, especially Emma Ferguson; the Council for Licensed Conveyancers, especially Stephen Ward; The Law Society and Michael Maher in particular; the Solicitors Regulation Authority, especially Maria Gibson; the Worshipful Company of Arbitrators, especially Gill Rushton.
- Academic institutions: the Centre for Socio-Legal Studies, especially Bettina Lange; the Institute of Historical Research, especially Jane Winters; University College London and Elizabeth Lomas in particular.
- Individual legal practitioners, academic historians and archivists: John Baker; Peter Bartlett; Tracey Calvert; Charlotte Clements; Becky Fanning; Denis Galligan; Rosemary Hunter; Nicholas le Poidevin; Michael Lobban; Lindsay McCormack, Lawrence McNamara; Jane Marshall; Richard Moorhead; Michael Moss; Linda Mulcahy; Renato Nazzini; Timothy Pitt-Payne; Michael Reynolds; Derek Roebuck; Murray Rosen; Alan Shipman; Maria Sienkiewicz; Judy Slinn; Lisa Webley.

A special thanks to those individuals who kindly reviewed and made excellent suggestions on how to improve, this book: Penny Baker, Michael Lobban, Elizabeth Lomas, Derek Roebuck, David Sugarman, Steven Whittle and Jules Winterton. And of course to William Twining, the inspiration behind the project and its guiding light.

# Acronyms and abbreviations

| | |
|---|---|
| AAA | American Arbitration Association |
| ABS | Alternative business structure |
| ACAS | Advisory, Conciliation and Arbitration Service |
| ACCA | Association of Chartered Certified Accountants |
| ADR | Alternative dispute resolution |
| AIIM | Association for Information and Image Management |
| AIM25 | Archives in London and the M25 area |
| ARA | Archives and Records Association |
| ARMA | Association for Research Managers and Administrators |
| BAC | Business Archives Council |
| BRA | British Records Association |
| BSB | Bar Standards Board |
| CALGG | Chief Archivists in Local Government Group |
| CEDR | Centre for Effective Dispute Resolution |
| CHS | Construction History Society |
| CIArb | Chartered Institute of Arbitrators |
| CILEx | Chartered Institute of Legal Executives |
| CLC | Council for Licensed Conveyancers |
| CMC | Civil Mediation Council |
| CPD | Continuing professional development |
| CPS | Crown Prosecution Service |
| CSLS | Centre for Socio-Legal Studies |
| DANGO | Database of Archives of Non-Governmental Organisations |
| EU | European Union |
| FOI | Freedom of Information |
| GDPR | General Data Protection Regulation |
| HE | Higher education |
| HMC | Historic Manuscripts Commission |
| HR | Human Resources |
| IALS | Institute of Advanced Legal Studies |
| ICA | International Court of Arbitration |
| ICC | International Chamber of Commerce |
| ICO | Information Commissioner's Office |
| ICSID | International Centre for Settlement of Investment Disputes |
| IRM | Information and records management |
| IRMS | Information and Records Management Society |
| ISL | Institution specialised to law |
| IT | Information technology |
| JPEG | Joint Photographic Experts Group (electronic image file) |
| KCL | King's College London |
| LLP | Limited Liability Partnership |
| LMA | London Metropolitan Archives |
| LRAR | Legal Records at Risk project |
| LSB | Legal Services Board |

| | |
|---|---|
| LSE | London School of Economics |
| MD | Managing Director |
| NGO | Non-Governmental Organisation |
| NHS | National Health Service |
| PAT | Pensions Archive Trust |
| PDF | Portable document format |
| PPT | Powerpoint format |
| PR | Public Relations |
| RICS | Royal Institution of Chartered Surveyors |
| RLEA | Records of Legal Education Archives |
| RPS | Records Preservation Section of the BRA |
| RTF | Rich text format |
| SAS | School of Advanced Study |
| SCA | Society of Construction Arbitrators |
| SLSA | Socio-Legal Studies Association |
| SRA | Solicitors Regulation Authority |
| TfL | Transport for London |
| TLS | The Law Society |
| TNA | The National Archives |
| UCL | University College London |
| UK | United Kingdom |
| UNESCO | United Nations Educational, Scientific and Cultural Organisation |
| USB | Universal serial bus |
| VAT | Value Added Tax |

# Glossary of terms

- Accession: material that comes into an archives as a gift, deposit or purchase; ownership or copyright may be legally transferred. A number of accessions may form one single collection with shared provenance e.g. the records of a business may be transferred to an archives over time.
- Alternative business structure (ABS): an entity that, while providing regulated reserved legal activities, allows non-lawyers to own or invest in law firms for the first time.
- Archive/archives: in the traditional definition the term 'archive/s' ('archives' can be either singular or plural), refers both to the repository where records of permanent value are stored and made available for research and to the records stored in it, comprising materials in any format created or received by a person, family, or organisation, public or private, in the conduct of their affairs and preserved because of the enduring value of the information they contain or as evidence of the functions and responsibilities of their creator.
- Archive repository: a professionally managed archive of records of permanent value made publicly available for research such as The National Archives (TNA).
- Archiving: the selection/appraisal, accessioning, storage and preservation, arrangement and description and provision of access to records of permanent value for all types of research through inspection and publication. Archiving should be distinguished from long-term, but finite, retention of records to support current business or legal requirements and should not be confused with sending records to cheaper offsite storage or moving data from a live system. The appropriation and indiscriminate use of the term by the Information Technology (IT) sector and most third-party records storage companies is a cause of much confusion.
- Born-digital records: records created in a digital format, as opposed to physical records that have been converted into a digital format (e.g. by scanning).
- Data: facts and statistics collected together for reference or analysis.
- Deaccessioning: the process by which a record is permanently removed from an archival collection.
- In-house archives: an archive repository of records of permanent value (often, but not always on-site) managed by the creating or inheriting institution or individual. Not to be confused with the allocation of a storage area for records no longer in regular use.
- Legal institution: any institution specialised to law, including: those providing legal services such as law firms and firms (including sole practitioners) of barristers' chambers, legal executives, licensed conveyancers, notaries, patent attorneys, trade mark attorneys, will writers; providers of ancillary legal services such as legal publishers and law stationers; legal charities; legal education and training institutions; legal membership associations and legal regulatory bodies.
- Legal instrument: any formally executed written document that can be formally attributed to its author, records and formally expresses a legally enforceable act, process or contractual duty, obligation, or right and therefore evidences that act, process, or agreement. Examples include deeds and wills.
- Legal records: all the records of any institution (or individual) specialised to law, including business records such as policy material, financial records, membership files, consultation papers and client records such as case/matter files, client documents and legal instruments. The term also encompasses the records of company legal departments and the papers of individual legal practitioners and academic researchers.
- Original documents: a term used by the legal profession to describe client documents deposited with a law firm e.g. deeds, wills, passports.
- Private sector: the part of a country's economy which consists of industries and commercial companies that are not owned or controlled by the government.
- Recordkeeping: the maintenance of a history of one's activities e.g. entering data; filing.
- Records: information, in any form, created, received and maintained as evidence and information by an organisation in pursuance of legal obligations or in the transaction of business.
- Records at risk: any record, regardless of format, whose future preservation, accessibility and security is uncertain, particularly records held outside of a recognised collecting archive institution, but not excluding records at risk from institutional failure of the record creator or the current custodian.

- Records disposal: the process of *either* destroying records once they no longer have any business or legal value *or* depositing them in an archive for permanent retention.
- Records management: the field of management responsible for the efficient and systematic control of the creation, receipt, maintenance, use and disposition of records, including the processes for capturing and maintaining evidence of and information about business activities and transactions in the form of records.
- Records store: in some large organisations (such as government departments or big businesses) the records store, as distinct from the archives, is a secure repository for semi-current records pending their disposal, as opposed to records of permanent value which are stored separately in an archives. In a number of organisations however, the two functions of semi-current records store and archives are combined for economy of effort and the term 'archive' or 'archives' is used to refer to both.
- Semi-current records: records which are no longer needed for day-to-day use but are still required for occasional business reference or which must be kept for a period of time by law before being destroyed.

# Introduction

> Archives sit at the heart of our collective understanding: who we are, where we came from, and, indeed, where we are going....Without records, we could not prove where and when we were born, or who owns the property we live in. We could not trace our ancestry, explore our collective and individual identities, or challenge established views of the past...without this collective memory – the evidence store for our histories – we could not hold governments and organisations to account.[1]

The Legal Records at Risk (LRAR) three-year project at the Institute of Advanced Legal Studies sought to facilitate the rescue for posterity of private sector legal records of archival value in England and Wales. Guided by an Executive Committee and Advisory Panel of experts in the fields of law, academic research and archives/records management,[2] it took as its starting point the famous legal historian F.W. Maitland's statement that:

> Legal documents, documents of the most technical kind, are the best, often the only evidence that we have for social and economic history, for the history of morality, for the history of practical religion.[3]

Taking as its definition of legal records *all the records of any institution (or individual) specialised to law, including business records such as policy material, financial records, membership files, consultation papers and client records such as case/matter files, client documents and legal instruments and including the records of company legal departments and the papers of individual legal practitioners and academic researchers*, the project focused on 20th- and 21st-century records, beginning with the assumption that legal records created in this period risk being lost. This risk is not only due to universal factors affecting all private sector records such as globalisation, mergers and acquisitions, digital obsolescence and neglect but because of issues potentially unique to the legal sector such as an over-emphasis on long-term client confidentiality, a lack of transparency about how the profession conducts its affairs and a very low awareness of information as an asset. This publication documents our achievements vis a vis the original project objectives and shows where further action research and a wider, truly national strategy is needed to fulfil the original vision of the project.

Five themes emerged during the course of the project:

1. The importance of good information and records management in a digital age. Records management training for staff and the employment of professionals to manage records management and archiving programmes are urgently needed, especially in the legal sector, where awareness is low of a) records as an asset b) the business benefits of good records management in terms of cost-effectiveness, efficiency, reputation and value to the institution and potential users and c) the assumption that 'archiving' records is purely about storage cost. Archiving records of value and destroying the dross are, on the contrary, the end products of records management, not only reducing costs but enhancing compliance and providing tangible benefits in terms of branding, public relations and reputation.
2. The special issues around rescuing digital records. Digital obsolescence, digital corruption, records duplication and poor controls for creating and storing records combined with the sheer quantity of records held in digital systems work against good management and archiving. While many organisations have procedures for the disposal of paper records (by destruction or archiving), many more have not yet considered how to manage the same procedures for records in digital form. Legal institutions on the whole are still quite wedded to the paper record so may ignore their digital counterparts, with consequences such as non-compliance, excess storage costs and eventual loss of access to information.
3. The disconnect between the legal, archives and research sectors over defining confidentiality. The legal sector in the main appears to conflate business confidentiality with protection of personal data under the umbrella of its obligation to protect client confidentiality and seems to think that this obligation persists in perpetuity. It does not seem to be aware that business secrets have a shorter life than personal data and that archives have a long history of experience in protecting both for as long as is required both in law and by depositors before allowing access (either restricted or open as appropriate) for research purposes. Academic researchers,

1 The National Archives: *Archives Unlocked: releasing the potential of our archives* (TNA, 2017) http://www.nationalarchives.gov.uk/documents/archives/Archives-Unlocked-Brochure.pdf.

2 See **Appendix I: Legal records at Risk Advisory Panel and Executive Committee members.**

3 F.W.Maitland, 'Why the History of English Law is not Written', reprinted in *Collected Legal Papers* I.480 (ed. H.A.L. Fisher, 1911).

too, are well aware of the need to undertake agreements to protect personal data or any other confidentiality requirements before being given access to information which is not generally available.[4]

4. The under-utilisation of legal records (other than court records and deeds) for research by users.[5] The research potential of legal records is very varied, so users need to be more aware of the extent, value and availability of legal records, contemporary and semi-current as well as those in archives. Potential users also need to know about the use and limitations of modern search engines such as The National Archives' (TNA) *Discovery*. It is in the interest of users to make their needs known and to actively support policies designed to preserve records of all kinds including legal records.
5. The need to identify and prioritise categories of legal records that are especially at risk. We found the following to be particularly endangered:
   - Legal records of relevance to a particular geographical area or specialist research interests respectively, previously collected by local authority and higher education (HE) archives.[6] These archives are now facing severe cuts in resources and, sometimes, lack of support from their own managing bodies, reducing their ability to continue to take in records outside their core collections policies. Thus there is no guarantee that more recent records of legal institutions which have been collected in the past or those of newer legal bodies will be preserved.
   - Records of legal institutions and professionals with a national focus based outside Greater London have no obvious archival repository in which to deposit records.[7]
   - Legal institutions themselves, with some shining exceptions,[8] are not maintaining in-house archives in the true sense and are avoiding making decisions on disposal of their own records. The records of membership/training/consultancy bodies and legal regulators are especially at risk.

The project sought two strategic solutions to the problems identified:

1. Many of the factors which cause private sector (including legal) records to be at risk are beyond the capacity of one short-term project to resolve and require a national, archives sector-led, strategy to save such records for posterity. We therefore collaborated with historical research and archive institutions such as TNA and the British Records Association (BRA) towards developing a national strategy to rescue private sector records at risk, including legal records. In doing so we additionally hoped to open the eyes of research communities to the rich, albeit often randomly gathered, harvest of legal records already available for research and alert them to what may be lost in the future without systematic preservation policies and practices.
2. We also attempted to raise the awareness of the legal sector of the potential value of its archives, not only for legal history but for national, local, social, diversity and genealogical research. We pointed out the value of the records as a business asset to legal organisations themselves in terms of compliance, public relations, branding, marketing, transparency and community engagement. We provided records management guidance aimed specifically at the legal sector and asked that it recognise both the historic and current importance of legal practice and policy to our national development and heritage by supporting the creation of a Legal Archives Trust to facilitate the rescue of legal records at risk.

In developing these strategic solutions the project also made a number of specific recommendations:

- The primary responsibility for records management, including the preservation and disposal of their records should normally rest with the private sector legal organisations themselves. Insofar, however, that many of these records are a potentially significant part of our national heritage, it is in the public interest that legal institutions and archives should collaborate and co-operate to facilitate the preservation of records of value.
- It is in the interests of the academic community and other potential users of legal records to take

4 The use of anonymised medical data for research being one obvious example.

5 Currently the main users of legal records, as far as we can tell, are genealogists and legal historians: the latter are few in number compared to researchers in other fields of history. LRAR's contention is that legal records (using our definition) have value for a huge variety of research fields – historical, social, geographical, local, national, political and for gender, race and diversity studies.

6 For details of records collected see **Appendix II: Legal records which are *not* at risk.**

7 See **Appendix III: Private sector legal institutions whose records might be at risk.**

8 See **Appendix IV: Dedicated 'legal' archives in England and Wales.**

an active role in monitoring archival collections policies and practice by fostering awareness of the scholarly value of many kinds of legal records and lobbying for their preservation.

- There needs to be an in-depth study of issues around confidentiality to resolve the concerns of the legal sector. The legal regulators should take the lead here.
- The legal sector should continue to be lobbied to understand the importance of its records not only for its own business benefit but for the safeguarding of our national heritage and to allocate resources to the management of its records and the preservation of those of value accordingly.
- The archives and records management community should be proactively advocating the benefits of good records management and preservation of archives to the private sector.

Clare Cowling, LRAR Project Director

# Chapter 1: Are private sector records more at risk than in the past?

The LRAR project was based on the premise that this is indeed the case. The following reports support the premise and were the starting point for LRAR.

## 1.1 The National Archives' 2009 report on business archives

The National Archives' *National Strategy for Business Archives* made the point that in England and Wales there is no unified approach to managing business records for historical development combined with very limited statutory requirements to maintain business archives. TNA has major holdings of business records largely generated by British industries nationalised in the 20th century, but the acquisition of private sector business records is beyond its statutory duty. This means that, unless businesses set up their own in-house archives, the preservation for posterity of business archives, which include the records of institutions specialised to law, is dependent on the capacity and willingness of local authority, HE or specialist archives to collect them.

TNA summarised the risks to business records thus:[1]

- Lack of professional staff. Only a tiny minority of British companies employ professional archivists and records managers to manage their records and therefore destruction decisions are often taken by company employees untrained in recordkeeping.
- Failing business. There is currently no systematic provision or guidance at national or local level for the records of failing businesses; records rescue work is ad hoc and reactive.
- Statutory limitations. There is no legislative requirement to keep records of historical interest even though they deliver cultural and socio-economic memory for future generations. Companies routinely destroy records, as they are often perceived as a liability to store and to make available for legal discovery. The Data Protection Act[2] is also often misinterpreted as an instruction to destroy any records that contain personal data.
- Provision for 21st-century companies. There is no clear picture of how the records of new companies, in particular internet-based companies, are being managed.
- Electronic records. While paper documentation of 19th- and 20th-century companies can be managed retrospectively, the electronic legacy generated in the recent past defies retrospective management and there is a serious risk of loss of born-digital company records of archival value. This issue needs to be addressed across the profession.

All of the above risks apply to legal records in the private sector. In the eight years since this report was published very little appears to have changed, other than steadily decreasing funding for archives leading to a reduced ability to proactively or reactively collect records.

## 1.2 The British Records Association's 2012 report on records at risk

The BRA's *Records at Risk* report emphasised that significant records of many private sector institutions, including legal, are at risk due to the worsening financial climate for archives combined with the proliferation of new forms of recordkeeping. The Report[3] noted that:

- There is currently an unwillingness or incapacity to take in archives in non-traditional formats, especially digital, but also film and sound.
- Only 25% of archive repositories are aware of records at risk within their territorial or subject area.
- 75% of repositories, including several London borough repositories, do not have the resources to actively survey undeposited records within their collecting area.

1 Katey Logan, Logan McCabe archive consultancy, *National Strategy for Business Archives* (TNA, Jul 2009) https://www.businessarchivescouncil.org.uk/materials/national_strategy_for_business_archives.pdf.

2 The Data Protection Acts 1998 and 2018 http://www.legislation.gov.uk/ukpga/1998/29/contents and http://www.legislation.gov.uk/ukpga/2018/12/contents/enacted.

3 British Records Association, *Records at Risk, A Report on the BRA Survey of Risks to Historical Records in the East of England and London Regions, Autumn 2010* (BRA, 2012) p. 3 http://www.britishrecordsassociation.org.uk/publications/reports/.

## 1.3 The 2014 pilot project on legal records at risk

In 2014 a pilot project on legal records at risk undertaken as a prequel to LRAR produced a *Report on Archive & Record Repositories* which agreed with the BRA's findings and also observed that

> 'Records relating to the law and the justice system are managed as part of the public records system, but material that is not subject to the provisions of the Public Records Acts and current legislation is under-represented in the archival domain.'[4]

The report emphasised the random nature of 'legal records' collecting by archives but also stressed the

> apparent lack of awareness of the importance of good recordkeeping systems for the legal sector's 'business records', which can be puzzling to an outsider, especially with the importance attached to ensuring that client records are dealt with appropriately. Further issues include the need for records management systems to be used properly and for guidance from the archives and legal sectors to be followed.[5]

The report noted that there are additional factors such as globalisation, confidentiality and legal professional privilege which apply to some legal records and may be a barrier to their preservation for research, plus recent developments in legal services which are changing the focus of legal provision.

## 1.4 Implications of the above for legal records

The implications of the gaps in archival provision are as follows:

- Loss of a significant part of our national heritage: private sector legal records in particular have a much wider value than just for students of law. The legal practitioner's role as an integral part of UK business, cultural and social development needs to be understood; therefore it must be studied and evaluated. Without relevant records this will be an uphill task. Furthermore, unless systematic efforts are made towards collecting private sector records, research using modern legal records will continue to be weighted towards the study of government policy, legislation and the courts, producing a one-sided historical picture of the United Kingdom (UK)'s legal framework. In short, we are in danger of losing a significant proportion of our legal heritage.
- Reputational risk: the good management of modern records and preservation of historic legal records is not only of value to researchers. It also enhances the reputation of the depositing organisation by:
  - Giving a clearer picture of the importance of private sector legal institutions in the development of the UK's legal and business framework.
  - Giving legal institutions a much-needed reputation for transparency and honesty.
  - Enhancing client confidence due to improved efficiency in client records management.
  - Reducing the public perception of the legal sector as arcane, secretive and elitist.

TNA summarises the benefits to businesses of maintaining archives (whether in-house or by transfer to a third-party archive repository) as follows:

> Across the globe communications and marketing teams are re-engineering corporate branding and identity to emphasise their pasts. Most successful companies have secret commercial weapons in the form of their archives, a sometimes under-used asset that can be used to increase brand awareness, build commercial identity and help grow business. Information is a powerful business tool that can be turned to corporate advantage. Companies already know that research and development information is valuable, but the knowledge, experience and investment locked in company archives is an asset that can underpin core business. Business archives contain the evidence that gives a company its edge or marks it out as different and special, making it stand out from its competitors.[6]

This, then, was the starting point of the LRAR project.

4 Gary Collins (Brass Paper Clip Consultancy) and Elizabeth Dawson (Archive Consultancy & Research), *Report on Archive & Record Repositories* (LRAR, 19 Apr 2015), p. 3 .

5 Ibid, p.9

6 TNA, Corporate Memory: A guide to managing business archives (http://www.nationalarchives.gov.uk/documents/information-management/corporate-memory.pdf ) (TNA, 2009).

# Chapter 2: The project plan

It was understood from the beginning that the success or failure of the project to achieve its objectives would primarily be dependent on a) the willingness to participate of legal institutions and practitioners and b) the capacity of archives to accept records identified as being of value.

## 2.1 Objectives

The initial plan in August 2015 when the project commenced was to improve archival provision for legal records at risk, mainly those created by private sector institutions. It would do so by general analysis of problems, targeted case studies, liaison and co-operation with stakeholders and other archival institutions. The project sought to recommend cost-effective, sustainable solutions for saving significant collections, stimulating changes of practice, avoiding duplication of effort, and raising awareness of the value of legal records at risk.

The specific project objectives were to:

- Broaden the concept of 'legal' records from the traditional definition of them as court records or legal instruments such as deeds to records of institutions (and individuals) specialised to law, including business records, mainly in the private sector.
- Identify categories of legal records of potential research value.
- Locate records which may be at risk and identify why they are at risk.
- Carry out case studies of the recordkeeping processes of selected institutions to demonstrate and address the issues identified.
- Provide generic recordkeeping advice and guidance to information owners.
- Seek out potential repositories for legal records of research value.
- Facilitate the process by which information owners reach agreement to deposit records with, or donate records to, those repositories via model agreements and allocation of costs.

## 2.2 Scope

The project focused on private sector legal records. Records of the courts and the legal records of central and local government bodies were largely excluded as their disposal is covered by legislation.[1]

'Legal records' to be investigated were defined as being in three broad groups: the business records of institutions specialised to law, practitioner case files, and those legal records created in the course of their business by private sector organisations. Legal institutions included the following categories: commercial service providers, including arbitration and other alternative dispute resolution services, law firms, barristers' chambers, legal executives, licensed conveyancers, patent attorneys, trade mark attorneys, notaries, actuaries and will writers; professional legal associations/ pressure groups; legal education and research bodies; charities associated with providing legal services; and providers of ancillary services such as legal publishers. The private and quasi-private papers of individual legal practitioners and professionals such as barristers, solicitors, law teachers and academic researchers were also within scope.

The project would target modern (20th–21st century) legal records in England and Wales; records in this category are especially at risk due to the dangers of digital obsolescence, meaning they might not survive in an accessible format – or at all – to be considered for permanent retention in an archive repository. The overall intent was to:

- identify records of potential archival interest which had not been transferred to an archive repository and may therefore be at risk and
- seek reasons for this and
- find solutions.

## 2.3 Assumptions

The project was set up based on the initial assumptions[2] that:

- There are major gaps in the collection of modern private sector legal records by archive repositories.

1 Specifically the *Public Records Act 1958* http://www.leglegal institutionation.gov.uk/ukpga/Eliz2/6-7/51 and the *Local Government Act 2000* .

2 Based largely on evidence in the documents described in **Chapter 1** of this report and on the findings of earlier projects into legal records (*Legal Records in the Commonwealth* and the *Records of Legal Education* projects in 1994 and 1998 respectively).

- Archive repositories in the main are not interested in systematically collecting private sector legal records as this category is usually ancillary to their core collections policies.
- Reduced funding for archives means that legal records are more at risk than ever. It might therefore be necessary/possible to seek funding to set up dedicated legal records repositories[3] collecting subject-specific material such as arbitration records.

The accuracy of these assumptions is assessed in **Chapter 8: Findings**.

## 2.4 Methodology

All the below were carried out concurrently.

- Evaluation of current research resources: online archive catalogues, research guides, websites of stakeholder organisations, recordkeeping policies, reports and legislation, best practice information and records management guidance and the guidance provided by the legal profession itself on managing and disposing of records would be examined and evaluated to inform the project by identifying generic risks to records, gaps in archival provision and the limitations of best practice guidance.
- Identifying just what we mean by 'legal records at risk': the concept of 'risk' was to be defined and the main contributors to records being at risk, with specific reference to legal records, identified.
- Identifying categories of legal records *not* at risk: an investigation was to be carried out into just which categories of modern private sector legal records could be said *not* to be at risk and could therefore be excluded from the project. This investigation would be undertaken primarily by searching TNA's *Discovery*[4] portal and other archive catalogues[5] to see which legal records have already been deposited in archives.
- Identifying categories of legal records which *are* at risk: using the information from *Discovery* et al and from reactions to initial contact approaches, compiling a list of categories of legal records potentially at risk and prioritising their rescue.
- Contact was to be established with the following stakeholders on the assumption that they would see the benefits of participating in the project:
  - Legal institutions
  - Archive repositories
  - Archives/records management societies and pressure groups
  - Research bodies, legal researchers and prominent legal practitioners.
- Dissemination of the project's objectives and achievements would be achieved via a website, presentations to interested bodies and articles in professional journals.
- Seminars would be held at which stakeholders from three sectors, legal, archival/records management and research, would be invited to contribute their ideas and experiences and discuss and recommend solutions to the various issues raised.
- Case studies: a number of legal institutions would be selected for in-depth case studies which could be used both as exemplars for other legal bodies wishing to manage and dispose of their records more systematically and as pilots for developing a strategy and process for transfer of records of value to archives.
- Generic guidance on information and records management, including advice on archiving records, would be provided on request to legal institutions to demonstrate the business benefits of managing and disposing of records effectively and thus to encourage participation in the project.
- Work to support a national records rescue strategy and process: standardised, generic processes and procedures to facilitate the transfer of records from legal institutions to archives would be drafted and circulated to major stakeholders. This work would support the development of a national strategy to rescue private sector records, including legal, in collaboration with TNA and the BRA.

3 In much the same way as the creation of the Records of Legal Education Archives at IALS as a result of the findings of the 1998 *Records of Legal Education* project that there was almost no archival provision for this category of records; see http://ials.sas.ac.uk/library/archives/about-archives-held-institute-advanced-legal-studies-ials/records-legal-education.

4 *Discovery* holds more than 32 million descriptions of records held by The National Archives and more than 2,500 archives across the country; see http://discovery.nationalarchives.gov.uk.

5 For details see **Bibliography.**

## 2.5 Quality control

An Advisory Panel of experts in three key areas (legal practitioners; academic researchers; archivists/ records managers) was established to provide advice, peer review, guidance and useful contacts as required. A smaller Executive Committee was set up to oversee the day-to-day progress of the project.

## 2.6 Resources and costs

The project was initially funded for two years, from September 2015 – September 2017. It was hoped at the outset that it would be possible to find extra funding for a) specific case studies and b) to extend the project.

Finance was allocated in the existing budget for research assistants to undertake specific case studies. As the project progressed, however, and it became obvious that it was going to take longer than anticipated to successfully engage with legal institutions and researchers, it was decided to only appoint one research assistant to manage a case study of modern construction arbitration records and allocate the rest of the money to extending the project. At the end of the two years sufficient funds were available to extend the project to the end of October 2018. Further limited funding was found to continue LRAR on a reduced scale until July 2019, primarily to facilitate publication of this report.

## 2.7 Risks and issues

Project dependencies: it was understood from the outset that the success of the project was dependent on the co-operation of the agencies contacted. Due to this dependency it was not possible to set exact project milestones and, as the project progressed, it became clear that some of the original objectives, such as facilitating the wide-scale rescue of individual sets of records, were not achievable.[6]

6 For details see **Chapter 8: Findings.**

# Chapter 3: Identifying legal records at risk

The methodology for defining legal records at risk was as follows:

## 3.1 Evaluating current research resources

The following online archive catalogues, recordkeeping policies, reports and legislation, best practice information and records management guidance and the websites and publications of relevant pressure groups and archive bodies were examined to identify current initiatives to rescue private sector records at risk:[1]

- International, national and sector policies, strategies and reports on recordkeeping. These included reports by the International Council on Archives, UNESCO, the Information Commissioner's Office (ICO), the Legal Services Board (LSB), TNA, the BRA and the Business Archives Council (BAC).
- Recordkeeping legislation and regulations were examined for specific relevance to legal records.
- Current guidance on archives and managing records: TNA, again, was a primary source for current best practice guidance on recordkeeping. Guidance provided by the legal sector was also trawled for the advice it provides to its members.
- Archive online catalogues. As mentioned above, TNA's *Discovery* portal in particular was regularly examined during the course of the project to seek out information on archive repositories and their collections policies, categories of legal records held in archives and records of individual legal institutions and practitioners in archives. The catalogues of local authority, HE archives and specialist legal archives were also investigated.
- Stakeholder organisations' websites, including those of a large number of legal institutions, were identified via keyword searches and then trawled for evidence of recordkeeping policies and practices and/or for references to in-house or external archives.

The evaluation of these resources informed the project by:

- Demonstrating the concerns of national and international organisations about the risks to private sector records.
- Showing existing archival provision for legal records.
- Defining gaps in archival provision for legal records.
- Indicating the extent – and limitations – of existing recordkeeping guidance.
- Demonstrating the number and variation of private sector legal institutions.

## 3.2 Defining just what we mean by 'legal records at risk'

*Classifying risks to records*: the Digital Preservation Coalition classifies a number of risk categories to digital collections of records in descending order of the danger of extinction.[2] These categories of risk could, with minor tweaking, equally be applied to paper records. The records in both paper and digital formats of many legal institutions fit into the category of

1 For details of all resources examined see **Bibliography.**

2 Digital Preservation Coalition, *The 'bit list' of digitally endangered species* (DPC, 2018) https://www.dpconline.org/our-work/bit-list. The categories are:

- EXTINCT – A collection/type is *Extinct* when there is no reasonable doubt that the last known example is completely inaccessible by all practical means and methods.
- CRITICALLY ENDANGERED – A collection/type is *Critically Endangered* when it is facing an extremely high risk of extinction in the immediate future, no recognized organisation is responsible for its care and there is no policy or plan in place for its preservation.
- ENDANGERED – A collection/type is *Endangered* when it is not *Critically Endangered* but is facing a very high risk of extinction in the near future, it is in the custody of a known institution but they have no evident policy, plan or funding in place for its preservation.
- VULNERABLE – A data group is *Vulnerable* when it is not *Critically endangered* or *Endangered* but is facing a high risk of extinction in the medium-term future, it is in the custody of a recognized preservation institution but there is insufficient policy or plan in place for its preservation, *or* a lack of funding or resources prevents its preservation.
- LOWER RISK – A collection/type is *Lower Risk* when it has been evaluated, does not satisfy the criteria for any of the categories *Critically Endangered*, *Endangered* or *Vulnerable*. Groups included in the *Lower Risk* category can be separated into three subcategories:
- Preservation Dependent – Collection/types which are the focus of a continuing specific preservation activity targeted in the custody of a recognized preservation institution, the cessation of which would result in the qualification for one of the threatened categories above within a period of five years.
- Near Threatened – Collections/types which do not qualify for *Conservation Dependent*, but which are close to qualifying for Vulnerable; the focus of a continuing specific preservation activity targeted, but sustained funding and resources for ongoing preservation are uncertain.
- Least Concern – Collections/types which do not qualify for *Conservation Dependent* or *Near Threatened*, in the custody of a recognized preservation institution with a policy or plan in place, and sufficient funding and resources for its ongoing preservation.

endangered (in other words, in the custody of a known institution with no evident policy, plan or funding in place for its preservation) for the reasons outlined below.

*Defining the main risks to legal records*: the project proposal[3] in 2016 summarised the following generic risks to private sector records which could also be applied to legal records: globalisation, mergers, destruction, neglect, downsizing, bankruptcy, dissolution and digital obsolescence. There was an assumption that repositories which were collecting legal records tended to focus too narrowly on legal instruments such as deeds at the expense of the administrative records of legal institutions. It was additionally assumed that the records of non-traditional providers of legal services and ancillary services[4] have been neglected by archives. It was further assumed, given the evidence of the earlier reports described in **Chapter 1**, that reduced resources in the current economic climate could mean that even where archive repositories *were* collecting legal records, their ability to do so in the future would be severely curtailed.

The above assumptions were tested as follows:

## 3.3 Identifying categories of legal records not at risk

To facilitate the rescue of legal records of value it was first necessary to identify which categories were at greatest risk. The project therefore carried out extensive research into just which private sector legal records were already held in archive repositories so as to a) identify where the gaps lay b) test the above assumption that private sector legal records were being neglected by archival bodies. This investigation was undertaken primarily by searching TNA's *Discovery* portal and other online and analogue archives catalogues. A case study into alternative dispute resolution records held in the TfL Corporate Archives was also undertaken to test the thesis that many private sector legal records form part of the business records of an organisation. Findings[5] at the close of the project were:

### *3.3.1 Records of legal institutions already held in archives*

### Records with a regional/local focus

Contrary to the original assumption that archives were not interested in legal records, we found that local authority archives appear to have been assiduous in collecting legal records of relevance to the history of the physical area covered by the archives. Records in this category meet the collections criteria of most local authority record offices, which is to acquire and make available for research records which demonstrate aspects of each county's social, political, economic, religious and cultural life. The focus of collecting is local interest; whether the records are 'legal' or not is irrelevant.

It was beyond the scope of LRAR to delve into whether such collections resulted from specific collecting campaigns by the archives,[6] from deposits from the BRA[7] or from accepting material on an ad hoc basis at the request of legal institutions facing dissolution or practitioners clearing out their attics/basements, but the following conclusions can now be made based on the records identified:

- The largest category of records of legal institutions held in archives is undoubtedly those of sole practitioner solicitors and law firms deposited in local authority archives, with 1,949 'record creators'; the vast bulk of these records comprises deeds and wills, many no doubt rescued from law firms moving premises and/or wishing to free up space and offered to archive repositories by the BRA. An attempt was made during the LRAR project to separate archive collections of the business records of law firms from collections which exist purely of random legal instruments to see how extensive such collections were; 147 such collections were tentatively identified.[8] The 'legal history' section in TNA's *Accessions to repositories*[9] also gives quite detailed descriptions of

3 William Twining, '*Legal Records at Risk*', LRAR funding proposal (29 Apr 2014).

4 Such as will writers, patent agents, alternative dispute resolution services, legal executives, legal publishers.

5 For a list of 1) records of legal institutions held in archives 2) business records of law firms in archives 3) records of individual legal practitioners and professionals in archives and 4) keyword categories of legal records held in archives see **Appendix II.**

6 Though it seems clear that some local authority archives did run such campaigns: Gloucestershire Archives, for example, holds the collections of 33 local legal bodies and Cumbria Archive Centre holds 30 (see **Appendix II s.1**).

7 The BRA was established as a charity in 1932 'to promote the preservation, understanding, accessibility and study of our recorded heritage for the public benefit' (http://www.britishrecordsassociation.org.uk/). One major activity was to physically rescue, store and list private sector records – primarily deeds and related client documents such as wills passed to the BRA by law firms and to transfer them to the relevant local authority record office. The BRA now no longer has the financial resources to maintain and manage this warehousing facility and is seeking, in consultation with LRAR, TNA and others to develop alternative procedures for rescuing records.

8 See **Appendix II s.2.**

9 TNA, *Accessions to Repositories in 2015 relating to legal history* (2015), http://www.nationalarchives.gov.uk/accessions/2015/15digests/legal.htm A sample is at **Appendix II s.3.**

annual collections of solicitors' records which show clearly that business records of solicitors and local legal associations *are* being collected by archives. The focus of collecting is of course local, not national (or indeed legal), relevance.

- The second largest category of archives of legal institutions collected, again by local authority archives, is that of other providers of legal services to local communities, primarily comprising the records of citizens' advice bureaux, law centres, chartered accountants and boards of arbitration.
- Records of professional legal associations and pressure groups such as local law societies: these appear to have been collected either as part of campaigns or as and when offered by those bodies to local authority archives. Records of professional associations which have not been deposited in archives may be assumed to be at risk, especially if they are nationally-focussed bodies which just happen to be held locally. There will of course be numerous local legal institutions whose records do not appear on the list and which could now be assumed to be at risk given the greatly reduced resources of local authority record offices to either proactively or reactively collect such records.
- Records of individual legal practitioners: collections might include personal papers, case papers and notes, copies of material amassed while a member of various legal organisations, press clippings and articles etc. TNA's *Discovery* lists 64,515 collections of 'personal papers'; it is not possible to filter these into any kind of comprehensive 'legal' category, though entries in *Discovery* under 'judges', 'solicitors', 'barristers' etc contain many collections of papers of individuals.[10] The vast bulk of 'personal papers' are held by archives other than TNA and fit into the 'local interest' or 'specialist' category; it was apparent from discussions with local repositories that if the papers of a prominent local legal practitioner were offered to an archives they would in all probability be accepted, while university archives still continue to collect the papers of prominent legal professionals related to their institution.

## Records with a national focus[11]

- The largest category of legal records of national relevance is that of archives of legal education bodies, the Records of Legal Education Archives (RLEA) at IALS, the bulk of which were rescued as part of the project to rescue legal education records some 15 years ago. Provided that the RLEA continues as a viable archives, records of these bodies will not be at risk.[12]
- Nationally-focused institutions based in Greater London: the London Metropolitan Archives (LMA) has collected, and has advised that it will continue to collect, records of value in this category.
- Records of some other nationally-focused institutions are either held in in-house archives or, if political or pressure groups, collected by universities with a special interest.
- Records of the legal regulators: the Faculty Office and the Institute of Chartered Accountants (England and Wales) have in-house archives and have deposited their archives in a repository respectively. The Council for Licensed Conveyancers (CLC) actively participated in a LRAR case study to identify its historical records and potentially deposit them in the LMA and the Association of Chartered Certified Accountants (ACCA) expressed an interest in the project. The rest[13] may have no archival provision for their own records or possibly for those of their predecessor bodies and must therefore be assumed to be at risk. All were contacted (some several times) seeking information about their records but only the CLC, ACCA and the Solicitors Regulation Authority (SRA)) engaged with LRAR.[14]
- The institutional archives of certain legal bodies such as the Inns of Court, The Law Society (TLS), the Worshipful Company of Arbitrators and the Institute and Faculty of Actuaries are also not at

10 See table at **Appendix II S. 4.**

11 For details of records in this category see **Appendix II s.1.**

12 The RLEA (http://ials.sas.ac.uk/library/archives/about-archives-held-institute-advanced-legal-studies-ials/records-legal-education) collects records of institutions concerned with promoting legal education, not the administrative or student records of university and other higher education law schools. The latter have not been included in this project as they form part of the business records of universities and should therefore be preserved as part of each university's corporate archives. To undertake a detailed investigation into just what records are being kept according to each university's archives policy would require a separate research project; it was beyond the scope of LRAR.

13 Bar Standards Board (for the Bar Council), CILEx Regulation (for CILEx), Intellectual Property Regulation Board (for the Chartered Institute of Patent Attorneys and Institute of Trade Mark Attorneys), Costs Lawyer Standards Board, SRA (for TLS).

14 For details see below under **Case studies**.

risk.[15] Discussions with archivists of most of the above indicate that collection of business records will continue despite reduced resources.

### *3.3.2 Keyword categories of legal records held in archives*

TNA's *Discovery* was regularly interrogated during the project using a number of 'legal' keywords.[16] Even allowing for the vagaries of relying on keyword searches and reliance on *Discovery*, which is only as comprehensive as the information it receives from repositories, the tables of records already held in archives clearly show that:

- There is a preponderance of central government legal records and court records, held in TNA.
- The largest collections of private sector legal records are those of deeds and wills, followed by solicitors' administrative records, probably reflecting the sterling rescue work of the BRA.
- Legal records of local interest have been, and continue to be, collected, either as offered or as part of finite campaigns, primarily by local authority and some specialist archives.

It should be noted that information on legal records already safely held in archives is only as up to date as the catalogues themselves; archive online catalogues are constantly refreshed to include new additions or exclude material which has been deaccessioned. There are also significant collections of legal records not at risk but which do not appear in online catalogues because:

- The catalogues of the relevant archives have not been published online. These include the archives of Ede & Ravenscroft, TLS, the Worshipful Company of Arbitrators and legal records in ecclesiastical archives. There will be others.
- Most archives have cataloguing backlogs and/or a policy of not cataloguing material closed to the public under, for example, the Data Protection Acts, so even though material is safely held it is not yet available for research.

## 3.4 Identifying categories of legal records which are potentially at risk

The categories of legal records listed above demonstrate the under-representation in archive catalogues of records of barristers' chambers, legal regulators and less high profile (but increasingly important) providers of legal services such as law centres, will writers, legal executives, patent attorneys and trade mark attorneys. The assumption, therefore, is that records in these categories are at risk. The records of alternative business structures (ABSs) are also not as yet represented; ABSs are of such recent creation that permanent preservation of their records for posterity is, we suspect, simply not on anyone's radar.

All institutions physically located outside Greater London but with a national focus are additionally at potential risk because there are no repositories willing to collect records in this category other than one or two in the HE sector (and their capacity to collect is being greatly reduced in the current economic climate).[17] Local authority archives will as a rule only take in records which represent activities within their local boundaries. This policy therefore excludes locally-based institutions with a national remit and the papers of local private practitioners with a nationwide or international focus. The LMA did express its willingness to accept records of institutions and individuals with a national or international focus, but only if they were physically located within Greater London.

During 2018 a list of legal institutions with records potentially at risk was compiled.[18] The list comprises the following categories (some of course overlap) and was generated simply by searching on the category in *Discovery* to see what, if any records had been archived and, if not, checking the websites of the institutions identified to see if their websites mention archives/records. Most were also contacted via email, but few responded:[19]

- Academic research centres
- Education and training providers
- Legal advice and guidance bodies
- Legal publishers
- Legal regulators
- Membership bodies
- Pressure groups

15 For a list of 'legal archives', including in-house repositories see **Appendix IV.**

16 See **Appendix II s. 5.**

17 Examples are given in **Chapter 8: Findings.**

18 See **Appendix III.**

19 For details see **Chapter 4: Engaging with Stakeholders.**

Commercial providers of legal services (law firms; conveyancers; accountants; insurers; dispute resolution providers; alternative business structures) were excluded from the list because they were simply too numerous to document individually.

This list is also by no means comprehensive as it primarily represents records of 'live' (in other words, still active) legal institutions identified by LRAR as *potentially* at risk at the time of writing given the lack of evidence from *Discovery* or on individual websites of records being deposited in an archive repository or held an in-house archive facility; additionally the lack of response means that at the time of writing we simply do not know whether or not they have their own in-house archives (in the true sense). Many of course, will store records in a warehouse, basement or lower-tier server; these records may be perfectly safe for the time being but not available for external research. It remains to be seen whether they will continue to be safe.

# Chapter 4: Engaging with stakeholders

The following stakeholders were contacted[1] by telephone, email and/or hard copy letter; where there was a response this was followed up as appropriate by questionnaires, face to face meetings or phone calls:

- Legal institutions to seek their co-operation in depositing records with archives.
- Archive repositories to ask for their support in collecting records of legal institutions and legal practitioners.
- Archives/records management societies and pressure groups to seek their support in a) publicising the project and b) helping to develop more systematic processes for collecting legal records.
- Research bodies, prominent legal researchers and legal practitioners to ask for their support in publishing the project and their input into the categories of legal records which they would find most useful in their research.

## 4.1 Contact with legal institutions

Using the knowledge of LRAR's Executive Committee and Advisory Panel and tools such as TNA's *Discovery* portal, an initial number of legal institutions were identified[2] whose records were of potential historical interest, but which might not have been either been stored in an in-house archives[3] or been transferred to an external archive repository and therefore could potentially be at risk. Initial contact letters went out to those legal institutions to establish a) whether the institution had considered/would consider archiving records of permanent historic value; b) if so, whether it required practical advice and assistance on how to manage this activity and c) offering that assistance.

A response, where received, was followed up via face to face interviews and questionnaires; selected institutions or individuals were offered hands-on assistance by project personnel in the form of an initial case study comprising a records survey and identification of records of value, followed by the brokering of an agreement to deposit records with an established archive repository.

The response rate as of June 2017 was as follows: 55 legal institutions were contacted; 12 responded. Four were dismissive of the project; one asked for (and was given) the specific help offered in the email and seven tentatively expressed some interest in the project.

Further sporadic attempts were made to contact legal institutions identified during 2017/18, but it was clear from the start that simply 'cold calling' or sending an email or hard copy letter outlining the benefits of involvement with LRAR was unlikely to generate a response. Nevertheless another exercise was carried out in April 2018 in which a further 23 legal bodies were contacted with a simple request to assist LRAR as an academic project by providing information as to whether their legal records were already held in an in-house or external archive or, if not, whether they might have an interest in preserving their records for posterity. Only one (negative) response was received.

In all 78 legal institutions were contacted by LRAR, some more than once. As a result of the responses received three case studies (for details see **Chapter 6**) were carried out, on the records of Chadwick Lawrence LLP, the CLC and an intervened firm held by the SRA. Discussions were also held with the records managers of two large London law firms, in which the main issue was described as management indifference to the potential benefits of preserving some records as archives accessible to the public.[4]

It was additionally soon realised that unless a guarantee could be made to responders at the outset that an archive repository would definitely be available to accept records, the original project objective to facilitate the rescue of a large number of records of legal institutions would not be achievable within the time available.

1 For a complete list see **Appendix V: Institutions and individuals contacted by LRAR.**

2 These institutions comprised representatives from the following categories: professional legal associations; legal regulators; pressure groups; educational and training bodies; providers of commercial legal services and legal publishers.

3 In the true sense of a repository for records of permanent value, not a basement or lower tier server where unwanted files are dumped en masse pending a decision on disposal.

4 One firm had an in-house paper archives with some documents dating back to the 15th century but the material was not catalogued in any meaningful way and the archives was not open to the public. The records manager was also worried about management and preservation of digital records, seen very much as the preserve of the IT department. The second firm had excellent management of its semi-current paper records and was developing a management and disposal policy for digital records; it held some old client documents in an in-house archives but had no plans to make them available to the public. Both firms stressed the confidential nature of the records and the unlikelihood of allowing the public any access.

## 4.2 Contact with archive repositories

Twenty-three repositories[5] were contacted. All expressed support for the project and all the local authority archives contacted were willing to accept collections of legal records of value relevant to their area. All, however, stated that in the current economic climate they could no longer afford to bankroll potential depositors and would now expect a) fairly accurate lists of records to be provided prior to deposit b) records to be in reasonable physical condition and c) a deposit or donation to be offered by the depositor towards the costs of transport, storage and cataloguing. Repositories further noted that due to diminished resources they were unable to proactively seek deposits of private sector records but would try to do so reactively where records were in immediate danger. Several were also unable or unwilling to collect born-digital records. All expressed the wish for some sort of national, co-ordinated leadership giving clear guidance into categories of records at risk and standard, generic procedures for rescuing such records in a cost-effective way. It was clear, therefore, that without a nationally led strategy to rescue private sector (including legal) records, collection would from now on be reduced, reactive and random.

## 4.3 Contact with archives/records management societies and pressure groups

The above were contacted to seek their support in a) publicising the project and b) helping to develop more systematic processes for collecting legal records. Requests for participation in the project were put out to 12 groups during the first weeks of the project via the various specialist email lists and letters to individual groups; an overwhelmingly positive response was received from all 12 contacts. All considered there was a need for a more systematic approach to collection and deposit and agreed with individual repositories that information owners should take more responsibility for the care of their records both before and during their disposal. The feeling was that the project should take a long-term approach, working with bodies such as TNA to develop a national strategy which should be publicised via seminars and articles.

## 4.4 Contact with research bodies, prominent legal researchers and legal practitioners

The above were contacted to ask for their support in publishing the project and their input into which categories of legal records they would find most useful in their research. We also sought to find out how accessible records in archives are to researchers and which records they would like to see rescued; 14 research bodies and 30 individuals were contacted via email, letter or telephone; of which about half responded. Successful contacts were followed up by further emails and/or face to face meetings. Some of these contacts resulted in invitations to speak at events or to run seminars; for results see **Chapter 7**.

We held two seminars on the use of modern legal records at the Centre for Socio-Legal Studies (CSLS) at the University of Oxford and participated in May 2017 in a joint BRA/Institute of Historical Studies seminar on the use of digital catalogues by researchers.

The impression received from the seminars, meetings and further email exchanges was:

- Researchers may be unaware of just what legal records are available in archives and how to search for them.
- Practitioners are concerned about the confidentiality implications of allowing legal records to be made available for research.

See **Chapter 9** for action taken by LRAR towards finding solutions to these issues.

## 4.5 Stakeholder responses to publicity generated

Project information was disseminated via a website, presentations to interested bodies and articles in professional journals.[6] The website includes the project's terms of reference, a blog, project documents such as questionnaires, case study reports, LRAR's best practice guidance, seminar proceedings and copies of presentations and articles.[7]

Ten articles were written, both for archival and legal journals; seven are currently reproduced on the website. The bulk of articles were published in legal or historical journals. Their theme was the need to preserve the UK's legal heritage and to redress the government-centric balance of legal records by rescuing material of value for posterity. The publicity

5 Comprising 6 local authority archives, 6 HE archives, 5 specialist archives, 4 business archives, 2 national archives and one diocesan archives.

6 For details of articles see **Appendix VI: Publicising the project.**

7 The LRAR website is here: http://ials.sas.ac.uk/research/areas-research/legal-records-risk-lrar-project.

generated by these articles primarily resulted in a number of ad hoc requests by legal institutions and individual practitioners for help in disposing of their records.[8]

Eight presentations on the project were given at the invitation of archival and records management pressure or educational groups; whilst useful in further publicising the project and collecting anecdotal evidence of generic issues around rescuing records from attendees, most of these presentations were simply preaching to the converted.

Of more potential value in raising awareness were presentations given at their request to the Legal Regulators' Research Forum and an Iron Mountain Legal Forum for law firms; few attendees were aware of the value of keeping archives and most were unaware of the recordkeeping services provided by local authority archives. Representatives from both groups expressed the desire for clearer guidance on confidentiality and records management, especially in relation to digital records. As a result of these two meetings LRAR drafted a number of guidance notes, including specific advice around confidentiality and the management of digital records and referred all the notes to the group representatives for comment and circulation[9].

## 4.6 Providing information and records management guidance

There is considerable guidance on recordkeeping and disposal already available from regulatory and membership bodies.[10] This guidance, however, while giving excellent general advice on policies and procedures, does not extend to explaining exactly how and by whom this work should be carried out. Guidance by the legal sector to itself is also primarily concerned with giving advice on keeping information confidential but does not specify for how long. Nor is there much advice on retention and disposal of legal records.

In 2017 LRAR published our first set of best practice information and records management advice and guidance[11] to help bridge this gap. Some of the guidance was written at the request of individual legal institutions and practitioners to plug perceived gaps or to condense relevant advice into one location.[12]

The guidance was provided to legal institutions to demonstrate the business benefits of managing and disposing of records effectively and thus to encourage participation in the project. This guidance included both advice currently provided by the legal institutions themselves to their stakeholders, generic advice from organisations such as TNA and advice specifically created by LRAR.

8 See **Appendix VII: Ad hoc requests to LRAR for help/advice/guidance.**

9 These guidance notes are reproduced in full in **Appendix VIII: LRAR information and records management guidance**, other than guidance around the management of email and shared drives, which is available in slightly amended form in **Annex II** of **Case study 1: records and recordkeeping in a publishing house** (see **Chapter 6**).

10 Including TLS, the SRA, the Bar Council, the Bar Standards Board, the CLC, the Institute of Barristers' Clerks, the Chartered Institute of Arbitrators (CIArb), the Centre for Effective Dispute Resolution (CEDR) etc.

11 The guidance is published on our website here: http://ials.sas.ac.uk/research/areas-research/legal-records-risk-lrar-project/lrar-information-and-records-management.

12 For details of this condensed advice see **Appendix VIII Guideline 1: Current advice available to legal institutions on managing and disposing of records.**

# Chapter 5: LRAR seminars

LRAR held five seminars over three years, three at IALS and two at the CSLS. The seminars aimed to encourage and facilitate discussion, debate and a more mutual understanding between the three sectors most likely to derive some benefit from the LRAR project: legal, academic and archival.

The two seminars at CSLS were held primarily so that LRAR could gain a better understanding of just what data is used by socio-legal researchers and so that socio-legal scholars could gain a better understanding of what archival resources are available.

The project director also gave a number of presentations at seminars held by stakeholder groups.

The seminar information packs and presentations were published on the LRAR website, along with a blog with impressions of seminar proceedings and recommendations.[1] Many of the presentations were given from notes or as PowerPoint slides; some have been rewritten as articles either by, or with the permission of, the original author. These articles and the seminar information packs will be found under each seminar at **Appendix IX.**

## 5.1 The first LRAR seminar: 'What do we mean by legal records at risk?'

Held at IALS on 10 December 2015, this seminar was designed to introduce the project and included a presentation describing TNA's work to save business archives at risk. The aims, methodology and projected outcomes of LRAR were outlined and a presentation on Business Archives at Risk was given by Alex Ritchie (Business Archives Advice Manager, Archives Sector Development). This was followed by a series of round table discussions on why legal records are at risk, contributory factors and recommended solutions. There were 25 attendees, primarily archivists, but with some legal practitioners and academic researchers.

The conclusions of the seminar are summarised as follows:[2]

- There is a need for a more co-ordinated archives strategy for the collection of private/business/legal records.
- Academic researchers and institutions could better communicate their records research needs to archives.
- The legal sector must take more responsibility for its records and be educated a) in their research potential in many fields as well as legal history and b) about the availability of repositories.
- The sector also needs better advice on records management. TLS and the SRA should be more proactive in guiding the profession in best practice. TNA should also provide guidance to help the SRA dispose of its Intervention Archives.
- Donations by depositing institutions to assist in covering transfer, storage and cataloguing costs (either one-off or on a regular basis) should be requested by archives.
- In-house archives of legal bodies seem to be conspicuous by their absence. Where they do exist they clearly demonstrate value for money to their organisations.
- A legal heritage function along the lines of the Wellcome Trust would be the ideal.

## 5.2 The second LRAR seminar: 'Information as an asset: the business benefits to providers of legal services of preserving records'

Held on 23 November 2016, the seminar used as its starting point the 2004 Clementi report, *Review of the regulatory framework for legal services in England and Wales*,[3] which suggested that it was time for the providers of legal services to act in a more business-like way. This seminar sought to demonstrate to attendees from the legal sector the benefits of managing business records and preserving those of value in archives. A number of excellent presentations demonstrated the clear benefits of managing – and archiving – information in accordance with best practice.

Presentations included a talk on the historian's perspective on the value of legal records; a demonstration of the cost versus the benefits of keeping business archives; a case study of the cost and efficiency savings which result from having a records management and archiving programme in a law firm and an explanation of the work of the Pensions Archive

1 http://ials.sas.ac.uk/research/areas-research/legal-records-risk-lrar-projectseminars and http://lrar.blogs.sas.ac.uk/2016/11/30/information-as-an-asset-the-business-benefits-to-providers-of-legal-services-of-preserving-records/.

2 For all the seminar material see **Appendix IX: the first LRAR seminar.**

3 Sir David Clementi, *Review of the regulatory framework for legal services in England and Wales, Final Report*, Dec 2004.

Trust, a potential model post-LRAR. The presentations were followed by two round table discussions on whether a) the business benefits of preserving legal records outweigh the risks and b) the benefit to legal organisations of investing in archival provision for records outweighs the effort involved. There were 25 attendees, evenly divided between legal practitioners/support staff, academic researchers and archivists/records managers.

The conclusions of the seminar are summarised as follows:[4]

The following business benefits, which apply equally to the proper management of current and semi-current records as well as preserving archives, were identified:

- Re-use of records for strategic planning, corporate, reputational benefits around community engagement, transparency and honesty, speedy and effective service to clients, better compliance with regulatory and legal requirements (especially around the management of client files) and an improved understanding of historical context.
- Business seen as caring about/part of the community, not removed from it.
- Good public relations – honesty, learning from mistakes etc.
- Better understanding by the public of the value of legal services.
- Removal of ongoing management costs if an external archive repository is used.
- Destroying the rubbish and keeping the good stuff saves money.

The following risks were accepted where records are preserved:

- Potential breaches of confidentiality and security.
- Litigation.
- Reputational damage.

It was agreed that these risks are caused primarily by poor information management but that reputational damage could also result from the publication of records containing politically incorrect content. It was suggested, however, that being honest and transparent about past mistakes could only benefit an organisation, otherwise rumour will take over ('what have they got to hide?'). Several seminar attendees felt that the legal profession's culture of secrecy unfortunately mitigated against transparency and that the profession at times seemed to be almost afraid of its own records instead of regarding them as a potential asset.

Solutions suggested included educating the profession about the value of its records as an asset and of their re-use potential plus lobbying by concerned practitioners, researchers and archivists to overcome the culture of secrecy.

## 5.3 The third LRAR seminar: 'Legal records, confidentiality and access: breaking down the barriers'

Held at IALS on 27 October 2017, this seminar was designed to address the specific issue of how client confidentiality affects the preservation in archives of records of research value and sought to find solutions to the issues raised.

Legal professionals, archivists and researchers all gave their views on whether and why client confidentiality precludes the deposit of legal records in archives. Presentations on the issues were given from the perspective of solicitors, barristers, researchers and archivists, followed by questions on particular problems put to an expert panel comprising the speakers. There were 18 attendees evenly divided between legal practitioners, academic researchers and archivists/records managers.

Points raised at the seminar included the following:[5]

1. There are legal and ethics issues around the management of client files, particularly the duty to keep client records confidential. The Data Protection Act and the General Data Protection Regulation (GDPR) also require personal data to be kept confidential but can be misinterpreted as an instruction that no personal data may be archived for future research.
2. Confidentiality of client records is, according to the members of the legal profession present, infinite, so a risk-based approach to releasing material for research is required. There are also issues over client ownership of documents which must be dealt with before records are made available for research.
3. Research ethics require better rules around: collection of data; use of data; storage of data and disclosure of data. Collection of data requires informed consent (why it is being collected; who

4 The full text of the seminar conclusions will be found in **Appendix IX: the second LRAR seminar.**

5 For all the seminar papers see **Appendix IX: the third LRAR seminar.**

will see it; how it will be used; how it will be confidentially destroyed). If the rules are relaxed what is the potential for harm? Informed consent of course can't be obtained from the dead, so a risk-based approach is needed. Information risk, however, diminishes over time. TNA usually imposes closure periods of 75–100 years on personal and some confidential data.

4. There is a need for clear guidance from the legal regulators on records ownership, records management and records disposal. At present there is very little. The changes imminent as a result of the GDPR (such as the requirement for legal institutions to draft and implement retention schedules) need to be more widely circulated within the legal profession. There is also a need for better guidance from the legal regulators on confidentiality and legal professional privilege – in particular definitive statements as to whether confidentiality obligations are in fact perpetual or, if not, when they lapse. The legal regulators should define client consent processes which are transparent about destruction and/or archival deposit of client documentation.
5. There is a mismatch between the public and private sectors over transparency. The public sector and some parts of the business sector are leaning heavily towards being more open and transparent; the legal sector is still leaning towards secretiveness. The latter is risk averse and out of step with recent trends in both government and business towards transparency, public accountability and community engagement.
6. The legal sector needs to be more aware of its responsibilities around good recordkeeping and to stop viewing information and records management as a separate overhead to be undertaken as an afterthought, if at all, instead of as an intrinsic part of running an organisation in the same way as Finance or Human Resources.
7. If the legal profession does not facilitate the preservation of records of value we will be left with a major gap in our historical record, undermining the understanding of the importance of legal developments to our nation's history. This is a major issue because the legal profession is an important part of our national heritage but its history is still under-represented in archives.

The lack of a consensus on whether any solution to the confidentiality issue was possible demonstrated the need for greater guidance, ideally from the legal regulators, on disposal of legal records.

## 5.4 The first LRAR seminar at CSLS: 'Legal Records at Risk 1914–2014: the use of unpublished data in socio-legal research'

Held on 25 April 2016, this was an introductory session to describe the aims, methodology and projected outcomes of the LRAR project and to suggest ways in which students could use legal records in archives to further their research. Attendees were either socio-legal researchers of long standing or postgraduate students.

Presentations included details of unpublished data used by socio-legal scholars, while the seminar information pack contained examples of unpublished sources used in socio-legal research. The seminar attendees agreed that greater awareness about the availability or otherwise of records could open up new topics for socio-legal researchers and/or stimulate lobbying by researchers to make information owners more aware of the potential value of their records.[6]

## 5.5 The second LRAR seminar at CSLS 'Use of unpublished documents in socio-legal research'

This seminar was held on 22 February 2017 for postgraduate students at the CSLS as a session of the Centre's *Theory and Method in Socio-Legal Research*, a course intended to develop an appreciation of law as a social phenomenon, to introduce influential theoretical perspectives and to consider the variety of methods by which socio-legal research questions might be addressed.

The seminar sought to demonstrate the importance of using primary source material in socio-legal studies and to show how the study of the recent past (using 20th- and 21st-century legal records held in archives) informs our analysis of the relationship between present day law and society, provides evidence of activities, tells us more about individuals, institutions and cultures and can even ensure justice. It gave practical examples of how to locate and use archival records and dispelled some of the myths around the selection, extent, subject matter, availability and accessibility of legal records in archives[7].

6 For the seminar papers see **Appendix IX: the first LRAR seminar at the CSLS.**

7 For the seminar papers see **Appendix IX: the 2nd LRAR seminar at the CSLS.**

## 5.6 Stakeholder group seminars

During the course of the project, the LRAR Director gave a number of presentations at seminars held by stakeholder groups as follows:

- Five presentations on the project were given to archival and records management pressure groups.[8] The purpose was to publicise the project and collect anecdotal evidence from seminar attendees on generic issues around rescuing records.
- Three presentations were given to archive students at University College London (UCL) seminars.[9] The purpose was to raise awareness of issues around identifying and rescuing private sector legal records for posterity.
- Presentations were given to the Legal Regulators' Research Forum on 1 December 2016 and an Iron Mountain Legal Forum for law firms on 2 March 2017: these were of considerable value in raising awareness, as few attendees were aware of the value of keeping archives and most were unaware of the recordkeeping services provided by local authority archives. As a result of these two seminars LRAR drafted a number of guidance notes and referred them to the group representatives for comment and circulation.[10]

Representatives from all groups expressed the desire for clearer guidance on confidentiality and records management, especially in relation to digital records.

Two articles have been compiled by the author using the original seminar presentations to give a flavour of issues raised which were particular to the three main categories of stakeholder: archival, research and legal; they are reproduced at **Appendix IX.**

## 5.7 What did these seminars achieve?

What value were these seminars in helping the project achieve its objectives? If nothing else the seminars clearly demonstrated:

1. The disconnect between archives/records management practitioners, researchers and legal practitioners over the potential value of legal records.
2. The under-use of, and lack of knowledge about, legal records already in archives
3. The confusion over defining certain legal tenets such as long-term client confidentiality.
4. The lack of interest on the part of the legal sector in preserving its own heritage.

The seminars did, therefore, assist LRAR in defining and targeting priorities as follows:

- The seminars made it clear that the legal sector was less aware than other private sector organisations of the business benefits of managing records and maintaining archives, saw client confidentiality as a barrier to the preservation of records for posterity and was not especially conscious of – or interested in – the existing services provided by archives. LRAR saw its role, therefore, as primarily one of raising awareness among the legal sector of a) the existence of archives b) the benefits of keeping good records and archives and c) how existing risks around issues such as confidentiality diminish over time. We also lobbied TNA and other archive groups such as the Information and Records Management Society (IRMS) to create advocacy programmes aimed at the private sector stressing the benefits of good records management.
- The seminars also confirmed what pre-LRAR investigations had discovered, namely that existing archives are struggling with drastically reduced resources, with the result that they are now expecting the private sector to take more responsibility (especially financial) for archiving records. In our opinion this is only right and proper, but it may mean that more records are at risk than hitherto, especially where private sector organisations are uninterested in the potential archival value of the information they create. Despite this lack of resources, all the archive attendees were eager to collect legal records of relevance to their collections policies but

8 Respectively to: the Archives in London and the M25 area (AIM25) Group on 3 November 2015; the London Archives Partnership on 30 November 2015; TNA's Collections Rescue Strategy Workshop on 10 February 2016; the IRMS Property Group on 23 March 2017 (jointly with the BRA); the Information and Records Management Society annual conference on 21 May 2018.

9 Respectively to: the International Centre for Archives and Records Management Research (ICARUS) – UCL on 25 February 2016; the Archives and Society Group – UCL on 19 April 2016; and a lecture to UCL Archives and Records Management students on 20 October 2017.

10 These guidance notes are reproduced in full on our website: http://ials.sas.ac.uk/research/areas-research/legal-records-risk-lrar-project/lrar-information-and-records-management.

required more co-ordinated direction and practical assistance, preferably from TNA but also from projects like LRAR.

- From comments by seminar attendees, we also noted that researchers are frequently unaware of just what legal records are already in archives and/or how to search for them. We therefore raised with TNA the need to expand the information on archives in its already magnificent *Discovery* portal[11] (such as including information on archive repositories' collection policies) and for archives in general to be more proactive in explaining the limitations of the services they can provide (such as explaining why not all documents are available online, why some are not open for access, why so many are uncatalogued, why many archives require advance booking etc). Collections policies should also be clear, unambiguous and published.

Practical outcomes:

- The creation of information and records management guidance by LRAR was a direct outcome of attendees' concern about confused or obscure messages from both the archival and legal sectors on how best to manage information.
- One legal institution requested that a case study of its records be undertaken following the records manager's attendance at the first LRAR seminar.[12]
- TNA has now facilitated the creation of a Records at Risk steering group[13] to examine exactly those issues raised at our seminars. LRAR cannot claim sole credit for this, of course, as many other factors were involved including lobbying from the BRA, the BAC and archive networks combined with TNA's own awareness of the need to find a way to further develop and expand – without extra resources – its existing crisis response process. We do, however, claim a role in influencing TNA's decision to undertake this initiative and we thank TNA for supporting LRAR by its attendance at our seminars and invitations to present at TNA's own records at risk seminars.

11 http://discovery.nationalarchives.gov.uk.

12 The CLC. As a result a case study of the CLC's records was carried out, records management advice (including a records retention and disposal schedule) proffered and a potential archive repository identified. This was undertaken at no cost to the CLC.

13 This group, though initially convened by TNA, is an independent body with TNA providing support as needed.

# Chapter 6: LRAR case studies

Following initial contact, some legal institutions were selected for in-depth case studies which could be used as exemplars for other legal institutions wishing to manage and dispose of their records more systematically. A number of case studies were undertaken and completed.[1]

## 6.1 Case study 1: Records and recordkeeping in a legal publishing house

Undertaken just prior to the official commencement of the LRAR project in September 2015, this pilot project set out to survey the paper and born-digital records of a legal publishing house based in the south-east of England. It sought to identify records of archival value and to make recommendations about their permanent retention. At the time of writing LRAR is still trying to persuade the publishing house to transfer its historic records to a local authority archives.

*Value to the LRAR project*: the case study clearly showed that legal publishers create and maintain records of potential research value.

*Value to the organisation of collaborating in the case study*: the organisation advised that the survey and recommendations were useful, and the resulting positive will to manage records better should result in an improvement of recordkeeping practices, especially around electronic records. There was an increased understanding in the organisation of the historic importance of its early and accruing record series.

## 6.2 Case study 2: Alternative dispute resolution records held in the TfL Corporate Archives

Completed in May 2016, this case study was undertaken to discover the extent of legal records, specifically alternative dispute resolution (ADR) records, in a business archives. The particular aim was to support the hypothesis that many legal records are located within business archives and must therefore be searched for under their business context.

*Value to the LRAR project*: the case study clearly showed that corporate archives do keep legal records where these are seen as pertinent to the core functions of the business and that they will readily make them available to researchers as soon as is appropriate (in other words once confidentiality and/or privacy issues have expired).

*Value to TfL of collaborating in the case study*: apart from the obvious value in generating publicity for the TfL Corporate Archives and its records, the study gave the Archives some external validation of its processes and resources. It also reassured the Archives staff that in the paper world they were not missing out on the acquisition of TfL's legal records, because LRAR's interview with the Head of TfL Legal demonstrated that the Legal department's process for disposing of paper records concurs with the current procedure of the Archives, which is to review and select records for the Archives from those deposited by the department in TfL's external storage facility. Finally, the leverage of an external body (especially one like the IALS) enabled access and conversations with TfL Legal that the Archives had often been hitherto unable to provoke, so they benefitted from the investigative work that LRAR undertook with them. It also gave the Archives an avenue to follow up on how to capture digital records in the future.[2]

## 6.3 Case study 3: The records of Chadwick Lawrence Solicitors

Completed in November 2016, the purpose of this case study was to survey the records and recordkeeping practices of a law firm based outside London which employed a professional archivist/records manager so as to evaluate the business benefits of employing professionally qualified persons to manage records.

*Value to the LRAR project*: the case study demonstrated conclusively LRAR's (and archives/records management pressure groups') thesis that there are clear business benefits to law firms in employing a professionally qualified records manager to a) tidy up legacy records b) create efficient procedures for managing records going forward and c) set up an in-house archives and records store serving the firm and, potentially, the public.

*Value to Chadwick Lawrence of collaborating in the case study*: the publication of the case study surely generated good public relations for the firm, demonstrating as it did how excellent its internal procedures for managing and disposing of records are. The value of the archives in providing information on request to departments within the firm was also a clear business benefit.

1 For the full case study reports see **Appendix X.**

2 Points made in an email from the TfL Corporate Archivist to LRAR, 22 Aug 2018.

## 6.4 Case study 4: Sub-project on domestic construction arbitration records

Completed in August 2017, this project was a preliminary exploration and feasibility study for a potential project in respect of arbitration records located in Great Britain/England and Wales.

The report of the sub-project concluded that:

- There are construction – and other – arbitration records which may be at risk.
- A wider survey needs to be undertaken of arbitral organisations' and individual arbitrators' records and archival homes identified for them.

*Value to the LRAR project*: a better understanding of just which categories of arbitration records may be at risk and the need for further research.

*Value to researchers of arbitration*: a better awareness of the gaps in preservation of arbitration records and the issues around confidentiality which may be hindering further research.

## 6.5 Case study 5: Records of the Council for Licensed Conveyancers (CLC)

Undertaken during 2016/17, the purpose of this case study was to gain an overview of the kinds of records held by a legal regulator, to understand the business drivers behind the management of its records and to demonstrate the business benefits to the CLC of making provision for the preservation of its archives.

*Value to the LRAR project*: the case study demonstrated the considerable amount of material of research value – primarily born-digital – held by the CLC and showed how keeping accurate metadata on records facilitates their eventual transfer to an archives. At the time of writing LRAR is hoping to broker an agreement for the transfer of CLC's records on an ongoing basis to LMA; this means that an important set of legal regulator's records will not be at risk of loss.

*Value to the CLC of collaborating in the case study*: the publication of this case study will provide external validation of the CLC's recordkeeping processes which are necessary to perform its regulatory function. LRAR's findings are that the CLC should be seen as a role model for other legal institutions, regulatory or otherwise, in its commitment to openness and transparency, its willingness to make its records available to the public as early as possible and its understanding that today's business record may be tomorrow's historical record and therefore needs to be managed and preserved.

## 6.6 Case study 6: Selected records of an intervened law firm in the Oxfordshire area

This case study, separately financed, was intended as a preliminary exploration and feasibility study for a major project to investigate a larger sample of records in the Intervention Archives managed by the SRA, to find archival homes for them and to draft an ongoing process to assist the SRA in disposing of records of value to archive repositories. It followed on from an earlier project by the BRA from 2012–14 to identify historical documents held by the SRA and arrange for their transfer to appropriate record offices. During the project about 500 cartons of records were examined and records of value identified (mostly client documents).[3] In 2016 LRAR and the BRA were represented on an interview panel to select a part-time fixed term archivist to arrange the transfer of the identified records to repositories.

LRAR had also discussed the Intervention Archives with the SRA in an attempt to provide some practical assistance, such as drafting standard terms of deposit to avoid the SRA having to negotiate different agreements with each archives. The case study itself was undertaken in 2017 and a confidential report sent to the SRA.

*Value to the LRAR project*: a better understanding of the issues the SRA faces when intervening in firms which have failed to manage their records effectively and the consequent problems faced by legal regulators such as the SRA in protecting the rights of users of legal services, including having to allocate considerable resources to keeping and managing intervened records for as long as necessary to fulfil obligations to users.

*Value to the SRA of collaborating in the case study*: LRAR noted the difficulties the SRA faces in its laudable attempts to deposit intervened records of value with archive repositories. Each repository has its own terms of deposit; LRAR is advocating that the Records at Risk group draft a standard agreement for deposit of records which will reduce the burden on organisations like the SRA of negotiating separate deposits each time.

3 Nat Alcock and Penelope Baker, 'The original documents project undertaken by the British Records Association and the Solicitors Regulation Authority/Law Society', *Archives Vol 1 no 130–1* (BRA, 2015).

## 6.7 Case study 7: Census of providers of legal services in Oxfordshire, 1900–present day

Commencing in April 2017 and separately financed, this case study aimed to map all private sector institutions specialised to law in Oxford and environs from 1900 to the present. At the time of writing this has not been completed, but much of the data will be useful for a new project on private sector records in Oxfordshire which may be at risk.[4]

## 6.8 Unsuccessful: case study of records of Inns of Court Barristers' Chambers

There is no doubt whatsoever that Chambers now have – or should have if they are following the Bar Council's and the Institute of Barristers' Clerks' own guidance[5] on records creation and management – quite a lot of material of potential research value. LRAR sought to engage with some of the Inns of Court Chambers in order to undertake one or two case studies with a view to brokering agreements for depositing Chambers records in the LMA. The Inns of Court Librarians and Archivists demonstrated support for the case studies and the Inner Temple Archivist worked to facilitate contacts with Chambers Practice Managers. Individual members of the Selden Society also tried to facilitate meetings between LRAR and Chambers or barristers. Unfortunately, however, all these attempts proved to be fruitless; records of barristers' chambers continue to remain a mystery.

## 6.9 Case study conclusions

The case studies demonstrated that:

- Legal records are readily available in company archives and must be searched for within their business context.
- Many of the business records of legal institutions are of potential research value and worth preserving.
- Legal institutions may be reluctant to deposit their records in an archive repository for a variety of reasons including confidentiality, loss of control, cost or simply a lack of interest in their own legal heritage.

4 This project commenced in December 2018 with funding from UCL Faculty of Laws.

5 For details see **Appendix VIII.**

# Chapter 7: Seeking to develop a national strategy to rescue legal records

Perhaps the most important of LRAR's findings was the understanding that little of long-term value could be achieved in isolation and within the lifespan of a finite project. We therefore sought to find ways to extend and widen the project's original purpose by working towards the creation of a national records rescue strategy.

## 7.1 Investigating the feasibility of creating a Legal Archives Trust

To find a new way to save legal records following the demise of the BRA's warehousing service for the records of law firms, LRAR and the BRA, together with LMA, talked with the Pensions Archive Trust, which has developed an excellent charitable model to facilitate the deposit of pensions records in the LMA, to see if a similar model could work for a 'Legal Archives Trust'. Such a Trust would work in partnership or collaboration with archive repositories in the UK to ensure the permanent preservation of material documenting the history, management and development of legal services and of institutions (and individuals) connected with the law for the use and benefit of present and future generations. LRAR has sought input from prominent legal practitioners and organisations[1] to:

- Determine whether a Legal Archives Trust funded by donations from legal stakeholders is a viable proposition.
- If so, to decide how to persuade legal institutions that such a Trust is in their interest.
- Recommend individuals with influence to serve as patrons.
- Decide how to set up and run the Trust, appoint trustees and achieve charitable status.

At the time of writing, alas, little interest has been shown by the recipients in developing this concept as a solution.

## 7.2 Beginning to develop a proactive legal records rescue strategy

Legal records rescue has until now primarily been undertaken reactively and on an ad hoc basis (such as when records come up for auction or legal bodies merge, dissolve or move to new premises). In collaboration with stakeholders, LRAR seeks to replace this with a proactive strategy and process as follows, possibly via a Legal Archives Trust model, by:

- Locating the records of legal bodies and legal professionals *before* their records become 'at risk'. This would be done by regional surveys to locate legal institutions and individuals and by contacting them to let them know of the archival services available. Collaboration with local authority and specialist archives is essential, probably via TNA and possibly the Chief Archivists in Local Government Group (CALGG), which has already offered to act as a conduit to local archives.
- Working with TNA, the BRA and other archives membership and pressure groups to address the issue of how to save private sector (including legal) records with no obvious archival home. A Legal Archives Trust could also lobby the legal sector on the need to take more responsibility for the preservation of its records.
- Offering guidance to legal institutions on good records management and digital continuity to ensure their records survive to reach an archives (as well as to improve their own efficiency and reduce costs). In 2017 LRAR contacted the IRMS to suggest that we join forces in a records management advocacy programme which could be continued post-LRAR. LRAR also drafted a strategy document[2] for consideration by the IRMS, which has agreed that lobbying private sector organisations to recognise the business benefit of good records management and archiving is needed.[3]

TNA, the BRA, the BAC, the Archives and Records Association (ARA), the IRMS and CALGG are key stakeholders, representing the government and local archive sectors, business and other private archives and professional archivists and records managers. LRAR has been in contact with all these bodies with the aim of jointly developing clear priorities

1 For a copy of the detailed proposal see **Appendix X paper 2.**

2 The document suggested a draft strategy as follows: that the IRMS run a major campaign to facilitate better records management in the private sector by advocating the business benefits of employing qualified professionals to manage digital and paper records; that the disconnect between archives and IRM professionals should continue to be actively whittled away (as is already happening through current archives/IRM postgraduate training programmes) via better communications and joint activities such as articles and seminars stressing that without good IRM there will be few archives to save in the future; and that IRM training be offered at a discount to those individuals in the private sector with responsibility for managing records.

3 Agreed with the IRMS Secretary on 30 July 2018.

and documented procedures for a) the identification and b) the collection of legal records of value. This forms part of a wider strategic piece of work being led by TNA on identifying and saving private sector records at risk as described below.

## 7.3 Standardising archiving procedures and processes

As legal institutions were put in contact with archive repositories the discrepancies in procedures for negotiation, transfer and deposit became increasingly apparent. In the case of organisations like the SRA, which has sought to deposit selected interventions records with a number of local authority archive repositories, these discrepancies have caused confusion and frustration at having to negotiate differing deposit agreements each time. LRAR therefore agreed with the BRA that it would be useful if a set of standard forms and procedures were developed which could be applied to all private sector bodies and individuals seeking to deposit records. The idea was mooted with some archives and received an enthusiastic reception, though it was considered that this was really something that TNA should lead on. LRAR hopes that the Records at Risk group will work on creating standard forms, terms and conditions and deposit agreements.

## 7.4 Liaising with TNA and other stakeholders to create a national private sector records rescue strategy

Once the project was underway it quickly became clear the issues affecting the rescue of legal records formed a microcosm of the global problem of how to save private sector records in general. It was obvious that we could not achieve any major ongoing strategic objectives in isolation and in the time available. LRAR therefore engaged with TNA, the BRA and other stakeholders to discuss the issue and seek solutions; as a first step we drafted a paper on working towards a strategy for the rescue of private sector records, including legal.[4] The Records at Risk Steering Group, on which LRAR is represented, was established to investigate this very issue.

This steering group was created partly as a result of considerable lobbying by LRAR, the BRA and other interested parties. It was established following two workshops in 2016 and 2017[5] at which LRAR and the BRA gave presentations describing the risks to legal records and the actions being taken to facilitate their rescue. Following the first workshop TNA commissioned an *Understanding Collections at Risk*[6] report on private sector records at risk to investigate whether there is a growing volume of archival material without a suitable, permanent home, and if this is the case, the extent to which this unpreserved material presents a risk to the national record and the archival sector. The report found that this was indeed the case, and recommended the creation of a steering group as a first step to scoping and addressing the challenges of collections at risk and of underrepresentation in archives.

According to the steering group's draft terms of reference[7], it will be:

> an advisory body that will consider and co-create with TNA appropriate steps to better manage the risks and challenges faced by vulnerable archive collections. The aim is to develop an activity plan for 2018–2019 possibly focusing on three themes for completion by 31st March 2019:
>
> a. Development of guidance and supporting case studies and the identification of a potential partner who might host this;
>
> b. Instigation of discussions with the academic, community and other interested constituencies to collect intelligence about vulnerable collections. Also identifying potential partners for the proposed advocacy and research;
>
> c. Exploring the potential to create a contingency fund that can be accessed at short notice to protect collections at immediate peril and who might lead hold and manage such a fund.
>
> The steering group will provide an open, independent and authoritative advisory voice working with TNA to engage with the archives sector and other interested stakeholders for the development of constructive and collaborative measures to mitigate the risks faced by vulnerable collections through sharing knowledge and supporting the development of appropriate case studies, guidance and training.

4 A copy of the paper is at **Appendix X: Developing a national strategy to rescue legal records paper 1.**

5 These workshops were attended by representatives from archives networks, funding bodies, higher education sector and stakeholders.

6 Caroline Williams, 'Understanding Collections at Risk' (report prepared for TNA, March 2017), *Archives: The Journal of the British Records Association* Vol 53 Issue 36.

7 The group's terms of reference have not yet been published, but no objection has been raised by members to their inclusion in this book.

The actions recommended above are similar to those undertaken by LRAR, the BRA and other archival pressure groups in the past, but on a much larger scale; we hope that under the aegis of TNA a truly national strategy to rescue private sector records of value, irrespective of subject category, will be achieved. The LRAR project director will continue to be a member of this group after the project is completed and will lobby to ensure that legal records are not overlooked.

# Chapter 8: Findings

Many of LRAR's findings about the risks to legal records could be applied to private sector records generally. Some, however, were unique to the legal sector. Both categories of risk are discussed below.

## 8.1 Identifying recordkeeping risks and issues common to all private sector organisations

### *8.1.1 Poor records management*

Despite (or partly as a result of? See next section) advances in IT, management and disposal of records in accordance with good practice continues to elude numerous organisations; legal bodies are no exception. Recent research indicates that the average information worker is still wasting large amounts of time searching for documentation and manually filing (or not filing at all) both paper and electronic material.[1] Records disposal (by which we mean either destruction/deletion or preservation in an archives) is often left to non-professionals[2] to undertake on top of the day job, with the result that it may not happen at all or, if it does, will be ad hoc and often without reference to best practice. Records of value will therefore not be identified in time to save them whilst records of no value may be retained unnecessarily, resulting in excess cost and compliance issues.[3]

National strategies are required to seek solutions. The proposed advocacy programme with the IRMS, as well as the expected advocacy work of the Records at Risk group, should progress this goal.

### *8.1.2 Digital continuity and digital obsolescence*

Born-digital records and problems of adaptation and continuity were a major concern of LRAR, as digital records pose a particular risk to any project seeking to rescue modern records. Most legal records of the past fifteen years or so will have been born-digital. Many larger institutions have sophisticated systems for dealing with their current digital records, but few will have been sensitive to the practical and scholarly value of those records as potential archives, which in turn means that many born-digital records will not survive to be collected by repositories. Poor recordkeeping may result in born-digital records becoming inaccessible through format change, corruption or simply losing the system manual; additionally the very lack of visibility of space issues around digital records increases their danger as many institutions simply don't see the need to dispose of their information efficiently (including making provision for permanent retention of valuable material).

This is a records management issue but is barely on the radar of many organisations. It was far beyond the resources of LRAR to find solutions, but the project did develop some generic guidance[4] on managing and disposing of born-digital records and liaised with national bodies such as TNA, which is seeking to find global strategies for dealing with the problem.

### *8.1.3 Confusion over the disposal of records in accordance with the provisions of the Data Protection Act and the General Data Protection Regulation (GDPR)*

Archivists will be familiar with private sector organisations' concerns over depositing personal data in repositories. At one LRAR seminar (see **s.8.2**) it was categorically stated by several legal practitioners that the legal requirement to keep personal data in client case files confidential supported the contention that such records could never be made available in archives. This misinterpretation of legislation requires clarification; the following recommendations on personal and confidential data may be of interest:

1 According to a recent International Data Corporation White Paper *Bridging the Information Worker Productivity Gap in Western Europe: New Challenges and Opportunities for IT* (IDC, 2012), UK businesses lose an average of two hours of their employees' working time every working day as follows:

- 57% of office workers spend an hour a day looking for missing documents
- 20% have to recreate documents that they couldn't find
- 56% of workers feel overwhelmed.

2 It may be of interest to note that in the few instances where LRAR was able to engage with legal institutions, it was usually the records manager who responded. In two cases the records managers left during the period of engagement and were not replaced; the engagement with LRAR then ceased. It should also be noted that employing professionally qualified records managers/archivists to undertake the necessary work often costs an organisation less than using other in-house employees such as paralegals and company secretaries, because archivists and records managers are no more costly – and indeed are sometimes cheaper – to employ and are often also willing to work part-time or be shared between organisations.

3 For examples see **Appendix XII: Legal records – horror stories.**

4 See **Appendix VIII** *Guideline 7: Advice to legal institutions on digital continuity and managing digital records.*

- At the 38th Session of the UNESCO General Conference in Paris in November 2015 it was agreed that:

  Where restrictions to accessing documentary heritage are necessary to protect privacy, human safety, security, confidentiality or for other legitimate reasons, they should be clearly defined and stated and be of limited duration. They should be underpinned by appropriate national legislation or regulation by including an appeals mechanism against such decisions.[5]

- The ICO has advised that Article 5 of the GDPR states:

  Personal data may be stored for longer periods insofar as the personal data will be processed solely for archiving purposes in the public interest, scientific or historical research purposes or statistical purposes.[6]

- The UK Secretary of State for Digital, Culture, Media and Sport responded to a parliamentary question on 3 November 2017 as follows:

  The General Data Protection Regulation (GDPR) and the Data Protection Bill permit such organisations to process personal data (including sensitive personal data) without consent, where necessary for 'archiving purposes in the public interest', subject to appropriate safeguards for the rights and freedoms of data subjects. It also exempts archiving services from complying with certain rights of data subjects (for example, rights to access, rectify or erase their data), where the exercise of such rights would seriously impair or prevent them from fulfilling their objectives.[7]

### 8.1.4 Lack of available archive repositories

In the current economic climate all archives, whether public or private, face severely reduced resources combined with competing demands for funding within their parent organisations. This in turn reduces their ability to proactively collect and make available for research records which do not fit exactly into their collections policies (and even some which do; see below). Current economic restraints have the further effect of stymying initiatives to set up new archives.

With specific reference to legal records, it was found that:

- The only archives in the UK dedicated to collecting a specific category of legal records, the Records of Legal Education Archives at IALS, did not have the capacity or the intention to expand its collections remit to take in categories of 'legal' records other than those specialised to legal education and might not in the current economic climate even be able to accept records from new legal education bodies.
- The Law Society Library, which holds the corporate archives, restricts its collections to TLS and SRA publications, ephemera and minutes and agenda papers from the Council, Boards, and selected policy making Committees; at the time of writing it has no capacity to retain born-digital records.[8]
- The Inns of Court archives, while still capable of receiving deposits of the business records of the Inns, are not able to expand their remit to include the records of individual barristers or barristers' chambers. This is, again, a resource issue, as all the Inn Archivists, when asked, expressed a desire to collect such records were they to have the capacity.
- HE archives may take in the papers of a legal professional or institution associated with the university, but the process is ad hoc and dependent on capacity and perceived relevance of the collection to the university's own interests.

5 UNESCO: 'Documentary Heritage in the Digital Era', *Resolutions of the 38th session of the General Conference* (Nov 2015), 38 C/Resolutions Annex V S 3.5, p.165 https://en.unesco.org/programme/mow/recommendation-documentary-heritage.

6 ICO, *Guide to the General Data Protection Regulation* (2018) https://ico.org.uk/for-organisations/guide-to-the-general-data-protection-regulation-gdpr/principles/?q=research.

7 *Archives: Public Interest: Written question – 111381* (2017) https://www.parliament.uk/business/publications/written-questions-answers-statements/written-question/Commons/2017-11-03/111381/.

8 According to the latest published version (2012) of its *Corporate Archive Policy*; see http://www.lawsociety.org.uk/support-services/library-services/corporate-archive/.

### 8.1.5 Reduced archival resources to collect records of London-based private sector organisations

The one public sector archives in London which is actively interested in collecting records of London-based institutions of both local and national significance (including legal), the LMA, has only limited resources to pursue this goal. The LMA, like every public sector archives, is suffering from reduced resources and is unable to proactively seek to rescue records at risk. As an example, a list of 49 London-based legal institutions[9] sent to LMA on 19 October 2017 by LRAR elicited the response that it had had contacts with none of the bodies listed except one of the law firms. Most of these institutions are current concerns; it is unlikely that LMA would have the resources to enter into ongoing records deposit agreements with all of them, even assuming they were willing to archive their records.

### 8.1.6 Lack of archive facilities to accommodate the records of institutions and individuals which have national significance, but which are physically located outside Greater London

There are many legal institutions and practitioners based outside London in this category but local authority archives will only collect records of relevance to their geographical area. This means a lack of provision for:

- Records of organisations located outside Greater London with a national or international focus.
- Records of individual legal practitioners and other professionals connected with the law who live/lived outside London but whose collections spread across county boundaries or have a national or international focus.
- Records of organisations which have moved to other areas or merged with organisations physically located in another area.

This issue is being, and will continue to be, raised at future meetings with the Records at Risk steering group, on which LRAR is represented (see **Chapter 9**) to seek solutions and will also be a major focus of any future Legal Archives Trust.

Some university archives and other specialist repositories (notably the RLEA at IALS) have collected records in the above category but may be unable to continue due to reduced resources.[10] It is beyond the scope of this project to approach every HE and specialist archives to clarify its collections policy and identify legal records of relevance to that organisation's interests which may be at risk and encourage deposits; the Records at Risk group and/or a Legal Archives Trust might be able to undertake this task.

### 8.1.7 The reduced ability of all UK archive repositories, public and private, to proactively seek to collect records due to drastically curtailed resources

Almost all repositories contacted advised that they face not only severely curtailed resources but reduced support from their management for collection of material outside their immediate remit. Unless the current economic climate changes it is unlikely that this obstacle will be overcome in the near future.[11] Most archives are now only able to respond reactively – if at all – when they discover that records are at imminent risk of destruction or sale to an outside bidder, by which time it may of course be too late. It should be pointed out, however, that all local authority archives contacted stated that they would continue to seek to collect private sector records despite reduced resources.

They did, however, express the opinion that the private sector should take more responsibility for the long-term care of its own records. TNA's 2017 *Understanding Collections at Risk* report suggested one route:

> A new concept being developed at TNA is that of 'emerging archives'... collections which will remain with their parent organisation, which will benefit from advice on good practice, development and funding and possible partnerships.[12]

9 Included in a list of private sector legal institutions whose records might be at risk at **Appendix III.**

10 Examples include UCL Archives, which has in the past collected the records of the British Maritime Law Association, but is now unable to accept further accruals (email to from the Head of Archives, 22 Nov. 2017) and LSE Library, Archives and Special Collections, which will no longer continue to collect records of mediation organisations (advised at meeting with LRAR project Director, 27 Apr. 2018); both due to changes in their collections policies.

11 One county archivist advised (email to LRAR, 17 Nov. 2018): 'We have undertaken some more systematic surveys [of records potentially at risk] in the past...However we haven't had the resources to carry out similar exhaustive surveys in recent years, chiefly because outreach and engagement activities are now a much greater part of our work than they were in the 1970s and 1980s and because the amount of new material coming in unsolicited, from new and existing depositors, is as much as we can handle generally. We now routinely ask depositors for voluntary donations towards the cost of processing their records although most do not respond. Given the financial climate, were we to embark on a survey of a particular type of record we would certainly emphasise the need for depositors to contribute to the cost of care of their records.'

12 Caroline Williams, *op cit.*

This recommendation chimes with the growing feeling amongst archivists[13] that profit-making institutions in particular (such as large London and regional law firms) should invest in their own in-house archives rather than expect the taxpayer to subsidise their recordkeeping (or sort out the lack of it), yet, almost unbelievably, LRAR has been unable to identify one major law firm with a professionally managed in-house archives open to the public as a matter of course. This contrasts sharply with the practice of most of the major UK banks, other commercial enterprises and membership organisations which have set up in-house archives, viewing them as a business benefit, and made the records available to researchers.[14]

What we currently have is a chicken and egg situation. It is pointless for LRAR to approach archives to collect the records of legal institutions if the institutions themselves will not engage with us. It is equally pointless to approach legal institutions unless we are confident that there is a repository ready to take in their records. Furthermore, archives now expect private sector institutions to manage their records better, both before and during deposit, and to accept some financial responsibility for records preservation; there is little evidence that this expectation will be met by legal institutions.

### *8.1.8 The changing role of the BRA and its Records Preservation Section (RPS)*

The changing role of the BRA, especially the RPS, is certainly a major factor affecting the rescue of private sector records, primarily legal records such as deeds. For over fifty years the RPS has acted as a warehouse and sorting facility for records, the majority of which were passed to the RPS by law firms, prior to transfer of those records to archive repositories. This storage, listing and archive transfer service was provided free of charge to organisations wishing to get rid of unwanted records. Due to changes in the economic climate[15] a professional service could no longer be provided and in 2016 the BRA decided the RPS could no longer continue to act as a storage and distribution hub.[16]

Over 2016 and 2017 LRAR and the BRA collaborated on drafting new procedures and processes in the hope that the RPS (with LRAR's assistance) would be able to act as a broker between private sector organisations and individuals wishing to deposit records with archives. LRAR accordingly referred a number of would-be depositors to the BRA during 2016–27.[17]

In 2018 the Chair of the RPS advised that continuing lack of resources meant it was unable to provide the proposed brokering service and now saw its role as comprising a first point of contact hub, giving guidance to enquirers on where and how to seek assistance in managing and disposing of records. The BRA is hoping that the new Records at Risk group will provide a more proactive service than the BRA can now provide. In the interim it is probably inevitable that some significant legal records will be lost.

## 8.2 Identifying obstacles specific to rescuing legal records for posterity

### *8.2.1 Client confidentiality and legal professional privilege*

All of the general issues faced by archivists when seeking to rescue private sector records apply equally to legal records. One obstacle which does seem unique to certain categories of legal records has, however, been identified. That obstacle is client confidentiality.

At our LRAR seminar on confidentiality and access in October 2017 we asked a gathering of legal professionals, researchers and archivists the following questions:

- Are client confidentiality and legal professional privilege real – or just perceived – barriers to rescuing legal records for posterity? In other words…
- Do client confidentiality and legal professional privilege last forever or are they finite?

Legal professionals articulated the issues around client confidentiality and access to records for research as follows:

13 Comments to the effect that the taxpayer should not continue to subsidise the archiving of records of law firms have been made at the two TNA records at risk seminars and in emails from local authority archives to LRAR; for example: 'As you cannot fail to be aware, local authority budgets are shrinking, and it is no longer appropriate to expect the taxpayer to cover the cost of solicitors' own neglect of their duty to their clients and their clients' records' (quoted in **Appendix XI: horror stories**).

14 The Bank of England, Barclays Bank, Lloyds Bank, Rothschild, Santander Group, BBC, BP, BT, British Airways, Diageo, Glaxo Smith Klein, The Guardian, Harrods, ITV, Marks and Spencers, Nestle, Network Rail, Pfizer, Prudential Group, Rolls Royce, Sainsbury, Transport for London and Unilever, to name just a few. The Royal Medical Colleges also have in-house archives. All are open to the public.

15 Including the loss of an Historic Manuscripts Commission (HMC) grant in 2000.

16 As stated in the *Minutes* of the BRA's 85th Annual General Meeting, 27 Oct. 2016.

17 See **Appendix VII.**

- There are legal and ethics issues around the management of client files, in particular the duty to keep client records confidential. The Data Protection Act and the GDPR also require personal data to be kept confidential.
- A 'solicitor must keep the affairs of clients … confidential except where disclosure is required or permitted by law or by the client'.[18] This duty of confidentiality applies equally to affairs of former clients and dead clients and outlasts executors or administrators.
- There is no time-limit.[19] Given that, according to some legal professionals, confidentiality never ends, perhaps the realistic question is: when does the risk reduce to minimal impact?
- Confidentiality may be breached merely by passing material to an archive.
- In the absence of a positive duty to assist archivists or to preserve documents, and without the express consent of the client, it is clear why legal professionals are reluctant to allow archives to collect their records. In other words, what's in it for them?

Researchers noted that:

- The use of data by researchers is governed by university and professional body codes of ethics and it is usual for academic researchers to need to go through a research ethics approval process before they are permitted to begin their research.
- Collection of data requires informed consent (why it is being collected; who will see it; how it will be used; how it will be confidentially destroyed). If the rules are relaxed what is the potential for harm? Informed consent of course can't be obtained from the dead, so a risk-based approach is needed.

Archivists noted that:

- The history of how the legal sector works is under-represented in archives and therefore in our national history and it should be in the profession's interest to correct this imbalance.
- There is a mismatch between the public, private and legal sectors over transparency. The public sector and some parts of the business sectors are leaning heavily towards being more open and transparent; the legal sector is still leaning towards secretiveness.
- Information risk diminishes over time. TNA along with the majority of archives, usually imposes closure periods of 100 years on personal or confidential data or data subject to legal professional privilege.[20]
- There is a need for better guidance from the legal regulators on confidentiality and legal professional privilege – in particular definitive statements as to whether confidentiality obligations are in fact perpetual or, if not, when they lapse.
- The legal regulators should define client consent processes which are transparent about destruction and/or archival deposit of client documentation.
- There is a need for generic templates to be made available to the legal sector when depositing records in archives, such as a standard deposit contract which includes access terms. Such templates ideally need to agree legal costs for dealing with access disputes.

Attendees asked how the emphasis on client confidentiality and concerns over reputational risk square with the historic practice of many law firms and some individuals to offload records en masse to local authority archives without any idea of the records' content; with leaving non-current client files containing personal data for decades in third-party repositories without any provision for appropriate, compliant disposal and with auctioning records off to the highest bidder.[21]

According to the legal sector, the duty of confidentiality applies equally to individual and corporate clients. While archivists agree with this tenet, they consider that the confidentiality of corporate records has a shorter shelf life than that of personal data, which is subject to the Data Protection Act and the GDPR.[22]

18 *Halsbury's Laws of England* (LexisNexis, 2015), 5th ed., vol. 65, para. 538.

19 This is an assumption made by most of the legal professionals to whom LRAR spoke. It is, however, nowhere stated in the legal regulators' rules and guidance or in legislation. Current guidance is summarised in *LRAR Guideline 4: advice to legal institutions on confidentiality and research access to records*, reproduced in **Appendix VIII**.

20 Where records are closed, the reason for closure is noted in *Discovery* against the individual record. Reasons given for closing records for longer than 20 years include: national security; law enforcement; health and safety; personal information; commercial interests; information provided in confidence; legal professional privilege.

21 Examples of all these practices are given in **Appendix XII.**

22 Archives as a general rule close corporate records for 20 years and personal data for 100 years before making them available for research. There will of course be exceptions.

The seminar did not reach any consensus on whether, why or how client documentation should be deposited in archives or on how long the obligation to respect client confidentiality lasts. The only agreement reached was that risk diminishes over time. This is fortunate for those archives which already hold the records of law firms or case notes of individual practitioners. Several of the legal practitioners present, however, stated categorically that undertakings of client confidentiality precluded *any* records (potentially even governance or business records) from being deposited in archives. This issue is too great for LRAR to tackle alone and it is hoped that TNA and/or a Legal Archives Trust might take up the challenge (see **Chapter 9**). The legal regulators also have a responsibility to clarify just how long client confidentiality should last.

### 8.2.2 The role of the legal regulators

It should go without saying that private sector legal regulators are concerned with the proper management and disposal of the records of the bodies they regulate. Certainly they all provide generic guidance on major concerns for the profession such as protecting confidential client records and, in most cases, some excellent advice on recordkeeping.[23] The regulators also meet regularly to thrash out mutual issues.[24] We have not, however, been able to establish just how the regulators undertake checks on whether their guidance is followed, other than in cases where non-compliance with confidentiality leads to disciplinary action or prosecutions. LRAR has also been unable to find any cases where poor records management has been cited as a factor when statistics on the reasons for legal interventions are published.[25] Some of the regulators are, however, well aware of the problems caused by poor recordkeeping, especially when it comes to adding to the cost to the regulators of interventions. On intervention, it is the regulator which must pick up the tab.

The SRA, as part of a consultation on how long to keep the records of intervened firms, noted in 2013:

> 'The SRA continues to encounter firms which have failed to manage their archives effectively. The SRA is seeing archiving contracts where law firms only pay costs to storage companies/third parties when files are deposited or extracted; so there is a cost to the firm attached to managing their archive properly and a financial incentive not to do so.'[26]

The CLC, which is also a regulatory body, noted during talks with LRAR that it has particular problems with the records of intervened firms where digital records have been stored on bespoke IT systems which are inaccessible without expensive forensic investigation. There are also problems accessing records stored in the Cloud or protected by ID verification checking systems. It is probable that the SRA faces the same issues.

In the CLC case study report LRAR recommended that legal regulators and the bodies they regulate would benefit if all regulated entities were required to include a contractual clause with Cloud providers (and indeed with any external information storage provider) specifying that, on contract expiry or firm closure (including intervention), the firm's records must be returned to the firm or, in the case of an intervention, passed to the regulator. Intervention procedures should also include taking custody of IT manuals and passwords.

### 8.2.3 Lack of transparency

The Legal Services Board (LSB), which oversees regulation of lawyers by the regulators, has publicly stated that two significant barriers that prevent consumers from accessing legal services are 'lack of information' and 'lack of trust'. In 2013 the Board noted that

> '...for many people, an initial barrier [to engagement with legal professionals] is lack of awareness and understanding of lawyers and the law...understanding is further clouded by the amount of legal jargon.'[27]

In examining why certain consumers consider and then reject seeking legal advice, one of the reasons cited in the report was that lawyers were seen as 'inaccessible'. To improve trust and increase the accessibility of legal services, the LSB's Choose and Use research suggested that:

23 Some of this guidance is listed in **Appendix VIII.**

24 A Legal Research Forum of regulators meets regularly. In 2017 the LRAR Director gave a well-received presentation to the Forum on the business benefits of archiving records.

25 The SRA cites the most common grounds for interventions as protecting the interests of the client or breach of accounts or code of conduct rules (http://www.sra.org.uk/sra/how-we-work/reports/moving-forward.page). Poor recordkeeping could well be a factor.

26 http://www.sra.org.uk/sra/consultations/file-retention-post-intervention.page

27 LSB, *Lowering barriers to accessing services report* (13 March 2016), p.7 http://www.legalservicesboard.org.uk/news_publications/publications/pdf/2016/20160331_Lowering_Barriers_Final_Report.pdf.

> 'Greater visibility and understanding of the role of the legal services regulatory and complaints bodies will provide reassurance and ultimately lead to greater trust.'[28]

Better transparency through making information about what they do and how they have worked in the past, available via archives, is one obvious solution to these issues.

It is debatable whether legal institutions as a whole view information as an asset; in fact, the reverse seems to be the case. At the second LRAR seminar in 2017 on the topic of information as an asset several seminar attendees expressed the view that legal entities, especially law firms, were too nervous over allowing historic material to enter the public domain to consider preserving records for posterity. The finding of the seminar was that there was additionally a lack of awareness of information as an asset, meaning that legal records have been under-utilised for branding or reuse for strategic planning or to ensure a speedy and effective service to clients or to enhance reputational benefits around community engagement, transparency and honesty. Certainly there does not seem to be any concerted action on the part of either regulators or membership bodies to promote the concept; again, this is in marked contrast to many businesses in the UK.[29]

### *8.2.4 Legal records not viewed as business records*

According to Wikipedia:

> 'a *business record* is a document (hard copy or digital) that records a business dealing. Business records include meeting minutes, memoranda, employment contracts, and accounting source documents. It must be retrievable at a later date so that the business dealings can be accurately reviewed as required.'[30]

This definition holds true for legal records, yet the legal sector does not appear to view its records in general as business records, nor its relationship with clients as a business one; this was identified as an issue by the Clementi report, which noted that:

> 'certain lawyers dislike being described as part of an industry. They see a conflict between lawyers as professionals and lawyers as business people. The idea that there is a major conflict is in my view misplaced. Access to justice requires not only that the legal advice given is sound, but also the presence of the business skills necessary to provide a cost-effective service in a consumer-friendly way.'[31]

Clementi suggested that it was time for the providers of legal services to become more businesslike:

> 'Research shows that complaints arise as much from poor business service as from poor legal advice... In developing business systems to minimise costs whilst maintaining high standards, there is no reason why lawyers should not work alongside those with other skills, for example in finance or IT.'[32]

The regulators did take note. In addition to facilitating the creation of alternative business structures as defined by the *Legal Services Act 2007*,[33] they also explicitly defined legal service providers as businesses. The *Bar Standards Handbook* defines a 'practice' as

> 'the activities, including business related activities, in that capacity, of: a) a practising barrister; b) a barrister exercising a right of audience in a Member State other than the United Kingdom pursuant to the Establishment Directive, or the European Communities (Lawyer's Practice) Regulations 2000; c) a BSB entity; d) a manager of a BSB entity e) an employee of a BSB entity.'[34]

28 Ibid., p. 9.

29 See, for example, the Hawley Committee 1995 consultative document for chairmen, chief executives and boards of directors: *Information as an Asset: the board agenda: checklist and explanatory notes*, developed on behalf of the KPMG IMPACT Programme by a committee under the chairmanship of Dr Robert Hawley, Chief executive of Nuclear Electric plc, which gives very specific advice on management, protection, use and disposal of corporate information.

30 https://en.wikipedia.org/wiki/Business_record. Astonishingly, Wikipedia was the only online definition of a business record which we could find, though there are many discussions online about what constitutes a business record.

31 Sir David Clementi, *Review Of The Regulatory Framework For Legal Services In England And Wales: Final Report* (Dec. 2004), p. 5.

32 Ibid, p. 6

33 https://www.legislation.gov.uk/ukpga/2007/29.

34 *Bar Standards Board Handbook* v. 3.2 (1 Feb 2018) p.268 https://www.barstandardsboard.org.uk/regulatory-requirements/bsb-handbook/ .

The *SRA Handbook* has an entire section devoted to 'You and your business'.[35] Yet judging from the descriptions (or lack of same) of records of law firms recently offered to archives, some legal service providers still have a way to go to catch up with the regulators' advice.[36]

Membership and legal research bodies also create minutes, financial and employment records and hold personal data on clients and members; they should therefore consider themselves to be businesses. Do they? The lack of interest in preserving records to show how they have functioned in the past and continue to function, in stark contrast to the efforts of many traditional businesses in the UK to publicise their heritage, suggests not.

### *8.2.5 Lack of interest in their own heritage*

As noted above, the legal sector appears to be unique among business organisations in the UK in that many of its constituents see no benefit – commercial, reputational or in terms of community engagement – in preserving its records for posterity. There are, for example, very few dedicated legal archives,[37] no major London law firm (as far as we know) maintains an in-house archive available to the public and/or bona fide academic researchers and the records of barristers' chambers, most alternative dispute resolution bodies, legal executives, patent agents, trade mark attorneys and will writers remain a mystery. The majority of legal institutions contacted by LRAR appeared to be uninterested in preserving their records for posterity.

Some law firms and a few other legal institutions do appear to have a limited sense of the value of their own heritage for public relations and have commissioned house histories or provided historical summaries of the institution's development on their website.[38] The word 'limited' is used advisedly; although it is clear that the firms' records must have been consulted in the course of compiling these histories, few of the firms identified as doing so have followed the exercise up by depositing records in archives and very few have publicised their own holdings of historical records (assuming any have survived in-house since the house histories were written), other than the occasional pdf of a 'historic' document on their website.[39]

Lack of interest was evident from the lack of response, or negative response, to contact emails and letters (often more than one) from LRAR, including approaches by the LRAR patrons. As of January 2018, 131 legal institutions were identified,[40] of which only 17 were *known* not to be at risk (in other words they have records in archives). Fifty-six legal institutions and 16 major London law firms were contacted; of the 11 legal institutions which replied only two responses were positive (resulting in tentative offers to take their records from the LMA), four were negative and five non-committal. Three law firms responded, all positively; one was put in touch with the BRA; the other two respondents were the firm records managers who sought to use LRAR guidance to interest their managers in preserving the firm's archives. LRAR also sought without success to engage barristers – especially barristers' chambers – with the project. It is clear that a high-level approach is needed, possibly from a Legal Archives Trust or the Records at Risk group (see **Chapter 9**).

### *8.2.6 Cost concerns*

Finally, during discussions with LRAR in 2017, cost was specifically cited by one legal institution[41] as a barrier to making records available for research. In the current economic climate it is unlikely that any legal institution, even a wealthy London law firm, would be amenable to spending money on setting up its own professional in-house archives or even to using archive/records management consultants to sort out legacy material, yet this is precisely what they should be doing to realise the potential of their records as business assets and reduce their records storage and compliance costs. Legal institutions have yet to be convinced of the benefits of preserving records for use in marketing and public relations, let alone making them available to public scrutiny. In this they lag behind other businesses which have set up in-house archives. A Legal Archives Trust could work towards raising awareness of the value of keeping archives, and we hope that TNA will also take this issue on board (see **Chapter 9**).

35 *SRA Handbook* v 19 (1 Oct 2017) 2nd Section https://www.sra.org.uk/solicitors/handbook/commencement.page.

36 See **Appendix XII.**

37 See **Appendix IV.**

38 See **Bibliography s.6** for examples of legal institutions which have published 'house histories' either in hard copy or online. Note that most include a 'history' or 'archive' section on their website, but in many cases this is either just a short paragraph or a link to recent events.

39 Genuine exceptions include the London Criminal Courts Solicitors Association, which publishes an online archive of documents dating back to 1922 on its website: see https://www.lccsa.org.uk.

40 Categories of legal institutions identified (some overlap) which might be without archival provision include: alternative dispute resolution (27); regulatory (21); membership (51); pressure groups (28); training (17); best practice advice (3); publishing (7); academic (1).

41 The SRA, which takes in the records of intervened law firms; the resource required to manage and dispose of these records appropriately is huge. It is to the SRA's credit that it has made efforts to arrange the deposit of some records with local authority archives despite the cost of doing so. The CLC has solved its own storage and cost issues around intervened records by simply destroying them all (other than legal instruments) after a set period of time.

## 8.3 Prioritising categories of legal records most at risk

As records at risk were identified, categories most at risk were prioritised as follows:

### *8.3.1 Private sector legal institutions' institutional records*

During 2018 LRAR compiled a specific list of legal bodies whose records are *not* known to be held in an archive repository and which therefore *might* be at risk.[42] One hundred and twelve legal institutions were identified; 21 had already been contacted during the course of the project (only two successfully) and another 30 were contacted in April 2018 (with only one response). This list might, we hope, form a basis for a targeted campaign by LRAR successor bodies to rescue at least some records.

### *8.3.2 Business records of law firms*

Though the BRA and local authority archives have in the past been remarkably successful in rescuing legal instruments such as deeds and wills offered by law firms, as evidenced by the vast numbers in archives listed in *Discovery*, they have been less so in collecting the business records of law firms themselves. There are notable exceptions to 'deeds only' collections, as evidenced by TNA's *Accessions to repositories*,[43] especially the business records of several London law firms held in LMA, but it does appear that collection of the business records of solicitors by archive repositories has primarily been on an as and when offered basis; this category of records could therefore be said to be at risk where law firms are unaware or unwilling to offer records to repositories. To this category must also be added the records of law firms which have been intervened in by the regulators.

Law firms may also be at risk due to mergers or closure; both factors can be triggers for firms to deposit records with local authority archives or pass them (until recently) to the BRA. There is no simple way to identify which records of which firms may be at risk due to these occurrences; the census of Oxfordshire legal institutions currently being undertaken (see **Ch 6 s.6.7**) may suggest a methodology for identifying such records.

### *8.3.3 Client case files*

As described above, this category of records has been known to filter through to archives, usually as random files of individual clients included in batches of unlisted records dumped on repositories by law firms or included in the 'personal' papers of legal practitioners. We are unaware of any complete or near-complete sets of client case files which have made their way into archives in the past and, given the express statements of some members of the legal sector that these records are permanently confidential, it seems most unlikely that any client file datasets would be offered to archives in the future. Ironically, better records management by legal institutions and greater awareness of the issue of long-term client confidentiality on the part of archive professionals will probably mean that fewer random client files make their way into archives. This is unfortunate, since case files (such as those produced by citizens' advice bureaux and law centres) can be valuable in their representation of marginalised and under-represented individuals and communities not documented in other classes of records.

### *8.3.4 Clients' documents and legal instruments*

Legal instruments (deeds, wills etc) held by law firms are now more at risk than in the past, partly due to the fact that the BRA no longer has the resources to act as a temporary repository for this material. Deeds and other client documents and, more rarely, the business records of law firms themselves, are also at risk from being offered for auction to the highest bidder by law firms, a somewhat dubious process (though mostly legal unless personal data or client files and documents are included in items for auction) which perpetuates the loss of our heritage.[44]

### *8.3.5 Records of legal institutions and practitioners physically located outside Greater London but with a wider than local focus*

Quite simply, these records are at risk because there is no existing repository with a remit to collect them. A list of institutions identified in this category was passed to TNA, which is compiling a schedule of private sector records at risk, in 2017.[45]

42 See **Appendix III.**

43 Annual accessions to repositories (ie lists of records deposited in archives) will be found here: http://www.nationalarchives.gov.uk/accessions/.

44 For a sample of records offered at auction see horror stories in **Appendix XII.**

45 Included in the list of organisations whose records may be at risk at **Appendix III.**

## *8.3.6 Barristers' chambers' records*

No records of Inns of Court chambers or regional barristers' chambers have been deposited in archives, though some records such as fee books may have been collected as part of the personal papers of individual barristers, judges etc.[46] This category of records has therefore been designated as being at high risk.

## *8.3.7 Individual legal practitioners' records*

One of the assumptions at the start of the project was that the personal papers of legal practitioners such as arbitrators, mediators, barristers and solicitors, which might contain valuable information relating to cases in which they were involved, would probably be stored in the garages, attics and basements of those practitioners and could therefore be said to be at risk. It was not possible to either prove or disprove this assumption, as, following offers in legal journals[47] to rescue such records, only four practitioners came forward with a selection of papers stored in their homes.[48] The records of these practitioners comprised a mix of personal material, copies of papers of cases or campaigns in which they were involved and what may be copies of the administrative records of bodies of which they were members.[49]

An examination of *Discovery* yielded a rich harvest of diaries, notebooks and personal papers of individual legal professionals and practitioners already deposited in archives.[50] At this stage it is not possible to generalise as to whether more recent records of individuals are at high risk, given the stated willingness of local authority and specialist archives to accept the relevant papers of prominent legal practitioners and the possibility that much material which may be held in attics etc duplicates records elsewhere (such as in institutional records). There are also questions around whether some records, such as case notes, should be retained long-term by practitioners in the first place and, therefore, whether it is appropriate to offer them to archives.[51]

## *8.3.8 Records of legal institutions with a regional focus*

This category of records (local law societies, legal associations and law centres) appears to have been collected by local authority archives whenever offered; the records may therefore be said only to be at risk where the local body is not aware of the services offered by archives. Certainly local authority archives seem to be aware of the existence of such bodies and would be happy to collect their records where resources permit. In its second attempt to contact legal institutions in April 2018 LRAR attempted to raise the awareness of some of these bodies to the existence of local authority archives and the services they offer.[52]

## *8.3.9 Records of legal institutions not on the list of records not at risk*

Given the fact that setting up an in-house archives is extremely costly, it must be assumed that all legal institutions not included in the 'not at risk' list and which have not engaged with LRAR hold records which are potentially at risk. This lack of engagement probably indicates nothing more than a wish not to be involved in a project outside the main remit of the legal institution, but it also demonstrates a lack of interest in preserving records – otherwise, presumably, there would have been at least a response to say that the legal institution does have/has deposited its records in an archives.

46 See **Appendix II.**

47 Via articles in TLS's *Gazette*, the Bar's *Counsel*, the CILEx journal, seminars etc.

48 See **Appendix VII** for details.

49 See **Appendix VII** for details.

50 See **Appendix II S. 4.**

51 See, for example, the instruction by CIArb quoted in **Appendix VIII** that 'all records, reports, or other documents received by a mediator, as well as all notes taken by the mediator during, with reference to, or for the purposes of, the mediation should be returned to the parties or kept secure until no longer needed for any purpose relating to the mediation and then destroyed' CIArb *Practice Guideline 1: Confidentiality in mediation*, p.1, http://www.ciarb.org/docs/default-source/ciarbdocuments/guidance-and-ethics/practice-guidelines-protocols-and-rules/mediation/1–guidelines-on-confidentiality-in-mediation.pdf?sfvrsn=4.

52 The contact emails stated: 'We are working with The National Archives and The British Records Association to develop a national strategy and procedure to rescue private sector records at risk, including legal records. This includes building a picture of just how many organisations consider that they hold records of potential research value but are a) unsure of how to dispose of them either by destruction/deletion or by placing them in an archive repository or b) how data protection, GDPR etc affect records retention. If you think your organisation may be in this category then do please let me know to ensure that your concerns are not overlooked. If you do, however, already have a suitable archival repository for your selected records of value, either in-house or with a recognised third-party repository (e.g. a local authority or specialist archive), I would be most grateful if you could inform me so that we can adjust the records at risk register accordingly'.

## 8.4 Conclusion

From the above contacts it was clear that the primary obstacles to the specific rescue of legal records were, in order of importance: a) client confidentiality issues b) lack of interest on the part of legal institutions and c) reduced archival resources.

It also became obvious quite early in the project that there were too many legal institutions with records at risk (assuming that non-responders and negative responders had no interest in their historic records) for the project, given its existing resources, to undertake any kind of systematic work to broker deposits of legal records with archives. The Executive Committee therefore agreed in February 2017 that there should be a change of emphasis from concentrating on specific categories of legal records to working towards a national strategy to rescue legal records at risk in general.

Private sector records are now undoubtedly more at risk than in the past due to the decreased resources of archive repositories to proactively collect them. Legal records must be included in this wider picture; LRAR and any successor initiative therefore needs to contribute to any national strategies or initiatives to identify and rescue private sector records at risk.

To summarise, current obstacles to the collection of private sector legal records are as follows:

- Concerns about client confidentiality.
- The attitude of the legal sector in general – uninterested in its own history and/or secretive about how it works and over-concerned with confidentiality.
- Poor recordkeeping by legal institutions resulting in the loss of valuable records.
- Poor understanding by legal institutions of information as an asset to be exploited.
- Misperceptions over the application of the Data Protection Act and the GDPR to records.
- Ownership issues where individuals have acquired business records and vice versa.
- Digital obsolescence.
- The changing role of the BRA.
- Reduced archival resources to undertake anything other than ad hoc records rescue work.
- The archive sector's resulting reactive, not proactive, attitude to rescuing private sector records.
- Gaps in archival provision for legal records which do not fit into existing collections policies.

Most of the above obstacles can be overcome through a combination of strategies to rescue private sector records in general and legal records in particular. Both are long-term solutions which will take time and resources to achieve.

# Chapter 9: Solutions

Again, many of the solutions outlined below apply to private sector records in general, but one or two are focussed solely on rescuing legal records.

## 9.1 The creation of a dedicated 'legal records' archives

At the beginning of the project investigating the feasibility of creating a 'legal archives' to collect, for example, arbitration records and papers of individual legal practitioners was mooted, partly based on the assumption (see **Chapter 2**) that archives were not collecting private sector legal records. This assumption was found to be somewhat flawed because:

- The trawl though TNA's *Discovery* portal uncovered thousands of private sector legal records, primarily held by local authority archives but also by some specialist and in-house archives.
- Most existing local authority archives contacted expressed their wish to continue to collect private sector material, including legal records, relevant to their location (despite reduced resources): something which they are well qualified and experienced to do.
- The LMA advised LRAR that it would collect, if offered, records of value of London-based and/or nationally focussed legal institutions and legal practitioners located in Greater London, in accordance with its *Collections Acquisition and Management Policy*.[1]
- Some specialist archives do collect specifically 'legal' records, notably the Records of Legal Education Archives at IALS. University archives collect the papers of prominent legal practitioners or academics connected to their university, as well as keeping their own business and student records, including those of law schools.[2]
- Many legal records – especially case files – form part of the business records of organisations and as such are not, and should not be, separated from their organisational context within archives simply because they are 'legal'. Nor are they necessarily catalogued as 'legal'. The TfL case study demonstrates this point.

Nevertheless, the project identified significant gaps in collections policies through which legal records may fall: they are summarised again as follows:

- Local authority archives will only collect records relevant to their physical area.
- Specialist 'legal' archives are very thin on the ground[3] and generally comprise in-house archives holding institutional records and other collections (e.g. papers of members) specifically relevant to those institutions. It is unlikely that any of these dedicated archives would have an interest in acquiring records outside their collections focus.
- Specialist, HE and local authority archive repositories are suffering from reduced resources.

In conclusion, if specialist archives cannot be found to collect legal records at risk which do not fit into current collections policies, creating a dedicated 'legal archives' in the UK may therefore still be the only way to rescue some legal records. It must be accepted, however, that setting up and permanently funding an archives is a) extremely costly and b) requires professional management; it is not simply a matter of finding a space and storing documents in that space. It is highly unlikely in the current economic climate that any funding would be found for such a venture. It would also be difficult to establish a collection policy other than for 'legal records that no existing archives wants', but it may become necessary to develop such a policy.

The legal sector could and should take some initiative here – it is in its own interests to preserve legal records to protect its reputation and enhance its image – and as a whole it undoubtedly has the resources.[4] If support for a national 'legal

1 The policy states that the LMA will acquire 'original records relating to a) the City of London or b) the Greater London area which are London-wide in significance, particularly those of: ....Private institutions including livery companies, clubs, schools, societies, charities, professional associations, pressure groups and other organisations....Businesses, Families, estates and notable individuals...National institutions whose headquarters are based in London and which complement existing holdings... We will add to our holdings by responding to offers of archives from institutions, businesses and individuals, including additional deposits/gifts from existing depositors and donors, and by actively seeking out archives which are at risk of loss, destruction or damage' (*Collections Acquisition and Management Policy*, City of London, London Metropolitan Archives, Dec 2017 https://www.cityoflondon.gov.uk/things-to-do/london-metropolitan-archives/about/Documents/collections-acquisition-and-management-policy.pdf).

2 See **Appendix IV.**

3 See **Appendix IV.**

4 A model which could – and should – be studied by our own legal associations is that of the Legal Archives Society of Amberta. Incorporated under the Societies Act of Alberta on 18 January 1990, it is an independent body with its own Board of Directors and Executive but is partly financed by the Law Society of Alberta. The Society collects the archival records of non-governmental legal organisations, representative law firms and individual pracitioners, and members of the judiciary in Alberta. The mandate of the Society is to preserve, promote and understand the evolution of law and society in Alberta. See https://albertaonrecord.ca/legal-archives-society-of-alberta.

records archives' is not forthcoming then at the very least the regulatory and membership bodies[5] and large, well-established law firms should consider the business benefits of creating in-house archives to service the organisation and which could be made accessible to the public on request.[6] Such archives should be managed by professionals, but resources could be shared between legal organisations or staffed on a part-time basis – both models already exist for the Royal Medical College archives and for many university archives. The in-house model has also been suggested as a potential solution in TNA's *Collections at Risk* report.

LRAR has attempted with limited success to raise the awareness of the legal sector as to the potential value of its records and the business need for professional management of all its records; the Records at Risk group and/or a Legal Archives Trust could lobby towards a more successful outcome.

## 9.2 Widening the collections focus of archives to include legal records

This was not found to be necessary as lack of interest on the part of archives in collecting legal records was simply not an issue. All archive repositories contacted expressed the desire to continue to collect private sector records, including legal records, relevant to their own geographical location or special area of interest. It was assumed that most 'legal' records would form part of the business records of donating organisations or the personal papers of individuals; they would not be singled out because of their legal focus but according to their historical value in demonstrating the functions/primary role and interests of the organisation or individual and their significance to local heritage. All repositories also expressed an interest in collecting legal records in the broader sense as well as documents such as deeds; nearly all local authority archives had for some decades been in regular receipt of deeds etc from the BRA. There are in fact many success stories in relation to the rescue of legal records by archives, albeit in an ad hoc rather than a systematic way.[7]

## 9.3 Facilitating the rescue of specific collections

As noted above, a primary obstacle to rescuing legal records at risk was found to be the unwillingness of legal institutions to make their records available for research or even to discuss the possibility of doing so. This lack of engagement meant that LRAR was able to identify far fewer records *known* to be at immediate risk than was originally anticipated.

LRAR was, however, contacted for advice at various times by individual legal institutions and legal or records management practitioners following seminars, presentations or the publication of articles. Requests for advice ranged from seeking to archive collections of records to guidance on how to better manage records. Most requests were for retention and disposal schedules to assist those in charge of the records to dispose of them appropriately, whether by destruction or permanent retention, in accordance with legislative, regulatory and business requirements. Given the variations in function and focus of legal institutions drafting a detailed schedule would have been an impossible task; however, an effort has been made to create retention schedules for categories of records of potential permanent value.[8]

A list[9] tracking the progress or otherwise of all ad hoc enquiries was compiled by LRAR. Several of these requests were referred to the BRA, since LRAR's remit was not to physically rescue records but to *facilitate* their rescue. With some requests, however, it was clear at that time that neither the BRA nor LRAR could provide immediate assistance and that a national strategy was necessary to rescue certain categories of legal records (such as locally-based records with a national focus). Our expectation is that TNA and the Records at Risk group will take the lead in developing a solution for these kinds of records.

## 9.4 Improving procedures for depositing records in archives

LRAR engaged with the archive membership/pressure groups such as CALGG to ascertain their opinions on the primary issues and obstacles to collecting private sector records. CALGG in particular agreed that reduced resources, space considerations (in some cases) and the relatively new expectation that organisations should continue to have some responsibility for their records post-deposit were the main issues.[10]

5 With apologies to those which we know *do* have in-house archives, including The Law Society, the Institute and Faculty of Actuaries and the Worshipful Company of Arbitrators. We trust the management of these organisations will continue to support their archives.

6 Such as the combined records store and archives of Chadwick Lawrence Solicitors described in the case study in **Chapter 6.** There are undoubtedly more of these (we simply cannot believe that all legal service providers are unaware of the potential value of their archives to their business), but we have been unable to find them.

7 For details see **Appendix XIII: Rescuing legal records – success stories.**

8 **See Appendix VIII LRAR** *Guideline 3: advice to legal institutions on identifying records of permanent research value.*

9 See **Appendix VII.**

10 'Some archives are now having to write to depositors to request 'maintenance payments' as it were for private collections on deposit, otherwise they may be returned. I think this is more an issue about financial sustainability rather than space, but it also shows a possible trend that would affect the deposit of large private collections.', email from the CALGG Chair to LRAR, 6 July 2017.

Space problems preventing archives from collecting records were less of an issue than originally assumed; physical space constraints in particular will gradually become less of a concern now that modern records are born-digital. Where archives are beginning to take a stand is over the attitude of depositors, especially law firms, which has often been simply to decide to dump records, unsorted and unlisted, on archives[11] and, in the past, on the BRA. Archivists are now, quite rightly, insisting that depositors take some responsibility for the proper management of their own records prior to transfer and offer at least a one-off contribution to the archives' costs.

This change is only partly caused by reduced resources; it also reflects the long overdue need for more efficient and cost-effective processes for collecting private sector material. As noted above, LRAR has a) suggested to the BRA and TNA that some generic forms and information material to facilitate this change in procedure should be drafted and b) advised legal institutions on the need for good records management and appropriate disposal. LRAR additionally provided ad hoc advice on records management and records transfer to legal institutions who had seen our publicity material and sought practical help in disposing of unwanted records.[12] This LRAR guidance is one small step; a national campaign to improve recordkeeping in the private sector is needed.

## 9.5 Seeking to widen research use of legal records

The impression received from seminars, meetings and email exchanges with academic researchers, primarily in the legal field, was that researchers were not always aware of just what legal records – other than 'official' documents such as court records and legal instruments – are available in archives or how to search for them.[13] The two seminars held at the CSLS tended to confirm this impression, with students conducting empirical studies using interviews and current data[14] (such as case files, media releases, public domain reports, position papers, submissions) as their preferred research methodology. The findings from the seminars were that students to date have encountered no issues around accessing relevant material, but they may not be fully aware of the existence of much accessible – and relatively modern – information already available in archives.

Anecdotal evidence from archivists suggests that the primary use of legal records such as deeds, wills, examination and membership records is genealogical. Archive repositories do keep statistics on categories of research, but not necessarily on which specific records are used; nor is research using legal records necessarily defined as 'legal'.[15]

LRAR considers that legal records could be of immense value for any and all categories of research.[16] In 2018 we sought to further engage the interest of research communities in the value of using legal records in archives.

TNA is seeking to improve the research skills of postgraduate students through its PAST (Postgraduate Archival Training Skills) programme.[17] Such programmes should assist academic researchers to 'discover' hitherto overlooked material in archives, including legal records.

## 9.6 Creating a working model specifically to rescue and preserve legal records

Below is an outline of what was done by LRAR towards a) creating a model to specifically rescue legal records and b) identifying what was achievable with or without the input of such a model by existing special interest groups and national bodies such as the Records at Risk group.

### *9.6.1 Creating a Legal Archives Trust*

In 2018 LRAR sought to set up a working party comprising representatives from the legal sector and the archives community to determine a) whether a Legal Archives Trust funded by donations from legal stakeholders is a viable proposition b) to decide how to persuade legal entities that such a Trust is in their interest) and c) how to set up the Trust, appoint trustees and achieve charitable status.[18] The concept was first mooted in August 2016, when LRAR, with the BRA, held a meeting with representatives from the LMA and the Pensions Archive Trust, which has developed an

11 See examples under horror stories at **Appendix XII**.

12 For details see **Appendix VII**.

13 'I doubt whether any textbook writers ever heard of any of these e-cases' quoted by a senior law lecturer and arbitrator in an email response on 9 May 2016 to my forwarding from TNA's *Discovery* a list of 20th-century arbitration cases and related records available in archives

14 Another question is whether this 'current data' ever finds its way into archives. If not, why not?

15 See Annex III of the TfL case study at **Appendix X** for examples of how researchers and research are categorised for statistical purposes.

16 The above case study demonstrates the unexpected use to which legal records could be put; one arbitration between TfL and a golf club not only threw up evidence of the workings of the club itself, but of the golfing handicaps of its members! Legal records will also, of course, provide evidence of the diversity (or lack of same) of the profession and of changes in practitioner and organisational attitudes to race, gender, class etc.

17 http://www.nationalarchives.gov.uk/about/our-research-and-academic-collaboration/events-and-training/postgraduate-archival-skills-training/.

18 For the Trust's draft statement of objectives see **Appendix X Paper 2**.

excellent charitable model to facilitate the deposit of pensions records in the LMA. At this meeting it was suggested that we approach the legal sector to see if a Legal Archives Trust might be set up to undertake similar records rescue work to the Pensions Archive Trust.

Specific contributions which such a Trust could make to the rescue of legal records include:

- Advocating the business benefits of good information and records management to legal institutions.
- Advertising the services offered by archives.
- Providing volunteer archivists to survey, evaluate and list records on-site prior to transfer.
- Brokering transfer and deposit arrangements between legal institutions and archives.
- Providing assistance to archives with cataloguing records.

We were unable to generate much interest in the idea on the part of the legal sector in the time available, but we are in discussion with some research organisations and of course TNA and the BRA to seek ways in which such a Trust could become a reality post-LRAR. One part of its strategy would be for the Trust to continue – and expand – the work historically done by the BRA to rescue records of local law firms. The emphasis will now be on saving the business records of the providers of legal services and, if appropriate, the papers of local legal practitioners.

### *9.6.2 Identifying and classifying institutions specialised to law*

LRAR identified numerous categories of private sector law-related institutions and organisations in England and Wales, including both those whose records are already in archives (but which could be a risk in the future due to reduced resources and/or changes to collections policies) and those which may have records at risk.[19] It is hoped that this information will help to inform strategic efforts not only by a potential Trust but by TNA, local authority and specialist archives to identify private sector legal records before they are at risk.

### *9.6.3 Rescuing records of local and national legal bodies and practitioners based in London*

LMA has already undertaken much work to recue some bodies in this category, but, again, is without the resources to proactively continue to do this. It has tentatively agreed to accept more records of value from London-based legal bodies provided a model, preferably along the lines of a Legal Archives Trust, could be set up to facilitate and fund the process.

### *9.6.4 Rescuing legal records without an obvious archival home*

We assume that the Records at Risk group will be seeking solutions to this problem. A Legal Archives Trust could assist by lobbying existing specialist archives to expand their collections policies so that records such as those of nationally focused bodies or individuals based outside greater London do not slip through the net.

### *9.6.5 Streamlining the records transfer process*

In 2017 LRAR sought to interest the BRA in drafting a set of protocols and process documents, including guidance to potential depositors on a) the categories of records which are of potential historical value b) how mutual contact is to be made between legal bodies and archives c) advice on prior evaluation and listing of records and d) probable costs and benefits. A standard set of forms and procedures to be used by archives when negotiating deposits with legal bodies could also be developed. This would be particularly valuable where ongoing deposit arrangements, especially of born-digital records, are to be agreed. It is now hoped that a Legal Archives Trust and/or the LRAR Director, as an ongoing member of the Records at Risk steering group post-2018, will be able to successfully lobby for the creation of more targeted guidance.

### *9.6.6 Developing a national records management advocacy strategy and programme*

LRAR considers that private sector organisations (including legal) need to be targeted to demonstrate the business benefit, including the reduction of information and compliance risk, of managing and disposing of their records according to best practice. LRAR has sought to begin this advocacy process via its seminars and publications and through liaison with TNA, the BRA and the IRMS. We must now hope that TNA and others will take the lead, though a Legal Archives Trust could certainly participate in any advocacy programme.

19 See **Appendix II** and **Appendix III.**

# Chapter 10: Conclusion

## 10.1 Summary of LRAR achievements to date

At its conclusion the project had:

- Identified current archival provision for legal records, including highlighting the existence in archives of records outside the traditional 'legal' definitions and in less obvious locations.
- Identified gaps in existing archival provision for legal records.
- Identified specific categories of legal records potentially at risk and gathered evidence as to reasons why they are at risk.
- Identified specific obstacles to the rescue of legal records at risk and suggested how they can be overcome.
- Provided hands-on help and advice to selected institutions and individual legal practitioners seeking to deposit records with archives.
- Achieved an undertaking from the LMA that records of nationally focused legal institutions and individual practitioners based in the Greater London area will, if of historical value, be accepted by LMA.
- Drafted a joint advocacy strategy with the IRMS to encourage better information and records management within private sector institutions, including legal bodies.
- Provided generic recordkeeping advice to legal information owners on request.
- Sought to publicise the value of the project to researchers and archivists, and the business benefits of participation in the project to legal information owners, via articles, presentations and running or participating in seminars.
- Begun work towards developing a model, the Legal Archives Trust, to rescue legal records once the project is wound up.
- Worked with TNA and other stakeholders, to develop a strategy to proactively collect private sector records, including legal. There has never been such a strategy in relation to legal records, with the sole exception of the creation of the Records of Legal Education Archives.

These are major, but only partial, successes. The development of a) a national legal records rescue strategy and b) a Legal Archives Trust or similar body capable of taking over LRAR's work[1] is essential if our legal heritage is not to be lost, but this work cannot be finalised within a period of three years. It may be that at the close of the project in July 2019 we will be nearer to achieving these goals and in a position to hand over negotiations to parties capable of continuing the work.

## 10.2 Did LRAR achieve its aims?

Partly. It clearly identified major categories of legal records at risk and the primary obstacles to their rescue. It noted that most risks to records applied to all categories of private sector records but that one or two were unique to legal records and as such it was primarily the responsibility of the legal sector to address those issues.

It found that collection of legal records in the past has been, with one or two notable exceptions, random, ad hoc and dependent on the interest of individuals or finite collection campaigns rather than systematic collections strategies. It recommended both long-term strategies and immediate processes for rescuing legal records but accepted that any achievements would be dependent on a) resources and b) engagement.

Will a national archives sector-led strategy to rescue private sector records (including legal) and/or a Legal Archives Trust whose specific purpose is to rescue legal records be successful? We can only hope so. If not the broader history of how the UK legal sector and legal policy and practice have developed and influenced government and society will be lost.

1 Hopefully the Records at Risk group.

# APPENDICES

## Appendix I: Legal Records at Risk Advisory Panel and Executive Committee members

### *Advisory Panel:*

| Name | Occupation |
|---|---|
| Penny Baker | Vice Chair, BRA |
| Sir Ross Cranston | High Court Judge |
| Clive Freedman Q.C. | Barrister, 3VB Barristers, Gray's Inn |
| Philip Gale | Head of Standards and Improvement Team, Archives Sector Development, TNA |
| Professor Michael Lobban | Professor of Legal History, LSE and Secretary of the Selden Society |
| Professor Julie McLeod | Professor in Records Management, University of Northumbria |
| Michael Maher* | Librarian, TLS |
| Antonia Moon | British Library |
| Professor Linda Mulcahy | Professor of Law, LSE |
| Juliet Oliver | General Counsel, SRA |
| Professor Martin Partington | Emeritus Professor of Law, University of Bristol /Law Commission (retired) |
| Murray Rosen Q.C. | Barrister, 4 New Square |
| Judith Slinn | Business History/Archivist, non-governmental organisations (NGOs) |
| Richard Wiltshire | Senior Archivist – Business Archives, LMA |
| Professor Jane Winters | Chair of Digital Humanities, School of Advanced Study (SAS) |
| Philip Wood Q.C. | Special Global Counsel, Allen & Overy |

* Michael Maher has since left TLS.

### *Executive Committee members*

| Name | Occupation |
|---|---|
| Avrom Sherr | Emeritus Professor, IALS |
| William Twining | Quain Professor of Jurisprudence Emeritus, UCL |
| Steven Whittle | Information Systems Manager, IALS |
| Jules Winterton | Director and Librarian, IALS |

# Appendix II: Legal records which are not at risk

## 1. Private sector legal institutions whose records are held in an archive repository

Source: primarily TNA's *Discovery* portal but also *DANGO*[1] (Database of Archives of NGOs). Unless otherwise stated the information has come from *Discovery*. The list comprises deposited records of professional associations, societies, pressure groups, academic institutes and charities/providers of non-commercial legal services to the public. Collections with a local focus outweigh nationally-focused collections[2]. The list does not include:

- Records of the large number of government and quasi-government legal bodies held in TNA.
- Records of the courts.
- Records of local government bodies.
- Records of commercial providers of legal services, including sole practitioners: law firms, solicitors, advocates, notaries, actuaries, insurance brokers and chartered accountants. These are simply too numerous to list (for figures see **s.5** of this appendix). Records of law stationers and legal publishers are included as an exception since they are relatively few in number. Another exception is a list attempting to distinguish deposits of business records of law firms in archives from deposits comprising only deeds and other client documents (see **s.2**).
- Records of law departments and law schools held in higher and further education archives unless classified in *Discovery* as separate entities.
- Individual references by another body to a legal institution.

It is hoped that, where the records of 'live' (i.e. still functioning) organisations are deposited, the relevant archives has an ongoing agreement with the organisation for continued deposit of records in accordance with standard archival practice. There are too many records in this category for a comprehensive check to be made; random enquiries have produced statements from some repositories that ongoing agreements *are* still in place but from others that the repository has, due to reduced resources or changes to collections policies, ceased to collect the records. This means that we cannot assume that more recent records of 'live' organisations on the list below are not at risk.

1 DANGO was a project funded by the Arts and Humanities Research Council and then the Leverhulme Trust. It provided information on the availability of records relating to NGOs and pressure groups active in the UK since 1945. The project ran until October 2011. All archive links which were checked for the project are broken. http://www.dango.bham.ac.uk.

2 Numbers at the time of writing were: of 512 legal institutions listed in the table, 342 were local, 147 had a national focus and 17 an international focus. Local institutions' records were overwhelmingly held by local authority archives while those of national and internationally-focused institutions were usually held by university or specialist repositories.

| Legal institution | Archive repository (England & Wales) | Focus |
|---|---|---|
| Aberystwyth Citizens' Advice Bureau | Ceredigion Archives | Local |
| Aberystwyth Marriage Guidance Council (RELATE) | Ceredigion Archives | Local |
| Abortion Law Reform Association | Wellcome Library | National |
| Abortion Rights | Collection held privately (source: DANGO) | National |
| Action Against Medical Accidents | Collection held privately (source: DANGO) | National |
| Actresses' Franchise League | London University: London School of Economics, The Women's Library | National |
| Agency of the Copyright Libraries | Cambridge University Library: Department of Manuscripts and University Archives | National |
| Aldershot Citizens' Advice Bureau | Hampshire Archives and Local Studies | Local |
| ALERT (Against Legalised Euthanasia Research & Training) | Collection held privately (source: DANGO) | National |
| Ammanford Citizens' Advice Bureau | Carmarthenshire Archive Service | Local |
| Ampthill Citizens' Advice Bureau | Bedfordshire Archives & Records Service | Local |
| Amnesty International (UK) | Warwick University: Modern Records Centre | National |
| Amnesty International: Bognor Regis Group | West Sussex Record Office | Local |
| Amnesty International: Bolton branch | Bolton Archives and Local Studies Service | Local |
| Amnesty International: Bournville branch | Birmingham: Archives, Heritage and Photography Service | Local |
| Amnesty International: Cartmel and Grange Group | Cumbria Archive Centre, Kendal | Local |
| Amnesty International: Central Birmingham branch | Birmingham: Archives, Heritage and Photography Service | Local |
| Amnesty International: Saffron Walden Group | Essex Record Office | Local |
| Amnesty International: Sheffield Group | Sheffield City Archives | Local |
| Amnesty International: Stratford upon Avon branch | Shakespeare Birthplace Trust | Local |
| Amnesty International: West Norfolk Group | Norfolk Record Office | Local |
| Amnesty International: Wolverhampton branch | Wolverhampton City Archives | Local |
| Anti-Common Market League | Hammersmith and Fulham Archives and Local History Centre | National |
| Anti-Corn Law League: Halifax | West Yorkshire Archive Service | Local |
| Anti-Slavery International | Oxford University: Bodleian Library, Special Collections | International |
| Artists' Suffrage League | London University: London School of Economics, The Women's Library | National |
| Ashton-under-Lyne and Stalybridge Suffrage Society | Tameside Local Studies and Archives | National |
| Ashton-under-Lyne Citizens' Advice Bureau | Tameside Local Studies and Archives | Local |
| Association for Legal Justice | Collection held privately (source: DANGO) | National |
| Association of Clerical, Technical and Supervisory Staff: legal workers' branch | London Metropolitan Archives: City of London | National |
| Association of Consulting Actuaries | London Metropolitan Archives: City of London | National |
| Association of Law Teachers | London University: Institute of Advanced Legal Studies, Records of Legal Education Archives | National |
| Association of Local Government Lawyers, Wakefield | West Yorkshire Archive Service, Wakefield | Local |
| Association of Women Magistrates: Gloucestershire | Gloucestershire Archives | Local |
| Association of Women Magistrates: Hampshire | Hampshire Archives and Local Studies | Local |
| Asylum Aid | Collection held privately (source: DANGO) | International |
| Bail for Immigration Detainees | Collection held privately (source: DANGO) | International |
| Bankruptcy Association | Collection held privately (source: DANGO) | International |
| Bangor Citizens' Advice Bureau | Gwynedd Archives, Caernarfon Record Office | Local |

| Legal institution | Archive repository (England & Wales) | Focus |
|---|---|---|
| Bar Council | London University: Institute of Advanced Legal Studies, Records of Legal Education Archives and Middle Temple Archive | National |
| Bar Human Rights Committee of England and Wales | Collection held privately (source: DANGO) | National |
| Barnard's Inn | Gray's Inn Archives | Local |
| Barnsley Citizens' Advice Bureau | Barnsley Archive and Local Studies Department | Local |
| Barnsley Womens' Suffrage Society | Sheffield City Archives | National |
| Barrow-in-Furness Citizens' Advice Bureau | Cumbria Archive and Local Studies Centre, Barrow | Local |
| Barry Citizens' Advice Bureau | Glamorgan Archives | Local |
| Basildon Citizens' Advice Bureau | Essex Record Office | Local |
| Bedford Citizens' Advice Bureau | Bedfordshire Archives & Records Service | Local |
| Berkshire Buckinghamshire and Oxfordshire Incorporated Law Society | Collection held privately: enquiries to The National Archives, Archives Sector Development | Local |
| Bethnal Green Citizens' Advice Bureau | Tower Hamlets Local History Library and Archives | Local |
| Biggleswade Citizens' Advice Bureau | Bedfordshire Archives & Records Service | Local |
| Birkenhead Citizens' Advice Bureau | Wirral Archives Service | Local |
| Birmingham Law Society | Birmingham: Archives, Heritage and Photography Service | Local |
| Blackburn Citizens' Advice Bureau | Lancashire Archives | Local |
| Blackpool Citizens' Advice Bureau | Lancashire Archives | Local |
| Blackwood Citizens' Advice Bureau | Gwent Archives | Local |
| Board of Conciliation and Arbitration for the Boot and Shoe Trade of Leicester | Record Office for Leicestershire, Leicester and Rutland | Local |
| Board of Conciliation and Arbitration for the Iron and Steel Trades of the North of England | Teesside Archives | Local |
| Bolton Incorporated Law Society | Collection held privately (source: Lesley Richmond & Bridget Stockford, *Company Archives* (1984)) | Local |
| Bolton Women's Local Government Association | Bolton Archives and Local Studies Service | Local |
| Bolton Women's Suffrage Association | Bolton Archives and Local Studies Service | National |
| Bradford Citizens' Advice Bureau | West Yorkshire Archive Service, Bradford | Local |
| Braintree and District Citizens' Advice Bureau | Essex Record Office | Local |
| Bridgend Citizens' Advice Bureau | Glamorgan Archives | Local |
| Bridgewater Citizens' Advice Bureau | Somerset Heritage Centre (South West Heritage Trust) | Local |
| Brighouse Citizens' Advice Bureau | West Yorkshire Archive Service, Calderdale | Local |
| Brighton Citizens' Advice Bureau | East Sussex Record Office | Local |
| Brighton Law Centre | East Sussex Record Office | Local |
| Bristol and West of England Society for Women's Suffrage | London University: London School of Economics, The Women's Library | National |
| Bristol Law Society | Bristol Archives | Local |
| Bristol Law Students Society | Bristol Archives | Local |
| British Association for Labour Legislation | London University: London School of Economics Library, Archives and Special Collections | National |
| British Institute of Human Rights | London University: King's College Archives | National |
| British Maritime Law Association | University College London Special Collections | National |
| Bury St Edmunds Citizens' Advice Bureau | Suffolk Record Office, Bury St Edmunds Branch | Local |
| Bury St Edmunds Justice and Peace Group | Suffolk Record Office, Bury St Edmunds Branch | Local |
| Butterworth & Co, law publishers | LexisNexis Butterworths and London Metropolitan Archives: City of London | International |
| Caernarfon area Citizens' Advice Bureau | Gwynedd Archives, Caernarfon Record Office | Local |

| Legal institution | Archive repository (England & Wales) | Focus |
|---|---|---|
| Caerphilly Citizens' Advice Bureau | Glamorgan Archives | Local |
| Cambridgeshire Law Society | Cambridgeshire Archives | Local |
| Cambridge University: Gonville and Caius Law Club | Cambridge University: Gonville and Caius College Archive | Local |
| Cambridge Womens' Suffrage Association | Cambridgeshire Archives | National |
| Campaign against Racist Laws | Collection held privately. Source: DANGO | International |
| Campaign for Homosexual Equality | London University: London School of Economics Library, Archives and Special Collections | National |
| Campaign for an Independent Britain | London University: London School of Economics Library, Archives and Special Collections | National |
| Campaign for the Limitation of Secret Police Powers | Sussex University Library (source: DANGO) | National |
| Canterbury Citizens' Advice Bureau | Kent History and Library Centre | Local |
| Carlisle and District Law Society | Cumbria Archive Centre, Carlisle | Local |
| Carlisle Law Society Library | Cumbria Archive Centre, Carlisle | Local |
| Carmarthen Citizens' Advice Bureau | Carmarthenshire Archive Service | Local |
| Carshalton Citizens' Advice Bureau | London Borough of Sutton: Archives & Local Studies | Local |
| Catholic Womens Suffrage Society | London University: London School of Economics, The Women's Library | National |
| Central National Society for Womens Suffrage | London University: London School of Economics, The Women's Library | National |
| Chapeltown Citizens' Advice Bureau | West Yorkshire Archive Service, Leeds | Local |
| Charles Bond Ltd, law publishers | London Metropolitan Archives: City of London | National |
| Chartered Accountants Benevolent Association | London Metropolitan Archives: City of London | National |
| Chartered Accountants' Charities Ltd | London Metropolitan Archives: City of London | National |
| Chartered Insurance Institute | In-house archives | National |
| Chartered Insurance Institute: Cambridge branch | Cambridgeshire Archives | Local |
| Chartered Insurance Institute: Carlisle branch | Cumbria Archive Centre, Carlisle | Local |
| Chartered Insurance Institute: Gloucester branch | Gloucestershire Archives | Local |
| Cheltenham Legal Association | Gloucestershire Archives | Local |
| Cheltenham Marriage Guidance Council (RELATE) | Gloucestershire Archives | Local |
| Chester and North Wales Incorporated Law Society | Cheshire Archives and Local Studies | Local |
| Chester Citizens' Advice Bureau | Cheshire Archives and Local Studies | Local |
| Chichester Citizens' Advice Bureau | West Sussex Record Office | Local |
| Children's Law Centre | Collection held privately. Source: DANGO | National |
| Chile Committee for Human Rights: Derbyshire area | Derbyshire Record Office | Local |
| Chiswick Citizens' Advice Bureau | Hounslow Library Local Studies Service | Local |
| Cinderford Citizens' Advice Bureau | Gloucestershire Archives | Local |
| Cirencester Citizens' Advice Bureau | Gloucestershire Archives | Local |
| Citizens' Advice Bureau: National Council | London Metropolitan Archives: City of London | National |
| Cleveleys Citizens' Advice Bureau | Lancashire Archives | Local |
| Coleford Citizens' Advice Bureau | Gloucestershire Archives | Local |
| Colwyn Bay Citizens' Advice Bureau | Denbighshire Archives | Local |
| Committee of Heads of University Law Schools | London University: Institute of Advanced Legal Studies, Records of Legal Education Archives | National |
| Commonwealth Legal Education Association | London University: Institute of Advanced Legal Studies, Records of Legal Education Archives | National |
| Commonwealth Legal Records Project | London University: Institute of Advanced Legal Studies, Records of Legal Education Archives | National |

| Legal institution | Archive repository (England & Wales) | Focus |
|---|---|---|
| Conscience (formerly Greater London Interdenominational Committee for the Release of Soviet Jewry) | University of Southampton Library | International |
| Conscience: Peace Tax Campaign | Bradford University: J.B. Priestley Library | National |
| Constitutional Reform Centre | London University: London School of Economics Library, Archives and Special Collections | National |
| Consultative Committee of Constitutional Women's Suffrage Societies | London University: London School of Economics, The Women's Library | National |
| Copeland Citizens' Advice Bureau | Cumbria Archive and Local Studies Centre, Whitehaven | Local |
| Council for the Amelioration of the Legal Position of the Jewess | University of Southampton Library | National |
| Council of Legal Education | London University: Institute of Advanced Legal Studies, Records of Legal Education Archives | National |
| Countryside Alliance | Museum of English Rural Life | National |
| Coventry Citizens' Advice Bureau | Coventry Archives & Research Centre | Local |
| Cwmbran Citizens' Advice Bureau | Gwent Archives | Local |
| Cynon Valley Citizens' Advice Bureau | Glamorgan Archives | Local |
| Darlington Citizens' Advice Bureau | Durham County Record Office | Local |
| Denton Citizens' Advice Bureau | Tameside Local Studies and Archives | Local |
| Derby Citizens' Advice Bureau | Derbyshire Record Office | Local |
| Derby and Derbyshire Citizens' Advice Bureau | Derbyshire Record Office | Local |
| Derby Society of Chartered Accountants | Derbyshire Record Office | Local |
| Devon and Exeter Incorporated Law Society | Devon Archives and Local Studies Service (South West Heritage Trust) | Local |
| Devonport Citizens' Advice Bureau | Plymouth and West Devon Record Office | Local |
| Dignity in Dying | Wellcome Library | National |
| Diss Citizens' Advice Bureau | Norfolk Record Office | Local |
| Dorchester Citizens' Advice Bureau | Dorset History Centre | Local |
| Dorking Citizens' Advice Bureau | Surrey History Centre | Local |
| Droylsden Citizens' Advice Bureau | Huntingdonshire Archives | Local |
| Dudley Citizens' Advice Bureau | Dudley Archives and Local History Service | Local |
| Durham Citizens' Advice Bureau | Durham County Record Office | Local |
| Dursley Citizens' Advice Bureau | Gloucestershire Archives | Local |
| East Anglian Society of Chartered Accountants Library | Norfolk Record Office | Local |
| East Grinstead Citizens' Advice Bureau | West Sussex Record Office | Local |
| East London Federation of the Suffragettes | International Institute of Social History | National |
| Eastwood and District Citizens' Advice Bureau | Nottinghamshire Archives | Local |
| Eccles Citizens' Advice Bureau | Salford City Archives | Local |
| Ecclesiastical Law Association | Herefordshire Archive and Records Centre | Local |
| Ede & Ravenscroft, tailors (including legal dress) | In-house archives | National |
| Education in Human Rights Network | London University: Institute of Education | National |
| Electoral Reform Society of Great Britain and Ireland | In-house archives; copies in Parliamentary Archives | National |
| Eminent Scholars Archive (scholars associated with the Faculty of Law at the University of Cambridge) | Cambridge University: Squire Law Library | Local |
| English & Scottish Law Fire and Life Assurance and Loan Association | London Metropolitan Archives: City of London | National |
| Equal Pay Campaign Committee | London University: London School of Economics, The Women's Library | National |

| Legal institution | Archive repository (England & Wales) | Focus |
|---|---|---|
| Equitable Life Assurance Society | Institute and Faculty of Actuaries; London Metropolitan Archives: City of London | National |
| Esher and Molesey Citizens' Advice Bureau | Surrey History Centre | Local |
| Ewell and Stoneleigh Citizens' Advice Bureau | Surrey History Centre | Local |
| Exeter Citizens' Advice Bureau | Devon Archives and Local Studies Service (South West Heritage Trust) | Local |
| Exeter Law Library Society | Devon Archives and Local Studies Service (South West Heritage Trust) | Local |
| Faculty Office | Lambeth Palace Library | National |
| Fareham Citizens' Advice Bureau | Hampshire Archives and Local Studies | Local |
| Farnborough Citizens' Advice Bureau | Hampshire Archives and Local Studies | Local |
| Fathers 4 Justice | Bishopsgate Institute | National |
| Fawcett Society | London University: London School of Economics, The Women's Library | National |
| Felixstowe Citizens' Advice Bureau | Suffolk Record Office, Ipswich Branch | Local |
| Feltham Citizens' Advice Bureau | Hounslow Library Local Studies Service | Local |
| Fleetwood Citizens' Advice Bureau | Lancashire Archives | Local |
| Flint Citizens' Advice Bureau | Flintshire Record Office | Local |
| Forest of Dean Citizens' Advice Bureau | Gloucestershire Archives | Local |
| Formby Citizens' Advice Bureau | Lancashire Archives | Local |
| Foundation for International Environmental Law and Development | Collection held privately (source: DANGO) | International |
| Freedom Defence Committee | International Institute of Social History | International |
| Gay Activists Alliance | London University: London School of Economics Library, Archives and Special Collections | National |
| Gay Liberation Front | London University: London School of Economics Library, Archives and Special Collections | National |
| Get Britain Out Campaign: Leeds branch | West Yorkshire Archive Service, Leeds | National |
| Get Britain Out Campaign: Leicestershire branch | Leicestershire, Leicester and Rutland, Record Office for | National |
| Gloucestershire and Wiltshire Incorporated Law Society | Collection held privately: enquiries to The National Archives, Archives Sector Development | Local |
| Gloucester Citizens' Advice Bureau | Gloucestershire Archives | Local |
| Gloucestershire Justices Dining Club | Gloucestershire Archives | Local |
| Gloucestershire Magistrates Association | Gloucestershire Archives | Local |
| Gloucestershire Marriage Guidance Council (RELATE) | Gloucestershire Archives | Local |
| Gloucestershire Probation Samaritan Trust Fund | Gloucestershire Archives | Local |
| Gray's Inn | In-house archives | Local |
| Great Yarmouth Citizens' Advice Bureau | Norfolk Record Office | Local |
| Greater London Citizens' Advice Bureau | London Metropolitan Archives: City of London | Local |
| Grimsby Citizens' Advice Bureau | North East Lincolnshire Archives | Local |
| Guildford and District Peace and Justice Network | Surrey History Centre | Local |
| Gwynedd Law Society | Gwynedd Archives, Caernarfon Record Office | Local |
| Hackney Abortion Campaign | Hackney Archives Department | Local |
| Haldane Society of Socialist Lawyers | London University: London School of Economics Library, Archives and Special Collections | National |
| Halifax Citizens' Advice Bureau | West Yorkshire Archive Service, Calderdale | Local |
| Hampstead Citizens' Advice Bureau | Camden Local Studies and Archives Centre | Local |
| Harpenden Citizens' Advice Bureau | Hertfordshire Archives and Local Studies | Local |
| Harrow Citizens' Advice Bureau | Harrow Local History Centre | Local |

| Legal institution | Archive repository (England & Wales) | Focus |
|---|---|---|
| Hebden Bridge Citizens' Advice Bureau | West Yorkshire Archive Service, Calderdale | Local |
| Herefordshire Breconshire and Radnorshire Incorporated Law Society | Collection held privately: enquiries to The National Archives, Archives Sector Development | Local |
| Hertford Citizens' Advice Bureau | Hertfordshire Archives and Local Studies | Local |
| Hertfordshire Law Society | Hertfordshire Archives and Local Studies | Local |
| Hinckley and District Boot and Shoe Arbitration Board | Record Office for Leicestershire, Leicester and Rutland | Local |
| Hitchin, Stevenage and District Women's Suffrage Society | London University: London School of Economics, The Women's Library | National |
| Holborn College of Law, Languages and Commerce | University of Westminster Archives | National |
| Holyhead Citizens' Advice Bureau | Archifau Ynys Mon /Anglesey Archives | Local |
| Homerton Social Democratic Club | International Institute of Social History | Local |
| Hove Citizens' Advice Bureau | East Sussex Record Office | Local |
| Howard League for Penal Reform | Warwick University: Modern Records Centre | National |
| Huddersfield Citizens' Advice Bureau | West Yorkshire Archive Service, Kirklees | Local |
| Hull Incorporated Law Society | Collection held privately: enquiries to The National Archives, Archives Sector Development | Local |
| Human Rights Society | In-house archives | National |
| Humberside Law Centre | Hull History Centre (Hull City Archives) | Local |
| Huntingdon Citizens' Advice Bureau | Huntingdonshire Archives | Local |
| Incorporated Council of Law Reporting for England and Wales | In-house archives | National |
| Inner Temple | In-house archives | Local |
| International Abolitionist Federation | London University: London School of Economics, The Women's Library | International |
| International Centre for the Legal Protection of Human Rights | Hull History Centre (Hull University Archives) | International |
| Institute and Faculty of Actuaries | In-house archives | National |
| Institute of Chartered Accountants England & Wales | London Metropolitan Archives: City of London | National |
| Institute of Employment Rights | In-house archives | National |
| International Association for Labour Legislation: Commission on Child Labour, British Section | London University: London School of Economics Library, Archives and Special Collections | International |
| International Association of Law Libraries | London University: Institute of Advanced Legal Studies, Records of Legal Education Archives | National |
| International Centre for the Legal Protection of Human Rights | Hull History Centre (Hull University Archives) | International |
| International Law Association | London University: Institute of Advanced Legal Studies, Records of Legal Education Archives | National |
| International Woman Suffrage Alliance | London University: London School of Economics, The Women's Library; Manchester University: University of Manchester Library; Smith College Library; New York Public Library: Manuscripts and Archives Division | International |
| International Year of Human Rights: Yorkshire committee | West Yorkshire Archive Service, Bradford | Local |
| Justice (British Section of the International Commission of Jurists) | Hull History Centre (Hull University Archives) | National |
| Justice Africa | Durham University Library, Special Collections | International |
| Justices Clerks Society: Essex Branch | Essex Record Office | Local |
| Kendal Citizens' Advice Bureau | Cumbria Archive Centre, Kendal | Local |
| Kent Law Society | Kent History and Library Centre | Local |

| Legal institution | Archive repository (England & Wales) | Focus |
|---|---|---|
| Kentish Town Citizens' Advice Bureau | Camden Local Studies and Archives Centre | Local |
| Kings Cross Citizens' Advice Bureau | Camden Local Studies and Archives Centre | Local |
| Kingston Citizens' Advice Bureau | Kingston History Centre | Local |
| Labour Campaign for Criminal Justice | London University: London School of Economics Library, Archives and Special Collections | National |
| Labour Campaign for Electoral Reform | In-house archives | National |
| Lambeth Mediation Service | Lambeth Archives | Local |
| Law Centres Federation/Network | In-house archives | National |
| Law Reversionary Interest Society Ltd | Collection held privately: *see* H.A.L. Cockerell & E. Green, *The British Insurance Business*, 1994 | National |
| The Law Society | In-house archives | National |
| Law Society Cricket Club | Surrey History Centre | Local |
| Law Students' Debating Society, London | London Metropolitan Archives: City of London | Local |
| Leasehold Enfranchisement Association | London Metropolitan Archives: City of London | National |
| Leeds Citizens' Advice Bureau | West Yorkshire Archive Service, Leeds | Local |
| Leeds Law Society | Collection held privately: enquiries to The National Archives, Archives Sector Development | Local |
| Leeds Law Students Society | West Yorkshire Archive Service, Leeds | Local |
| Legal Action Group | In-house archives | National |
| Legal Skills Research Group | London University: Institute of Advanced Legal Studies, Records of Legal Education Archives | National |
| Leicestershire and Northamptonshire Society of Chartered Accountants | Record Office for Leicestershire, Leicester and Rutland | Local |
| Leicestershire and Rutland Board of Conciliation and Arbitration for the Boot and Shoe Trade | Record Office for Leicestershire, Leicester and Rutland | Local |
| Leicester Citizens' Advice Bureau | Record Office for Leicestershire, Leicester and Rutland | Local |
| Leicestershire Law Society | Record Office for Leicestershire, Leicester and Rutland | Local |
| Leigh Park, Portsmouth Citizens' Advice Bureau | Portsmouth History Centre | Local |
| Letchworth Citizens' Advice Bureau | Hertfordshire Archives and Local Studies | Local |
| Lewes Citizens' Advice Bureau | East Sussex Record Office | Local |
| LexisNexis Butterworths | In-house archives | National |
| Liberty, civil liberties and human rights campaigning organisation | Hull History Centre (Hull University Archives) | National |
| Lincoln's Inn | In-house archives | Local |
| Lincolnshire Incorporated Law Society | Lincolnshire Archives | Local |
| Liverpool Citizens' Advice Bureau | Liverpool Record Office | Local |
| Liverpool Incorporated Law Society | Liverpool Record Office *and* held privately: enquiries to The National Archives, Archives Sector Development | Local |
| Liverpool Society of Chartered Accountants | Collection held privately | Local |
| Llanelli Citizens' Advice Bureau | Carmarthenshire Archive Service | Local |
| London Beth Din | London Metropolitan Archives: City of London | Local |
| London Court of Arbitration | London Metropolitan Archives: City of London | Local |
| London Criminal Courts Solicitors Association | In-house (online archive) | Local |
| London Labour Council for Adult Suffrage | International Institute of Social History | National |
| London Magistrates Clerks Association | London Metropolitan Archives: City of London | Local |
| London National Society for Womens Suffrage | London University: London School of Economics, The Women's Library | National |
| London National Society for Womens Suffrage: Whitechapel and St George's in the East branch | London University: London School of Economics, The Women's Library | National |

| Legal institution | Archive repository (England & Wales) | Focus |
|---|---|---|
| London National Society for Womens Suffrage: Wimbledon branch | London University: London School of Economics, The Women's Library | National |
| London University: King's College London, Centre for Medical Law and Ethics | London University: King's College Archives | Local |
| London University: King's College London School of Law | London University: King's College Archives | Local |
| London University: King's College London School of Law student records | London University: King's College Archives | Local |
| Long Eaton Citizens' Advice Bureau | Derbyshire Record Office | Local |
| Lower Broughton Citizens' Advice Bureau | Salford City Archives | Local |
| Lundwood Citizens' Advice Bureau | Barnsley Archive and Local Studies Department | Local |
| Lydney Citizens' Advice Bureau | Gloucestershire Archives | Local |
| Macclesfield Citizens' Advice Bureau | Cheshire Archives and Local Studies | Local |
| Magistrates Association | Magistrates Association | National |
| Magistrates Association: East Sussex branch | East Sussex Record Office | Local |
| Magistrates Association: Monmouthshire branch | Gwent Archives | Local |
| Magistrates Association: Wiltshire branch | Wiltshire and Swindon History Centre | Local |
| Maidstone Citizens' Advice Bureau | Kent History and Library Centre | Local |
| Manchester Law Clerks Friendly Society | Manchester Archives and Local Studies | Local |
| Manchester Law Society | Collection held privately: enquiries to The National Archives, Archives Sector Development | Local |
| Manchester Men's League for Women's Suffrage | Manchester University: University of Manchester Library | National |
| Manchester Society for Women's Suffrage | Manchester Archives and Local Studies | National |
| Manchester Society of Chartered Accountants | Manchester Library *and* Local Studies and held privately: enquiries to The National Archives, Archives Sector Development | Local |
| Manchester University, Faculty of Law Archive | Manchester University: University of Manchester Library | Local |
| Manx Penal Reform Group | Manx National Heritage Library & Archives | Local |
| Marriage Law Reform Society | Collection held privately: see Cook & Waller, *Sources in Contemporary British History*, vol 1, 1994 | National |
| Marriage Law Reform Society: Sheffield Committee | Sheffield City Archives | Local |
| Mediation UK | London University: London School of Economics Library, Archives and Special Collections | National |
| Melksham and District Citizens' Advice Bureau | Wiltshire and Swindon History Centre | Local |
| Merseyside and West Cheshire Area Citizens' Advice Bureau | Merseyside Record Office | Local |
| Metropolitan Counties Anti-Abolition Campaign: London Office | Tyne and Wear Archives | Local |
| Mid Bedfordshire Citizens' Advice Bureau | Bedfordshire Archives and Records Service | Local |
| Mid Surrey Law Society | Surrey History Centre | Local |
| Mid Wales Law Society | Powys County Archives Office | Local |
| Middle Temple | In-house archives | Local |
| Middlesex Justices' Dining Club | London Metropolitan Archives: City of London | Local |
| Midsomer Norton Citizens' Advice Bureau | Somerset Heritage Centre (South West Heritage Trust) | Local |
| Millom and District Citizens' Advice Bureau | Cumbria Archive and Local Studies Centre, Whitehaven | Local |
| Milton Keynes Citizens' Advice Bureau | Centre for Buckinghamshire Studies | Local |
| Monmouthshire Magistrates | Gwent Archives | Local |
| National Abortion Campaign | Wellcome Library | National |

| Legal institution | Archive repository (England & Wales) | Focus |
|---|---|---|
| National Family Mediation | London University: London School of Economics Library, Archives and Special Collections | National |
| National Marriage Guidance Council (RELATE) | In-house archives and London Metropolitan Archives: City of London | National |
| National Poor Law Officers Association | Warwick University: Modern Records Centre | National |
| National Poor Law Officers Association: Birmingham and district branch | Birmingham: Archives, Heritage and Photography Service | Local |
| National Poor Law Officers Association: Cambridgeshire and Isle of Ely branch | Cambridgeshire Archives | Local |
| National Poor Law Officers Association: North Lancashire branch | Manchester Archives and Local Studies | Local |
| National Referendum Campaign | Parliamentary Archives | National |
| National Society for the Prevention of Cruelty to Children (NSPCC) | In-house archives (source: Cook & Waller, *Sources in Contemporary British History*, vol 1, 1994) | National |
| NSPCC: Bromley and District branch | Bromley Historic Collections | Local |
| NSPCC: Burton upon Trent and District Branch | Staffordshire and Stoke-on-Trent Archive Service: Lichfield Record Office | Local |
| NSPCC: Bury St Edmunds branch | Suffolk Record Office, Bury St Edmunds Branch | Local |
| NSPCC: Capel Bangor branch | Ceredigion Archives | Local |
| NSPCC: Great Yarmouth committee | Norfolk Record Office | Local |
| NSPCC: Keighley committee | Keighley Local Studies Library | Local |
| NSPCC: Liverpool branch | Liverpool Record Office | Local |
| NSPCC: Llangollen branch | Denbighshire Archives | Local |
| NSPCC: Maldon branch | Essex Record Office | Local |
| NSPCC: Southend-on-Sea and South East Essex branch | Essex Record Office | Local |
| National Society for Womens Suffrage | London University: London School of Economics, the Women's Library | National |
| Nationality of Married Women Committee | London University: London School of Economics, the Women's Library | National |
| National Union of Women's Suffrage Societies | Cumbria Archive Centre, Carlisle; London University: London School of Economics, the Women's Library; Manchester Archives and Local Studies; Manchester University: University of Manchester Library | National |
| National Union of Women's Suffrage Societies: Bedford branch | Bedfordshire Archives & Records Service | National |
| National Union of Women's Suffrage Societies: Bolton branch | Bolton Archives and Local Studies Service | National |
| National Union of Women's Suffrage Societies: Carmarthen branch | Carmarthenshire Archive Service | National |
| National Union of Women's Suffrage Societies: Clitheroe branch | Lancashire Archives | National |
| National Union of Women's Suffrage Societies: Great Yarmouth branch | Norfolk Archives | National |
| National Union of Women's Suffrage Societies: Keswick branch | Cumbria Archive Centre, Carlisle | National |
| National Union of Women's Suffrage Societies: LLangollen branch | National Library of Wales: Department of Collection Services | National |
| National Union of Women's Suffrage Societies: Nottingham and Notts branch | Nottinghamshire Archives | National |
| National Union of Women's Suffrage Societies: Penarth branch | Glamorgan Archives | National |

| Legal institution | Archive repository (England & Wales) | Focus |
|---|---|---|
| National Union of Women's Suffrage Societies: Portsmouth branch | Portsmouth History Centre | National |
| National Union of Women's Suffrage Societies: Southampton branch | Southampton Archives Office | National |
| National Union of Women's Suffrage Societies: West Cambridgeshire branch | Cambridgeshire Archives | National |
| National Women Citizens Association | London University: London School of Economics, The Women's Library | National |
| National Women Citizens Association: Ambleside branch | Armitt Library and Museum | Local |
| National Women Citizens Association: Beckenham branch | Bromley Historic Collections | Local |
| National Women Citizens Association: Beddington, Wallington and Carshalton branch | London University: London School of Economics, The Women's Library; London Borough of Sutton: Archives & Local Studies | Local |
| National Women Citizens Association: Birmingham branch | Birmingham: Archives, Heritage and Photography Service | Local |
| National Women Citizens Association: Bolton branch | Bolton Archives and Local Studies Service | Local |
| National Women Citizens Association: Cambridge and district branch | Cambridgeshire Archives | Local |
| National Women Citizens' Association: Canterbury branch | Canterbury Cathedral Archives | Local |
| National Women Citizens Association: Cardiff branch | Glamorgan Archives | Local |
| National Women Citizens Association: Chorley branch | London University: London School of Economics, The Women's Library | Local |
| National Women Citizens Association: Coulsdon and Purley branch | London University: London School of Economics, The Women's Library | Local |
| National Women Citizens Association: Crawley branch | London University: London School of Economics, The Women's Library | Local |
| National Women Citizens Association: Dulwich branch | London University: London School of Economics, The Women's Library | Local |
| National Women Citizens Association: Maidstone branch | London University: London School of Economics, The Women's Library | Local |
| National Women Citizens Association: Morecambe and Heysham branch | London University: London School of Economics, The Women's Library | Local |
| National Women Citizens Association: North West federation | London University: London School of Economics, The Women's Library | Local |
| National Women Citizens Association: Portsmouth branch | Portsmouth History Centre | Local |
| National Women Citizens Association: Preston branch | Lancashire Archives | Local |
| National Women Citizens Association: Ruskin Park branch | London University: London School of Economics, The Women's Library | Local |
| National Women Citizens Association: St Marylebone branch | City of Westminster Archives Centre | Local |
| National Women Citizens Association: Southern federation | London University: London School of Economics, The Women's Library | Local |
| National Women Citizens Association: Stockton Thornaby and district branch | Teesside Archives; London University: London School of Economics, The Women's Library | Local |
| National Women Citizens Association: Sutton and Cheam branch | London University: London School of Economics, The Women's Library | Local |
| New Inn | Middle Temple Library and Archive | Local |
| New Milton Citizens' Advice Bureau | Hampshire Archives and Local Studies | Local |
| Newcastle Citizens' Advice Bureau | Tyne and Wear Archives | Local |

| Legal institution | Archive repository (England & Wales) | Focus |
|---|---|---|
| Newcastle Legal Discussion Society | Tyne and Wear Archives | Local |
| Newcastle upon Tyne Incorporated Law Society | Tyne and Wear Archives | Local |
| Newcastle upon Tyne Law Students Society | Tyne and Wear Archives | Local |
| Newport Citizens' Advice Bureau | Gwent Archives | Local |
| Norfolk and Norwich Incorporated Law Society Library | Norfolk Record Office | Local |
| Northampton Citizens' Advice Bureau | Northamptonshire Record Office | Local |
| North and West Wiltshire Marriage Guidance Council (RELATE) | Wiltshire and Swindon History Centre | Local |
| North Bedfordshire Citizens' Advice Bureau | Bedfordshire Archives and Records Service | Local |
| North of England Society for Women's Suffrage: Ashton-under-Lyne and district branch | Tameside Local Studies and Archives | National |
| Nottingham Chartered Accountants Students Society | Nottinghamshire Archives | Local |
| Nottingham, Derby and Lincoln Society of Chartered Accountants | Nottinghamshire Archives | Local |
| Nottingham Society of Chartered Accountants | Nottinghamshire Archives | Local |
| Nottinghamshire Law Society | Collection held privately: enquiries to The National Archives, Archives Sector Development | Local |
| Okehampton and District Citizens' Advice Bureau | Devon Archives and Local Studies Service (South West Heritage Trust) | Local |
| Oldham Women's Suffrage Society | London University: London School of Economics, The Women's Library | National |
| Ollerton Citizens' Advice Bureau | Nottinghamshire Archives | Local |
| Oswestry Citizens' Advice Bureau | Shropshire Archives | Local |
| Oxford Citizens' Advice Bureau | Oxfordshire History Centre | Local |
| Parents Against Injustice | Collection held privately: See Cook & Waller, *Sources in Contemporary British History*, vol 1, 1994 | National |
| Parity (pension equality organisation) | Hull History Centre (Hull University Archives) | National |
| Parliamentary Committee for Women's Suffrage | Manchester University: University of Manchester Library | National |
| Penrith Citizens' Advice Bureau | Cumbria Archive Centre, Carlisle | Local |
| Petersfield Citizens' Advice Bureau | Hampshire Archives and Local Studies | Local |
| Pimlico Citizens' Advice Bureau | City of Westminster Archives Centre | Local |
| Plymouth, Stonehouse and Devonport Law Students Society | Plymouth and West Devon Record Office | Local |
| Plymouth Citizens' Advice Bureau | Plymouth and West Devon Record Office | Local |
| Pontypool Citizens' Advice Bureau | Gwent Archives | Local |
| Poole Citizens' Advice Bureau | Dorset History Centre | Local |
| Portsmouth and District Law Clerks Association | Portsmouth History Centre | Local |
| Potters Bar Citizens' Advice Bureau | Hertfordshire Archives and Local Studies | Local |
| Preston Citizens' Advice Bureau | Lancashire Archives | Local |
| Preston Law Debating Society | Lancashire Archives | Local |
| Prison Reform Trust | In-house archives (source: Cook & Waller, *Sources in Contemporary British History*, vol 1, 1994) | National |
| Prolife Alliance | Collection held privately (source: DANGO) | National |
| Programme for Reform of the Law on Soliciting | Warwick University: Modern Records Centre | National |
| Ramsey Citizens' Advice Bureau | Huntingdonshire Archives | Local |
| Reading Citizens' Advice Bureau | Berkshire Record Office | Local |
| Records of Legal Education Project | London University: Institute of Advanced Legal Studies, Records of Legal Education Archives | National |

| Legal institution | Archive repository (England & Wales) | Focus |
| --- | --- | --- |
| Republic (Republic Campaign Ltd), London | Bishopsgate Institute | National |
| Rhyl Citizens' Advice Bureau | Denbighshire Archives | Local |
| Rights of Women | London University: London School of Economics, the Women's Library | National |
| Ringwood and Fordingbridge Citizens' Advice Bureau | Hampshire Archives and Local Studies | Local |
| Rossendale Citizens' Advice Bureau | Lancashire Archives | Local |
| Robert Yorston, law stationer | The National Archives | National |
| Royal Institution of Chartered Surveyors | City of Westminster Archives Centre | National |
| St Albans District Citizens' Advice Bureau | Hertfordshire Archives and Local Studies | Local |
| St Marylebone Citizens' Advice Bureau | City of Westminster Archives Centre | Local |
| St Neots Citizens' Advice Bureau | Huntingdonshire Archives | Local |
| Salford Citizens' Advice Bureau | Salford City Archives | Local |
| Salisbury Marriage Guidance Council (RELATE) | Wiltshire and Swindon History Centre | Local |
| Scriveners' Company, Newcastle | Tyne and Wear Archives | Local |
| Selly Oak Citizens' Advice Bureau | Birmingham: Archives, Heritage and Photography Service | Local |
| S.G. Field, law stationer | Shakespeare Birthplace Trust | Local |
| Sheffield and District Society of Chartered Accountants | Collection held privately: See Wendy Habgood, *Chartered Accountants in England & Wales*, 1994 | Local |
| Sheffield District Incorporated Law Society | Collection held privately: enquiries to The National Archives, Archives Sector Development | Local |
| Shelter: National Campaign for the Homeless | Bishopsgate Institute | National |
| Shelter: National Campaign for the Homeless – Bedford Group | Bedfordshire Archives and Records Service | Local |
| Shelter Cymru | National Library of Wales: Department of Collection Services | Local |
| Shoe Trade Board of Arbitration | Northamptonshire Record Office | Local |
| Shrewsbury and Central Shropshire Citizens' Advice Bureau | Shropshire Archives; Bishopsgate Institute | Local |
| Sidmouth and District Women's Suffrage Society | Devon Archives and Local Studies Service (South West Heritage Trust) | National |
| Skipton Citizens' Advice Bureau | Craven Museum and Gallery | Local |
| Society for Advanced Legal Studies | London University: Institute of Advanced Legal Studies, Records of Legal Education Archives | National |
| Society of Labour Lawyers | London University: London School of Economics Library, Archives and Special Collections | National |
| Society of Public Teachers of Law (now Society of Legal Scholars) | London University: Institute of Advanced Legal Studies, Records of Legal Education Archives | National |
| Society of Scrivener Notaries (formerly Society of Public Notaries of London) | London Metropolitan Archives: City of London | National |
| Socio-Legal Studies Association | London University: Institute of Advanced Legal Studies, Records of Legal Education Archives | National |
| Solicitors Benevolent Association: Gainsborough | Lincolnshire Archives | Local |
| Solicitors Law Stationery Society Ltd, printers and publishers | Collection held privately: See Lesley Richmond & Bridget Stockford, *Company Archives*,1984 | National |
| Somerset Law Society | Somerset Heritage Centre | Local |
| South East Staffordshire Citizens' Advice Bureau | Staffordshire and Stoke-on-Trent Archive Service: Lichfield Record Office | Local |
| South East Surrey Law Society | Surrey History Centre | Local |
| South Manchester Law Centre | Manchester Archives and Local Studies | Local |

| Legal institution | Archive repository (England & Wales) | Focus |
|---|---|---|
| South Wales and Monmouthshire Society of Chartered Accountants | Glamorgan Archives | Local |
| South Wansdyke Citizens' Advice Bureau | Somerset Heritage Centre (South West Heritage Trust) | Local |
| Southwark Citizens' Advice Bureau | London Metropolitan Archives: City of London | Local |
| Stafford Citizens' Advice Bureau | Staffordshire and Stoke-on-Trent Archive Service: Staffordshire County Record Office | Local |
| Staines Citizens' Advice Bureau | London Metropolitan Archives: City of London | Local |
| Stalybridge Citizens' Advice Bureau | Tameside Local Studies and Archives | Local |
| Staple Inn | Gray's Inn Archives | Local |
| Status of Women Committee | London University: London School of Economics, the Women's Library | National |
| Stevens & Sons Ltd, law publishers | Collection held privately: enquiries to The National Archives, Archives Sector Development | National |
| Stratford-on-Avon Citizens' Advice Bureau | Shakespeare Birthplace Trust | Local |
| Stroud Citizens' Advice Bureau | Gloucestershire Archives | Local |
| Sunbury and Shepperton branch Citizens' Advice Bureau | Surrey History Centre | Local |
| Sunderland Anti-Corn Law Association | Tyne and Wear Archives | Local |
| Sunderland Law Students Society | Tyne and Wear Archives | Local |
| Sussex Law Society | East Sussex Record Office | Local |
| Sweet & Maxwell Ltd, law publishers and booksellers | In-house archives and University of Reading: Special Collections | International |
| Swinton and Pendlebury Citizens' Advice Bureau | Salford City Archives | Local |
| Swiss Cottage Citizens' Advice Bureau | Camden Local Studies and Archives Centre | Local |
| Tariff Reform League: Brighton and Hove Branch | Collection held privately: enquiries to West Sussex Record Office | National |
| Tariff Reform League: Kidderminster Branch | Oxford University: Bodleian Library, Special Collections | National |
| Taunton Citizens' Advice Bureau | Somerset Heritage Centre (South West Heritage Trust) | Local |
| Todmorden Anti-Corn Law Association | West Yorkshire Archive Service, Calderdale | Local |
| Todmorden Citizens' Advice Bureau | West Yorkshire Archive Service, Calderdale | Local |
| Torquay Citizens' Advice Bureau | Devon Archives and Local Studies Service (South West Heritage Trust) | Local |
| Tory Campaign for Homosexual Equality | London University: London School of Economics Library, Archives and Special Collections | National |
| United Kingdom National Committee of Comparative Law | London University: Institute of Advanced Legal Studies, Records of Legal Education Archives | National |
| United Law Clerks Society | London Metropolitan Archives: City of London | National |
| United Law Debating Society | Camden Local Studies and Archives Centre | Local |
| University College London School of Public Policy: Constitution Unit | British Library, Manuscript Collections | National |
| University of Wales Aberystwyth Department of Law | Aberystwyth University | Local |
| Uxbridge Citizens' Advice Bureau | Hillingdon Local Studies, Archives and Museums Service | Local |
| Wakefield Law Society | West Yorkshire Archive Service, Wakefield | Local |
| Wales for the Assembly Campaign | Swansea University: Richard Burton Archives and National Library of Wales: Department of Collection Services | National |
| Walsall Citizens' Advice Bureau | Walsall Local History Centre | Local |
| Waltham Forest Citizens' Advice Bureau | Waltham Forest Archives | Local |

| Legal institution | Archive repository (England & Wales) | Focus |
|---|---|---|
| Walton, Weybridge and Hersham Citizens' Advice Bureau | Surrey History Centre | Local |
| Warrington Law Society | Livewire Warrington Library and Archive Service | Local |
| Watford Citizens' Advice Bureau | Hertfordshire Archives and Local Studies | Local |
| Welwyn Garden City Citizens' Advice Bureau | Hertfordshire Archives and Local Studies | Local |
| West Hampstead Citizens' Advice Bureau | Camden Local Studies and Archives Centre | Local |
| West Midlands Association of Women Solicitors | Birmingham: Archives, Heritage and Photography Service | Local |
| West Surrey Law Society | Surrey History Centre | Local |
| Westminster Citizens' Advice Bureau | City of Westminster Archives Centre | Local |
| Weston-super-Mare Citizens' Advice Bureau | Somerset Heritage Centre (South West Heritage Trust) | Local |
| Weymouth and Portland Citizens' Advice Bureau | Dorset History Centre | Local |
| Whitehaven Citizens' Advice Bureau | Cumbria Archive and Local Studies Centre, Whitehaven | Local |
| Whitehaven Incorporated Law Society | Cumbria Archive and Local Studies Centre, Whitehaven | Local |
| Wigan Citizens' Advice Bureau | Wigan Archives and Local Studies | Local |
| Wiltshire Probation Trust | Wiltshire and Swindon History Centre | Local |
| Winchester Citizens' Advice Bureau | Hampshire Archives and Local Studies | Local |
| Wolverhampton Citizens' Advice Bureau | Wolverhampton City Archives | Local |
| Wolverhampton Law Centre | Wolverhampton Archives and Local Studies | Local |
| Wolverhampton Marriage Guidance Council (RELATE) | Wolverhampton City Archives | Local |
| Women for Westminster | London University: London School of Economics, the Women's Library | National |
| Women for Westminster: Bournemouth branch | London University: London School of Economics, the Women's Library | National |
| Women Living Under Muslim Laws - International Solidarity Network | Collection held privately (source: DANGO) | International |
| Women's Freedom League | London University: London School of Economics, the Women's Library | National |
| Women's Local Government Society | London University: London School of Economics, the Women's Library and London Metropolitan Archives: City of London | Local |
| Women's Provisional Club | London University: London School of Economics, the Women's Library | National |
| Women's Publicity Planning Association | London University: London School of Economics, the Women's Library | National |
| Womens Rights Campaign | London University: London School of Economics, the Women's Library | National |
| Worcester and Worcestershire Incorporated Law Society | Worcestershire Archive and Archaeology Service | Local |
| Worcester Citizens' Advice Bureau and Worcester Housing and Benefits Advice Centre | Worcestershire Archive and Archaeology Service | Local |
| Worcester Law Students Society | Worcestershire Archive and Archaeology Service | Local |
| Workington Citizens' Advice Bureau | Cumbria Archive and Local Studies Centre, Whitehaven | Local |
| Worshipful Company of Arbitrators | In-house archives | National |
| Worshipful Company of Scriveners, London | London Metropolitan Archives: City of London | Local |
| Worsley Citizens' Advice Bureau | Salford City Archives | Local |
| York Citizens' Advice Bureau | Explore York Libraries & Archives | Local |
| Yorkshire Law Society | North Yorkshire County Record Office | Local |

## 2. Law firms whose administrative records have been deposited in archives

Source: TNA's *Discovery* was examined using the advanced search facility to link the keywords 'solicitor', 'firm' and 'records'. There were 4,422 hits for records in archives other than TNA; many of these hits, however, were multiple entries for the same firm. Once these were removed, entries where it was obvious from the description that the collection comprised *solely* client documents such as deeds and wills deposited by the client with the solicitor were further excluded. The remainder, listed below, are assumed to hold administrative records of the firm and/or its predecessors (such as correspondence, cash books, day books, bills, diaries, insurance papers, property transactions, schedules of documents, indexes to client papers) and client files (as opposed to solely documents belonging to clients). With one or two exceptions, the collections are held in local authority archives.

| Firm | Records | Repository |
|---|---|---|
| Adams and Remers of Lewes, solicitors | Firm's and clients' papers | East Sussex Record Office |
| Addison, Jesson and Copper, solicitors of Walsall | Clients' papers | Staffordshire and Stoke-on-Trent Archive Service: Staffordshire County Record Office |
| Andrews and Hepworth, Pewsey, solicitors | Firm's Records, Dixon and Mason | Wiltshire and Swindon History Centre |
| Ashurst Morris Crisp and Company | Records of the firm and its predecessors | London Metropolitan Archives: City of London |
| Awdry, Douglas and Bailey, solicitors | Records of | Wiltshire and Swindon History Centre |
| Awdrys, solicitors of Chippenham | Firm's Records | Wiltshire and Swindon History Centre |
| Bannister and King, formerly Bernard, King and Sons, solicitors of Stourbridge, Worcestershire | Firm's and clients' papers | Staffordshire and Stoke-on-Trent Archive Service: Staffordshire County Record Office |
| Baxter and Somerville, solicitors of Doncaster | Firm's and clients' papers | Doncaster Archives |
| Beale & Co., solicitors | Firm's and clients' papers | Birmingham: Archives, Heritage and Photography Service |
| Blaker, Son and Young of Lewes, solicitors | Firm and clients' records | East Sussex Record Office |
| Blandy & Blandy, solicitors | Clients' records | Berkshire Record Office |
| Bond Pearce and Co., solicitors | Property and estate papers | Plymouth and West Devon Record Office |
| Branson and Bramley, solicitors of Sheffield | Firm and clients' records | Sheffield Assay Office |
| Brethertons of Rugby, solicitors | Firm and clients' records | Warwickshire County Record Office |
| Brockbank and Helder, solicitors of Whitehaven | Firm and clients' records | Cumbria Archive and Local Studies Centre, Whitehaven |
| Brockbank and Tyson, solicitors of Whitehaven | Firm and clients' records | Cumbria Archive and Local Studies Centre, Whitehaven |
| Brookes and Badham, solicitors, Tewkesbury | Firm and clients' records | Gloucestershire Archives |
| Brundrett & Co. of 10 Kings Bench Walk, solicitors | Clients' papers | East Sussex Record Office |
| Bull, solicitors, Newport Pagnell | Firm and clients' records | Centre for Buckinghamshire Studies |
| Campbell, Brown & Ledbrook of Warwick, solicitors | Internal records of the firm and of Greenway and Partners, and their predecessors + client records | Warwickshire County Record Office |
| Carne-Hill & Wedd, solicitors | Firm and clients' records | Somerset Heritage Centre (South West Heritage Trust) |
| Chanter, Burrington & Foster, Barnstaple | Firm and predecessor records | North Devon Record Office (South West Heritage Trust) |
| Charles Sheppard and Sons of Battle, solicitors | Coronership of the Rye District of East Sussex and predecessor jurisdictions | East Sussex Record Office |
| Chaundler and Co. | Office diaries of the firm | Bedfordshire Archives & Records Service |

| Firm | Records | Repository |
|---|---|---|
| Clark and Co., solicitors, Snaith | Firm and clients' records | East Riding of Yorkshire Archives and Local Studies Service |
| Coles and James, solicitors, Eastbourne | Firm and clients' records | East Sussex Record Office |
| Collyer Bristow, solicitors | Firm and clients' records and records of predecessors | London Metropolitan Archives: City of London |
| Cooper, solicitors of Henley-on-Thames and Marlow | Firm and clients' records | Oxfordshire History Centre |
| Cornish & Birtill, solicitors | Firm and clients' records | Cornwall Record Office |
| D. J. Mason and Company, solicitors, of Workington | Firm and clients' records | Cumbria Archive and Local Studies Centre, Whitehaven |
| Dawes, Son and Prentice of Rye, solicitors | Firm's and clients' papers | East Sussex Record Office |
| Dibb Lupton & Co., solicitors, Leeds | Clients' papers and predecessor firms' records | West Yorkshire Archive Service, Leeds |
| Donne, Mileham and Haddock of Brighton, solicitors | Firm's and clients' papers | East Sussex Record Office |
| Drake and Lee of Lewes, solicitor | Archive of | East Sussex Record Office |
| Eaton, Smith and Downey, solicitors, Huddersfield, Incorporating Laycock, Dyson, and Laycock | Firm's and clients' papers | West Yorkshire Archive Service, Wakefield |
| Elwell & Son, Highworth, solicitors | Firm's and clients' papers | Wiltshire and Swindon History Centre |
| Ennions, solicitors, Newmarket | Firm's and clients' papers | Suffolk Record Office, Bury St Edmunds Branch |
| Eversheds, solicitors, Norwich | Business records and client papers | Norfolk Record Office |
| F.B. Hancock & Co., solicitors | Firm's and clients' records | Warwickshire County Record Office |
| F.H.C. Hannam Clark and Son, solicitors of Gloucester | Firm's and clients' records | Gloucestershire Archives |
| Farnfield & Nichols, solicitors, Gillingham and Warminster | Firm's records | Dorset History Centre |
| Farnfield and Nicholls, solicitors, of Warminster | Solicitors' business records | Wiltshire and Swindon History Centre |
| Farrer & Co., solicitors, London | Records including Somerset deeds | Somerset Heritage Centre (South West Heritage Trust) |
| Fitzhugh Gates of Brighton, solicitors | Client's papers | East Sussex Record Office |
| Fosters, solicitors | Accounts, business records, clients papers and manorial records, incl predecessor firms | Norfolk Record Office |
| Freshfields, solicitors | Papers re the firm's work as solicitors to the Bank of England | Bank of England Archive |
| G. F. Lodder & Sons, solicitors | Business papers | Shakespeare Birthplace Trust |
| George Wintringham Cutts, solicitor and Commissioner for Oaths, Bognor Regis | Office ledger | West Sussex Record Office |
| Goldingham and Jotcham, solicitors | Firm's and clients' records | Gloucestershire Archives |
| Grays, solicitors | Deeds and papers rel to ecclesiastical matters, manorial records, incl predecessor Gray, Dodsworth & Cobb firm | Borthwick Institute for Archives: University of York |
| Greene and Greene | Firm's records | Suffolk Record Office, Bury St Edmunds Branch |
| Gudgeons, Peecock & Prentice, solicitors | Manorial records, firm's financial records and clients' papers | Suffolk Record Office, Ipswich Branch |
| Guillaume and Sons, solicitors | Property and firm records | London Metropolitan Archives, City of London |

| Firm | Records | Repository |
|---|---|---|
| H.F.T. Gough and Co., solicitors, of Whitehaven | Firm's and client records | Cumbria Archive and Local Studies Centre, Whitehaven |
| Hallam, solicitors, Kirkby Stephen | Petty sessions records; letter books, day books, account books, cash books of the firm C.19th-20th | Cumbria Archive Centre, Kendal |
| Hand, Morgan and Owen, solicitors of Lichfield and Stafford | Firm's and clients' records | Staffordshire and Stoke-on-Trent Archive Service: Staffordshire County Record Office |
| Hartley and Worstenholme, solicitors, Castleford | Firm's and clients' records | West Yorkshire Archive Service, Wakefield |
| Harveys of Bristol | Schedules of legal records and documents belonging to Cockburn Smithes and Co delivered to the firm | Bristol Archives |
| Harward and Evers, solicitors, Stourbridge | Firm's and clients' records | Staffordshire and Stoke-on-Trent Archive Service: Staffordshire County Record Office |
| Hasties of London, solicitors | Firm's and clients' records | East Sussex Record Office |
| Heath and Blenkinsop | Firm's and clients' records, incl predecessor records | Warwickshire County Record Office |
| Hinckley, Birch and Brown, solicitors | Firm's and clients' records | Staffordshire and Stoke-on-Trent Archive Service: Lichfield Record Office |
| Hinckley, Birch and Exham, solicitors, Lichfield | Firm's papers | Staffordshire and Stoke-on-Trent Archive Service: Lichfield Record Office |
| Hodgson, solicitors and clerks of the peace, Carlisle | Firm's and clients' records | Cumbria Archive Centre, Carlisle |
| Holmes, Campbell & Co. | Business papers | West Sussex Record Office |
| Hooper and Fletcher | Firm's papers | Bedfordshire Archives & Records Service |
| Horne, Engall and Freeman, Staines, solicitors | Firm and clients' records | London Metropolitan Archives: City of London |
| Howlett and Clarke of Brighton, solicitors | Firm's and clients' papers | East Sussex Record Office |
| Howson and Mason, solicitors of Workington | Diary of member of firm, financial records | Cumbria Archive and Local Studies Centre, Whitehaven |
| J.D. Langton & Passmore, solicitors, London | Firm and clients' records incl records of predecessor Whale & Wates and George Whale of Woolwich and successor firm of Stoneham Langton & Passmore | London Metropolitan Archives: City of London |
| John Musgrave, solicitor and businessman, Wasdale Hall, Netherwasdale | Correspondence and accounts | Cumbria Archive and Local Studies Centre, Whitehaven |
| Justice and Pattenden, solicitors | Firm and clients' records | London Metropolitan Archives: City of London |
| Kinneirs, Solicitors, Swindon | Firm and client papers | Wiltshire and Swindon History Centre |
| Knight and Sons, solicitors of Newcastle under Lyme | Firm's and client records. Business papers not forming part of above sections. Partnership agreements | Staffordshire and Stoke-on-Trent Archive Service: Staffordshire County Record Office |
| Langport solicitor | Records from a solicitors' office in Langport | Somerset Heritage Centre (South West Heritage Trust) |
| Large & Major | Firm's and clients' records | Warwickshire County Record Office |
| Layton & Co., solicitors | Papers | Merseyside Record Office |
| Lee and Pembertons, solicitors | Firm's and client records | London Metropolitan Archives: City of London |
| Little and Hutton, solicitors | Records of clients of Little and Hutton and of the Little family | Gloucestershire Archives |

| Firm | Records | Repository |
|---|---|---|
| Longmore, solicitors, of Hertford | A miscellaneous collection from the offices including title deeds, manorial and estate records, with additional and family papers, 1465 – 1936 | Hertfordshire Archives and Local Studies |
| Longmore, Sworder and Longmore, solicitors, Hertford | Clients' records | Suffolk Record Office, Bury St Edmunds Branch |
| Manby and Steward, solicitors of Wolverhampton | Papers re partnership in firm of Wine and Spirit Merchants at Wolverhampton: dissolution of partnership | Staffordshire and Stoke-on-Trent Archive Service: Staffordshire County Record Office |
| May, May and Merriman, solicitors | Firm and clients' records | London Metropolitan Archives: City of London |
| Meek Stubbs and Barnley | Financial Records of the firm | Teesside Archives |
| Menneer, Idle and Brackett, solicitors of St Leonards | Coronerships of Hastings Borough, and the Rye District and Eastern District of East Sussex | East Sussex Record Office |
| Milne, Moser & Sons, solicitors, Kendal | Firm's and clients' papers | Cumbria Archive Centre, Kendal |
| Moore and Tibbits | Client papers | Warwickshire County Record Office |
| Osborne, Ward, Vasall and Abbot, solicitors of Bristol | Litigation papers | Somerset Heritage Centre (South West Heritage Trust) |
| Paine and Brettell, solicitors of Chertsey | Firm's and clients' records | Surrey History Centre |
| Paisley and Co., solicitors, Workington | Client papers | Cumbria Archive and Local Studies Centre, Whitehaven |
| Paper and Fovargue of Battle, solicitors | Firm's and clients' papers | East Sussex Record Office |
| Parker, Garrett and Co. | Property records and firm's correspondence | London Metropolitan Archives: City of London |
| Parrott and Coales, solicitors | Firm's records and clients' papers | Centre for Buckinghamshire Studies |
| Penley, Milward and Bayley, solicitors, Dursley | Office records and Hale family documents | Gloucestershire Archives |
| Penny and Harward, Bampton | Firm records | Devon Archives and Local Studies Service (South West Heritage Trust) |
| Perring & Co., solicitors | Records of firm and its predecessors + client papers | East Sussex Record Office |
| Peter, Peter and Sons, solicitors | Client records | Cornwall Record Office |
| Phillips and Creswick, Chippenham, solicitors | Firm's and clients' papers | Wiltshire and Swindon History Centre |
| Pitts Tucker, solicitors of Barnstaple | Firm's records | North Devon Record Office (South West Heritage Trust) |
| Potter Family of Walsall, solicitors and local land agents | Records of various firms | Walsall Local History Centre |
| Proctor and Horden, solicitors of Chard | Client records | Somerset Heritage Centre (South West Heritage Trust) |
| Raper and Fovargue of Battle, solicitors | Firm's and clients' papers | East Sussex Record Office |
| Reed, Graham & Little, solicitors of Penrith | Firm's and clients' records | Cumbria Archive Centre, Carlisle |
| Reginald Rogers & Son, solicitors | Firm's and clients' records | Cornwall Record Office |
| Rigby, Rowley and Cooper, solicitors, King Street, Newcastle | Firm's and clients' records | Staffordshire and Stoke-on-Trent Archive Service: Staffordshire County Record Office |
| Rivington and Son | Clients' papers | London Metropolitan Archives: City of London |
| Robinson, Till & Oakley, solicitors | Firm's and clients' records, records of predecessor firms | East Riding of Yorkshire Archives and Local Studies Service |
| Royle James Bird (Chamberlins), solicitor | Firm day books and accounts, records of predecessor firms and clients' papers | Suffolk Record Office, Lowestoft Branch |

| Firm | Records | Repository |
|---|---|---|
| Rye and Leman of London, solicitors | Clients' papers | East Sussex Record Office |
| S.C. Warden and Tompkins, solicitors, of Stratford-upon-Avon | Clients' papers | Shakespeare Birthplace Trust |
| Salwey and Rickards, solicitors, Ludlow | Records of the firm | Shropshire Archives |
| Sheffield solicitor's office | Records | Sheffield City Archives |
| Shelly and Johns, solicitors | Firm's and clients' records | Plymouth and West Devon Record Office |
| Sheppard and Son of Battle, solicitors | Firm's clients' account ledgers | East Sussex Record Office |
| Slatter Son and More, solicitors of Stratford-upon-Avon | Records of the firm and clients | Shakespeare Birthplace Trust |
| Smith and Sons, solicitors of Nailsworth | Firm's and clients' records | Gloucestershire Archives |
| Smythe Etches and Co, later Lee Crowder and Co, solicitors of Birmingham | Firm's and clients' records | Birmingham: Archives, Heritage and Photography Service |
| Solicitors' papers | Attorney's Diary or Journal; attorney's ledger; other misc | Liverpool Record Office |
| Spear and Sons of Plymouth, solicitors | Client files | Cornwall Record Office |
| Sprott and Sons of Mayfield, solicitors | Firm's and clients' papers | East Sussex Record Office |
| Stanton Croft and Co, solicitors | Client files | Tyne and Wear Archives |
| Stephens and Lindsay, solicitors, Winchcombe | Firm's and clients' papers | Gloucestershire Archives |
| Storey Perry and Firth, solicitors | Deeds and clients papers, incl predecessor firms, and misc business records | West Yorkshire Archive Service, Calderdale |
| Sydney Bonner Scott, solicitor | Firm's and clients' papers | Bath Record Office |
| Talbot and Company, solicitors of Burton upon Trent | Firm's and clients' papers | Staffordshire and Stoke-on-Trent Archive Service: Staffordshire County Record Office |
| Taunton solicitor's firm | Records of a Taunton firm of solicitors | Somerset Heritage Centre (South West Heritage Trust) |
| Tennant, Nevin and Greenwood, solicitors, Dewsbury | Records | West Yorkshire Archive Service, Bradford |
| Toller Staunton, solicitors of Leicester | Records of | Leicestershire, Leicester and Rutland, Record Office for |
| T.P. & J.W. Tyacke, solicitors | Firm's and clients' records | Cornwall Record Office |
| Truman Hanbury Buxton and Co. Ltd | Firm and clients' records incl history of the firm notes | London Metropolitan Archives: City of London |
| Turner & Debenham, solicitors, St Albans | Firm and clients' records | London Metropolitan Archives: City of London |
| Tweedale, Sons and Lees, solicitors | Clients' records | Oldham Local Studies & Archives |
| Wace, Morgan & Salt, solicitors, Shrewsbury | Firm's and clients' papers | Shropshire Archives |
| Waugh and Musgrave, solicitors of Cockermouth | Firm's records | Cumbria Archive and Local Studies Centre, Whitehaven |
| Whitfords of St. Columb Major | Firm and client papers, predecessor files Paynter and Whitford, Solicitors | Cornwall Record Office |
| Whyley and Piper, solicitors | Bills | Bedfordshire Archives and Records Service |
| Wilkinson and Co., solicitors of Walsall | Firm's records and clients' papers | Staffordshire and Stoke-on-Trent Archive Service: Staffordshire County Record Office |
| William Balcombe Langridge of Lewes, solicitor and Clerk of the Peace | Deed of co-partnership | East Sussex Record Office |
| Willis, Fairthorne and Clarke, solicitors and attorneys at law | Business papers | London Metropolitan Archives: City of London |

| Firm | Records | Repository |
|---|---|---|
| Wilmot and Co., solicitors | Firm's records and clients' papers | Gloucestershire Archives |
| Wilson and Son solicitors | Solicitor's business records | Wiltshire and Swindon History Centre |
| Witham Weld & Co. | Firm's and predecessor records | Lancashire Archives |
| Woodbridge and Sons, Uxbridge, solicitors | Firm's and client records | London Metropolitan Archives: City of London |
| Woolcott and Co., solicitors, 5 Grange Road, West Kirby | Firm's and client records | Wirral Archives Service |
| Wynne Baxter Godfree (formerly Wynne Baxter, Hillman and Carter) Of Lewes, solicitors | Firm's and clients' papers | East Sussex Record Office |
| Yates & Co. solicitors | Newspaper advertisement book of Yates & Co., solicitors | Liverpool Record Office |

## 3. Major accessions to repositories in 2017 relating to legal history

**Source:** TNA's *Accessions to repositories*[3]. TNA publishes a list of accessions annually, based on returns sent in by archive repositories. The returns are classified under various subject headings, including 'legal history'. Legal records will doubtless also be located in the records of institutions listed under headings such as 'Building and construction' 'Business', 'Politics', 'Publishing', 'Religion', 'Sport'. 'Legal history' returns for 2017 are listed below.

### *Local*

### Archifau Ynys Mon / Anglesey Archives

William Owen Williams (fl1903–1986), prison officer: papers and photographs rel to his employment at Beaumaris Gaol c1900–1986 (WM/2602)

S R Dew Prothero Williams, solicitors: papers rel to the Paynter family c1762–1940 (WDBC)

### Ayrshire Archives

Gilmour, Inglis & Allan, solicitors, Stewarton: ledger 1946–1955 (17/018)

### Bath Record Office

Wansdyke Petty Sessions: additional records transferred from Somerset Record Office, incl registers, minutes, adoptions and accounts rel to Keynsham, Kilmersdon and Temple Cloud petty sessional divisions 1847–1985 (1202)

### Berkshire Record Office

Abingdon Borough Petty Sessions: court registers 1905–1974 (PS/A)

Abingdon Petty Sessions: court registers 1939–1974 (PS/AC)

Faringdon Petty Sessions: court registers 1934–1973 (PS/F)

Moreton and Wallingford Petty Sessions: additional register 1968–1970 (PS/MW)

Wantage Petty Sessions: court registers 1934–1974 (PS/WT)

### Berwick-upon-Tweed Record Office

Wallace Green Gaol, Berwick: plans 1847 (BRO 2456)

### Bury Museum and Archives

Bury Magistrates Court: registers for fines court, magistrates, enforcement and juvenile court 1986–1997 (A17)

### Conwy Archive Service

Arthur Benjamin Roberts, solicitor: legal papers and corresp rel to properties in Llanwst and Llandudno c1890–1955 (CX655)

3 http://nationalarchives.gov.uk/accessions/.

## Dorset History Centre

Blandford Forum Magistrates Court: additional licensing registers 1970–1996 (PS/BF)

Bournemouth Magistrates Court: rates, community charge and council tax registers, with licensing registers and registers of clubs and licences, with some Poole premises (1980–2000) 1960–2008 (PS/BH)

Bridport Magistrates Court: licensing registers 1960–1990 (PS/BT)

Christchurch Magistrates Court: licensing registers 1983–1995 (PS/CC)

Dorchester Magistrates Court: licensing registers 1970–1996 (PS/DO)

East Dorset Magistrates Courts: registers for courts at Bournemouth, Poole, Wareham and Wimborne, bound into combined volumes 2002–2007 (PS/ED)

Poole Magistrates Court: licensing registers 1960–1996 (PS/PL)

Shaftesbury Magistrates Court: licensing registers 1960–1990 (PS/SY)

Sherborne Magistrates Court: licensing registers 1960–1990 (PS/SH)

Wareham Magistrates Court: licensing registers 1960–1990 (PS/SH)

Weymouth Magistrates Court: licensing registers 1962–1995 (PS/WY)

Wimborne Magistrates Court: licensing registers 1960–1996 (PS/WM)

Licensing registers for all Dorset courts (but not Poole or Bournemouth) 1987–1990 (PS/DT)

Additional licensing and club registers for all Dorset courts (incl Poole but not Bournemouth) 1980–2000 (PS/DT)

## Dudley Archives and Local History Service

FT Goodman & Son, solicitors, Halesowen: deeds 1728–1971 (C9965)

## East Dunbartonshire Archives: Kirkintilloch

St Matthew's RC Primary School, Bishopbriggs: file rel to corporal punishment case heard by the European Court of Human Rights 1980–1986 (2017/12)

## East Sussex Record Office

Attree & Sons, solicitors, Brighton: letters (5) 1813–1839 (12915)

Attree & Sons, solicitors, Brighton: letters to (7) Thomas Attree and successors 1774–1837 (12784)

Lawson Lewis Blakers, solicitors: deeds of Wilbees in Arlington, 1654–1923, and of Providence Chapel, Lewes, 1664–1968 1654–1968 (12818)

Rooks, Rider & Co, solicitors: deeds of Broadreed Farm, Mayfield 1590–1770 (12806)

Battle Petty Sessions: magistrates' court registers 1988–2006 (12998)

Bexhill Petty Sessions: Magistrates' Court Registers 1988–2006 (12998)

Brighton and Hove Magistrates' Division: records 1982–1997 (12934)

Brighton County Court: bankruptcy deeds and registers 1914–1983 (12999)

Brighton Magistrates Court: Affiliation papers and Adoption Register c1960–1970 (12796)

Eastbourne and Hailsham Magistrates' Division: records 1982–1997 (12936)

Eastbourne and Hailsham Magistrates' Division: Eastbourne Magistrates' Court minute books, court registers, juvenile court registers 1957–1992 (12941)

Eastbourne and Hailsham Magistrates' Division: magistrates' court registers 1988–2006 (12998)

Eastbourne Borough Petty Sessions: magistrates' court registers 1988–2006 (12998)

Hailsham Petty Sessions: magistrates' court registers 1988–2006 (12998)

Hastings and Rother Magistrates Court: records 1982–1997 (12936)

Hastings and Rother Magistrates Division: magistrates' court registers 1988–2006 (12998)

Lewes and Crowborough Magistrates' Division: records 1982–1997 (12936)

Lewes Petty Sessional Division: records (12936)

Sussex Eastern Magistrates' Division: magistrates' court registers 1988–2006 (12998)

## Edinburgh City Archives

Police Service of Scotland: records 2013 (1069)

## Explore York Libraries & Archives

City of York Council: Legal Property records, Social Care records, Coroners Records and Contracts from Guildhall 16th-20th cent

## Gloucestershire Archives

Gloucestershire Constabulary: additional offence books, stolen and found property books, offenders' record cards and publications c1875–2001 (Q)

## Gwent Archives

Francis & Co, solicitors, Chepstow: letter books , financial records and manorial records c1890–1970 (D6336)

Blackwood Police Station: photographs, constabulary reports, Benevolent Fund Register and other papers c1920–2010 (D6268)

## Hampshire Archives and Local Studies

Warner and Richardson, solicitors, Bishop's Waltham: client and business records c1800–1950 (116A17)

HM Prison, Haslar: register of appellants, scrapbook, chaplain's journal, photographs 1962–2015 (46A17)

## Herefordshire Archive and Records Centre

Unnamed solicitor, Herefordshire: ledgers 1838–1888 (DA53)

## Isle of Man Public Record Office

High Court of Justice of the Isle of Man, Civil division: records incl petitions, actions, minute books, distributions and receipts, entry books and ledgers 1800–1916 (A81)

## Leicestershire, Leicester and Rutland, Record Office for

Melton Mowbray Petty Sessions: register 1885–1888 (DE9308)

## Liverpool Record Office

Liverpool 8 Law Centre: case files 2006–2007 (ACC 7116)

Liverpool Clerk of the Peace: calendar of prisoners in the House of Corrections 1851 (354 QUQ/2/36A)

## Manchester Archives and Local Studies

Bagshaw & Son, solicitors, Manchester: records 1848–1951 (2017/51)

## Norfolk Record Office

Allens, Gadge & Gilbert, solicitors, Loddon: additional clients' records, incl papers rel to the Loddon and Langley Nursing Association, records for Loddon Town Hall Company Ltd, records for various Drainage Boards, Loddon Tax Division and County Court and maps and plans 1697–1980 (MC 3212)

## North East Lincolnshire Archives

Len Rayner (fl 1960–2015), police constable: scrapbook on Tex, award winning police dog 1960–2015 (1440)

## Northamptonshire Archives

Corby Magistrates Court: registers of court, clubs and licensing 1962–1994

Daventry Magistrates Court: registers incl court, clubs and licensing c1960–2000

Kettering Magistrates Court: registers incl court, youth court, clubs and licensing c1960–1988

Northampton Magistrates Court: additional registers incl court, youth court, clubs and licensing 1903–1990

Northamptonshire Police: records incl committee minutes, daily occurrence books, civil defence files, licensing records, order books, individual officers' journals 1840–2013 (NCPF)

Oundle and Thrapston Magistrates Court: club registers 1961–1985

Towcester Magistrates Court: additional registers rel to court, clubs and licensing 1980–1999

Wellingborough Magistrates Court: additional records incl court, youth court, clubs and licensing 1960–2002

Quarter Sessions volume entitled 'London & North Western Railway company vs. Potterspury Union Rating Appeal (Parish of Wolverton)' N261 (1894–1895)

## Nottinghamshire Archives

Nottingham Quarter Sessions: minutes, vols 5–7 1966–1971 (9128)

## Oxfordshire History Centre

Oxfordshire Magistrates Court: court records (6568)

## Staffordshire and Stoke-on-Trent Archive Service: Staffordshire County Record Office

Burton County Magistrates Court: licensing registers 1950–1995

Burton Magistrates Court: Adult, Youth and Family Court registers, licensing registers 1972–1999

Cannock and Penkridge Magistrates Court: orders for maintenance 1922–1958

Cannock Magistrates Court: licensing registers and orders for maintenance 1964–1995

Cannock, Rugeley and Seisdon Magistrates Court: Adult, Youth and Family Court registers, licensing registers 1992–1999

Lichfield and Brownhills Magistrates Court: licensing registers 1919–1974

Lichfield Magistrates Court: Adult and Youth Court registers, licensing registers 1970–1999

Rugeley Magistrates Court: Adult and Youth Court registers 1994–1999, licensing registers 1992–1999; orders for maintenance 1934–1967 1934–1999

Seisdon Magistrates Court: licensing registers 1959–1999

Stafford Borough Magistrates Court: licensing registers 1962–1981

Stafford County Magistrates Court: licensing registers 1962–1981

Stafford Magistrates Court: Adult, Youth and Family Court registers, licensing registers 1976–1999

Stone Magistrates Court: licensing register 1962–1989

Tamworth Borough Magistrates Court: licensing registers 1930–1962

Tamworth Magistrates Court: Adult and Youth Court registers, licensing registers 1939–1999

Wilnecote Magistrates Court: licensing registers 1938–1965

## Surrey History Centre

Mortlake Petty Sessions: additional records incl minutes, chairman's book, legal aid cases 1858–1972 (7947)

## Tyne and Wear Archives

Houghton le Spring Magistrates Court: records incl court and adoption registers 1959–1994 (MG.HS)

Sunderland Magistrates Court: adoption registers 1927–1990 (MG.SU)

Sunderland County Borough Petty Sessions: adoption registers 1927–1953 (MG.SUC)

## Warwickshire County Record Office

Magistrates' court registers for Alcester, Kenilworth, Kineton, Nuneaton, Rugby, Shipston, Stratford on Avon, Warwick and Leamington and Mid-Warwickshire courts 1960–1990 (CR4867)

## West Sussex Record Office

Magistrates Court registers for West Sussex 2006–2007 (18753)

## West Yorkshire Archive Service, Calderdale

Halifax Borough Police: reminiscences of borough police force from police officers and war reserve constables 1938–1954 (WYC:1854)

## West Yorkshire Archive Service, Wakefield

Bradford County Court: ledgers, summonses and court books 1840–1969 (CC9)

## Wiltshire and Swindon History Centre

Rollestone Prison, Larkhill: collected research materials and article by Martin Shallcross on history of Rollestone Prison, incl board of visitors' minutes and corresp 1980–81, when manned by the army during a strike by the Prison Officers' Association 1980–2017 (4400)

### Wolverhampton City Archives

William Sturges & Co, solicitors, London: clients deeds 1794–1841 (Acc No 2826)

## *National*

### British Library, Manuscript Collections

Philip Carteret Webb (1702–1770), barrister, antiquary and politician: documents rel to the trial of John Wilkes for seditious libel and counter proceedings 1763–1764 (Add MS 89273)

Charles Harvey (fl 1830–1840), solicitor, of Spanish Town, Jamaica: papers rel to the compensation claims of Thomas Breakenridge, late owner of the Philips Valley Estate, Port Royal, Jamaica, lodged under the West India Compensation Account 1822–1841 (Add MS 89260)

### National Library of Scotland, Manuscript Collections

Henry Cockburn (1779–1854), Lord Cockburn Scottish judge: notebook and journal 1821–1837 (Acc.13863)

Compendium of Sir George Mackenzie of Rosehaugh's 'Lawes and Customes of Scotland in Matters Criminall...', written and abridged by M. Wardrobe, Bathgate 1706 (Acc.13875)

Robert Cook: legal thesis and genealogical records 1676 (Acc.13798)

### Search Engine (National Railway Museum)

James Gates (fl 1903–1932), railway police officer: papers and notebooks recording criminal activity on Midlands Railway 1903–1932 (2017–7120)

## *Special*

### Bishopsgate Institute

Free Talha Campaign: records incl papers and ephemera 2006–2014 (FREETALHA)

## *University*

### Bristol University Information Services: Special Collections

15 fragments of leaves of Gratian's 'Decretum', by an unknown scribe 13th cent (DM2736)

### Oxford University: Bodleian Library, Special Collections

Val M Warren (c1890–1970), police officer: journal while on secondment from the Metropolitan Police to Freetown, Sierra Leone, to inspect and instruct in policing 1919–1920 (MS 12380)

Sir John Fischer Williams (1870–1947), international lawyer: letters to his wife 1922–1929 (MS. 12598)

### Trinity College Dublin

John Scott (1739–1798), Earl of Clonmell, barrister and judge: legal notebooks 1772–1797 (TCD MS 11561)

Arthur Rose Vincent (1876–1956), politician and barrister: personal corresp (copies) 1902–1932 (TCD MS 11562)

# 4. Personal and quasi-personal papers of individual legal practitioners and academic professionals held in archives

Source: TNA's *Discovery* was first examined in October 2017 using the keywords listed below and then again in April 2018**,** isolating numbers of records listed under 'record creator' and then selecting 'personal' and 'diaries' (note: judges' notebooks are not classed as personal papers or diaries but as court records; see **s.5** below). 'Personal' papers contain such diverse records as correspondence, lecture notes, minutes of meetings, certificates and press cuttings, with some professional papers mixed in; 'diaries' include notebooks (other than judges'). There were too many hits to list individuals by name. More entries were identified in 2018. At the time of writing the categories of individual with the most collections of private papers in archives are, in numerical order, judges (400), lawyers (283), barristers (277) and solicitors (224).

| Category of legal professional | **Number of hits** |
|---|---|
| Academic lawyer | 3 |
| Adjudicator | 1 |
| Advocate | 70 |
| Arbitrator | 4 |
| Attorney | 69 |
| Attorney General | 27 |
| Bailiff | 7 |
| Barrister | 277 |
| Barristers' clerk | 1 |
| Chartered accountant | 7 |
| Clerk of the Peace | 8 |
| Conveyancer | 2 |
| Coroner | 7 |
| Insurance broker | 4 |
| Insurer | 11 |
| Judge | 400 |
| Jurist | 42 |
| Justice | 113 |
| Justice of the peace | 10 |
| Law stationer | 1 |
| Law student | 1 |
| Law teacher | 1 |
| Lawyer | 283 |
| Legal clerk | 3 |
| Legal practitioner | 2 |
| Legal secretary | 2 |
| Magistrate | 34 |
| Mediator | 1 |
| Notary | 1 |
| Police | 125 |
| Professor of Civil Law | 8 |
| Professor of Common Law | 1 |
| Professor of Comparative Law | 1 |
| Professor of International Law | 4 |
| Professor of Law | 24 |
| Professor of Legal History | 1 |
| Scrivener | 1 |
| Solicitor | 224 |

## 5. Keyword categories: legal records held in archive repositories

Source: TNA's *Discovery* was initially examined in April 2017 and then again at various times from April 2018 using the keywords listed below. To show the breadth of legal records held in archive repositories, the table shows all hits for all dates and all UK archives, including TNA, Irish and Scottish archives. Hits may simply refer to a mention of the legal institution, practitioner or event or may include the collections of information owners (in other words, an institution or individual); where the latter is the case this is noted in column 5 under 'record creators'. Some hits may also be irrelevant (such as where a proper name is the same as the keyword). Some records may still be unavailable for access; where individual records are closed the reason for this[4] and the length of time may be viewed against the entry in *Discovery*.

Note: figures are constantly being refreshed by TNA, so may not correlate between the time of collection and the time of publication; additionally the numbers in the table below may not appear to be consistent. What is clear is that at the time of writing the categories with the greatest number of hits (over 1 million in each case) are, starting with the most, court records, wills, probate records and deeds. Other than deeds, which are overwhelmingly held by local authority record offices, the bulk of the records in the above categories are held by TNA. Where 'other' archives hold more records than TNA the majority comprise the aforesaid deeds plus conveyances and oaths, the records of solicitors, magistrates, lawyers, coroners, bailiffs, barristers, attorneys, actuaries and notaries and those of local legal associations and organisations. In all, almost 13 million records which could be classified as 'legal' are listed, of which approximately 7 million are held by TNA and the remainder by local authority or specialist archives.

TNA also provides 'Legal Records' guides[5] as follows: (selection only; excludes court records):

- Barristers
- Business history
- Companies
- Crime and criminals
- Deeds
- Law and order
- Lawyers
- Probate
- Solicitors

It should also be noted that there are significant numbers of legal records not at risk but not referenced below because:

a. The catalogues of the relevant archives have not been integrated with *Discovery* at the time of writing. These include the archives of Ede & Ravenscroft and The Law Society, legal records in ecclesiastical archives and libraries and records in company archives such as those of Transport for London. There will be others.

b. Many collections already held in archives are awaiting cataloguing, in which case they are usually (with some exceptions) not listed in *Discovery*.

| Keyword term | Hits all dates and all archives | Hits TNA | Hits other archives | Record creators | Sample records |
|---|---|---|---|---|---|
| **Academic lawyer** | 6 | 0 | 6 | 3 | Papers of individuals |
| **Actuary** | 3,717 | 3,326 | 391 | 23 | Actuaries' reports; correspondence |
| **Adjudicator** | 6,220 | 4,178 | 2,042 | 6 | Schemes; cases; orders; adjudicators' reports |
| **Admiralty law** | 14 | 11 | 3 | 0 | Prizes; notes; law officers |
| **Advocate** | 13,845 | 11,824 | 2,021 | 91 | Papers of individual advocates; correspondence |
| **Arbitral award** | 104 | 104 | 0 | 0 | Awards |
| **Arbitrator/Arbitration** | 25,264 | 18,129 | 7,135 | 28 | Arbitration awards; proceedings; cases; agreements; appeals; arbitration tribunals |
| **Arbitration board** | 292 | 273 | 14 | 4 | Board minutes and papers |
| **Arbitration tribunal** | 1,788 | 1,747 | 41 | 5 | Reports; proceedings; awards |
| **Attorney** | 83,375 | 53,492 | 29,883 | 182 | Case files; correspondence; personal papers |

4 Reasons for closing records for longer than 20 years could include: national security; law enforcement; health and safety; personal information; commercial interests; information provided in confidence; legal professional privilege

5 See under http://www.nationalarchives.gov.uk/help-with-your-research/research-guides-keywords/

| Keyword term | Hits all dates and all archives | Hits TNA | Hits other archives | Record creators | Sample records |
|---|---|---|---|---|---|
| **Attorney general** | 30,221 | 27,522 | 2,699 | 31 | Commissions; cases |
| **Bailiff** | 39,317 | 13,817 | 25,500 | 25 | Accounts, primarily |
| **Barrister** | 4,452 | 1,638 | 2,814 | 298 | Fees books; cash account books; diaries; personal papers; photographs |
| **Barristers' chambers** | 1 | 1 | 0 | 0 | Visit by royal commission to |
| **Barristers' clerk** | 485 | 145 | 340 | 1 | Evidence to courts; correspondence |
| **Bankruptcy** | 26,939 | 20,636 | 6,303 | 10 | Proceedings; reports; client papers |
| **Canon law** | 197 | 83 | 114 | 0 | Mss; treatises; commissions on |
| **Central Criminal Court** | 17,949 | 17,763 | 186 | 1 | Registered files; depositions; calendars of prisoners |
| **Chartered accountant** | 599 | 54 | 545 | 14 | Records, including case files, of individual chartered accountants |
| **Chartered accountants** | 1,242 | 252 | 986 | 209 | Records of and references to individual businesses and associations |
| **Citizens' advice bureau** | 1,522 | 41 | 1481 | 174 | Records of and about citizens' advice bureaux |
| **Civil court** | 126 | 91 | 35 | 0 | Case files; ordinances; photos |
| **Civil law** | 382 | 186 | 196 | 9 | Agreements; legislation; personal papers |
| **Claims** | 137,123 | 92,986 | 44,137 | 31 | Case files; claims commissions |
| **Client** | 13,911 | 479 | 13,432 | 0 | Client files; cases; ledgers; bills; wills; deeds. Majority are solicitors' papers |
| **Clerk of the court** | 747 | 235 | 512 | 0 | Letter books; appointments; certificates; correspondence |
| **Clerk of the peace** | 21,276 | 905 | 20,371 | 8 | Quarter sessions records; accounts |
| **Common law** | 7,162 | 6,685 | 478 | 2 | Minutes; note books |
| **Common Market law** | 2 | 2 | 0 | 0 | Government files |
| **Comparative law** | 40 | 37 | 3 | 2 | Committees; correspondence; studies |
| **Competition law** | 31 | 31 | 0 | 0 | Reviews; reforms |
| **Conciliation** | 5,557 | 4,904 | 653 | 20 | Minutes and papers of conciliation boards and committees; schemes; bills |
| **Constitutional law** | 1 | 0 | 1 | 0 | Letter re |
| **Construction arbitration** | 182 | 105 | 77 | 0 | Awards; proceedings |
| **Construction law** | 3 | 2 | 1 | 0 | Correspondence re |
| **Contract** | 117,947 | 63,466 | 54,481 | 38 | Council contracts; construction contracts; building contracts; sales contracts; publishing contracts; contract registers; contract ledgers; contracts books |
| **Contract dispute** | 699 | 274 | 425 | 0 | Minutes; correspondence; contracts |
| **Contract law** | 11 | 110 | 1 | 0 | Correspondence; arrangements; regulations |
| **Conveyance** | 136,734 | 12,447 | 124,287 | 1 | Individual conveyances held by law firms |
| **Conveyancer/ conveyancing** | 3,138 | 379 | 2,759 | 10 | Conveyancing fees; costs; books; papers |
| **Copyright** | 134,620 | 131,930 | 2,690 | 7 | Reports; correspondence; cases |

| Keyword term | Hits all dates and all archives | Hits TNA | Hits other archives | Record creators | Sample records |
|---|---|---|---|---|---|
| **Coroner** | 96,724 | 43,986 | 52,739 | 469 | Court proceedings; appointments; registers |
| **Coroners Court** | 749 | 9 | 740 | 1 | Case files; inquest books |
| **County Court** | 11,586 | 5,196 | 6,390 | 255 | Proceedings |
| **Court** | 3,994,930 | 3,335,774 | 659,157 | 1,621 | Court proceedings |
| **Court clerk** | 287 | 14 | 273 | 0 | Minute books; papers |
| **Court interpreter** | 7 | 3 | 4 | 0 | Use of |
| **Court of Admiralty** | 69,002 | 67,962 | 1,040 | 5 | Proceedings |
| **Court of Bankruptcy** | 8,126 | 8,029 | 97 | 2 | Proceedings; affidavits |
| **Court of Petty Sessions** | 75 | 4 | 71 | 0 | Proceedings |
| **Court of Quarter Sessions** | 10,521 | 128 | 10,393 | 1 | Proceedings |
| **Court of Stannaries** | 4,115 | 0 | 4,115 | 0 | Papers; accounts |
| **Court registrar** | 299 | 21 | 278 | 0 | Accounts; appointments |
| **Court reporter** | 2 | 1 | 1 | 0 | Proceedings; publications |
| **Court stenographer** | 1 | 1 | 0 | 0 | Court Stenographer Act |
| **Criminal Court** | 18,046 | 17,829 | 217 | 1 | Ordinances; case files; depositions |
| **Criminal law** | 1,094 | 798 | 296 | 0 | Amendments to act; revisions; reports |
| **Deeds** | 1,076,456 | 167,853 | 908,604 | 17 | Title deeds and estate papers |
| **Devolution** | 4,571 | 3,761 | 811 | 2 | Commissions; government files; bills; correspondence |
| **Diocesan Court** | 597 | 4 | 593 | 0 | Act books; fees; minutes; decisions |
| **Diocesan legal** | 28 | 0 | 28 | 0 | Legal papers in county record offices |
| **Dispute** | 52,049 | 27,507 | 24,542 | 1 | Local disputes; industrial relations disputes; trade disputes |
| **Dispute resolution** | 15 | 14 | 1 | 0 | Procedures |
| **Ecclesiastical Court** | 606 | 204 | 402 | 1 | Fees; depositions; petitions; case lists |
| **Ecclesiastical law** | 93 | 9 | 84 | 0 | Books; mss; treatises |
| **Employment law** | 25 | 22 | 3 | 0 | Government files; committees |
| **European Court of Human Rights** | 156 | 152 | 4 | 0 | Individual cases |
| **European Court of Justice** | 293 | 293 | 0 | 0 | Registered files; appointments |
| **Family Court** | 398 | 36 | 362 | 4 | Registers; reviews |
| **Family law** | 579 | 1228 | 451 | 0 | Acts; bills; reports; reviews |
| **Financial law** | 1 | 0 | 1 | 0 | Fragments of a local book re |
| **High Court** | 210,727 | 207,529 | 3,198 | 21 | Proceedings |
| **History of law** | 1 | 0 | 1 | 0 | History of law in Horsham |
| **Human rights** | 9,926 | 9,626 | 300 | 13 | Government files; commissions |
| **Inquest** | 59,229 | 38,859 | 20,370 | 0 | Inquest proceedings |
| **Insolvency** | 6,489 | 1,508 | 4,981 | 10 | Records of insolvency services; rules; proceedings; cases |
| **Insolvency court** | 8 | 5 | 3 | 0 | Papers; correspondence |

| Keyword term | Hits all dates and all archives | Hits TNA | Hits other archives | Record creators | Sample records |
|---|---|---|---|---|---|
| **Insolvency practitioner** | 1 | 0 | 1 | 1 | Merger of licensed practitioner with another law firm |
| **Insurance** | 422,340 | 68,037 | 354,303 | 554 | Ledgers; journals; accounts; minutes |
| **Insurance broker** | 343 | 254 | 89 | 8 | Correspondence; accounts |
| **Insurer** | 422,340 | 68,037 | 354,303 | 551 | Financial papers; correspondence |
| **Intellectual property** | 75 | 72 | 3 | 1 | Mostly government files |
| **International arbitration** | 63 | 32 | 31 | 1 | Agreements; awards; correspondence |
| **International law** | 1,152 | 1,042 | 110 | 4 | Commissions; opinions; progress |
| **Judge** | 36,900 | 25,133 | 11,769 | 413 | Notebooks; notes; registers of judges; photographs of judges and chambers; judges of competitions; personal papers |
| **Judges' notebooks** | 406 | 236 | 170 | 0 | Notebooks in court cases |
| **Juror** | 13 | 2 | 11 | 0 | Lists of jurors |
| **Jurisprudence** | 127 | 20 | 107 | 7 | Papers of individuals; reports; lectures |
| **Jurist** | 344 | 116 | 228 | 43 | Returns of jurists; commissions; personal papers |
| **Jury** | 32,799 | 5,213 | 27,586 | 5 | Petitions; jury lists; jury books |
| **Justice** | 231,652 | 184,722 | 46,931 | 218 | Papers of individuals; pressure groups; justices of assize |
| **Justice of the peace** | 4,299 | 777 | 3,522 | 10 | Official papers; personal papers; correspondence; diaries; notebooks |
| **Justices' notebooks** | 41 | 25 | 16 | 0 | Notebooks in court cases |
| **Law and order** | 1,873 | 1,589 | 284 | 1 | Government papers; reports |
| **Law book** | 23 | 6 | 17 | 0 | Publications; requests for copies |
| **Law bookseller** | 27 | 10 | 17 | 0 | Insurance papers; wills |
| **Law centre** | 47 | 33 | 14 | 3 | Records of and about law centres |
| **Law clerk** | 381 | 268 | 113 | 3 | Committees; minutes; letters |
| **Law days** | 91 | 27 | 64 | 0 | Individual occurrences |
| **Law department** | 697 | 669 | 28 | 0 | Correspondence with/re |
| **Law faculty** | 9 | 8 | 1 | 0 | Correspondence with/re |
| **Law firm** | 22 | 4 | 18 | 0 | Correspondence with individual law firms |
| **Law librarian** | 1 | | 1 | 0 | Letter to an individual |
| **Law officer** | 721 | 697 | 24 | 0 | Appointments; opinions |
| **Law publisher** | 2 | 1 | 1 | 0 | Correspondence |
| **Law reform** | 1,276 | 938 | 338 | 3 | Correspondence; minutes |
| **Law reporting** | 19 | 14 | 5 | 1 | Commissions; correspondence |
| **Law reports** | 1,311 | 438 | 873 | 0 | Law reports and associated documents |
| **Law school** | 407 | 200 | 207 | 0 | Correspondence and reports re law schools |
| **Law society** | 2,425 | 1,978 | 447 | 41 | Correspondence with and records of various local law societies |
| **Law stationer** | 349 | 78 | 271 | 3 | Account books; personal papers |
| **Law student** | 69 | 20 | 49 | 1 | Students' notebooks; letters; student files |

| Keyword term | Hits all dates and all archives | Hits TNA | Hits other archives | Record creators | Sample records |
|---|---|---|---|---|---|
| **Law teacher** | 1 | | 1 | 1 | Papers of one individual |
| **Law tutor** | 2 | 1 | 1 | 0 | Correspondence re individuals |
| **Lawsuit** | 16,328 | 11,244 | 5,084 | 0 | Individual lawsuits |
| **Lawyer** | 5,842 | 1,386 | 4,456 | 328 | Lawyers' accounts; bills; correspondence of and about; personal papers |
| **Legal** | 216,778 | 98,843 | 117,937 | 164 | Council legal dept records; legal papers of companies; solicitors' records; deeds; estate papers; legal aid papers; contracts; legal advice |
| **Legal artefacts** | 91 | 2 | 89 | 0 | Physical artefacts |
| **Legal association** | 3,745 | 850 | 354,303 | 4 | Correspondence; reports |
| **Legal case** | 2,154 | 372 | 1,782 | 0 | Case files; mostly property disputes |
| **Legal clerk** | 20 | 3 | 17 | 2 | Applications; diaries; correspondence |
| **Legal department** | 6,605 | 4,656 | 1,949 | 14 | Correspondence and papers of central and local government departments |
| **Legal dispute** | 248 | 45 | 203 | 0 | Individual case papers and reports |
| **Legal education** | 591 | 572 | 19 | 5 | Government policy files; records of legal education bodies |
| **Legal ephemera** | 62 | 0 | 62 | 0 | Ephemera |
| **Legal executive** | 343 | 336 | 7 | 1 | Statutory declarations; leases; wills |
| **Legal forms** | 24 | 11 | 13 | 0 | Forms books; procedures |
| **Legal history** | 26 | 7 | 19 | 1 | Research notes; correspondence |
| **Legal photographs** | 1,144 | 368 | 89 | 0 | Photographs |
| **Legal practice** | 1,317 | 27 | 1,290 | 1 | Mainly papers re individual legal practices |
| **Legal practitioner** | 2 | 0 | 2 | 2 | Papers of individuals |
| **Legal professional privilege** | 4 | 4 | 0 | 0 | Select committees on |
| **Legal publication** | 3 | 1 | 2 | 0 | Notes on publications |
| **Legal records** | 62,758 | 7,604 | 55,155 | 2 | Legal records held within collections (companies; businesses; societies; estates) |
| **Legal reform** | 19 | 14 | 5 | 0 | Correspondence; committees |
| **Legal regulation** | 3 | 2 | 1 | 0 | Submissions; cases |
| **Legal research** | 31 | 28 | 3 | 0 | Research files; correspondence |
| **Legal secretary** | 64 | 36 | 28 | 2 | Appointments; reports; correspondence |
| **Legal services** | 5,729 | 4,854 | 875 | 9 | Board and commission minutes; accounts; bills |
| **Legal system** | 63 | 51 | 12 | 0 | Descriptions of various legal systems |
| **Legislation** | 78,759 | 72,754 | 6,006 | 16 | National and local government papers; personal papers re |
| **Letters patent** | 16,840 | 7,589 | 9,251 | 0 | Individual letters patent |
| **Licensed conveyancer** | 2 | 1 | 1 | 0 | Complaints |
| **Litigation** | 4,932 | 2,318 | 2,614 | 3 | Case files |
| **Local government law** | 27 | 7 | 20 | 0 | Administration of |

| Keyword term | Hits all dates and all archives | Hits TNA | Hits other archives | Record creators | Sample records |
|---|---|---|---|---|---|
| **Magistrate** | 66,398 | 15,033 | 51,365 | 283 | Notebooks; examination books; meetings records; personal papers; court records |
| **Magistrates' Court** | 34,664 | 345 | 34,319 | 230 | Minutes books; registers; fees books |
| **Magistrates' notebooks** | 414 | 372 | 42 | 0 | Court notebooks |
| **Manor Court** | 86,379 | 8,049 | 78,330 | 1 | Court rolls; administration |
| **Maritime arbitration** | 1 | 1 | 0 | 0 | Commission in China - papers re |
| **Maritime Court** | 8 | 7 | 1 | 0 | Reports |
| **Maritime law** | 132 | 110 | 22 | 1 | Conferences; agreements |
| **Mediation** | 2,536 | 2,068 | 468 | 9 | Records of mediation services; foreign mediations files |
| **Medical law** | 10 | 8 | 2 | 0 | Amendments to acts; correspondence |
| **Multi-disciplinary practice** | 1 | 1 | 0 | 0 | Advice on |
| **National security law** | 1 | 1 | 0 | 0 | Review of Brazilian law |
| **Notary/notaries** | 3,653 | 1,758 | 1,895 | 22 | Records of individual notaries; instruments; appointments |
| **Oaths** | 30,211 | 9,081 | 21,130 | 6 | Records of oaths sworn |
| **Old Bailey** | 8,022 | 5,601 | 2,421 | 1 | Sessions papers |
| **Ombudsman** | 1,581 | 1,552 | 29 | 13 | Government files; individual cases |
| **Paralegal** | 10 | 10 | 0 | 0 | Evidence given at coroner's inquest into the London bombings |
| **Partnership agreements** | 383 | 39 | 344 | 0 | Partnership agreements between businesses |
| **Patent agent** | 58 | 9 | 49 | 0 | Agents' correspondence and fees re patent applications |
| **Patent attorney** | 2 | 1 | 1 | 0 | Applications |
| **Patents** | 853,214 | 830,615 | 22,599 | 51 | Patent office records; individual patents |
| **Patents law** | 12 | 9 | 3 | 0 | Correspondence; amendments |
| **Police/policing** | 183,767 | 132,758 | 51,009 | 371 | Subject files; administrative records |
| **Poor Law** | 155,118 | 94,651 | 60,467 | 430 | Poor Law papers; borough records; parish records; poor Law unions |
| **Private investigator** | 3 | 2 | 1 | 0 | Individual cases |
| **Probate** | 1,519,582 | 1,221,362 | 298,220 | 51 | Registered copies of wills; correspondence; probate registry records |
| **Pro bono** | 36 | 6 | 30 | 0 | Grants; correspondence |
| **Professor of civil law** | 44 | 6 | 38 | 8 | Letters; accounts |
| **Professor of common law** | 1 | 0 | 2 | 1 | Papers of individual |
| **Professor of law** | 30 | 15 | 15 | 24 | Correspondence and personal papers |
| **Property law** | 16,297 | 9.193 | 7,104 | 0 | Cases; deeds |
| **Quasi-judicial** | 26 | 24 | 2 | 0 | Functions; definitions; decisions |
| **Referenda** | 702 | 28 | 674 | 0 | Campaigns; returns |
| **Referendum** | 879 | 667 | 212 | 2 | Election material; pamphlets; campaigns |
| **Regulator/regulation** | 140,063 | 67,401 | 72,664 | 38 | Specific regulations |
| **School of law** | 19 | 5 | 14 | 0 | Correspondence and reports re schools of law |

| Keyword term | Hits all dates and all archives | Hits TNA | Hits other archives | Record creators | Sample records |
|---|---|---|---|---|---|
| **Scrivener** | 5,868 | 3,287 | 2,581 | 17 | Returns; reports |
| **Solicitor** | 457,890 | 144,685 | 313,206 | 1,949 | Deeds; estates papers; wills; correspondence; accounts; photographs |
| **Suffrage** | 8,459 | 146 | 8,313 | 41 | Minutes; correspondence |
| **Supreme Court** | 350,227 | 349,641 | 586 | 126 | Registers; ordinances; correspondence |
| **Terrorism law** | 1 | 1 | 0 | 0 | Review of terrorism legislation |
| **Trade mark** | 1,095 | 292 | 803 | 2 | Registrations, registers, applications |
| **Trade mark attorney** | 0 | 0 | 0 | 0 | |
| **Tribunal** | 43,076 | 40,511 | 2,566 | 82 | Papers, awards and minutes of: arbitration tribunals; land tribunals; industrial tribunals; rent tribunals; military tribunals; local tribunals; one-off tribunals such as Aberfan |
| **Votes/voting** | 4,816 | 1,885 | 2,931 | 1 | Voting papers; lists; oversees |
| **Will writer/willwriter** | 0 | 0 | 0 | 0 | |
| **Wills** | 1,848,453 | 1,381,836 | 466,618 | 2 | Wills held by solicitors; registered copies of wills |
| **Women's suffrage** | 7,136 | 25 | 7,111 | 14 | Minutes; correspppndence; diaries |

# Appendix III: Private sector legal institutions whose records might be at risk

The list below comprises legal institutions in the following categories (some overlap):

- Academic research centres
- Education and training providers
- Legal advice and guidance bodies
- Legal publishers
- Legal regulators
- Membership bodies
- Pressure groups

Sinart Creative/Shutterstock.com

Commercial providers of legal services (law firms; conveyancers; accountants; insurers; dispute resolution providers; alternative business structures) are excluded because they are simply too numerous to list. By way of demonstration, as of 2017 there were 139,624 practising solicitors registered in the UK[1] and as of 2014 there had been 219 alternative business structures licensed by the SRA.[2] As of March 2018 the Bar Standards Board (BSB) had licensed 16,258 registered barristers in England and Wales and a further 50,912 unregistered barristers.[3] As of 2018 the Chartered Institute of Legal Executives (CILEx) had around 20,000 members, who were either paralegals, legal professionals, or qualified chartered legal executive lawyers (of which there were around 7,500).[4]

At the time of writing there were 104 organisations on this list, 75 with a national focus, 25 with an international focus and 4 with a local focus; of the nationally/internationally focused organisations 46 are based outside Greater London (or give no address) and therefore have no obvious archive repository available to accept their records. If contacted by LRAR the organisations (48 in all) are marked with an *. Where they engaged with LRAR brief details are included on the list.

This list is by no means comprehensive or accurate as it only represents, with one or two exceptions, records of 'live' (in other words, still active as far as we can tell) legal institutions identified by LRAR as *potentially* at risk at the time of writing: in other words there is no mention in TNA's *Discovery* or on their own websites of any records being deposited in an archive repository or held an in-house archive facility; additionally the lack of response from many legal institutions means that we simply do not know whether or not they have their own in-house archives (in the true sense). Many of course will store records in a warehouse, basement or lower-tier server pending a decision on disposal; these records may be perfectly safe for the time being but not available for external research.

All institutions physically located outside Greater London but with a national or international focus are additionally at potential risk because there are no repositories willing to collect records in this category other than one or two in the HE sector (and their capacity to collect is being greatly reduced in the current economic climate).

For legal institutions, both live and defunct, which *do* have archival provision for all or some of their records at the time of writing see **Appendix II S.1.**

Legal institutions seeking to deposit their records in an archives should act as follows:

- Those with a national or local focus located in Greater London should contact the London Metropolitan Archives (https://www.cityoflondon.gov.uk/things-to-do/london-metropolitan-archives/Pages/default.aspx)
- Those whose primary focus is legal education should contact the Records of Legal Education Archives at the Institute of Advanced Legal Studies (https://ials.sas.ac.uk/library/archives/about-archives-held-institute-advanced-legal-studies-ials/records-legal-education)
- Those which form part of, or are connected to, a higher or further education institution should contact that institution's archives.

1 As advised by TLS in its Annual Statistics Report 2017: https://www.lawsociety.org.uk/communities/the-city/articles/annual-statistics-report-2017/.

2 As noted on the SRA's website here: https://www.sra.org.uk/sra/how-we-work/reports/research-abs-executive-report.page.

3 BSB Annual report 2017/18 p.2 https://www.barstandardsboard.org.uk/media/1945100/bsb_annual_report_2017-18.pdf.

4 https://www.cilex.org.uk/media/interesting_facts/facts__figures.

- Those with a local or regional focus should contact their local authority archives. For a list see The National Archives' http://discovery.nationalarchives.gov.uk/find-an-archive.

| Name | Current location | Category | Focus | Date established | Records at risk? | Website |
|---|---|---|---|---|---|---|
| Academy of Experts* | London | Membership; ADR; accreditation, training, support and guidance | National | 1987 | Not known | https://www.academyofexperts.org/ |
| Agricultural Law Association* | Leicester-shire | Membership; education; consultancy | National | c.1977 | Not known | http://ala.org.uk/#_blank |
| Arbitral Women* | Not stated | ADR pressure group; membership | International | 1993 | Not known | http://www.arbitralwomen.org/ |
| Arbitration Club* | London | ADR; Membership; Pressure group | National | 2008 | Not known | https://www.arbitrationclub.org.uk/home |
| Association of Business Recovery Professionals (R3)* | London | Membership; education and training | National | Not known | Not known | https://www.r3.org.uk/ |
| Association of Chartered Certified Accountants (ACCA)* | London | Membership; education and training | National | 1904 | Does not have an archives but has engaged with LRAR re its records | http://www.accaglobal.com/uk/en.html |
| Association of Child Abuse Lawyers (ACAL) | London | Membership; Pressure group | National | 1997 | Not known | http://www.childabuselawyers.com/#_blank |
| Association of Corporate Trustees* | London | Education and training | National | 1974 | | http://www.tact.uk.net/ |
| Association of Costs Lawyers (ACL)* | Norfolk | Legal regulator; Membership; Pressure group | National | 1977 | Not known | http://www.associationofcostslawyers.co.uk/ |
| Association of Lawyers for Children* | Surrey | Membership body; legal training; pressure group | National | Not known | Not known | http://www.alc.org.uk/#_blank |
| Association of Leasehold Enfranchisement Practitioners* | Folkestone | Membership; legal services | National | Not known | Not known | http://www.alep.org.uk/ |
| Association of Muslim Lawyers | Based at University of Oxford | Membership; pressure group | National | 1995 | Not known | Website no longer active; no contact details available |
| Association of Pension Lawyers | St Albans | Membership; pressure group | National | 1984 | Pensions Archive Trust is in contact with APL re its records | http://www.apl.org.uk/ |
| Association of Probate Researchers* | London | Membership | National | 2016 | Not known | https://www.a-p-r.org/ |

| Name | Current location | Category | Focus | Date established | Records at risk? | Website |
|---|---|---|---|---|---|---|
| Association of Women Solicitors London* | London | Membership | National | 1992 | Not known | http://awslondon.co.uk/ |
| Association of Women Solicitors Manchester* | Manchester | Membership | Local | Early 1980s | Not known | http://www.awsmanchester.org.uk/ |
| Bankruptcy Association | Lancashire | Legal advice; publishing | National | 1983 | Not known | http://www.theba.org.uk/ |
| Bar Standards Board | London | Legal regulator | National | 2010 | Not known | https://www.barstandardsboard.org.uk/ |
| Black Women's Rape Action Project | London | Pressure group | National | 1991 | Not known – website archived | http://womenagainstrape.net/black-womens-rape-action-project |
| Bracton Centre for Legal History Research, University of Exeter | Devon | Academic research | International | Not stated | Not known | http://socialsciences.exeter.ac.uk/law/research/groups/legalhistory/ website defunct |
| British Association for Sport and Law* | London | Membership; education | National | Not stated | Not known | https://www.britishsportslaw.com/ |
| British German Jurists Association | Surrey | Membership | International | 2006 | Not known | http://www.bgja.org.uk/#_blank |
| British Italian Law Association* | London | Membership; education and training | International | 2012 | Not known | http://www.bila.biz/ |
| Campaign against Criminalising Communities | Not stated | Pressure group | International | 2001 | Website archived by the UK Web Archiving Consortium | http://www.campacc.org.uk/ |
| Centre for Effective Dispute Resolution* | London | Conflict resolution consultancy | International | 1990 | Does not have an archives but has engaged with LRAR re its records | https://www.cedr.com/ |
| Centre for Child and Family Law Reform, University of London | London | Academic pressure group | National | 2009 | Not known | https://www.city.ac.uk/law/research/centre-on-child-and-family-law-reform |
| Centre for Legal Leadership | Not stated | Training for in-house lawyers | National | Not stated | Not known | http://www.legalleadership.co.uk/ |
| Centre for Socio-Legal Studies, University of Oxford * | Oxfordshire | Academic research | International | 1970s | LRAR has suggested CSLS contact Oxford University archives re its records | https://www.law.ox.ac.uk/centres-institutes/centre-socio-legal-studies |

| Name | Current location | Category | Focus | Date established | Records at risk? | Website |
|---|---|---|---|---|---|---|
| Centre for Law, Justice & Journalism, City University London | London | Academic research | International | Not stated | Not known | https://www.city.ac.uk/centre-for-law-justice-and-journalism |
| Centre of Construction Law, King's College London* | London | Academic research | National | 1987 | LRAR has suggested CCL contact KCL Archives re its records | https://www.kcl.ac.uk/law/research/centres/construction/about.aspx |
| Centre on the Legal Profession, University of Westminster | London | Academic research | National | Not stated | Not known | https://www.westminster.ac.uk/centre-on-the-legal-profession |
| Chambers & Partners | London | Legal publisher | International | 1990 | Not known | https://www.chambersandpartners.com/ |
| Chartered Institute of Arbitrators (CIARB)* | London | Membership; training | International | 1915 | Not known | http://www.ciarb.org/ |
| Chartered Institute of Legal Executives (CILEX)* | Bedfordshire | Membership | National | 1892 | Not known | https://www.cilex.org.uk/ |
| Chartered Institute of Loss Adjusters (CILA)* | London | Membership; Advice; education | National | 1941 | Not known | http://www.cila.co.uk/ |
| Chartered Institute of Patent Attorneys (CIPA) * | London | Legal regulator; Membership; Training | National | 1882 | Not known | http://www.cipa.org.uk/ |
| Chartered Institute of Taxation | London | Membership and training | National | Not known | Not known | https://www.tax.org.uk/homepage |
| Chartered Institute of Trade Mark Attorneys (CITMA)* | London | Legal regulator; Membership | National | 1934 | Not known | https://www.citma.org.uk/ |
| CILEx Regulation* | Bedfordshire | Legal regulator | National | 2007 | Not known | https://www.cilexregulation.org.uk/ |
| City Legal Information Group | London | Membership; support | National | 1976 | Not known | https://clig.org/home.html |
| City of London Law Society * | London | Membership | Local | 2007 | Not known | http://www.citysolicitors.org.uk/index.php?option=com_content&view=article&id=71&Itemid=464 |
| City of London Solicitors' Company * | London | Membership | Local | 1909 | Not known | https://www.citysolicitors.org/ |
| Civil Mediation Council* | London | ADR service provision; pressure Group | National | Not known | Not known | http://www.civilmediation.org/ |
| Commercial Litigators' Forum* | London, New York & Moscow | Pressure group | International | 2002 | Not known | http://commercial litigatorsforum.com/ |

| Name | Current location | Category | Focus | Date established | Records at risk? | Website |
|---|---|---|---|---|---|---|
| Commonwealth Lawyers' Association | London and abroad | Membership; pressure group | International | 1986 | Not known | https://www.commonwealthlawyers.com/ |
| Conveyancing Association | Newport, Wales | Membership; pressure group | National | Not stated | Not known | http://www.conveyancingassociation.org.uk/ |
| Costs Lawyer Standards Board* | Manchester | Legal regulator | National | 2010 | Not known | https://clsb.info/ |
| Council for Licensed Conveyancers* | London | Legal regulator | National | 1985 | Does not have an archives but has engaged with LRAR re its records | http://www.clc-uk.org/ |
| Criminal Law Solicitors' Association | Brighton | Membership; pressure group | National | 1990 | Not known | https://www.clsa.co.uk/ |
| Dispute Mediation Consultancy | Hampshire | Mediation consultancy | National | 2008 | Not known | http://www.dispute-mediation.co.uk/ |
| Employment Lawyers Association | Middlesex | Membership | National | 1992 | Not known | http://www.elaweb.org.uk/#_blank |
| Environmental Law Association | Devon | Membership; pressure group | National | 1988 | Not known | https://www.ukela.org/ |
| Expert Evidence | London | Mediation consultancy | National | 1984 | Not known | http://www.elaweb.org.uk/#_blank |
| Families Fighting for Justice | Liverpool | Pressure group | National | 2008 | Not known | https://familiesfightingforjustice.org/ |
| Family Law Bar Association* | Sussex | Membership; pressure group | National | Not stated | Not known | http://flba.co.uk/ |
| Family Mediators Association (FMA) | Devon | Training; mediation consultancy | National | 1988 | Not known | https://thefma.co.uk/ |
| Fish Legal* | Leominster | Pressure group | National | 1940s | Does not have an archives but has engaged with LRAR re its records | http://www.fishlegal.net/ |
| Global Legal Group | London | Legal publisher | International | 2002 | Not known | https://www.glgroup.co.uk/ |
| Hammicks Legal Information services | Hampshire | Legal publisher | International | 1968 | Not known | https://www.hammickslegal.com/live/ |
| Hart Publishing* | Oxfordshire | Legal publisher | International | 1996 | Does not have an archives but has engaged with LRAR re its records | https://www.bloomsburyprofessional.com/uk/hart/ |
| Human Rights Lawyers Association | London | Membership; pressure group | National | Not stated | Not known | https://www.hrla.org.uk/ |

| Name | Current location | Category | Focus | Date established | Records at risk? | Website |
|---|---|---|---|---|---|---|
| Immigration Law Practitioners' Association (ILPA)* | London | Membership; pressure group | National | 1984 | Not known | http://www.ilpa.org.uk/ |
| Information Law and Policy Centre | London | Research | International | 2015 | Not known, but IALS has an in-house archives | https://ials.sas.ac.uk/research/research-centres/information-law-policy-centre |
| Insolvency Lawyers' Association | London | Membership; pressure group | National | 1989 | Not known | http://www.ilauk.org/ |
| Insolvency Practitioners Association* | London | Legal regulator; Membership; training | National | 1961 | Not known | http://www.insolvency-practitioners.org.uk/ |
| Institute of Barristers Clerks* | London | Self-regulatory body; Membership; training | National | 1922 | Not known | https://www.ibc.org.uk/ |
| Institute of Family Law Arbitrators | Not stated | Arbitration consultancy | National | Not stated | Not known | http://ifla.org.uk/ |
| Institute of Information Security Professionals | Not stated | Membership; accreditation | National | Not stated | Not known | https://www.iisp.org/imis15 |
| Institute of Paralegals | London | Membership; standards setting | National | 2003 | Not known | https://theiop.org/ |
| Institute of Patentees and Inventors | London | Membership | National | 1919 | Not known | http://www.theipi.org.uk/ |
| Institute of Professional Will Writers* | West Midlands | Self-regulatory body | National | 1991 | Not known | office@ipw.org.uk |
| Intellectual Property Regulation Board | London | Legal regulator | National | Not given | Not known | https://ipreg.org.uk |
| International Dispute Resolution Centre Limited (IDRC) | London | Arbitration consultancy | National | 2000 | Not known | https://www.idrc.co.uk/ |
| International Law and Human Rights Society – London | London | Academic; membership | National | Not stated | Not known | https://www.bppstudents.com/organisation/6334/ |
| Islamic Human Rights Commission | London | Pressure group | National | 1997 | Not known | http://www.ihrc.org.uk/ |
| LawCare | Essex | Charity offering legal advice | National | 1997 | Not known | https://www.lawcare.org.uk/ |
| Law for Life* | London | Educational charity | National | Not stated | Not known | http://www.lawforlife.org.uk/ |
| LawinSport | London | Legal publishing; education | International | | | https://www.lawinsport.com/ |

| Name | Current location | Category | Focus | Date established | Records at risk? | Website |
|---|---|---|---|---|---|---|
| Lawyers for Better Business | Not stated | Pressure group | International | Not stated | Not known | http://www.l4bb.org/pages/home.php |
| The Legal 500 | London | Legal publishing | International | 1990s | Not known | https://www.legal500.com/ |
| Legal Education and Training Group* | Not given | Pressure group; training | National | Not stated | Not known | http://www.letg.org.uk/about |
| London Court of International Arbitration | London | Dispute resolution | International | 1981 | Not known, but LMA holds records of predecessor body | http://www.lcia.org/ |
| London Maritime Arbitrators Association* | London | Membership | Local | 1960 | Not known | http://www.lmaa.london/ |
| National Association for Youth Justice | Not given | Pressure group | National | 1995 | Not known | http://thenayj.org.uk/ |
| National Association of Licensed Paralegals* | London | Membership; training | National | 1987 | Not known | https://www.nationalparalegals.co.uk/ |
| Notaries Society* | Suffolk | Membership | National | 1882 | Not known | https://www.thenotariessociety.org.uk/ |
| Prime | Not stated | Training (work experience) | National | Not stated | Not known | https://primecommitment.co.uk/ |
| Relate | Not stated | Counselling, including legal advice | National | 1988 | Records of predecessor body in LMA | https://www.relate.org.uk/ |
| Reprieve | Not stated | Pressure group | International | 1999 | Not known | https://reprieve.org.uk/ |
| Resolution (formerly the Solicitors' Family Law Association) | Kent | Membership (family lawyers) | National | Not stated | Not known | http://www.resolution.org.uk/ |
| Social Housing Law Association* | London | Membership; pressure group | National | 2005 | Not known | http://www.shla.org.uk/ |
| Society for the Protection of Unborn Children | London | Pressure group | National | 1967 | Not known | https://www.spuc.org.uk/ |
| Society of Conservative Lawyers | Suffolk | Think tank on law and legal issues for the Party | National | 1947 | Not known | http://www.conservativelawyers.com/ |
| Society of Construction Arbitrators* | Not stated | Membership; pressure group | National | 1983 | Not known | https://www.constructionarbitrators.org// |
| Society of Construction Law | Leicester-shire | Membership; pressure group | National | 1983 | Not known | https://www.scl.org.uk/ |
| Society of Licensed Conveyancers | Northants | Membership; pressure group | National | Not stated | Not known | http://www.conveyancers.org.uk/ |
| Society of Professional McKenzie Friends Ltd | Wolver-hampton | Membership; self-regulation | National | Not stated | Not known | http://www.mckenziefriends.directory/index.html |

| Name | Current location | Category | Focus | Date established | Records at risk? | Website |
|---|---|---|---|---|---|---|
| Society of Trust and Estate Practitioners | London | Membership; training | International | 1991 | Not known but has an in-house history | https://www.step.org/ |
| Society of Will Writers* | Lincolnshire | Self-regulatory body; membership | National | Not stated | Not known | https://www.willwriters.com/ |
| Solicitors Assistance Scheme | Not stated | Advice and support to solicitors | National | Early 1970s | Not known | http://www.thesas.org.uk/ |
| Solicitors International Human Rights Group (SIHRG) | Surrey | Pressure group | International | Not stated | Not known | https://sites.google.com/a/sihrg.org/solicitors-international-human-rights-group/Home |
| Solicitors Regulation Authority* | London and Birmingham | Legal regulator | National | 2007 | Not known; archives of TLS, from which the SRA split in 2007, held by TLS | http://www.sra.org.uk/home/home.page |
| Sport Resolutions UK* | London | Membership; training; dispute resolution services | National | 1997 | Not known | https://www.sportresolutions.co.uk/ |
| Tax Justice Network | Buckingham-shire | Pressure group | International | 2003 | Not known | https://www.taxjustice.net/ |
| UK and Ireland Notarial Forum | Not stated | Membership; pressure group | International | 1992 | Not known | http://www.ukinf.org.uk/ |
| UK Centre for Animal Law* | London | Membership; pressure group | National | Not stated | Not known | http://www.alaw.org.uk/ |
| UK Environmental Law Association | Surrey | Membership; pressure group | National | 1988 | Not known | https://www.ukela.org/#_blank |
| UK Mediation* | London and Derbyshire | Training; dispute resolution services | International | 1999 | Not known | https://www.ukmediation.net/ |
| Women against Rape | London | Pressure group | National | 1976 | Not known – website archived | http://womenagainstrape.net/black-womens-rape-action-project |
| Wildy & Sons | London | Legal publisher | International | 1830 | Not known | http://www.wildy.com/ |
| Worshipful Company of Chartered Accountants in England and Wales* | Oxfordshire | Livery Company | National | 1977 | Not known | http://liverydatabase.liverycompanies.info/networks/549/index.html |
| Young Legal Aid Lawyers* | London | Membership; pressure group | National | Not stated | Not known | http://www.younglegalaidlawyers.org/ |

# Appendix IV: Dedicated 'legal' archives in England and Wales

Sebastian Duda/Shutterstock.com

Source: primarily TNA's *Discovery* portal; also *DANGO* and the websites of some of the institutions listed. Nearly all are in-house archives of institutional records, with some special collections in HE archives.

| Name of repository | Location | Records collected |
|---|---|---|
| Centre for English Legal History | Faculty of Law, 10 West Road, Cambridge CB3 9DZ | The Centre is acquiring its own extensive collection of historical works, ranging from treatises and law reports to manuscript materials and other documents.<br>Pending the acquisition of an appropriate physical space in which to house these materials, the process of collecting together and cataloguing the Centre's materials has yet to begin (source: Centre's website) |
| Gray's Inn Archives | Honourable Society of Gray's Inn 8 South Square, London | Holds Gray's Inn records |
| Inner Temple Library | Inner Temple, London EC4Y 7DA | Holds manuscripts and Inner Temple records |
| Institute and Faculty of Actuaries | Staple Inn Hall, High Holborn London WC1V 7QJ | In-house archives and also collects papers of individual actuaries |
| Human Rights Society (HRS) | Mariners Hard, High Street, Cley-next-the-sea, Holt NR25 7RX | In-house archives |
| Institute of Chartered Accountants (England and Wales) | Chartered Accountants' Hall Moorgate Place, London EC2R 6EA | Holds some in-house material (e.g. biographies), though its own organisational archive is at LMA and some special collections are held at John Rylands Library |
| Law Centres Network | Floor 1, Tavis House, 1–6 Tavistock Square, London WC1H 9NA | In-house archives of predecessor body Law Centres Federation (source: DANGO) |
| The Law Society Historical Archive | The Law Society, 113 Chancery Lane London WC2A 1PL | Meetings, Council and committee minutes; information on disciplinary matters involving solicitors, and lots of unusual items and information on the early days of the Law Society and the solicitors' profession |
| Legal Action Group | National Pro Bono Centre 48 Chancery Lane London WC2A 1JF | In-house archives |
| Lincoln's Inn Library and Archives | The Honourable Society of Lincoln's Inn, Treasury Office London WC2A 3TL | The Archives are departmentally part of the Library but form a separate collection of the Inn's own historical records distinct from the Library's manuscript collections and are in the care of a professional archivist. Includes records of solicitors acting for the Inn |

| Name of repository | Location | Records collected |
|---|---|---|
| London Criminal Courts Solicitors Association (LCCSA) | LCCSA Administrator<br>29 Church Vale<br>London N2 9PB | In-house. Publishes an online archive of documents and published material dating back to 1922 on its website |
| Middle Temple Library and Archive | Middle Temple, Sir Louis Blom-Cooper Floor, Ashley Building, Middle Temple Lane London EC4Y 9BT | The Archive consists primarily of the administrative, financial, membership and property records of the Inn since 1501. There is also a small section of deposited papers. Generally the Archive does not contain personal or professional records of its members, neither does it contain records or reports of trials |
| Records of Legal Education Archives | Institute of Advanced Legal Studies, Charles Clore House<br>17 Russell Square, London<br>WC1B 5DR | Archives of institutions and individuals connected to legal education |
| Worshipful Company of Arbitrators | 98 Elm Road<br>Kingston-upon-Thames<br>Surrey<br>KT2 6HU | In-house archives |

# Appendix V: Institutions and individuals contacted by LRAR

Kachka/Shutterstock.com

Note: functions may overlap, in which case the organisation is placed under its primary function

## *Legal professional associations*

Academy of Experts
Agricultural Law Association
Arbitral Women
Arbitration Club
Association of Business Recovery Professionals
Association of Corporate Trustees
Association of Costs Lawyers
Association of Lawyers for Children
Association of Probate Researchers
Association of Women Solicitors London
Association of Women Solicitors Manchester
Bar Council
British Association for Sport and Law
British Italian Law Association
Chartered Institute of Arbitrators (CIArb)
Chartered Institute of Legal Executives (CILEX)
Chartered Institute of Loss Adjusters
Chartered Institute of Patent Attorneys (CIPA)
Chartered Institute of Trade Mark Attorneys (CITMA)
City of London Law Society
City of London Solicitors' Company
Family Law Bar Association
Immigration Law Practitioners' Association (ILPA)
Insolvency Practitioners Association
Institute of Barristers Clerks
Institute of Professional Will Writers
London Criminal Courts Solicitors' Association
London Maritime Arbitrators Association (LMAA)
Notaries Society
Social Housing Law Association
Society of Construction Arbitrators
Society of Will Writers
Sport Resolutions UK
The Law Society
Worshipful Company of Arbitrators
Worshipful Company of Chartered Accountants in England and Wales
Worshipful Company of Solicitors of the City of London
Young Legal Aid Lawyers

## *Legal regulators*

Association of Chartered Certified Accountants
Bar Standards Board
CILEx Regulation
Cost Lawyers Standards Board
Council for Licensed Conveyancers
Institute of Chartered Accountants in England and Wales
Intellectual Property Regulation Board
Legal Ombudsman
Legal Services Board
Legal Services Consumer Panel
Solicitors Regulation Authority

## *Legal consultancy services*

Centre for Effective Dispute Resolution
Civil Mediation Council
Fish Legal
Law Centres Network
Law for Life
UK Mediation

## *Legal education*

Legal Education and Training Group

## *Legal publishers*

Hart Publishing
Oyez Professional Services

## *Law firms*

Allen & Overy
Ashurst Solicitors
Baker & McKenzie LLP
Chadwick Lawrence LLP
Clifford Chance
CMS-Cameron McKenna LLP
DLA Piper UK
Fieldfisher LLP
Fiona Bruce Solicitors
Freshfields Bruckhaus Deringer
Hempsons
Hogan Lovells
Linklater
Norton Rose Fulbright
Sheridans
Slaughter & May
Withers Worldwide

## *Archival membership and pressure groups*

AIM25 (Archives in London and the M25 area)
Archives and Records Association (UK and Ireland) (ARA)
ARA Section for Business Records
British Records Association
Business Archives Council
Chief Archivists in Local Government Group (CALGG)
CIRCA Trust (Construction Industry Resource Archive)
City Archivists Group
City Livery Companies Group
Information and Records Management Society (IRMS)
IRMS Property Group
London Archives Partnership
Pensions Archive Trust
The National Archives: Archives Sector Development

## *Archive repositories*

Bank of England Archives
Devon Archives and South West Heritage Trust
Barclays Group Archives
Diocese of Ely Parish Giving and Records Office
Durham University Archives and Special Collections
Gray's Inn Archives
Guardian News & Media Archive
Hertfordshire Archives and Local Studies
Inner Temple Library
National Archives of Ireland
Gloucestershire Archives
King's College London Archives
Lincoln's Inn Library
London Metropolitan Archives: City of London
Middle Temple Library and Archive
London School of Economics: Archives and Special Collections
London School of Economics: Women's Library
Oxfordshire History Centre
Records of Legal Education Archives, IALS
Surrey History Centre
The National Archives
Transport for London Corporate Archives
University College London: Library Services – Archives and Special Collections

## *Research bodies and institutions*

A2SN Archives and Artefacts Study Network
Association of Business Historians
British Association for Local History
Centre for International Business History
Centre for Socio-Legal Studies,University of Oxford
Charity Finance Group
Construction History Society
Department of Information Studies, University College London
Institute of Education, University College London
Institute of Historical Research, School of Advanced Study, University of London
Northumbria University, Department of Computer and Information Sciences
Royal Historical Society
Selden Society
Society of Legal Scholars
Socio-Legal Studies Association

## *Archivists, legal researchers, legal practitioners and administrators*

Bill Abraham, university administrator
Sarah Aitcheson, archivist
Dr Nat Alcock, researcher
Mike Anson, archivist
Professor Diamond Ashiagbor, law teacher
Sian Astill, archivist
Robert Atholl, archivist
Professor Rosemary Auchmuty, law teacher
Richard Bailey, solicitor
Professor Sir John H. Baker Q.C., legal historian
Penelope Baker, archivist
Nick Barratt, librarian
Professor Peter Bartlett, law teacher
Francis Boorman, legal researcher
Robert Bourns, solicitor
Geoffrey Browell, archivist
Philip Britton, law teacher
Philip Bouchier, archivist
Michael Buck, solicitor
Tracey Calvert, lawyer
Julie Carpenter, archivist
Sarah Cartwright, records storage warehouse administrator
Sarah Cates, records manager
Sarah Chubb, archivist
Margaret Clay, librarian
Dr Charlotte Clements, history teacher
Gary Collins, archivist
Sharon Cooper, legal administrator
Nellie Cosmetatu, university administrator
Julie Courtenay, archivist
Sir Ross Cranston, judge
Elizabeth Dawson, archivist
Michael Driver, historian
Magdalen D'Silva, legal researcher
Becky Fanning, archivist
Emma Ferguson, archivist/records manager
Dr Mark Forrest, archivist
Christopher Francis, records manager
Clive Freedman Q.C., barrister
Dr Ruth Frendo, archivist
Philip Gale, archivist
Professor Denis Galligan, law teacher
Mark George Q.C., barrister
Maria Gibson, legal administrator
Simon Guild, information compliance administrator
Keith Harcourt, historian
Professor John Harrington, law teacher
Alan Herbert, pensions trustee
Ellen Higgs, archivist
Guy Holborn, librarian
Isobel Hunter, archivist
Professor Rosemary Hunter, law teacher
Jamie Hunt, legal administrator
Mohammed Ismail, barrister
Hannah James, archivist/records manager
Fiona Kearney, records manager
Bettina Lange, law teacher
Nicholas Le Poidevin Q.C., barrister
Professor Michael Lobban, law teacher
Dr Elizabeth Lomas, information governance teacher
Lizzie Lunn, archivist
Lindsay McCormack, archivist
Melissa McGreechan, archivist
Professor Julie McLeod, records management teacher
Dr Lawrence McNamara, law teacher
Karl Mackie, mediator
Professor Imelda Maher, law teacher
Michael Maher, librarian
Jane Marshall, solicitor
Philippa Mole. archivist
Sinead Moloney, legal publisher

Antonia Moon, librarian
Professor Richard Moorhead, law teacher
Jonathan Morris, lawyer
Tina Morton, archivist
Professor David Mosey, law teacher
Professor Michael Moss, archives teacher
Professor Linda Mulcahy, law teacher
Professor Renato Nazzini, law teacher
Juliet Oliver, solicitor
Michael Page, archivist
Lucy Palmer, researcher
Professor Martin Partington, law teacher
Geoff Pick, archivist
Celia Pilkington, archivist
Timothy Pitt-Payne Q.C., barrister
Mark Priddey, archivist
Dr Michael Reynolds, arbitrator
Alex Ritchie, archivist
Sir Bernard Rix, judge
Professor Derek Roebuck, legal historian
Murray Rosen Q.C., barrister
Gill Rushton, archivist
Robin Scally, records manager
Thomas Seymour, barrister
Professor Avrom Sherr, law teacher
Alan Shipman, records manager
Maria Sienkiewicz, archivist
Jonathan Sims, librarian
Judy Slinn, researcher
Fleur Soper, archivist
Dunstan Speight, librarian
Bob Stanley, information compliance administrator
Neil Stewart, librarian
Professor David Sugarman, law teacher
Richard Thomas CBE, lawyer
Simon Thomson, records manager
Tamara Thornhill, archivist
Anna Towlson, archivist
Stuart Tyler, archivist
Dr Michael Waibel, law teacher
Stephen Ward, legal administrator
Professor Lisa Webley, law teacher
Kate Wheeler, archivist
Lesley Whitelaw, archivist
Steven Whittle, university administrator
Richard Wiltshire, archivist
Professor Jane Winters, history teacher
Jules Winterton, university administrator
Philip Wood Q.C., barrister
Conor Wyer, university administrator

# Appendix VI: Publicising the project

ra2studio/Shutterstock.com

## *LRAR website*

(http://ials.sas.ac.uk/research/areas-research/legal-records-risk-lrar-project)

Includes a blog, the case study reports, best practice guidance, details of seminars and reprints of published articles.

## *Articles*

For copies of most articles see http://ials.sas.ac.uk/research/areas-research/legal-records-risk-lrar-project/lrar-project-publications

- Blurbs publicising the project were published in the *IALS Annual Review* and the *SLSA Newsletter*.
- 'Legal Records at Risk Project', published in the *BRA Newsletter* March 2016
- 'Is our legal heritage at risk? What might be done to rescue private sector legal records', joint article by Clare Cowling and Michael Reynolds published May 2016 in *The Law Society's e-newsletter*
- 'Our legal heritage at risk: rescuing private sector legal records', article for *Amicus Curiae* published August 2016
- 'Legal records at risk: does the legal profession care about preserving its heritage?' published in the September Issue 16 of the *Legal Information Management Journal*
- 'Is the history of how the Bar works being lost?' published on November 15 in the *Inner Temple Newsletter Issue 46*
- 'Legal records at risk: what should be done to rescue private sector legal records?' published in the October 2016 issue of the BRA Journal, *Archives Vol LI*
- 'Is our legal heritage at risk? What might be done to rescue private sector legal records', published in the January 2017 issue of the *CILEx Journal*
- 'Is the history of how the Bar works being lost?' published in the March 2017 issue of the Bar Journal *Counsel*
- 'Private sector records at risk: rescuing legal records', published in the May 2017 issue of the *IRMS Bulletin Issue 197*
- 'Legal Records at Risk (LRAR) summary project report 26/09/2017', published on the LRAR website https://ials.sas.ac.uk/sites/default/files/files/Research/LRAR/2017-09-01_LRAR_two_year_progress_report_summary.pdf

# Appendix VII: Ad hoc requests to LRAR for help/advice/guidance

Dim Tik/Shutterstock.com

This table was drawn up not only to track these requests during the course of the project but to indicate:

- The source from whence the request came (meetings, seminars, articles etc) to help determine how effective we have been in publicising the project.
- The type of request: e.g. about archiving or records management.
- Where it was clear that LRAR could not further assist (given that our remit was not to physically rescue records but to facilitate their rescue) and that a wider – possibly national – strategy is required to rescue legal records. In these cases the request was usually referred to the BRA.

The requests have been anonymised. One request was from a legal regulator; four were from law firms; five from individual legal practitioners and one from a commercial service provider. Where the enquiry was a general one about depositing records in an archives, all contact ceased when we asked for a list of records to be provided.

| Category of legal institution | Request | Advice and progress | Date of original enquiry | Source |
|---|---|---|---|---|
| London-based regulatory body | Would like to be involved in LRAR with a view to archiving records and improving records management | Case study undertaken in 2016 and records referred to LMA. Awaiting confirmation from the organisation that they are liaising with LMA | 11/12/15 | The organisation's records manager attended LRAR seminar on 10/12/15 |
| London law firm | Disposal of historic records | With BRA, visited firm to give advice on 22 Sept 2016 | 03/05/16 | Referred to LRAR by Lincoln's Inn Library |
| Personal and quasi-official papers of a Hertfordshire solicitor | Miscellaneous, but primarily papers from his time as an officer of a prominent London legal membership organisation | Sent original list to Hertfordshire Archives which refused to take as focus of papers is not local. Then referred to BRA which sent an archivist to list the papers in more detail on 27 Nov 2016. Sent new list to LMA which also refused to take as focus not national/ London based enough – stalemate. Issue raised with TNA | 07/07/16 | Referred to LRAR by RLEA Archivist |

| **Category of legal institution** | **Request** | **Advice and progress** | **Date of original enquiry** | **Source** |
|---|---|---|---|---|
| Third-party records storage company | Want to scan and destroy law firm's records held in warehouse – need advice on which documents can and cannot be scanned within the legal profession | Advised that 'Original Documents' would have to be kept in hard copy (deeds, wills, leases, passports etc) given that they are not the firms' to process without permission as they belong to the client. Any other material (such as their own business records) is legally admissible in scanned form provided it has been scanned to BS 10008 standard | 13/12/16 | Article in *IRMS Bulletin* May 2017 |
| Cheshire law firm | Documents going back hundreds of years – want to send to archives | Referred to BRA | 21/02/17 | *TLS Gazette* article 20/2/17 |
| London law firm | Want to archive client files (and retrieve if necessary) | Referred to BRA | 03/03/17 | Not stated but probably *TLS Gazette* article 20/2/17 |
| Yorkshire law firm | Historic practice files of defunct law firm to be archived | Referred to BRA | 06/03/17 | Not stated but probably *TLS Gazette* article 20/2/17 |
| Ireland-based archivist | Worried that we might encourage digitisation and destruction of original law firm papers | Advised that we would never recommend destruction of original material already in archives following digitisation | 07/03/17 | *TLS Gazette* article 20/2/17 |
| Manchester barrister: papers of a Manchester Chambers plus personal papers | Files relating to the administration of the Chambers | Asked LMA if they would take – refused as Chambers not London-based. Offered to contact Manchester Archives 5 May 2017 – no response from requestor | 21/03/17 | Article in *Counsel* Mar 2017 |
| Inns of Court Barrister | Would like to see his Chambers' records archived – how to go about it? | Sent advice on how we would undergo a case study plus guidance on DPA and confidentiality 22 Jun 2017 – acknowledged but no further progress | 08/05/17 | Inner Temple Archives Committee circulated our suggestion to Inns of Court Chambers re archiving records with LMA |
| Insurance underwriter located in Cambridge | Wants an archives to take complete (hard) copies of all the expert reports and advice letters that he prepared for solicitors during a fairly recent period of about 12 years | Asked for a file list to send to the BRA – not received | 09/08/17 | Referred to LRAR by the Squire Library, Cambridge |
| Wiltshire-based barrister | Seeking an archives to take his case notes, including pleadings and opinions, plus some notes from his time as a judge | Suggested he contact either the BRA or Wiltshire Archives and include a file list | 29/09/18 | Article in *Counsel* Mar 2017 |

# Appendix VIII: LRAR information and records management guidance

garagestock/Shutterstock.com

The following guidance notes were produced partly at the request of individual legal institutions and practitioners seeking more detailed advice on recordkeeping than was readily available from their own organisations, the regulators and membership organisations but also to condense the information and records management advice already available for the legal sector and to begin to fill the gaps in available advice.

These guidelines were produced between April and September 2017. They were always viewed as works in progress and were placed on the LRAR website as discussion drafts for review by interested parties and subject matter experts: see http://ials.sas.ac.uk/research/areas-research/legal-records-risk-lrar-project/lrar-information-and-records-management

Guidelines 8 and 9 are not reproduced in this appendix because they are included, slightly amended, as appendices to Case study 1: records and recordkeeping in a legal publishing house (see **Appendix X**).

## *Contents:*

# Guideline 1: Current advice available to legal institutions on managing and disposing of records

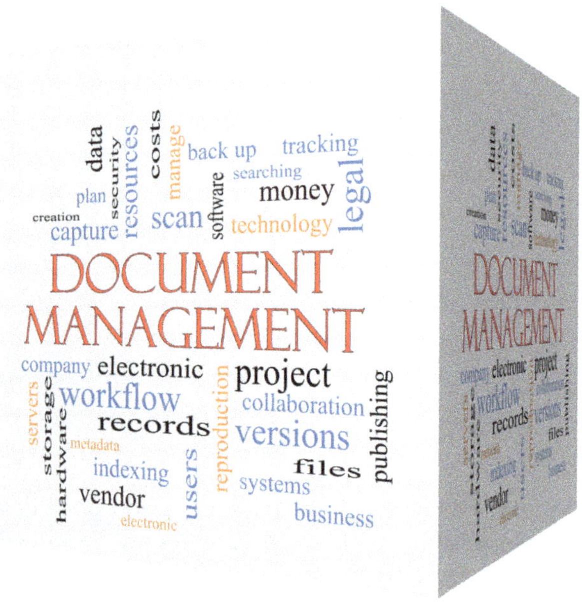


Keith Bell/Shutterstock.com

All organisations, whether public or private, have a duty to their clients and stakeholders to manage the records they hold effectively and in compliance with relevant legislation or regulations. The legal profession is no exception. This guideline seeks to summarise published advice at this time, both generic and targeted to legal practitioners, on best practice in managing information and records in the UK.

It is recommended that institutions specialised to law wishing to improve their information and records management (IRM) familiarise themselves with both the specific guidance provided by the representatives of and regulators for their legal specialism and with generic advice provided by IRM experts such as The National Archives.

## *Part 1: Guidance from the legal profession to its members*[1]

*Arbitrators and mediators*: the guidance below primarily covers confidentiality emphasising the confidential nature of arbitration and mediation proceedings as follows:

- International Court of Arbitration: *Arbitration Rules, Mediation Rules*, especially Article 9: Confidentiality https://cdn.iccwbo.org/content/uploads/sites/3/2017/01/ICC-2017-Arbitration-and-2014-Mediation-Rules-english-version.pdf.pdf
- European Commission, *European Code of Conduct for Mediators*, 2004 http://ec.europa.eu/civiljustice/adr/adr_ec_code_conduct_en.pdf
- Chartered Institute of Arbitrators: *Practice Guideline 1: Confidentiality in mediation*, 2007. This guideline also advises (p.1) that records should be destroyed or returned to the parties following a decision: https://www.ciarb.org/media/4171/practice-guideline-1-confidentiality-in-mediation-2007.pdf
- Civil Mediation Council: *Guidance note no 1: mediation confidentiality*, 8th July 2009: https://www.clerksroom.com/downloads/286-Confidentiality-Guidance-Note.pdf

*Barristers*: the *BSB Handbook* v. 3.2, 1st February 2018, recommends (p.268) that a recordkeeping policy be drawn up to identify compliance and records retention requirements. https://www.barstandardsboard.org.uk/regulatory-requirements/bsb-handbook/

*Licensed Conveyancers*: the Council for Licensed Conveyancers' *Handbook* advises on maintenance of proper records, compliance and retention of financial records. https://www.clc-uk.org/handbook/

*Notaries: the Faculty Office Code of Practice for Notaries* has rules for Recordkeeping and File Storage (Chapter 17),

1 Note: links may have changed or disappeared since the time of writing. All links were rechecked before publication.

including advice on records destruction or transfer to an archive approved by the Master of the Faculties. http://www.facultyoffice.org.uk/notary/code-of-practice/ especially http://www.facultyoffice.org.uk/chapter/recordkeeping-and-file-storage/

*Patent Attorneys and Trade Mark Attorneys*: the Chartered Institutes of Patent Attorneys and Trade Mark Attorneys have produced joint *Business practice guidance* on ownership, storage and confidentiality of files: https://www.citma.org.uk/site-search.html?q=confidentiality+of+files

*Solicitors*: The Law Society provides a great deal of good advice on managing records, including the following Practice Notes https://www.lawsociety.org.uk/support-services/advice/practice-notes/

- *Business continuity*
- *Closing down your practice: regulatory requirements*
- *Depositing records and documents with public sector archives* (note: this practice note has disappeared from TLS's website but copies are available from the BRA)
- *File closure management*
- *File retention: trusts*
- *File retention: wills and probate*
- *Who owns the file?*

The Solicitors Regulation Authority gives advice on good business practice, confidentiality and recordkeeping in the following:

- *Code of Conduct*, 2011 https://www.sra.org.uk/solicitors/handbook/code/content.page
- *Handbook*, v 19, 1 Oct 2017 https://www.sra.org.uk/solicitors/handbook/welcome.page
- The *Statement of solicitor competence*, 11 Mar 2015, also includes a section (Section D) on the need to 'keep, use and maintain accurate, complete and clear records, including:

  (a) Making effective use of information management systems (whether electronic or hard copy), including storing and retrieving information

  (b) Complying with confidentiality, security, data protection and file retention and destruction requirements'.

  http://www.sra.org.uk/solicitors/competence-statement.page

LexisNexis provides guidance on retention and disposal of records here: http://www.lexisnexis.com/applieddiscovery/lawlibrary/whitePapers/ADI_WP_DocRetentionDestruction.pdf and here: https://www.lexisnexis.com/applieddiscovery/lawlibrary/whitePapers/ADI_WP_ElementsOfAGoodDocRetentionPolicy.pdf

Lexcel also gives advice on file and case management here: *England and Wales Standard v.6 for legal practices* (downloadable from The Law Society website: https://www.lawsociety.org.uk/search/?q=Lexcel+standard)

Individual law firms have published excellent guidance for legal practitioners in specific areas of document management e.g.:

- Bristows LLP in conjunction with Iron Mountain, *Document Retention Guide*, United Kingdom 2013
- Herbert Smith, *Document Retention in England and Wales: law, practice and cross-border issues*, UK, 2011
- Herbert Smith Freehills, *Document Retention: an International Review*, Legal Guide, Second Edition, 2013 https://www.herbertsmithfreehills.com/latest-thinking/document-retention-an-international-review

*Will writers*:

- The Society of Will Writers' *Code of Practice* specifies that procedural records and records of transactions must be kept, including a written record of complaints (s.8.7): https://www.willwriters.com/code-of-practice/. The Society also publishes a *Practitioner's Guide to file retention* which contains advice on what information in addition to wills should be included in a client file and when files can be disposed of: https://www.willwriters.com/?s=file+retention.
- The Institute of Professional Willwriters' Code of Practice gives guidance on the correct storage and protection of client records: https://www.ipw.org.uk/code-of-practice

## *Part 2: Generic information and records management advice*

There is a plethora of both international and UK-specific IRM guidance publicly available to private sector organisations, though care should be taken to distinguish disinterested advice from that which, though often very sound, may be offered as part of an advertising campaign for the sale of bespoke services and storage systems. A small selection of best practice guidance provided by IRM practitioner organisations in the UK is listed below. Excellent advice is also available from international IRM organisations such as AIIM (Association for Information and Imaging Management) and ARMA International and commercial service providers like Iron Mountain.

*The National Archives* offers detailed and comprehensive guidance here on numerous topics such as managing information risk, managing digital records including emails and disposing of records: http://www.nationalarchives.gov.uk/information-management/.

*The Archives and Records Association (ARA)* has produced the excellent *Don't Risk It! Know Your Records Campaign* including a toolkit aimed specifically at individuals with recordkeeping responsibilities within organisations: https://www.archives.org.uk/?view=article&id=533:dont-risk-it-know-your-records-campaign&catid=18&ZItemid=406

*The Information and Records Management Society (IRMS)* has produced a number of guides on topics such as data security, digital records preservation, records retention and disposal, developing IRM programmes and standards and outsourcing IRM: https://irms.org.uk/page/resources

*The Information Commissioner's Office (ICO) offers* advice for organisations in both the public and private sectors on data protection and privacy and electronic communications. It also produces a wide range of leaflets, briefing notes, guides and training materials for both individuals and organisations, plus a selection of CDs and DVDs.

In 2014 the ICO gave a specific warning and clear advice to barristers and solicitors on ensuring the security of the information they hold, following a number of data breaches (**ICO blog** 5 August 2014). The ICO publicly names and shames organisations and individuals which have been found guilty of such breaches.

# Guideline 2: Advice to legal institutions on disposing of records

Cartoon Resource/Shutterstock.com

"Are you sure that hitting it with a baseball bat will work?"

This guideline has been produced by LRAR[2] to give advice and assistance to institutions specialised to law seeking practical help in disposing of their unwanted records. There are *two* ways to undertake this activity:

1. By destroying/deleting the bulk of records once they are no longer required for business use or to comply with legal retention stipulations; and
2. By preserving a small proportion of records of permanent value in an archives, either in-house or by deposit in an external facility, where they will, once all confidentiality and other requirements have expired, be available for research or reuse.

It should be clearly understood that moving paper records en masse to a warehouse/basement or storing digital records on a lower tier server is not archiving (notwithstanding the hijacking of the term by the IT community and third-party storage providers) but an interim measure to reduce storage costs pending disposal. If records are left indefinitely in storage costs mount, it is harder to find information and compliance risk increases.

The business benefits of destroying redundant information are obvious: they include storage cost savings, reduced duplication and improved accuracy of records, faster information retrieval, less wastage of staff time, reduced compliance risk and reduced information security risk, resulting in a more efficient service to clients and stakeholders.

The business benefits to legal bodies of preserving records of permanent value and making them available for research in an archives include:

- Internal: reuse of records for strategic planning, corporate branding, community engagement; compliance with regulatory and legal requirements (especially around the management of client files); removal of ongoing costs where an external archive repository is used and an improved understanding of historical context.
- External: the legal body seen as caring about/part of the community; good PR – the institution gaining a reputation for transparency, honesty, learning from mistakes; rebuttal of damaging myths about the legal profession and legal services; underwriting the institution's accountability to society and the regulators on which its legitimacy exists and a better understanding on the part of the public of the value of legal services.

## *Checklist for institutions specialised to law seeking to dispose of records*

Any legal body experiencing the following problems: spiralling storage costs, space problems, difficulties locating relevant information, non-compliance with the Data Protection Act or information security breaches should seek

2 The LRAR project seeks to develop a national strategy and process to rescue private sector legal records of potential research value which are at risk of loss through globalisation, digital obsolescence, lack of interest on the part of their information owner or lack of archival resources.

expert help. The most cost-effective measure is to appoint a full- or part-time professionally qualified records manager to institute and run an ongoing programme of records management and disposal. If this is not deemed possible at the time, LRAR recommends (and can provide contacts details for) using a professional records management/archives consultancy service to undertake the records disposal project; a professional service will prevent project creep and unwarranted costs. The project can be undertaken in-house, but will inevitably take longer and cost more than necessary if inexperienced persons are seconded from their day jobs to do the work. Whichever course is chosen, the following checklist should be followed:

### Basic records disposal checklist

- A survey of the records the institution wishes to dispose of (in both paper and electronic format), including their function and value to the institution, should be undertaken.
- An appraisal of the records (paper and digital) should then be carried out to determine whether they are redundant or of potential research value. This appraisal should also include clarification of business need and specify legislative retention requirements.
- A detailed report should be presented to senior management on the records, their storage and physical condition/format and recordkeeping costs. A records retention schedule should be included recommending either destruction or deposit in an archives.
- Once the recommendations are approved by senior management, an appropriate repository should be approached to accept the selected records as listed. The repository will advise the institution about conditions of deposit, standard access/closure periods and charges (e.g. for transport of records). Any special confidentiality requirements on the part of the institution and options for an ongoing deposit agreement with the repository for records of value as they become surplus to the institution's requirements should be raised at this point.
- Once a deposit agreement is reached, the repository will arrange to collect the records.

### Ongoing records management checklist

To prevent the same issues, unnecessary costs and risks recurring in the future, the institution should consider employing a professional to:

1. Regularly survey and assess *all* the institution's records and information management requirements to assist in space planning, IT planning, business continuity planning and legislative compliance (e.g. with the Data Protection Act).
2. Draw up, update and monitor compliance with, a retention and disposal schedule for *all* records which will provide directions for disposal of records by destruction or deposit in an archives at the appropriate time.
3. Provide practical recordkeeping advice on, e.g., document management, email management, IT systems selection, off-site storage requirements (e.g. paper records; cloud storage), information security and on particular issues such as digital media storage, digital continuity, physical conservation of paper and scanning.

# Guideline 3: Advice to legal institutions on identifying records of permanent research value

At last he had found the Regulatory Guidelines.

This guideline seeks to assist institutions specialised to law and individual legal practitioners to decide which of the information they hold may be of value to future researchers and could therefore be offered to an archive repository. It is a work in progress and will be added to as more records of permanent value are identified.

## *What do we mean by 'legal records'?*

The LRAR project seeks to broaden the concept of 'legal' records from the traditional definition of them as court records or formal documents such as deeds to the governance and business records of private sector institutions specialised to law.[3] In doing so, it seeks to rescue and find an archival home for any and all private sector legal records which are of potential research value, whether for legal research or for national or local social, geographical, gender, race or genealogical study.

## *Where will a researcher find legal records?*

There is a dearth of private sector legal records available for research in UK archives and little systematic collection of records of private sector institutions specialised to law. A researcher seeking to find and evaluate records documenting the development of non-governmental legal services in the UK and their impact on cultural and social change or national and local history will find it an interesting exercise, to say the least.

Legal records will be found in:

- The National Archives (TNA), which systematically collects and holds records of the courts, the legal records of government bodies and records of public sector legal institutions, some of which may have previously been private or later been privatised. It also holds personal or quasi-personal papers of judges and other prominent legal practitioners who have held a public role.
- There are a few in-house collections of 'legal archives' maintained by institutions specialised to law to keep their business records of historic value, which they may make available to the public.[4]

3 Such as law firms, barristers' chambers, legal executives, arbitrators and mediators, patent agents, licensed conveyancers, will writers and ancillary bodies such as legal stationers and law publishers.

4 These are: Ede & Ravenscroft; Faculty Office; Human Rights Society; Inns of Court; Institute and Faculty of Actuaries; Law Centres Network; Legal Action Group; LexisNexis Butterworths; The Law Society. (Source: The National Archives' *Discovery*). At the time of writing not one UK law firm has been located which maintains an in-house archive routinely opened to the public.

- Some university special collections departments collect and hold the archives of legal bodies[5] or prominent legal practitioners and researchers.
- Businesses with in-house archives will keep their own legal records where these are of interest.[6]
- Local authority archives have for many years collected private sector legal records, but on an ad hoc and random basis. The principal category of 'legal' records held in these archives comprises deeds deposited by law firms with the British Records Association (BRA) for later distribution to local archives, not the records of the law firms themselves. The BRA has since discontinued this process but will continue to advise law firms on deposit of their records with archives.

Collection of private sector legal material is not systematic. It depends on a) the legal institution/individual information owner knowing about archives and contacting them b) the will and capacity of the archives to take the records c) how proactive the archives is in its collecting. Some archives, therefore, hold the records of institutions specialised to law or the papers of prominent legal practitioners and some do not. LRAR seeks to change this random harvesting process by devising a national strategy for the systematic collection and preservation of private sector legal records.

## *Where should private sector information owners look to deposit their records?*

- National and Greater London legal institutions: London Metropolitan Archives collects archives relating to the City of London and to the Greater London area which are of London-wide significance. It also collects the records of national institutions, primarily those whose headquarters are based in London.
- Regional or local bodies such as law firms: the local authority record office should be approached.
- Records of legal education bodies: the Records of Legal Education Archives at IALS.

## *Which records should be retained permanently in-house or offered to an archives?*

The permanent preservation of records of research value should not be confused with the need to retain some administrative records to meet legislative requirements or business reference,[7] or with retention of client files, essential for as long as the relationship lasts. Many legal institutions maintain either in-house or externally hosted facilities to store such records; a small number may combine their in-house store with an archive used for business reference which they may also make available to the public on demand. Where such a facility is not available, an external archives repository should be considered.

## *Categories of legal records of potential research value*

The categories of records listed in the schedules below are considered by LRAR to be of probable research value and should be preserved in their original order and in the format in which they were originally created, whether paper or digital.[8] Categories may overlap as many institutions have combined responsibility for e.g., membership and regulatory functions or provide legal consultancy and education services.

The schedules are designed purely as a guide. Many categories of records not included below may need to be kept for specified times for legal or business reasons or because the relevant institution considers that they have special value. Each legal body should make – and document – its own decisions as to disposal of *all* its records by either destruction once all use is exhausted or by permanent retention in an archival repository (in-house or third party).

Notes on access issues which should be considered when preserving records in archives will be found in Guideline 4: advice to legal institutions on confidentiality and research access to records.

5 Notably the archives of several educational bodies in the Records of Legal Education Archives at IALS, the archive of the British Institute of Human Rights at KCL Archives, the British Maritime Law Association archive at University College London Special Collections; London Court of International Arbitration records at London Metropolitan Archives; Mediation UK and National Family Mediation records at The LSE Library, Archives and Special Collections; the Howard League for Penal Reform archive at Warwick University Modern Records Centre.

6 See, for example, arbitration records held by the Transport for London Corporate Archives http://ials.sas.ac.uk/sites/default/files/files/Research/LRAR/2016-05-23_TfL_case_study_report_final.pdf

7 For example, financial, Human Resources, facilities, audit and other administrative records, which will have to be kept for varying amounts of time but many of which will have little or no research value. Where there is doubt the prospective archive repository should be contacted for advice.

8 Many archive repositories now have, or are making arrangements to create, a digital archive facility.

## *Schedules of records of permanent value*

1. Barristers' chambers
2. Institutions providing legal services
3. Professional membership associations
4. Legal regulators
5. Legal education and research institutions
6. Individual legal professionals and practitioners

## *1. Barristers' chambers*

| **Record category** | **Sample records of value** |
|---|---|
| Complaints and enquiries | • Annual reports of complaints and enquiries received<br>• Complaints and enquiries files: representative samples of unusual complaints and enquiries e.g. which resulted in major changes to a Chamber's internal procedures or external image* |
| Corporate governance | • Agenda, minutes and papers of Board/Council and Committee meetings<br>• Agenda, minutes and papers of Annual General Meetings<br>• Business plans<br>• Organisation charts<br>• Diaries<br>• Biographies of Chambers' barristers<br>• Regulations and rules<br>• Registers of members' interests<br>• Directories of members of Chambers |
| External relations management | • Design and control of Chamber's corporate identity<br>• Consultation papers<br>• Seminars and conventions organised by the Chambers<br>• Published material (retain one copy only)<br>• Websites (retain regular snapshots) |
| Finance | • Fees books<br>• Annual report and accounts |
| Procedures and policies | • Policy and strategy documents<br>• Standards<br>• Procedures<br>• Handbooks<br>• Best practice guidance notes |
| Training and education | • Policy files<br>• Registers of pupils<br>• Pupillage files – samples (e.g. of prominent pupils) could be preserved for research with permission of the individual* |

## *2. Institutions providing legal services*

Includes records of organisations such as law firms, law centres, arbitration and mediation institutions, licensed conveyancers, legal executives, costs lawyers, insolvency practitioners, notaries, patent and trade mark attorneys, scriveners, will writers, consultancy firms.

| Category | Sample records of value |
|---|---|
| Client records | • Case files: unusual or high profile cases*<br>• Client documents (wills, deeds etc) where these cannot be returned to the client<br>• Client case registers or databases #<br>• Client care policy and procedures |
| Complaints and enquiries | • Annual reports of complaints and enquiries received<br>• Complaints and enquiries files+ |
| Corporate governance | • Certificate of incorporation or registration as a company<br>• Agenda, minutes and papers of Board/Council and Committee and Senior Management Team meetings<br>• Partnership regulations and rules<br>• Corporate risk registers<br>• Business plans<br>• Organisation charts<br>• Biographies of officers/partners |
| External relations management | • Design and control of corporate identity<br>• Consultation papers<br>• Marketing campaigns<br>• Seminars and conventions organised by the firm<br>• Published material<br>• Websites (regular snapshots) |
| Finance | • Annual report and accounts |
| Procedures and policies | • Policy and strategy documents<br>• Procedures |
| Relations with regulators | • Accreditation records<br>• Practising certificate<br>• Monitoring and investigations files |
| Training and development | • Policy and frameworks files<br>• Training programmes which resulted in major changes |

## *3. Professional membership associations*

| Record category | Sample records of value |
|---|---|
| Corporate governance | • Charters, Constitution and bye-laws<br>• Agenda, minutes and papers of Board/Council/Senior Management Team and Committee meetings<br>• Minutes of Annual General Meetings<br>• Memorandum of Understanding<br>• Regulations and Rules<br>• Corporate risk registers<br>• Registers of members' interests<br>• Business plans<br>• Organisation charts |
| External relations | • Design and control of the organisation's corporate identity<br>• Consultation papers<br>• Seminars and conventions organised by the organisation<br>• Published material<br>• Websites (regular snapshots) |
| Finance | • Annual report and accounts |

| Record category | Sample records of value |
|---|---|
| Membership | • Directories of members<br>• Biographies of officers or prominent members<br>• Members' files – samples (e.g. of prominent members' files) could be preserved for research with permission of the individual* |
| Procedures and policies | • Corporate policy and strategy documents<br>• Standards/Codes of Conduct/Handbooks<br>• Procedures<br>• Best practice guidance notes |
| Training and education of members | • Policy and frameworks files<br>• Training programmes which resulted in major changes |

## *4. Legal regulators*

| Category | Sample records of potential research value |
|---|---|
| Complaints and enquiries | • Annual reports of complaints and enquiries received<br>• Complaints and enquiries files+ |
| Corporate governance | • Charters, Constitution and bye-laws<br>• Agenda, minutes and papers of Board/Council and Committee meetings<br>• Agenda, minutes and papers of Annual General Meetings<br>• Corporate risk registers<br>• Business plans<br>• Organisation charts<br>• Biographies of officers |
| External relations | • Design and control of the regulator's corporate identity<br>• Consultation papers<br>• Seminars and conventions organised by the regulator<br>• Published material<br>• Websites (regular snapshots) |
| Finance | • Annual report and accounts |
| Procedures and policies | • Policy and strategy documents<br>• Standards<br>• Codes of Conduct<br>• Procedures<br>• Handbooks<br>• Best practice guidance notes |
| Regulatory | • Annual Regulatory return<br>• Regulatory risk registers<br>• Licensing registers<br>• Monitoring records+<br>• Investigations+<br>• Interventions+ |
| Training and education of licensed members | • Policy and frameworks files<br>• Training programmes which resulted in major changes |

## *5. Legal education and research institutions*

| Category | Sample records of potential research value |
|---|---|
| Corporate governance | • Constitution and bye-laws<br>• Agenda, minutes and papers of Board/Council and Committee meetings<br>• Agenda, minutes and papers of Annual General Meetings<br>• Chairpersons' and secretaries' correspondence |
| External relations | • Design and control of corporate identity<br>• Consultation papers and schemes<br>• Seminars and conventions organised by the association<br>• Published material<br>• Websites (regular snapshots) |
| Finance | • Annual report and accounts |
| Membership | • Registers, directories and lists of members<br>• Membership rules<br>• Members' files – samples (e.g. of prominent members' files) could be preserved for research with permission of the organisation or individual* |

## *6. Individual legal professionals and practitioners*

Includes personal and quasi-personal records of individual arbitrators, mediators, barristers, solicitors, legal executives; will writers, patent agents, licensed conveyancers, legal educators, legal administrators.

| Category | Sample records of potential research value |
|---|---|
| Client records* | • Case notes<br>• Correspondence with clients |
| Consultancy and research | • Papers as an officer or member of a legal organisation+<br>• Consultancy documents<br>• Mss of own research papers and publications |
| Correspondence* | • General correspondence with other organisations or individuals |
| Court or tribunal records~ | • Copies of submissions<br>• Copies of awards<br>• Copies of evidence<br>• Case notes |
| Personal papers* | • Career records<br>• Educational records<br>• Private and social life papers |

* Records containing personal data are closed by all archive repositories for 75–100 years unless permission to release the material earlier for research is given by the data subject. Anonymised data may be made available for research by special arrangement. Depositors may also stipulate their own confidentiality rules. If records are covered by guarantees of client confidentiality or legal professional privilege they may need to be closed for longer than 100 years.

# Such records are of interest to social historians in particular; where anonymised, information in such databases may be made available for research under Section 33 of the Data Protection Act 1998

+ Sampling of these records might be appropriate e.g. of complaints and enquiries which resulted in major changes to the firm's internal procedures or external image.

~ Archives will not as a rule accept duplicates of material held elsewhere unless annotated. Alternative dispute resolution tribunals may also stipulate that documents, communications or correspondence submitted by the parties or the arbitrators/mediators be destroyed or returned to the relevant parties.

# Guideline 4: Advice to legal institutions on confidentiality and research access to records

Tashatuvango/Shutterstock.com

## *Legal records and historical research*

Private sector 'legal' records have never been collected systematically in the UK other than by a very small number of specialist archives.[9] Collecting in the local authority archives sector has tended to be ad hoc (i.e. as and when individuals or legal bodies such as law firms decide to clear out some of their records). As a result research using legal records is inevitably weighted towards the pre-20th-century study of government policy, legislation and the courts, producing a historical picture of the UK's legal framework and legal services which is skewed towards the policies and actions of central government. One reason for this dearth of private sector legal records may be the legal profession's legitimate concerns about record confidentiality and a mistrust of or misunderstanding about how archive repositories respect and manage this, plus the reluctance of archives to accept deposits of records with unfeasibly long closure periods. These issues, and how to resolve them, are discussed below.

## *Legal records and confidentiality*

The Legal Records at Risk project seeks to broaden the concept of 'legal' records from the traditional definition of them as court records or formal documents such as deeds to the business records of private sector institutions with a connection to the law such as law firms, barristers' chambers, regulators, membership bodies, pressure groups and educational bodies as well as to legal records created and held by businesses, companies, charities etc. 'Business records' will include corporate governance records, policy and procedures files, marketing, public relations and accounting records; as such they will be bound by the usual conditions of commercial confidentiality and the Data Protection Act. In this respect the records of a legal institution should not be treated any differently to the records of other private sector organisations when seeking to make them available for research and so there should be no particular confidentiality problems in depositing them in archives. There is, however, one exception to this rule as follows.

## *Legal professional privilege and client confidentiality*

All client information is held by legal institutions under a long-term obligation of confidentiality.[10] Legal service providers are bound by their professional codes of conduct to keep client and complaints information confidential (see the end of this guideline). This may be the primary reason both for the reluctance of legal providers to make *any* information about their work available for research despite the fact that many of their records will not be subject to client confidentiality. It may also explain why archive repositories may not wish to collect and store such records where unfeasibly (in archival terms) lengthy closure periods are demanded.

## *How long does client confidentiality last?*

The question is whether this guarantee of confidentiality is in perpetuity or for a limited (in archival terms) period. None of the Codes of Conduct listed at the end of this guideline specify a length of time, so the next question is whether there is a tacit assumption of confidentiality in perpetuity, and whether this has ever been challenged.

9 Such as the Archives of the Inns of Court, the Law Society and the Records of Legal Education Archives. Not to be confused with the almost universal practice followed by institutions of depositing their non-current records en masse in a warehouse, basement or lower-tier server for indefinite storage.

10 The 2004 Clementi Report *Review of the regulatory framework for legal services in England and Wales* describes confidentiality thus (p.23): 'The codes of conduct of the legal professional bodies generally require lawyers to keep clients' affairs confidential. Communications between a client and his lawyer may be subject to Legal Professional Privilege (i.e. certain communications between a client and legal adviser in the context of obtaining legal advice or assistance are protected from disclosure, even in legal proceedings).'

'Actionable Breach of Confidence' is a useful baseline for discussion. An action for breach of confidence can only be brought by a deceased person's personal representative – i.e. executor or administrator. Once that person can be proved or presumed dead (say 82 years after death of the data subject, if we assume that a personal representative must be at least 18 – though 16 might be safer), there is no legal risk in releasing the information. This may be useful in dealing with confidentiality for individual clients but is more problematic for companies, which do not 'die' unless they are wound up or dissolved. It is not an insuperable barrier to eventual release of client information but it may well be an obstacle too far for archive repositories, which as a rule simply cannot afford to sit on material for hundreds of years until they can make it available.

Legal bodies presumably have a responsibility not to transfer client information to a third party unless and until the files are no longer subject to an obligation of confidence (i.e. the client has died and the time limit for all legal actions has expired or the company has been dissolved/wound up), when they can legally be destroyed or sent to an archive repository.

It appears to be easier to say that this responsibility implies confidentiality in perpetuity than to make decisions as to when client files become redundant and can safely be disposed of. Yet client files cannot be held indefinitely, not least because where individual clients are concerned such retention would be in breach of the Data Protection Act.[11] LRAR suggests, therefore, that legal institutions and practitioners look afresh at the way in which they manage their client files and make carefully considered decisions as to disposal.

## *Archives and confidentiality*

Established archive repositories[12] have well developed techniques for dealing with 'sensitive' records, including closure periods and conditions on access and use; they operate under strict confidentiality guidelines and follow The National Archives' advice to close all records for at least 20 years and personal data for 100 years.[13]

Deposit agreements: any legal institution or individual depositing records with an archives can also stipulate their own confidentiality requirements (though the archives, equally, can refuse to accept records with an unfeasibly long closure period). Where a private sector organisation deposits records in an archives an agreement is always drawn up specifying the length of time the records should be closed to public access unless the depositor is happy with the archives' own standard access rules.

Standard closure periods based on confidentiality applied by archive repositories, after which records may be made available for research, are as follows:

- Records in general: all records held by an archives are closed for 20–30 years other than material already in the public domain or for which permission for earlier access has been given by the depositing organisation/individual.
- Commercial confidentiality: usually assumed to expire after 20–30 years, unless a specific stipulation is made by the depositing body that the relevant records should be closed for a longer period.
- Personal data: the Data Protection Act specifies that the term 'personal data' only applies to the data of living individuals, so archives close such data for 75–100 years as recommended by The National Archives. Once the data subject is deceased or presumed deceased the Act no longer applies. In certain circumstances personal data may be examined for bona fide research purposes provided a legally binding guarantee of anonymisation is signed, or research bodies may redact personal data to make it available.[14] In other words, client confidentiality is not an insuperable barrier to making client data available for research.

There is, therefore, no reason for any legal institution to be concerned that an archive repository will not professionally manage access to deposited records.

## *Confidentiality Codes of Conduct and Practice Guidelines*

**The Bar:** the *BSB Handbook* (https://www.barstandardsboard.org.uk/regulatory-requirements/bsb-handbook/ ) states in S12:

11 See Schedule 1 and the 8 Data Principles, in particular Principle 5: 'Personal data processed for any purpose or purposes shall not be kept for longer than is necessary for that purpose or those purposes.'

12 The term 'Archive repositories' in this guideline refers to places where archival records (ie collections of records selected for long-term preservation as evidence of the activities of organisations or individuals) are stored, preserved and made accessible. The term does not refer to the mass storage of information in third-party records stores, basements or lower tier servers pending disposal.

13 TNA Code of practice for archivists and records managers under Section 51(4) of the Data Protection Act

14 Section 33 of the Data Protection Act 1998 refers

> The regulatory objectives of the Bar Standards Board derive from the Legal Services Act 2007 and can be summarised as follows... 'that the affairs of clients are kept confidential' and rC106 'All communications and documents relating to complaints must be kept confidential'.

**Solicitors**: the *Solicitors' Code of Conduct 2011* (https://www.lawsociety.org.uk/support-services/advice/articles/solicitors--code-of-conduct-2011/) states in Ch 4 Client confidentiality:

> Firms are required to have effective systems and controls in place to identify risks to client confidentiality and to mitigate those risks... Protection of confidential information is a fundamental feature of your relationship with clients. It exists as a concept both as a matter of law and as a matter of conduct. This duty continues despite the end of the retainer and even after the death of the client.

**Arbitrators:** institutions have their own rules e.g. Article 30(1) of the *Rules* of the London Court of International Arbitration (https://www.lcia.org/Dispute_Resolution_Services/lcia-arbitration-rules-2014.aspx) states:

> Unless the parties expressly agree in writing to the contrary, the parties undertake as a general principle to keep confidential all awards in their arbitration, together with all materials in the proceedings created for the purpose of the arbitration and all other documents produced by another party in the proceedings not otherwise in the public domain - save and to the extent that disclosure may be required of a party by legal duty, to protect or pursue a legal right or to enforce or challenge an award in bona fide legal proceedings before a state court or other judicial authority.

**Mediators:** the Chartered Institute of Arbitrators' *Practice Guideline 1: Confidentiality in Mediation* (https://www.ciarb.org/media/4171/practice-guideline-1-confidentiality-in-mediation-2007.pdf) states:

> Save as required or permitted by law... the Institute, the parties, their representatives, their advisors and the mediator(s) shall keep confidential all information (whether given orally, in writing or otherwise) produced for, or arising out of or in connection with, the mediation passing between any of the participants and between any of them and the mediator made for the purposes of the mediation, including the fact that the mediation is taking place or has taken place...The mediator's duty to protect the confidentiality of the mediation proceedings commences with the first communication to the mediator, is continuous in nature, and does not expire upon the termination, for whatever reason, of the mediation under Rule 11. The mediator's duty extends to all information relating to the mediation proceedings, even indirectly, such as previous invitations and/or negotiations leading to mediation, terms of the agreement to mediate, appointment of mediators and performance, or non performance, of the settlement agreement. All records, reports, or other documents received by a mediator, as well as all notes taken by the mediator during, with reference to, or for the purposes of, the mediation should be returned to the parties or kept secure until no longer needed for any purpose relating to the mediation and then destroyed.

**Conveyancers**: Outcome 3.6 of the Council for Licensed Conveyancers' *Code of Conduct* (https://www.conveyancer.org.uk/wp-content/uploads/clcSiteMedia/Code-of-Conduct.pdf) requires that: 'Clients' affairs are treated confidentially (except as required or permitted by law or with the Client's consent)'.

**Notaries:** Ch. 17 *Recordkeeping and file storage* (http://www.facultyoffice.org.uk/chapter/record-keeping-and-file-storage/) of the Master of Faculties *Code of Practice* states: 'A notary's records are as a general principle confidential [Practice Rule 23.6]'.

**Patent attorneys and Trade Mark attorneys**: the Chartered Institutes of Patent Attorneys and Trade Mark Attorneys have produced joint guidance on ownership, storage and confidentiality of files: https://www.citma.org.uk/site-search.html?q=confidentiality+of+files

**Will writers:** the **Institute of Professional Willwriters'** *Code of Practice* (https://www.ipw.org.uk/code-of-practice) **states** at **S.5.1:** 'Members shall act with independence and integrity, maintain proper standards of work and keep the affairs of the Client confidential'.

# Guideline 5: Advice to legal institutions on the business benefits of depositing records in an archives

### *What is the issue and why should legal institutions care?*

Dilen/Shutterstock.com

Private sector 'legal' records have never been collected systematically in the UK other than by a very small number of specialist archives.[15] Collecting in the public archives sector has tended to be ad hoc (i.e. as and when individuals or legal bodies such as law firms decide to clear out some of their records). As a result research using legal records is inevitably weighted towards the pre-20th-century study of government policy, legislation and the courts, producing a historical picture of the UK's legal framework and legal services which is skewed towards the policies and actions of central government. Does this matter?

All the major UK banks, commercial companies such as Unilever, Diageo and Marks and Spencers, non-governmental bodies such as Transport for London, Network Rail, the Royal Medical Colleges and numerous religious and charitable institutions recognise the financial and reputational benefits of running their own in-house archives, yet legal institutions, it seems, do not. Why is this and does it matter?

Unless systematic efforts are made towards collecting private sector legal records in the same way as other private sector records we are in danger of losing a significant proportion of our legal heritage. Does this matter? We believe it does.

### *Why are institutions specialised to law reluctant to preserve their archives?*

#### The cost factor

Cost, understandably, is a major factor behind any legal institution, large or small, deciding not to create and maintain an in-house archives. Yet this does not explain why legal institutions may be reluctant to deposit records in an archive repository such as a local authority record office. Record offices do not charge for their services, though they may – and indeed should – seek a financial contribution from depositors towards the cost of deposit. This is negligible compared to the year-on-year cost of storing information in third-party records stores or on-site pending eventual destruction, yet many legal institutions either are not aware that county record offices will collect, preserve and eventually make accessible their historic records at minimal cost and/or prefer to pay for indefinite storage in a warehouse or basement. Why?

#### The confidentiality factor

One reason may be the undertaking law firms and barristers' chambers, for example, make to their clients to keep their information confidential. The long-term confidentiality rules which apply to client files do not, however, apply to the business records of legal bodies – and these are just as important historically as client records, if not more.[16]

15 Such as the Archives of the Inns of Court, the Law Society and the Records of Legal Education Archives. Not to be confused with the almost universal practice followed by institutions of depositing their non-current records en masse in a warehouse, basement or lower-tier server for indefinite storage.

16 For examples of business records of historical value see The Law Society's Practice Note: Depositing records and documents with public sector archives (15 December 2010).

All archives have well developed techniques for dealing with 'sensitive' records, including closure periods and conditions on access and use; they operate under strict confidentiality guidelines and follow The National Archives' advice to close all deposited records for at least 20 years and personal data for 100 years.[17] Any legal institution depositing records with an archives can also stipulate its own more stringent confidentiality requirements.

## The embarrassment factor

Another, more understandable, reason is concern about embarrassment/reputational damage, even in relation to records over 20 years old. An institution may be reluctant to make records available to the public because some might reveal former mistakes or contain statements or notes which are politically incorrect by today's standards. This is in fact a short-sighted argument, since denying access to archives does not stop the stories from being there. Archives in fact have the potential to help draw a line under a distasteful aspect of the company history.[18]

In other words, legal bodies should be encouraged to see their archives as business assets rather than liabilities. Most businesses now recognise that they should be seen to be good corporate citizens and be transparent. Part of that should be allowing access to their archives and the history of their business, even if it does mean revealing links to practices which are now disapproved of. The alternative is being viewed as having something to hide.

## *Why should legal institutions care about their archives? What's in it for them?*

We understand that legal practitioners are busy people and that appraising the potential research value of records is rarely a top priority when running a business. Yet managing one's business records efficiently so as to reduce costs and provide a good service to clients is, or should be, a high priority. Archives are simply the end of the process.

Lack of awareness in business of the value of archives and their management leads to:

- Under-utilisation of business records and history as a marketing and client relations tool and for involvement in wider corporate social responsibility projects.
- The unwitting destruction of important business records, particularly at periods of change, such as merger, acquisition and buy-outs.
- Loss of records that could be used to provide legal protection or safeguard Intellectual Property rights and trademarks.
- Legal bodies ignoring and/or destroying their own heritage.

## *What are the business benefits of archiving records?*

The business benefits of preserving legal records of permanent value include:

### Commercial benefits:

- Reducing the time it takes to locate information of importance.
- Reuse of records for strategic planning, corporate branding, firm histories etc.
- Removal of ongoing management costs if an external archive is used.
- Reducing storage costs – including IT costs – as records are systematically disposed of.
- Better compliance with regulatory and legal requirements, especially around the management of client files and personal data in general.
- An improved understanding of the institution's historical context.

### Reputational benefits:

- Giving a clearer picture of the importance of private sector legal institutions in the development of the UK's legal and business framework.
- Gaining a reputation for enhanced transparency, honesty and community involvement.
- The business seen as caring about/part of the community, not removed from it.
- Greater client confidence due to improved efficiency in client records management.

17 TNA Code of practice for archivists and records managers under Section 51(4) of the Data Protection Act, 2007.

18 'In any organisation…there will also be elements of which people may not be so proud. Practices which were just a part of life 300 years ago may be frowned upon now. Decisions made 40 years ago which seemed right at the time turned out to be the wrong choice with the benefit of hindsight. And sometimes, as we all know, people have been downright dishonest…But if we deny access to the archives, we deny access to the other side of the story too. And there is always the danger that by not letting people in, they will automatically assume the worst.' Maria Sienkiewicz (Group Archivist, Barclays Group Archives): 'Take the 109 bus and bring a packed lunch': Confidentiality, reputation and logistics – the challenges and opportunities of opening up business archives,' Presentation at the Business Archives Council conference 2014.

- Good public relations – honesty, learning from mistakes etc.
- Better understanding by the public of the value of legal services.

TNA summarises the benefits to businesses of maintaining archives (whether in-house or transfer to a third-party archive repository) as follows:

> Across the globe communications and marketing teams are re-engineering corporate branding and identity to emphasise their pasts. Most successful companies have secret commercial weapons in the form of their archives, an often under-used asset that can be used to increase brand awareness, build commercial identity and help grow business. Information is a powerful business tool that can be turned to corporate advantage. Companies already know that research and development information is valuable, but the knowledge, experience and investment locked in company archives is an asset that can underpin core business. Business archives contain the evidence that gives a company its edge or marks it out as different and special, making it stand out from its competitors.[19]

## *Does the benefit outweigh the effort involved?*

There are three options open to legal institutions wishing to dispose of records:

Option 1: store them en masse in a basement, warehouse or 'archive' server and – eventually – destroy them. This is always more costly than implementing disposal rules in a timely fashion, especially as regards digital records, which are more expensive to keep over time than physical formats because the IT systems they are stored in will need regular and costly upgrading or replacement to ensure continued accessibility. Blanket destruction, already practised for many digital records (e.g. emails) due to the perceived cost of selecting material for long-term retention, can result in a loss of business continuity as crucial records (such as contracts) are inadvertently lost.

Option 2: set up an in-house archives for material of value and destroy the rest once it becomes redundant. Setting up and managing an in-house archives is expensive, but can certainly justify the cost (Barclays Bank recently saved upwards of £1 billion by being able to produce historic records held in its archives for a court case[20]).

Option 3: deposit valuable records in a third-party archives such as a county record office and destroy the rest once it becomes redundant. Transferring records to an external archives costs institutions very little in the larger scheme of things other than some effort and planning on the part of the information owners to engage with archives.

## *Conclusion*

There is a cost to archiving records but this is minimal compared to the cost and risks of indiscriminate storage of all records, including rubbish, or of blanket destruction. It is also outweighed by the commercial and reputational benefits of making sure that records of archival value are preserved for posterity.

19 TNA, Corporate Memory: A guide to managing business archives, 2009.

20 See presentation by the Barclay's Group Archivist here: http://ials.sas.ac.uk/sites/default/files/files/Research/LRAR/LRAR_2nd_Seminar Presentations_Nov_2016.pdf.

# Guideline 6: Advice to legal institutions on the business benefits of an information and records management programme

DRogatnev/Shutterstock.com

## *What is the issue and why should institutions specialised to law care?*

The international standard on records management (ISO 15489) defines records management as a field of management responsible for the efficient and systematic control of the creation, receipt, maintenance, use and disposition of records. Historically records have been managed within organisations as follows:

- When paper records were the primary format, most organisations recognised the need for centralised registration and management of records, including enforcement of rules for their creation, filing, retrieval and disposal followed by all staff.
- As electronic records began to be created, 'hybrid' management systems were developed, usually on an ad hoc basis, with paper still being seen as the primary, managed, 'record' and electronic records somehow 'belonging' to their individual creators, meaning that it was not seen as necessary to have rules for their management.
- Now that records are principally maintained in born-digital format this historic lack of management has led to chaos in most organisations. Most digital records are still held in unstructured systems (i.e. in Microsoft Office folders or email) with little guidance to staff on how to manage them. Where there has been a recognition of the need for better management IT systems are procured at high expense and configured or customised to suit the requirements of individual departments rather than the overall needs of the organisation. And there is rarely a central department or even an individual responsible for ensuring the appropriate management of *all* information held in *all* IT and paper systems and creating the rules for doing so.
- Organisations quite rightly pay for qualified and experienced legal practitioners, IT professionals, auditors, accountants, knowledge managers and so on, yet only exceptionally do they invest in professional records management practitioners. Even where some rules and guidance have been created,[21] the day-to-day management of information is still left to individuals, who may or may not have some basic records management training but do not see this function as part of their core work.

There is one simple fact which has to be recognised if organisations are to fulfil their obligations to stakeholders and work efficiently: *information does not manage itself.*

## *What is an information and records management (IRM) programme?*

In practical terms an IRM programme means:

- The creation, implementation and application of rules for the day to day creation and filing of information.
- Efficiency and economy in the management of information and records by facilitating cost-effective space and storage of both physical and digital records.

21 Some organisations may, for example, have guidance on document naming, version control or email management.

- The regular, orderly elimination of large amounts of records that have no value once their administrative usefulness has expired.
- The preservation of records of permanent value as part of the corporate history.
- The recognition of information as an asset rather than an overhead.
- All the above controlled and monitored via organisation-wide IRM rules and policies which are fully supported by senior management.

## *What are the objectives of an IRM programme?*

Implementing a programme will result in:

- Cost effective management of records stores for physical records.
- A 'less-paper' office.
- Assured control of electronic records.
- A central function to offer advice and manage records/archiving/disposal processes.
- Clear guidance on how to file and retrieve records, what to keep and what to dispose of to meet business and stakeholders' requirements.

## *What does an IRM programme cost?*

The only significant cost is the employment of a records management professional or professionals to a) establish and b) run the programme. It cannot be emphasised too strongly that this kind of programme requires professionally qualified people in just the same way as managing IT systems or providing legal services to clients.

## *What are the business benefits of an IRM programme?*[22]

Quick wins: a records manager should be able to almost immediately reduce storage costs by disposing of obsolete paper records. With the co-operation of IT the records manager should also be able to supervise the deletion of redundant digital records and backup tapes and the decommissioning of obsolete IT systems. The records manager should also be able to reduce duplication and confusion over versions by setting rules for storage of digital records.

Long-term gains: a professional records manager will, in consultation with stakeholders, develop consistent rules and guidelines on:

- document and folder naming
- version control
- records classification
- security classification
- email management
- social media management
- scanning
- retention and disposal
- archiving

And advise on:

- Facilitation of a 'less-paper' and eventually paper-free office
- IRM requirements for IT systems
- IRM contractual requirements (e.g. for external records stores; Cloud storage)
- IRM and regulatory recordkeeping requirements
- Staff training in best practice

The long-term nature of a programme of this kind is not to be underestimated but significant cost savings and improvements to processes and staff awareness should be possible quite quickly, *provided the programme has the full support of senior management*. This last is crucial as there will be considerable staff resistance to new ways of working corporately rather than as individuals. There may also be resistance on the part of administrative support areas such as IT, Audit, HR and Facilities to what could be seen as interference in 'their' way of doing things. If senior management is not fully on board with the IRM programme there is little point in setting one up in the first place.

22 See the case study of how instituting an IRM programme benefitted Chadwick Lawrence LLP at http://ials.sas.ac.uk/research/areas-research/legal-records-risk-lrar-project/lrar-case-studies.

## *What part does disposing of records play?*

Destroying redundant information and archiving the remainder (in the true sense of preserving a significantly small proportion of records of permanent value in an archive repository for long-term business use and public research) is the end product of IRM. Neither destruction nor archiving is possible to carry out efficiently unless an IRM programme is in place to ensure continuity and consistency of the necessary processes.

The business benefits of destroying redundant material are obvious: they include:

- Storage cost savings
- Reduced duplication
- Faster retrieval of important records
- Less wastage of staff time
- Reduction of risk and a better service to clients through legislative compliance and improved information security.

The business benefits of preserving legal records of permanent value (and making them available for research once all confidentiality requirements have expired) include:

- Reuse of records by the legal body for strategic planning, corporate branding, community engagement, speedy service to clients, better compliance with regulatory and legal requirements (especially around the management of client files) and an improved understanding of historical context, including the potential for publishing a history of the organisation.
- The business seen as caring about/part of the community, not removed from it.
- Good PR – a reputation for transparency, honesty, learning from mistakes etc.
- Better understanding by the public of the value of legal services.
- Removal of ongoing management costs where records are deposited in an external archive repository.

## *Conclusion*

There is a cost to managing information and records properly but:

- Institutions specialised to law should be doing this work anyway as part of best practice and regulatory requirements.
- The initial set-up costs will speedily be outweighed by streamlined business processes, increased staff efficiency, storage savings and better assurances on legal and general information compliance to protect the interests of staff and stakeholders.
- Clear business ownership of certain records and data will be established which will be advantageous in the event of a future split or merger.
- The historical archives documenting the history of the organisation will be protected even in the event of a merger or split.

# Guideline 7: Advice to legal institutions on digital continuity and managing digital records

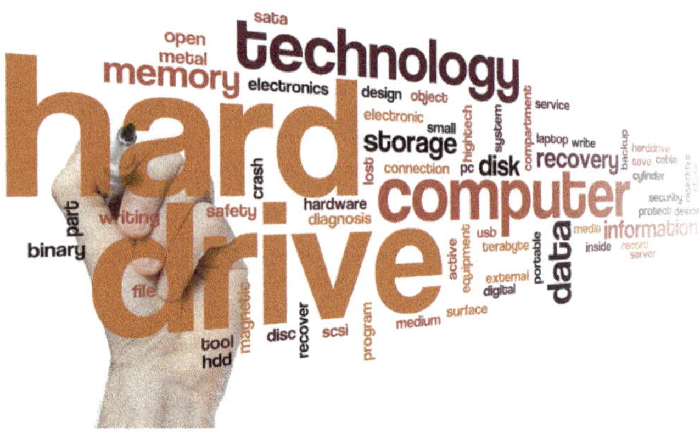


ibreakstock/Shutterstock.com

Most information and data created or managed by institutions specialised to law are now born-digital. Existing technology does not, however, always provide adequate solutions to the challenges of digital working. We risk losing key information and corporate knowledge. Information is hard to find, and if it is found, may lack an 'administrative history' – the context necessary to interpret it. It may exist in many formats and be duplicated many times and, after an astonishingly short space of time, it may become inaccessible through digital obsolescence.

Information compliance and records management requirements need to be included in all IT systems planning from the beginning, not added on as an afterthought or when a system nears obsolescence, when it may be too late to save valuable records. *This is a particular issue for client files, which may have to be accessible for decades.*

**Disclosure and information risk**

It should always be remembered that all surviving information (including data in backup tapes, databases, line of business systems, shared or personal drives and email) is potentially disclosable under the Data Protection Act (where there is personal data) or in connection with a litigation disclosure process.

Not managing information properly heightens risk and cost, especially around e-disclosure for litigation purposes.

There is also a risk that digital information will not be accepted in a UK court if it has not been managed in accordance with best practice standards like BS 10008:2014 Evidential Weight and Legal Admissibility of Electronic Information.

Where information and records management requirements are not clearly defined from the beginning systems quickly become overloaded, particularly if there are no automated disposal rules to allow deletion of documents and data. Some sort of bulk 'archiving' action may then have to be taken by IT to reduce the storage problem.

This 'archived' information also needs to be subject to clear management and disposal rules, otherwise the costs of retaining all data indefinitely and unnecessarily (and, where personal data is involved, potentially in violation of Principle 5 of the Data Protection Act) – and of having to locate, retrieve, assess and produce it – will continue to spiral.

<table>
<tr><th colspan="2">Disposing of digital records – deleting, purging and archiving</th></tr>
<tr><th>What is 'Archiving'?</th><th>How do we safely dispose of digital information?<br>By either archiving or deletion</th></tr>
<tr><td>
In the IT world archiving means the bulk removal of information and data to cheaper storage once it is either a) no longer needed for day to day work or b) the system in which it is stored becomes overloaded. This is a temporary solution to reduce storage costs. It does not solve the issue of how long to keep the information; if it is kept indefinitely the cost of storage, management and retrieval will spiral in exactly the same way as the costs of keeping paper records.
Archiving in the true, professional sense means the selection of (usually about 5%) of those records of an individual or organisation which have permanent research value and their deposit in an archive repository (either in-house or third party) which will make them available for research once any sensitivity has expired. The remaining 95% of records can be destroyed once the organisation/ individual no longer needs them.
In the paper world such records were not deposited in an archive until their business use had expired. In the digital world this may not be possible as the records could well have disappeared or become inaccessible through digital obsolescence before they can be collected for deposit. Digital records are therefore more at risk than their paper counterparts.
This risk means that, where a legal organisation or practitioner knows that some digital records have permanent value as an asset, they should:
a. identify and tag them on creation or receipt;<br>
b. ensure that the system and format in which they are stored will render them accessible over the long-term; and<br>
c. arrange for the archives to take custody of them before they become inaccessible through system decommissioning or data migration.
</td><td>
The regular disposal of digital information and data when no longer needed means that the fiscal, legal, operational and historic value of records has been identified (preferably on creation), that deletion or archiving rules have been put in place and that information risk and storage costs are consequently reduced.
<h3>Deleting obsolete digital information:</h3>
<ul>
<li>All individuals within organisations are capable of – and should regularly delete – redundant material so that ephemeral data and documents are not stored unnecessarily (e.g. drafts, duplicates, inaccurate material, obsolete versions and old reference material).</li>
<li>All organisations should maintain and implement regularly updated information retention and destruction schedules and instruct their IT departments on when to purge redundant material.</li>
<li>The Archivist or Records/Information Manager should be involved in all planning for new, or decommissioning of old, IT systems and for any 'archiving' by IT.</li>
</ul>
<h3>Archiving digital information</h3>
<ul>
<li>For in-house archives the Archivist should have full access to IT systems to enable early selection of information of permanent value.</li>
<li>Where an organisation has a deposit arrangement with a third-party archives the deposit agreement should specify:</li>
</ul>
d. frequency of digital deposits (e.g. annually);<br>
e. method of deposit (eg secure file transfer protocol; encrypted USB or hard drive);<br>
f. format of deposits (e.g. PDF);<br>
g. closure periods and<br>
h. the arrangements the archives will make to ensure accessibility and digital continuity over time.
</td></tr>
</table>

# Appendix IX: Seminar papers and presentations

Janos Levente/Shutterstock.com

The appendices below include:

a. Biographical notes on all speakers.
b. Talks which have been paraphrased either by the original authors or the LRAR Director with the authors' permission.
c. Information packs for attendees containing useful background reading.
d. Summaries of group discussions and responses to questions put to panels of experts.

All information, unless otherwise stated, was up to date at the time of the seminars. The seminar information packs and original presentations are on the LRAR website: http://ials.sas.ac.uk/research/areas-research/legal-records-risk-lrar-project/lrar-seminars and a blog with impressions of seminar proceedings and recommendations will be found here: http://lrar.blogs.sas.ac.uk/2016/11/30/information-as-an-asset-the-business-benefits-to-providers-of-legal-services-of-preserving-records/

## *Seminar contributors: biographical notes*

**Peter Bartlett** is the Nottinghamshire Healthcare National Health Service (NHS) Trust Professor of Mental Health Law, School of Law and Institute of Mental Health, University of Nottingham. Following two degrees in philosophy at the University of Toronto, he read law at Osgoode Hall Law School of York University, Canada. After his call to the bar in 1988, he served as Law Clerk to the Justice of the Ontario High Court and then as research associate to the Ontario Enquiry on Mental Competency. He obtained his doctorate in 1993 and joined the School of Law at the University of Nottingham, where in April 2005 he was appointed to the Nottinghamshire Healthcare NHS Trust Chair in Mental Health Law. Professor Bartlett's research interests are primarily in the area of mental disability (including psycho-social disability/mental illness and learning disability), both in England and Wales and internationally. He has provided advice regarding law reform in Lesotho and Bosnia and Herzegovina, and for six years (four as chair) served on the board of the Mental Disability Advocacy Center (MDAC), a human rights organisation based in Budapest. From 2013–14, he was specialist advisor to the House of Lords Post-Legislative Scrutiny Committee on the Mental Capacity Act. His research interests include the Mental Health Act 1983 (England and Wales), the Mental Capacity Act 2005 (England and Wales), and the European Convention on Human Rights and the UN Convention on the Rights of Persons with Disabilities. He is also interested in the history of law and psychiatry, particularly in England.

**Tracey Calvert** is a lawyer who specialises in professional ethics, regulatory and legal compliance issues. She was previously employed by The Law Society as a senior ethics adviser and was part of the policy team at the Solicitors Regulation Authority which drafted the SRA *Handbook*. She now runs her own consultancy business, Oakalls Consultancy Limited, providing compliance services to other lawyers. She has written a number of books, is on the boards of the Legal Compliance Association and TLS's Legal Compliance Bulletin, an officer of the professional ethics committee of the International Bar Association and a contributor to *Cordery on Legal Services*.

**Clare Cowling** is an Associate Research Fellow of the IALS, where the LRAR project was based, and was the project Director. She has been an archivist and records manager for over 40 years in Australia and the UK and has also managed two earlier projects on legal records under the supervision of William Twining: the Legal Records in the Commonwealth project, completed in 1994 and the Records of Legal Education project, which resulted in the establishment of the Records of Legal Education Archives at IALS in 2001.

**Emma Ferguson** has worked in the Archives and Records Management profession since 2007 in a number of different sectors. Emma graduated from The University of Manchester in 2005; following this she volunteered in the Archives and Special Collections department at the John Rylands University Library, Manchester. She was a Graduate Trainee in Archives and Library studies at The John Rylands Library in 2008 and then successfully gained a place on a master's degree in Archives and Records Management at the University of Liverpool, graduating in 2010. Her first post-qualification position was at the General Medical Council in a short-term contract as Records Officer. Emma was then offered the position of Archivist at Chadwick Lawrence Solicitors LLP, based in West Yorkshire, where she still currently works, in 2011 and was promoted to Head Archivist in 2012.

**Philip Gale** is the Head of Standards and Improvement Team at The National Archives, which has the responsibility to develop and deploy effective standards and good practice to support the effective care of and access to archives. The key standards it works with are Archive Service Accreditation and standards relating to Places of Deposit for Public Records. Since training at the University of Liverpool in 1983, Philip has held a variety of archival and records management posts with the Glamorgan Archives Service, Warwickshire Record Office, Bedfordshire and Luton Archive Service, the former Corporation of London Records Office and the Church of England Record Centre. He has a keen awareness of the importance of archives as an asset for supporting business operations and reputations as well as their wider historical and cultural significance for their owners and wider society.

**Denis Galligan** is Professor of Socio-Legal Studies and a Professorial Fellow of Wolfson College, University of Oxford. He is the Jean Monnet Professor of European Public Law at the Universita' degli Studi di Siena and a visiting professor at the Woodrow Wilson School of Public and International Affairs at Princeton University. He is a member of the board of directors of the Foundation for Law, Justice, and Society, an independent institution affiliated with the Centre for Socio-Legal Studies and based at Wolfson College. His books include *Law in Modern Society* and *Western Concepts of Administrative Law*.

**Bettina Lange** is an Associate Professor of Law and Regulation at the Centre for Socio-Legal Studies, University of Oxford. Bettina was a Jean-Monnet Fellow at the European University Institute, Florence, Italy from September 2004 to January 2005. She has carried out consultancy work for the Environment Agency for England and Wales on trust-based environmental regulation.

**Nicholas Le Poidevin Q.C.** is a barrister practising in London. He specialises in private client work, both contentious and non-contentious, appearing in some of the leading cases in trusts and estates in recent years, both in England and offshore, and has a particular expertise in the conflict of laws. He speaks and writes extensively on the law of trusts and estates and has for several editions been a senior editor of *Lewin on Trusts*. He has a strong interest in legal history and is editing for the Selden Society a collection of 15th-century law reports. A Bencher of Lincoln's Inn, he chairs its Library Committee and is keen to maintain and expand the Library's holdings of historical material, both printed and manuscript.

**Elizabeth Lomas** is a Senior Lecturer in Information Governance at University College London. Her research currently focuses on the research needs for the digital evidence base (RecordDNA https://recorddna.wordpress.com/) and developing tools to aid the navigating of information management and compliance challenges for society and business. She has particular expertise in information rights law and its application in practice. She undertakes small scale consultancy projects and currently these are increasingly focusing on GDPR. She is a member of the Advisory Council on National Records and Archives and the Deputy Chair of the Forum on Historical Manuscripts and Research.

**Jane Marshall** was admitted as a solicitor in 1978 and following a period working abroad has spent her professional career in the City. She specialises in corporate pensions law and has been involved in a wide variety of work, both contentious and non-contentious, ranging from international, privatisation and public sector work to public takeovers and regulatory disputes. A founder member of the Association of Pension Lawyers, she was a partner in a boutique pensions firm and a large national firm before becoming a partner of Macfarlanes LLP. Following her retirement from full-time practice in 2014 she now runs her own consulting firm. She is a Court member of the University of Dundee and a Liveryman of the Worshipful Company of Glovers of London. An author and speaker on pensions matters, with a particular interest in funding, regulatory and governance issues, she became a director of the Pensions Archive Trust in 2015.

**Michael Reynolds** is a solicitor and chartered arbitrator. He is currently the Module leader, International Dispute Resolution BPP University College London and a Visiting Senior Fellow at the London School of Economics. He has more than 30 years' experience in European antitrust law with Allen & Overy. He has represented a large number of corporations from the United States, Japan and Brazil and other international clients before the European Commission in merger control, cartel and unilateral conduct cases. He acted for Sun Microsystems in their complaint against Microsoft, leading to one of the most complex antitrust cases ever brought by the Commission. He has been involved in over 20 of the major cartel cases brought by the Commission including one of the first cases on cartel settlements. He was President of the International Bar Association (IBA) from 2013 until 2015 and past Chair of the IBA Antitrust Committee.

**Alex Ritchie** is a business archives specialist. Until March 2018 he was the Business Archives Advice Manager, Archives Sector Development, The National Archives. Prior to taking up this post he was, for 25 years, the Senior Curatorial Officer at the Royal Commission on Historical Manuscripts, responsible for maintenance of the National Register of Archives until its merger with the Public Record Office to form The National Archives in 2003.

**Derek Roebuck** is a solicitor who has taught and practised law in England, New Zealand, Australia, Papua New Guinea and Hong Kong. He is the editor of Arbitration, the Journal of the Chartered Institute of Arbitrators. Derek is Senior Associate Research Fellow at the IALS and Guest Professor at the People's University of China. He was formerly Professor of Law (comparative law) in Australia, Papua New Guinea and Hong Kong. He has written over 40 books on law, legal history and language, including the seven-volume Peking University Press bilingual texts on Hong Kong contract, criminal law and procedure. Recently he has written on the history of dispute resolution: *A Miscellany of Disputes* (2000), *Ancient Greek Arbitration* (2001), *The Charitable Arbitrator: How to Mediate and Arbitrate in Louis XIV's France* (2002) and *Roman Arbitration* (2004). He is now working on early English arbitration.

**Maria Sienkiewicz** qualified as an archivist in 1996 and spent eight years working in archives, libraries and museums in the public sector before moving to Barclays Bank as Group Archivist in 2004. Based in Manchester, Maria reports to the Company Secretary, and leads a team of four staff, who are responsible for the management of those records the Bank wishes to keep permanently. The archives comprise both hard copy and digital records and are used by a wide variety of Barclays business units around the world. The archives are also available for use by the public.

**Judy Slinn** read Philosophy, Politics and Economics at St Anne's College, Oxford. Since then she has researched and written about many aspects of business across a wide range of manufacturing and service industries in the UK, Europe and North America. She has written the histories of several of London's international law firms, including Freshfields, Linklaters, Clifford Chance, Ashurst and most recently the firm that is now Hogan Lovells. Over the last decade her research focused on innovation and globalisation in the pharmaceutical industry and more recently on corporate governance, the latter resulting in the publication (with Laura Spira) of *The Cadbury Committee: A history* (OUP 2013). Until retirement she was Reader in Business History at the Oxford Brookes University Business School. She continues as an associate editor and writer for the *New Oxford Dictionary of National Biography*, as she has been since its inception.

**William Twining** is patron of the Legal Records at Risk project, which was his brainchild. He was Quain Professor of Jurisprudence at UCL from 1983 until 1996; after a period as Research Professor he became Emeritus in 2004. He has held chairs in Belfast and Warwick and numerous visiting appointments. At the start of his career William taught for seven years in Sudan and Tanzania. He has maintained an interest in Eastern Africa, and more broadly the Commonwealth, ever since. He has studied and taught in several leading UK and American law schools. A prominent member of the Law in Context movement, he has contributed especially to jurisprudence, evidence and proof, legal method, legal education, intellectual history and legal archives. His recent work explores the implications of globalisation for legal scholarship and legal theory. Central themes include the variety and complexity of legal phenomena; that many so-called global processes and patterns are sub-global, linked to empires, diasporas, alliances and legal traditions; that diffusion, legal pluralism, and surface law are important topics for both analytical and empirical jurisprudence; that, in a world characterised by profound diversity of beliefs and radical poverty, the discipline of law needs to engage with problems of constructing just and workable supra-national institutions and practices; and that adopting a global perspective challenges some of the main working assumptions of Western traditions of academic law. He was awarded the 2016 Halsbury Legal Award for Academic Achievement.

**Lisa Webley** was at the time of the seminar a Senior Fellow at IALS and Professor of Empirical Legal Studies at the University of Westminster. She is now the Chair in Legal Information and Research, Birmingham Law School. She undertakes research on legal ethics, the legal profession and access to justice and was until recently on the University Research Ethics Committee which had oversight of all research in the University. She is Secretary of the International Association of Legal Ethics and General Editor of the journal *Legal Ethics*. She is the incoming co-director of the Legal Education Research Network.

# The first LRAR seminar: 'What do we mean by legal records at risk?', 10 December 2015

ESB Professional/Shutterstock.com

## 1. Project outline – aims, methodology and expected outcomes (William Twining and Clare Cowling)[1]

The project's scope is to identify records of private sector institutions specialised to law (ISLs) in England and Wales, 1913–2014, that are at risk and facilitate their rescue. The category of ISLs is broadly and flexibly interpreted. An initial census of legal institutions provides the 16 major categories, including providers of legal services, arbitration, providers of ancillary services (such as law publishers, legal stationers) and professional and specialist organisations/associations. Sub-categories of providers of legal services include alternative dispute resolution, especially arbitration-mediation services, barristers, insolvency practitioners, licensed conveyancers, multi-disciplinary practices, notaries, patent attorneys, pro bono legal services (including law school clinics), scriveners, solicitors, trade mark attorneys and will writers.

The project feeds upon the following earlier work:

- *Legal Records in the Commonwealth* (Twining, Quick, Cowling and others): national archives' policies in relation to (mainly public sector) legal records.
- *Records of Legal Education*: report and creation of archives at Institute of Advanced Legal Studies (Cowling, Winterton, Twining and others).
- *Records at Risk* BRA Report: the starting point of the project

A pilot project carried out from 2013–15 provided the rationale and plans for a major project or programme. It included:

- A preliminary study about records of international commercial arbitration which concluded that they are inadequately provided for.
- A report on actual and potential repositories for significant records of ISLs and problems relating thereto (Collins-Dawson).
- Preparatory work for the project as a whole, including selective bibliography, background material, and ten briefing papers for possible sub-projects.
- A case study of the records of one law publisher.
- A preliminary review of problems for ISLs of adjusting to the digital age.

The LRAR Project itself started on 1 September 2015, based at IALS and funded by two years 'seed money' for the Director and some research assistance. Substantial fundraising will be needed over the next two years. LRAR is an action-research project conducted mainly by archivists. The programme will proceed on three levels:

1. Systematic analysis of problems of preservation of legal records at risk. Planned outcome: a report/short book marrying jurisprudence and the law in action with archival best practice.
2. Study of situation, issues and problems relating to selected particular categories and sub-categories of ISLs. Study of potential archival significance of differentiated types of ISL records in relation to various kinds of users
3. Raising awareness and general guidance re significance, selection and preservation of records of

1 The text of this article is a slightly amended version by the authors of their original Powerpoint presentation and is reproduced with their permission.

ISLs; identification of suitable repositories, including matching of specialist and niche institutions with appropriate repositories in liaison, where possible, with potential users e.g. linking individuals or firms specialising in entertainment law with historians of popular culture and potential repositories.

4. Case studies and dealings with particular institutions among selected categories. Analysis of problems; guidance on retention schedules, digital records etc; facilitation of transfer.

The project will not collect records. It does not assume that general archival principles and methods will need much adaptation to most categories of ISLs. The main focus is on gaps in provision for many categories, sub-categories and individual ISLs.

Progress to date: scoping the project. We have contacted all the major archive pressure groups, plus individual archives with a particular interest, most historical/research societies and institutions, The Law Society, the Solicitors Regulation Authority, 10 major London law firms and c.20 smaller/ancillary ISLs. We have also begun to create a database of ISLs and possible gaps in archive provision, set up a website and drafted two questionnaires.

Progress to date: identifying potential ways forward. We have begun to identify categories of legal records of research value, potential case studies, user research requirements, potential repositories, further funding opportunities, digital archiving possibilities and ways to raise the project's profile.

## 2. Business Archives at Risk (Alex Ritchie)

Alex spoke about business records at risk, making the following points:

- In 2009 TNA set up a Crisis Management Team to devise a national strategy for business archives at risk. The team works in collaboration with the Business Archives Council (BAC) and the Archives and Records Association (ARA). The Team currently has 10 staff, who monitor the collapse of businesses and seek to rescue records. It has had notable success, with 22 deposits in archive repositories from 86 cases where records were at risk e.g. Comet and Woolworths.
- TNA manages an index of business records, based on the old National Register of Archives.
- In-house business archives currently comprise 33% of all corporate archives, primarily in banking, alcohol and retail. There is an appreciation by these businesses of the potential of their archives for branding and reuse.
- TNA has also undertaken a survey of architectural, building and construction records.

## 3. Seminar handout: Legal Records at Risk (William Twining)

### The Project

**Scope**: records of private sector institutions specialised to law (ISLs) in England and Wales, 1913–2014, that are at risk. The category of ISLs is broadly and flexibly interpreted.

**ISLs census**: **16 categories of institutions**, including providers of legal services, arbitration, providers of ancillary services (e.g law publishers, legal stationers), professional and specialist organisations/ associations.

**Sub-categories: providers of legal services**

a. Primary providers of legal services: alternative dispute resolution, especially arbitration-mediation services, barristers insolvency practitioners, licensed conveyancers, multi-disciplinary practices, notaries, patent attorneys, pro bono legal services (including law school clinics) scriveners, solicitors, trade mark attorneys, will writers.

b. Secondary providers of legal services (sub-level 2 – distinguish professional/ paraprofessional/ mixed/other).

### Pilot Project 2013–15

- Rationale and plans for a major project or programme.
- Preliminary study about records of international commercial arbitration. Conclusion: inadequately provided for. There are no insuperable obstacles to establishing an international archive, probably in the United States (on hold).
- Census: identification and taxonomy of private sector ISLs divided into 16 categories with sub-categories (see above). Nearly complete.

- Report on actual and potential repositories for significant records of ISLs and problems relating thereto. (Collins-Dawson).
- Preparatory work for the project as a whole, including selective bibliography, background material, and ten briefing papers for possible sub-projects.
- Case study of one law publisher (almost complete).
- Preliminary review of problems for ISLs of adjusting to the digital age.

## 4. Round table discussion topic 1: What do we mean by 'legal records at risk'? Are legal records now more at risk than in the past? If they are at risk, what are the contributory factors?

After a lively debate the following findings were agreed:

- The Records Preservation Section of the BRA will no longer be able to act as a holding area for hard copy records of solicitors' firms. This may mean records are lost.
- The recordkeeping guidance of regulatory bodies like the Solicitors Regulation Authority is excellent but needs updating and the regulators need to monitor best practice more proactively to encourage better records management.
- Digital issues – same issue as with other records plus digital continuity. There may be special issues around accessing the digital records of intervened firms.
- Lack of recognised value in legal records by the information owners.
- Sale of legal records at auction (despite confidentiality/ownership issues).
- Records may be at risk of becoming invisible e.g. marriage settlements early 19th century – mid 20th century.
- Barristers' records: there is already a historical black hole with this category. Barristers do not appear to have an interest.
- Concerns about confidentiality do not appear to be a major issue, though some archives (e.g. LMA) are now refusing to take in any records closed for more than 20 years due to storage costs.
- Success story – justices' notebooks are retained by the Supreme Court (if offered by the judge) and will be made available for research. It is hoped The National Archives will accept custody.[2]

## 5. Round table discussion topic 2: What hitherto neglected/at risk categories of legal records would researchers use if the records were readily available? In what areas of research might these records be significant and useful?

Findings included:

- Questions of use – for scholars or for owners or both? Deeds, estate maps and manorial records are of recognised value to genealogists.
- Need for academic support and input. Historical mapping – interest of economic historians in arbitration. Legal historians and socio-legal studies: need to engage historians in collaborative projects.
- Use of seminars like this as means of engagement.
- Need to alert academic researchers to the potential value of legal records (i.e. create a demand).
- Better publicity as to the location of legal records already available for research.
- Run a project with PhD students?
- More events like the BAC's 'Meet the Archivists' sessions or Sheffield University Centre for Archival Practice student inductions.

2 Editor's note: since this seminar an examination of TNA's *Discovery* portal has shown that at the time of writing there are 447 sets of judges'/justices' notebooks held in TNA and local authority archives. See http://discovery.nationalarchives.gov.uk.

## 6. Round table discussion topic 3: Given the current economic climate, how can the collection and care of legal records by archives and libraries be facilitated?

Findings included:

- Need for a more co-ordinated archives strategy for the collection of private/business/legal records.
- Need for industry sponsorship of archiving projects – how to advocate for archives.
- Need to differentiate types of solicitors' practice, especially specialist and niche practices in order to identify institutions connected with the law whose records may be of special archival interest.
- More digitisation would create more demand.
- More funding for digitisation and cataloguing projects is needed.
- Donations by depositing institutions to assist in covering transfer, storage and cataloguing costs (either one-off or on a regular basis) should be requested.
- Academic researchers and institutions could better communicate their research needs to archives.
- The BRA intends to widen its scope to offer more guidance to law firms on the potential archival value of their business records.
- The legal profession must take more responsibility for its records and be educated a) in their research potential in many fields as well as legal history and b) about the availability of repositories.
- A legal heritage function along the lines of the Wellcome Trust would be the ideal!

# The second LRAR seminar: 'Information as an asset: the business benefits to providers of legal services of preserving records', 23 November 2016

TarikVision/Shutterstock.com

## 1. Introductory notes to the seminar (Clare Cowling)

The 2004 Clementi report: *Review of the regulatory framework for legal services in England and Wales* suggested that it was time for the providers of legal services to act in a more business-like way:

> Research shows that complaints arise as much from poor business service as from poor legal advice... In developing business systems to minimise costs whilst maintaining high standards, there is no reason why lawyers should not work alongside those with other skills, for example in finance or IT.[3]

To these skills the Legal Records at Risk project adds the skill of information and records management.

Recent developments (changes to legal services; globalisation) have transformed our legal framework, yet no concerted effort has as yet been made to protect and preserve private sector records which document these changes. The Legal Records at Risk project, led by IALS and working in collaboration with the legal profession, the research community and archives, including TNA and the BRA, seeks to develop a national strategy to identify and preserve our legal heritage and to save modern (20th- and 21st-century) private sector legal records in the UK that may be at risk.

What are the specific benefits to institutions specialised to law of managing their records effectively and preserving those of value for internal and external research? Here are just a few which were explored in this seminar, along with suggestions as to how they can be achieved:

- cost and efficiency savings
- business continuity
- improved client confidence
- service to justice
- enhanced reputation
- community engagement

## 2. The value of preserving legal records: the historian's perspective (Judy Slinn)

### *Solicitors' archives: the case for preservation*

Thirty years ago the senior partner of the London law firm Wilde Sapte wrote an introduction to his firm's history, with an explanation of the decision to research and publish it at that time:

3 Clementi Report, p. 8.

> The increase in the size of firms of solicitors in London today.... Together with the specialisation imposed on modern solicitors by reason of the complexity of business life, has radically changed the nature of legal practice....The change is continuing and accelerating with the development of sophisticated machinery and communications.[4]

Wilde Sapte was by no means the only law firm to recognise the changes driving the profession in new directions. The abolition in 1967 of the limit of 20 on the number of partners had opened the way for the creation of much larger firms, which in turn allowed the greater specialisation and internationalisation increasingly required by large corporate clients. These changes, which were both aided and stimulated by technological development, led a number of large, mainly London-based, law firms to publish their histories in the last two decades of the 20th century; they included Freshfields, Linklaters & Paines, Slaughter and May, Norton Rose, Clifford Chance, Ashurst and Vizards. These firms – and those who followed in their footsteps later wanted not only to capture the essence of the legal practices of the smaller partnerships which had dominated the profession for more than a century. They also wished to preserve, enhance and pass on a sense of continuity and identity for future generations in the firm, albeit in a very different environment.

### *Records in the archives*

For the historian researching the history of a law firm its own records ideally provide a basic structure of the account; these would include partnership agreements together with information on the organisation and structure of the firm. As firms grew larger more formal structures where the decisions made on management and policy matters were recorded replaced the informal and largely unrecorded decision-making of the senior partner(s).

The historian also needs to know about partners and staff as well as the offices from which the firm had practised over the years. Photographs and other memorabilia – for example relating to office social events, such as dinner menus – often put flesh on the bones as well as painting a vivid picture of changing office practices and social customs. Oral history in the shape of interviews with partners and staff who have been with the firm for long periods of time enlivens the past and frequently points the contrast between past and present. Last but by no means least the firm's accounts. Reconstructing the practice from client records, to understand who the clients were, and the kind of work done for them is essential. For the years before 1945 some of this information may be sparse or no longer in existence: in London and other UK cities enemy action destroyed office premises and much or all that was in them.

In some cases, however, relevant records may be found surviving with the clients. Banks have usually been great keepers of records; Coward Chance (Clifford Chance since 1987) had a large banking practice in the 19th century and the firm's clients provided information on its work. Freshfields' offices in Old Jewry suffered a direct hit, destroying virtually all their archives. The firm had, however, acted for the Bank of England since early in the 18th century and the Bank's documents enabled much of the practice to be reconstructed. This included, for example, the large number of forgery cases the firm managed during the wars with France (1797–1821) when the use of gold was suspended.[5] The official Law Reports of course can also be a useful source of information on the firm's practice.

## 3. Hidden gems or skeletons in cupboards: making the most of business archives (Maria Sienkiewicz)[6]

Barclays Bank can trace its foundation back to two goldsmith bankers, John Freame and Thomas Gould, who set up shop in Lombard Street, London in 1690. In 1736, James Barclay became a partner, and the partnership eventually became Barclay, Bevan, Tritton and Co. In 1896, that partnership merged with 19 other private family banks to form Barclay and Co. Ltd. Through the 20th century, other banks and building societies amalgamated into Barclays, an international business was established, the UK's first credit card was launched and an investment banking business was built up.

As a result of this long, and very mixed, history, the archives is fairly extensive and surprisingly varied. In addition to the standard minute books, accounts and records relating to personnel and premises you might expect in a business archive, we also hold much personal material. Many of our founding banks were established by Quakers, and they all knew each other. Important and influential Quaker families like the Barclays in London, the Gurneys in East Anglia and the Backhouses in the north east were all involved in other businesses, politics and a variety of good causes. The correspondence in our collection speaks as much about this as it does about banking.

Even the standard banking records have uses far beyond expectations. Our customer ledgers for the bank of Goslings and Sharpe of Fleet Street run from 1717 to 1896, containing the details of the income and expenditure of thousands of people. These records are frequently consulted by people researching a specific individual, family or business. The

4 A.G. Salmon, *The History of Wilde Sapte*, 1985.

5 Judy Slinn, *A History of Freshfields*,1984.

6 The text of this article is based on the author's original Powerpoint presentation at the seminar and is reproduced with her permission.

National Trust, for example, has been able to use the account of the Earl of Bristol to track payments to Capability Brown and Gainsborough, enabling them to date the landscaping of the gardens, and the painting of a portrait at Ickworth.

The collection also includes a great many pictorial items, ranging from 19th-century portraits to 20th-century advertising, a large number of films and a variety of artefacts, such as early computers, credit cards, signs, strong boxes and firearms, which were used for security purposes in the 18th and 19th centuries.

More recently, we have started collecting items which we may not strictly think of as archival, but which have value to the Bank. A good example of this are customer leaflets. These are the leaflets which advertise our products and set out the terms and conditions under which those products are provided. Ordinarily, we might only elect to collect a sample of these, to show what sort of thing the Bank was doing and what the branding looked like. However, the recent rise in customer complaints means that these documents have taken on greater significance as they are needed to properly decide claims.

In 2009 they proved to be crucial in the test case between the Office of Fair Trading[7] and the banks in deciding the fairness of charges for unauthorised overdrafts. The Supreme Court's decision in favour of the banks meant that the potential for millions of customers to reclaim billions of pounds in charges was prevented. This was only possible thanks to the banks being able to produce their terms and conditions in court. The value of the archives in preserving and making this material accessible was beyond dispute.

Of course, not every benefit an archive brings to a business is so tangible. So what other benefits do we bring the Bank?

I should explain at this point that we do cross the boundary between archivist and historian, much more so than an archivist in, for example, a local authority service would expect to do. For many people within the Bank, when they contact us with a question, they don't expect to be sent a list of potentially relevant archives which they can come to our office to search through to find the answer. They don't even expect to be sent digital images of archives which may contain the answer. They expect the answer. This means that some of our enquiries may take days of research.

The more serious ones usually come from the Bank's Legal teams, Chief Executive or Corporate Secretariat. They usually involve some sort of litigation, internal review, request from our regulators, or some statutory function. They always come with a tight deadline and thanks to the wonders of modern technology we don't have to risk sending important documents down to London. Now one of us gets to stand at the scanner and scan it all so that it can be emailed.

As much as I hate standing at the scanner at 7 o'clock on a Friday evening, the fact that we can respond to these requests is, for me, the ultimate reason we exist. The archives, coupled with our knowledge and expertise, is being used in the most direct way to enable the business to function and that is the very core of business archives.

The slightly less serious enquiries (or should that be serious in a different way?) come from colleagues working in Public Relations and Marketing, who have recognised that our long past has a value in enhancing our brand and reputation. Since 2012, the archives have been involved in a number of campaigns which have celebrated our history and used it as a source of inspiration.

There has been content on barclays.com and on the Bank's social media platforms; a series of films about the archives were available on the intranet and, in 2015, Barclays celebrated its 325th anniversary with a series of events, including an archive exhibition at the Annual General Meeting. The following year, Barclaycard marked its 50th anniversary, which gained a great deal of media attention, including a feature on Radio 4 and colour spreads in many national newspapers. The anniversary received an overwhelmingly positive response, much of it focussed around Barclaycard's eye-catching 1960s publicity – material that was only available thanks to the archives.

In support of all of these initiatives we have hosted numerous visits to the archives by colleagues from marketing and external designers, we have answered hundreds of enquiries and we have given presentations to a variety of groups across the Bank.

We were also able to leverage this appreciation of our history to achieve something that had been an aim of ours for a long time – an archive website. Featuring stories from our history and thousands of images of archives, including our entire UK branch network photographic collection and Barclays' annual reports back to 1896, the website serves to provide quick answers to some of our frequently asked questions, and provide access to material previously only available in our office. In its first year (March 2015 to March 2016) the website attracted over 32,000 unique visitors from around the world. By sharing our unique resource with a global audience we were able to support Barclays' commitment to the global community in which it operates.

Obviously, our website does not provide the answer to every question. External enquiries range from simple family history queries to complex academic research. Many of the simpler enquiries we choose to answer remotely – we are

7 Office of Fair Trading (OFT) *v* Abbey National plc & Ors [2009] UKSC 6 (25 November 2009): http://www.bailii.org/uk/cases/UKSC/2009/6.html [2010] 1 All ER 667, [2009] UKSC 6, [2010] 1 Lloyd's Rep 281, [2009] 3 WLR 1215, [2010] 1 AC 696.

located on an industrial estate in Manchester. It's not easy to get to and many of our enquirers would spend a lot longer travelling than they would looking at archives.

Those external enquirers conducting more in-depth research are encouraged to visit in person, and they usually want to, but as we have no dedicated searchroom staff, a researcher means one of our team spending the day in our searchroom, which is something we're happy to do, but can be quite a drain on our already limited resources. However, our enquirers frequently comment on how they did not expect such a great service from a big corporation so it all feels more than worthwhile.

It is important to remember though that there may be risks as well as benefits in keeping archives. Barclays is an organisation with over 300 years of history, and like any organisation that old, some of it's good and some of it's bad. There are those who might argue that retaining the evidence of past wrongdoings is storing up trouble for the future. I would disagree.

Barclays' history in South Africa, for example, is not something that will ever be looked upon positively, but surely that only makes it more important that we understand what happened. If an organisation is serious about becoming more trusted, responsible and transparent, then a professionally managed archive can only be an asset.

We do also need to be aware of the context in which we operate. We are not an academic archive, operating within an environment where the nuances of historical debate are allowed space to breathe. Too often, any story involving a large corporation is reduced to an attention-grabbing and potentially ruinous headline. A good example is the accusation of being founded on the profits of the slave trade which is levelled at Barclays with alarming regularity. The truth is that one of our early partners, David Barclay did end up owning slaves as the result of a debt that was owed to him. Barclay freed the slaves, provided the funding to train them in trades and relocated them from Jamaica to Philadelphia. We have letters in the archive written by Barclay in which he talks about this and they are a fascinating resource. While they are freely available to anyone who might wish to see them, the sad fact is that we do not go out of our way to publicise them as we might wish because we don't want to attract any hostility.

I believe that a properly managed archive can only ever be an asset to any business wishing to portray itself as a responsible corporate citizen. Even if there are activities recorded there that you'd rather weren't, history has taught us that it's by far easier to be honest and open, to learn from the past and move on.

## 4. From 'big boxes' to digitisation: the business benefits of employing a professional archivist at a law firm (Emma Ferguson)[8]

Chadwick Lawrence Solicitors is a broad-based modern solicitors firm proud of our Yorkshire heritage. We are trusted across the region to have the knowledge and experience to help in any legal situation – we are Yorkshire's Legal People. As a large firm in Yorkshire we recognise the importance of creating a positive social impact, through both our exceptionally high level of service and first-rate legal advice, but also through supporting the community through charity events and sponsorships. We currently have seven office branches, with over two hundred members of staff. We hold business records relating to finance, human resources, compliance and risk management; governance records such as board minutes and policy and strategic records; and client records such as matter files, wills, title deeds and grants of probate.

The 'Chadwick Lawrence Way' is a term used to refer to the culture of the firm, incorporating our values, standards and behaviours. The firm's mission of 'being the best at what we do' is something that governs all areas of work and shapes our day to day activities and decisions. Recently, the archives department was asked to deliver three objectives that reflect the core aims of our work that fit in directly with the firm's vision and values.

They are to 1) proactively work with fee earners and secretaries (our customers), encouraging and supporting them to follow archive policies and procedures and to promote the advantages of doing so; 2) deal with external client requests in a professional, efficient and timely manner; 3) keep fee earners and secretaries (our customers) up to date with the status of internal requests and the expected timescales of completion, to have regular and open communication with requestors, and to promote the archive service as being reliable, trustworthy and approachable. The archives department is a crucial component in ensuring that the firm meets the needs of its clients and also its employees and the objectives clearly demonstrate the ethos behind our work.

Chadwick Lawrence has undergone a lot of change over the past seven years, including a change in Managing Partner and the acquisition of two other law firms. The firm is growing each year in terms of client base and staff members and as a result the volume of records, files and original documents that are being created and archived is consistently increasing. The expanding nature of the firm was the initial driving force behind my employment with Chadwick

8 The text of this article is based on the author's original Powerpoint presentation at the seminar and is reproduced with her permission.

Lawrence in 2011. Management staff had come to a realisation that the archives needed to be regulated in the same way that other support areas within the firm were. Items were not being located and retrieved as quickly as they needed to be, which was having a direct impact on the quality of the service that the firm was able to offer to clients. Backlogs of files waiting to be archived were building up at each office and consequently locating a file was often an impossible task. Prior to my commencing employment with the firm, each office branch had their own way of archiving and storing files. This had worked to an extent in the firm's earlier days when it was a smaller operation, but the lack of standardisation was now causing problems. Files were stored in numbered boxes, with archival records created on a mixture of index cards, ledgers, and Microsoft Access databases. Some files were simply stored in 'big boxes' which were labelled as 'big box 1, big box 2' etc, with no actual record of what each box contained, and as a result all of the 'big boxes' had to be searched through whenever a file was requested. Similarly, it was often hit and miss whether the documents were ever logged out to someone once located.

Only one person at each office knew the 'archiving' system for that specific branch and if this employee was ever away from work, then no one else in the firm knew how or where to locate the archived documents. Requests for items to be retrieved were received in an ad hoc manner, with very little information provided that would help us to locate the file. It soon became clear that a homogenised way of working was needed across the firm and that things had to change. Understandably, I had to tread lightly at first as staff were protective of the systems that had been in place for many years. Before doing anything else, I conducted a survey of all the records at each office to establish what kinds of records the firm produced, what was retained and destroyed and how items were physically archived, stored and then retrieved. Upon reporting back to Management, I was promoted to Head Archivist and set about creating an organised, consistent and compliant archives and records management service that would be of great benefit to the firm.

One of the first changes that I made was to set up an archives department email address and inbox, so that all requests to retrieve items from storage were sent to a central email account. We have been quite strict with this over the years and everyone now knows to use the archives@chadlaw email address if they have any archival queries. I also created standardised forms for staff to use when requesting or returning items to and from storage, or when sending new material to us to be archived. Secondly, upon researching different software packages, I discovered that the firm's case management system actually had an archive catalogue already built within it, but this had not ever been utilised and the majority of people within the firm did not even know that it existed. I realised that this was an opportunity for the department and set about redesigning the catalogue so that it had the required fields and functions, including a check in and check out system and provenance and storage location fields. A large part of designing and implementing the catalogue was spent working with internal and external IT staff and there was a lot of trial and error and going back and forth with testing, which could be frustrating when things didn't work out exactly as planned or took longer than originally thought. However, the end result is that the firm now has an archive catalogue which is used to create records of newly archived items and crucially all members of the department now create the records in a standardised way on the one catalogue. Everyone in the firm can access the catalogue and see exactly what we have in storage for a particular client and request items directly from it. This means that items can instantly be located and retrieved and that documents are checked in and out of storage as part of this process, allowing a history of the movement of each document to develop. The firm is currently looking at launching a new case management system across all sites and I am involved in developing a new archive cataloguing system on this, so the work begins again!

We now have a thriving archives department that has a key place within the firm's structure, and I am line manager of four full-time archivists. We have one off-site storage unit where the archived files are stored and also have converted basements in two of the offices for archives storage – all of which are ordered and designed in the same manner, making it easy for any of us to locate an item from any location. In the majority of cases, items are retrieved and with the requestor on the same day or the day after that the request is made. As a result the client and customer (fee earners) satisfaction rates are high. We are the first point of contact for client queries regarding their archived documents and we are often able to answer their query without having to involve a fee earner, which allows our colleagues to concentrate on their ongoing case work. For the more complicated queries, we take the clients details, retrieve the relevant documents from storage and pass the query onto a designated fee earner who can then advise the client with all of the information to hand and charge for the work as necessary. We get a lot of feedback and praise from clients because we offer a prompt, accurate and professional service to them and they are reassured that their documents are being safely and securely stored, yet are accessible to them at any time. This also generates a lot of repeat business for the firm.

Due to the expanding nature of the firm, the number of documents that we archive each month has increased over the past few years. In 2016, we archived 10,387 client files, which increased to 13,196 in 2017. To date in 2018 we have archived 7,438 files, so we are well on the way to improving on last year's figures. This is only a small aspect of our role – so far in 2018, we have archived 1,567 original documents and dealt with 959 requests to retrieve archived documents from storage. By providing a professional and efficient in-house archives service, we are saving the firm a lot of expense and inconvenience in having to outsource the archives service to an external company, which often charges per item retrieved from storage and according to how many deliveries are required each day. I compile the archive figures for a monthly Heads of Department report, which is an opportunity for me to showcase the work that we do and demonstrate how invaluable the archives department has become to the firm and how improving the efficiency of the records management and archival processes has had such a positive effect across the board.

Since January 2015 I have been actively involved with strategic management and forward planning, which has heightened my own profile and the presence of the archives department within the firm. Working with the Compliance Officer for Legal Practice, I now conduct quarterly Archive and Risk Management training sessions for all new starters, which is a great opportunity to inform staff of who we are, how to request and return items to us and why it is so important for staff to send client files to us to be archived as soon as the case is complete. I have also written policies for file retention and destruction, the file closing process and emergency planning, all of which are reviewed and updated on a yearly basis and stored on SharePoint so that all staff members within the firm have access to them. I have also recently been involved in the implementation of the GDPR across the firm.

There have obviously been obstacles to overcome since I started at Chadwick Lawrence as I have implemented a lot of change since my appointment, but these have now been accepted and embraced across the firm as the benefits of those changes are clear for all to see. Work for the archives department will never be finished and it is continually evolving. Just when I think that things are running smoothly, we will take over another firm with very little notice and find ourselves in charge of 10,000 new wills for instance that have to be slotted into our archive system, so there's never a dull day. The plan for the next year is to start digitising files, rather than archiving the physical paper copy. I have written proposals and budgets for this which are being considered by the Board and we are currently in talks with an external scanning company which will scan the files to BS10008 standards.[9] This will be another major change for the firm in its working practices. However, digitisation will mean that client files can be instantly accessed by anyone (permissions granted) at any time, so we will be reducing the waiting time for receiving a file again, from one days wait to instant access. We are planning on trialling this with one department and if all goes as planned it will then be gradually branched out across the firm. If this can be successfully achieved then the archives department will certainly have come a long way from the days of the 'big box' approach.

The business benefits of employing a professional archivist for Chadwick Lawrence have been invaluable, with long standing benefits currently being appreciated and plans for future development in progress that will again be invaluable to the firm. Employing a professional archivist in a law firm is quite an unusual occurrence, but doing so has stimulated positive change and raised awareness of the value of the records across the whole firm, whilst simultaneously demonstrating that it is a forward thinking and adaptable business that crucially is always looking for ways to improve the service on offer to clients. Everyone now knows what the archives department is, where to find us, what we do and crucially why we do it – for the benefit of the firm, its staff, its clients and the wider community.

## 5. A model for the future? The work of the Pensions Archive Trust (PAT) (Jane Marshall)[10]

### *Why PAT?*

A pensions archive, which collects and stores material on UK company and personal pensions, might be considered of limited interest and relevance. And yet it is a good example of the potential significance of the work of archivists in the commercial world, extending well beyond the historical and academic context of the documents involved.

Over the last 30 years, commercial life has changed beyond recognition in response to technology, social change and globalisation. Anyone whose legal career began in the early 1980s will remember attempting to decipher telex messages and completing transactions with bank drafts. More fundamentally, the law itself has continued to evolve to meet these challenges. Developments in occupational law and regulation in particular occurred in rapid succession over that period. UK work place pensions were once regarded as a remarkable success story. Steady growth in private sector coverage and benefits accelerated in the 1970s and 1980s. In the 1990s and for a variety of reasons the tide began to turn. Now, and in spite of vast resources that continue to be invested in pension provision, newspaper headlines are likely to be all that the general public knows about company schemes. An understandable response to past failures perhaps, but obscuring the bigger picture: pension schemes and sponsoring employers have created security and prosperity for millions of workers and their dependants. Aging populations mean that the search for long-term savings and protection mechanisms will continue. If we have indeed entered an age of populism, the need for an accurate and wide-ranging record of past successes and failures is key. PAT collects and preserves the material that provides that record.

9 British Standards Institution, *BS 10008:2014 Evidential weight and legal admissibility of electronic information: specification* (BSI, 2014).

10 The text of this article is based on the author's original Powerpoint presentation at the seminar and is reproduced with her permission.

## What does PAT do?

PAT has three main objectives:

- To gather relevant records in a permanent archive;
- To ensure the security and accessibility of those records and to create a central reference point;
- To educate the general public, policy makers and others on all aspects of occupational and personal pension provision.

In order to achieve these objectives, PAT has organised itself so as to combine knowledge and understanding of pensions with expertise in the management of archives. Established as a charitable company limited by guarantee, its directors are people with long experience of and interest in pension provision, including pensions managers, advisers and academics. The PAT board meets regularly (five times in the year ending 31 August 2016). A number of leading members of the pensions community are involved as presidents and vice presidents. Professional archivists turn PAT's aspirations into reality through a partnership agreement with London Metropolitan Archives (LMA), one of the largest archives in the country. While LMA is funded and managed by the City of London, the PAT archive is operated as a national resource. Digitisation of some material is already underway which will facilitate access, although financial resources will largely dictate what can be done and when. The relationship with LMA is central to the success and professionalism of PAT. PAT's archive is held within LMA's own collections. Items can be ordered in advance and inspected there. The pensions and professional archive strands of PAT are operated seamlessly. PAT and LMA jointly fund a graduate intern who provides archival services to PAT, subject to appropriate LMA supervision and guidance. The graduate receives paid training and a good foundation for his or her future career and in addition to professional archive work is given practical experience in management and regular reporting. A Joint Liaison Committee consisting of representatives of PAT and LMA and the graduate intern meets following board meetings.

## Origins of PAT

PAT came about principally because of one individual. Alan Herbert, now the Chairman of PAT, had the original idea and the connections, skill and persistence to carry it out. In 2001, Alan had attended the 25th anniversary celebrations of a company whose business was computerised pensions administration. It occurred to him how much pensions had changed over that period and how much more change was likely to follow. It was therefore important to record the evolution of work place pensions, along with the legislative and tax framework and the contribution of employers, individuals and representative and professional bodies. Soundings taken over a 12 month period established that there was general support, and towards the end of 2002 a steering group was established. It met for the first time in January 2003. During that year discussions took place with several universities on a possible location for the archive and two years later in 2005 an appeal was launched to meet the costs of establishing the archive and the running costs. The rest is history.

## What material does PAT hold?

PAT holds a wide range of material including formal legal pensions documents (trust deeds and rules, deeds of amendment and deeds of adherence) scheme reports and accounts, explanatory material and membership records. It also holds archives of bodies such as the Pensions and Lifetime Savings Association (formerly the National Association of Pension Funds) the Association of Consulting Actuaries, the Society of Pension Professionals and the Pensions Management Institute. Reports, responses to consultations, the resolution of technical issues and practical concerns, and the successes and failures of policy and regulation can all be tracked. PAT also holds important work on financial and investment matters, most notably the George Ross Goobey archive and continues to collect material from new sources. The Association of Pension Lawyers, which has done much to facilitate the development of the law in this area, has recently offered to contribute and work is underway in order to identify the scope of the material to be donated.

## Current and future challenges

PAT confronts a threefold challenge. First, it must engage with those who have material to contribute, explaining the value of PAT and its objectives so as to obtain the fullest collection practicable. For the reasons set out above, PAT believes that its collections are particularly relevant for the development of future policy. The second challenge relates to individual and commercial confidentiality, data protection and personal sensitivities and the last, predictably and inevitably, is financial. All of these are, of course, closely connected. Unless people are convinced of the value of a pensions archive, it is all too easy to use confidentiality or data protection as reasons for non-engagement, without exploring whether and to what extent these issues can be managed. And without wide engagement and support, the future financial viability of PAT will in turn become a concern. Much work is undertaken in relation to confidentiality and disclosure when material is being prepared for inclusion. Sometimes initial concerns fall away. Substantial disclosure requirements already exist: in practice much is already in the public domain, and full disclosure may be an easy additional step. Some material is affected by data protection and legal requirements which are scrupulously observed. The ability to separate particular information from a collection and restricting access to it can, equally, be used to overcome commercial or other sensitivities. It is usually sufficient to delay access – the number of years is agreed in discussion. A growing belief in transparency in public and commercial life, wherever possible, chimes with the work of PAT. Applying modern standards to past practice may be uncomfortable – but facts trump misconceptions every time.

## 6. Information pack attachment 1: current guidance available to the legal profession on managing and disposing of records[11]

Below is a limited selection of recordkeeping advice specifically aimed at providers of legal services. A more comprehensive guide to such advice is in preparation.

It is recommended that legal institutions also familiarise themselves with the detailed and comprehensive guidance offered by The National Archives: http://www.nationalarchives.gov.uk/information-management/

**Arbitrators and mediators**: the guidance below primarily deals with confidentiality, but also advises that records should be destroyed or returned to the parties following a decision.

- International Court of Arbitration: the ICC Rules of Arbitration Article 1: Confidentiality
- Chartered Institute of Arbitrators (CIArb) : Practice guideline 1: Confidentiality in mediation

**Barristers**: the *BSB Handbook* recommends that a record keeping policy be drawn up to identify compliance and records retention requirements.

**Licensed Conveyancers**: the Council for Licensed Conveyancers' *Handbook* advises on maintenance of proper records, compliance and retention of financial records.

**Solicitors**: The Law Society provides a great deal of good advice on managing records, including the following Practice Notes:

- Depositing records and documents with public sector archives
- Retention of wills and probate practice note
- Retention of trusts practice note
- Information security
- Business continuity
- Data protection
- File closure management

The Solicitors Regulation Authority gives advice on good business practice, confidentiality and recordkeeping in the following:

- SRA *Code of Conduct 2011*
- SRA *Handbook*
- Closing down your practice: regulatory requirements

LexisNexis provides comprehensive guidance on managing records in the following document:

- Records Management: Current Issues in Retention, Destruction, and E-Discovery

Is this good advice being followed?

11 All references to documents and hyperlinks were correct at the time of the seminar.

## 7. Information pack attachment II: Sample records of potential research value held by providers of legal services

| Category | Records of potential research value (samples only) |
|---|---|
| Client management | Policy and procedures<br>Client documents: deeds, wills etc*<br>Case files+ |
| Corporate management | Minutes of meetings<br>Annual Report and Accounts<br>Business plans<br>Organisation charts<br>Published biographies e.g. of partners, members |
| External relations management | Design and control of corporate identity<br>Consultation papers<br>Seminars and conventions organised by the organisation<br>Published material (retain one copy only)<br>Websites (retain regular snapshots) |
| Finance | Fees books |
| Governance | Regulations and rules<br>Registers of interests<br>Directories of members/partners<br>Documentation of legal framework<br>Partnership regulations and rules<br>Certificate of incorporation or registration as a company<br>Memorandum and articles of Association<br>Incorporation as a limited company |
| Procedures and policies | Policy and strategy documents<br>Standards<br>Procedures<br>Handbooks<br>Best practice guidance notes |
| Training and education | Policy files |

* Should be returned to client on termination of relationship. If this is not possible could be offered to a local archives.
+Though selected case files could well be of considerable research interest, confidentiality guarantees made to clients often preclude any consideration by the information owners of making them accessible for research, even in the very long term. If archivists and researchers are concerned by this and wish for such records to be preserved solutions such as anonymisation or lengthy closure periods (100 years plus) could be recommended.

## 8. Information pack attachment III: Success stories: private sector legal records which have been saved for research in archives

Source: primarily The National Archives' *Discovery* portal.

### *Archives of legal institutions*[12]

This list does not include records of the large number of government and quasi-government legal bodies held in TNA.

| Legal entity | Archive repository |
|---|---|
| Association of Law Teachers | Records of Legal Education Archives, IALS |
| Board of Conciliation and Arbitration for the Boot and Shoe Trade of Leicester | Record Office for Leicestershire, Leicester and Rutland |

12 The above list is a sample only, based on what had been uncovered at the time of the seminar. For a full list see **Appendix II.**

| Legal entity | Archive repository |
|---|---|
| Board of Conciliation and Arbitration for the Iron and Steel Trades of the North of England | Teesside Archives |
| Brighton Law Centre | East Sussex Record Office |
| British Institute of Human Rights | Kings College London Archives |
| British Maritime Law Association | University College London Archives and Special Collections |
| Committee of Heads of University Law Schools | Records of Legal Education Archives, IALS |
| Commonwealth Legal Education Association | Records of Legal Education Archives, IALS |
| Commonwealth Legal Records Project | Records of Legal Education Archives, IALS |
| Council of Legal Education | Records of Legal Education Archives, IALS |
| Ede & Ravenscroft | In-house archives |
| Faculty Office | In-house archives |
| Bar Council | Records of Legal Education Archives, IALS and Middle Temple Archives |
| Gray's Inn | In-house archives |
| Hinckley and District Boot and Shoe Arbitration Board | Record Office for Leicestershire, Leicester and Rutland |
| Howard League for Penal Reform | Warwick University: Modern Records Centre |
| Human Rights Society | In-house archives |
| Inner Temple | In-house archives |
| Institute and Faculty of Actuaries | In-house archives |
| International Association of Law Libraries | Records of Legal Education Archives, IALS |
| International Law Association | Records of Legal Education Archives, IALS |
| Lambeth Mediation Service | Lambeth Archives |
| Law Centres Network | In-house archives |
| The Law Society | In-house archives |
| Legal Action Group | In-house archives |
| Legal Skills Research Group | Records of Legal Education Archives, IALS |
| Leicestershire and Rutland Board of Conciliation and Arbitration for the Boot and Shoe Trade | Record Office for Leicestershire, Leicester and Rutland |
| LexisNexis Butterworths | In-house archives |
| Lincoln's Inn | In-house archives |
| London Court of Arbitration | London Metropolitan Archives: City of London |
| Mediation UK | LSE Library, Archives and Special Collections |
| Middle Temple | In-house archives |
| National Family Mediation | LSE Library, Archives and Special Collections |
| New Inn | Middle Temple Archive |
| Records of Legal Education Project | Records of Legal Education Archives, IALS |
| Royal Institution of Chartered Surveyors | City of Westminster Archives |
| Shoe Trade Board of Arbitration | Northamptonshire Record Office |
| Society for Advanced Legal Studies | Records of Legal Education Archives, IALS |
| Society of Public Teachers of Law (now Society of Legal Scholars) | Records of Legal Education Archives, IALS |
| Society of Scrivener Notaries | London Metropolitan Archives: City of London |
| Socio-Legal Studies Association | Records of Legal Education Archives, IALS |
| South Manchester Law Centre | Manchester Archives and Local Studies |
| United Kingdom National Committee of Comparative Law | Records of Legal Education Archives, IALS |
| Wolverhampton Law Centre | Wolverhampton Archives and Local Studies |

## *Arbitrators' records in archives (20th–21st century)*

Most arbitrators' records will be found within the business records of the organisations to which they provided services, and must therefore be searched for under their individual names or other occupations (e.g. as judges). Only four discrete collections of 'arbitrators' records as such for this period were found using *Discovery*:

| Name | Records | Archive repository |
|---|---|---|
| Edwards, Leslie (b 1945), engineer and arbitrator | 1975–1978: papers rel to the construction of Marsa shipyard at Malta | Institution of Civil Engineers |
| Fry, Sir Edward (1827–1918), Knight, judge, arbitrator and zoologist | family corresp<br>1834–1935: personal and family corresp<br>1895–1901: diaries of prison visits | Cambridge University: King's College Archive Centre<br>Cambridge University Library: Department of Manuscripts and University Archives<br>Warwick University: Modern Records Centre |
| Guillebaud, Claude William (1890–1971), economist and arbitrator | 1927–1972: personal papers and corresp | Cambridge University: St John's College Library |
| Marsh, Arthur (1922–1999), academic and industrial arbitrator | c.1960–1991: papers rel to work as industrial arbitrator | Warwick University: Modern Records Centre |

## *Barristers' records in archives (20th–21st century):*

Records of individual barristers should also be searched for under their individual names or subsequent occupations. Only four discrete collections of barristers' business records for this period were found using *Discovery*:

| Name | Records | Archive repository |
|---|---|---|
| Bagge family, barristers | Fee books, 1900–1923 | Norfolk Record Office |
| Adrian Herbert Head, barrister and Norfolk circuit judge | Notes and case papers relating to his legal practice and as a circuit judge, 1951–1955 | Norfolk Record Office |
| J.J. Somerville, barrister | Diaries, ledgers and cash account books, 1930–1967 | Lancashire Archives |
| J.C. Whitebrook, barrister, Lincolns Inn | Correspondence and papers, 20th c. | Camden Local Studies and Archives Centre |

## *Solicitors' records in archives (20th–21st century)*

For this period, *Discovery* lists 1,500 collections of records of individual solicitors and law firms available for research in local archives in England and Wales. The collections mostly comprise 'Client records' – deeds, leases and other property or probate documents originally belonging to clients, but there are also some business records. No 'client case files' were located in the course of this search.

The LMA in particular holds many collections of solicitors' business records; some sample entries are listed below.

| Firm | Records |
|---|---|
| Ashurst Morris Crisp, solicitors | Records including accounts, correspondence, copy-out letters, photographs, plans and deeds, 1685–1999 |
| Chamberlayne, A.R., solicitor | Office books, accounts and miscellaneous papers, 1853–1924 |
| Collyer-Bristow and Company, solicitors | Company and client administration records, 1781–1975 |
| Gilbert Samuel & Co, solicitors | General ledgers and cash journals, 1902–1971 |
| Maude & Tunnicliffe, solicitors | Business records, 19th–20th c. |
| Warrens, solicitors | Letter books, bills books, manor books and ledgers, 1774–1930 |
| Woodbridge and Sons, solicitors, Uxbridge | Family, business and client records, 1636–1953 |

## 9. Information pack attachment IV: Not so successful stories – auctioning of legal records and other tales of woe...

### *Records for sale...*

Below is a sample of 'solicitors' papers' offered at public auction, courtesy of TNA's manuscript Sales Monitoring Service. TNA keeps an eye on all auctions and notifies the relevant record office when something comes up in which the record office might be interested. The record office will then bid, but only if it has sufficient funds or time to apply for a grant before the auction. For an advertisement of a current sale see https://www.the-saleroom.com/en-gb/auction-catalogues/lloyd-cameron-and-partners/catalogue-id-srtheau10073/lot-b1afc31d-65ca-4b08-8389-a6be00e5deb1

| |
|---|
| 199: solicitors bill book, Chard, Somerset., 1802–1809 |
| 164: Cheltenham Solicitor Clerks day book, 1832–1834 |
| 116: Cheltenham solicitors: letter book, 1839–1846 |
| 134: Solicitor's bill book of John Reed Clarke, Chard area, 1802–1809 |
| 86: Cheltenham solicitor's bill book (prob TV Banner), 1827–1830 |
| 74: London lawyer's bill book, 1786–1809 |
| 74: Warwickshire solicitor's notebook, 1700–1800 |
| 457: Account book of Roberts & Carter, solicitors, Barnstaple, 1834–1837 |
| 131: Banner, Thomas Vaughan, solicitor, Cheltenham: bill book, 1827–1830 |
| 166: John Reed Clarke, solicitors, Chard: bill book and index of clients, 1802–1809 |
| 28: Hall, Robert, lawyer: ms legal commmonplace book, 1713 |
| 486: Legal case notebook, 1824 |
| 147: Solicitors ledgers for firm (Francillon and Willott?) in Dursley, Glos listing clients and cases, 1868–1915 |
| 109: Lewis & Lewis solicitors of Ely Place corresp including blackmail letters and details of payments relating to royal, noble and celebrity scandals (Quantity not given), 1800–1950 |
| 320463130450: Thorp & Dickson solicitors Alnwick legal papers (15 bundles), 1800–1850 |
| 320463132564: Legal papers of Robert Thorp, Northumberland rel to Foster v Burrell, 1810–1820 |
| 128: Forster, solicitor of Aylsham, client corresp (several hundred items), 1883–1886 |
| 136: Wymondham legal corresp, files, lunatic asylum papers, court papers, 1800–1950 |
| 138: Bodenham & James, solicitors Hereford, letters received (100), 1860–1869 |

### *Comments from five local record office archivists on deposits of solicitors' records, 2015–16*[13]

### Information not seen as an asset?

> We would actually find it impossible to take a large collection these days as we have no room and because they are generally a terrible mess they take a huge amount of resources to make them usable...we do worry that many important documents are being destroyed particularly as land is registered and deeds are destroyed. Of course there are issues with preserving client files for historical purposes as I doubt any clients have given their consent to that and there are issues with solicitors not understanding the ownership of the material that they send us. The general attitude seems to be 'we don't want this you can have it if you want as a gift' without them understanding it is not their property and therefore we can only take it on deposit in case the owner turns up and claims it. It is increasingly difficult for us to keep track of who are the current firms responsible for our older deposits as firms merge and change and as far as I am aware no firm has contacted us about the material they have deposited with us since the moment it left their premises so I think you can safely say that they do not consider them an asset to the firm and feel no link to them once they believe the file closed.

13 The entries listed are extracts from emails sent to the LRAR project director by local authority archivists.

## Confidentiality issues?

There was one notable disaster in acquisition which was when a large collection was accepted unconditionally and was found to contain masses of rather uninteresting and fairly recent (e.g. still subject to DPA) records. It appears we can't give them back, we can't sample or destroy them, the firm has never requested anything back – and they've never been catalogued. I suspect the more general problem is just a simple lack of historical awareness by lawyers. I wonder how you could make reading that nice practice note[14] compulsory? I think you may also be right in believing there may be confidentiality issues – perhaps solicitors don't understand that archivists deal with DP and other aspects of record security all the time. I suppose the most basic aspect of all this is that everyone is so busy – the preservation of [records] totally peripheral to the work of the lawyers. Other than by making an archival element to the CPD points system (perhaps it could be part of a wider record-keeping agenda?) I'm not sure how best to go about changing the status quo.'

## Problems with client files?

I was appointed in January 2015 to complete...an 18-month National Cataloguing Grants funded project to catalogue the records of a historic law firm. This included a large accession (383 boxes) made in 1998 consisting mostly of client papers. Due to the time constraints, there was not time to catalogue in great detail (although this would not have been desirable in hindsight) and the project was designed to include a significant contribution from volunteers. The approach that was adopted was that it was not appropriate for volunteers to work with client papers so they were directed towards deeds and sale particulars while I catalogued the client papers. This work was completed with the Data Protection Act in mind but with a broad intention to make the records as accessible as possible....Because of how concerned the firm were about client confidentiality, the partners were invited to look at the catalogue to agree access restrictions. The result is that on one of the catalogues, clients papers dated 1900 or later may only be accessed with permission of the firm...There were two separate concerns from the firm a) complaint to legal ombudsman for breach of confidentiality from the descendent of a client and b) bad publicity from the impression that they would advise clients then make details public later on. We have since been offered additional deposits from the firm, but declined to collect additional client papers.

## Taking advantage of the taxpayer?

In my experience:

- Solicitors have extremely poor recordkeeping as far as older client records are concerned – the records can be kept in appalling conditions and in a state of disorder.
- They don't recognise the ongoing historic value of what they hold and may therefore destroy records.
- As an alternative to destruction, they are often happy to deposit with the local record office, but at no cost to themselves. This means that the financial burden falls to the record office (usually the local authority) to assess, transport, list, package and repair the documents – with the solicitors often imposing timescales for removal of the records at entirely their own convenience! As you cannot fail to be aware, local authority budgets are shrinking, and it is no longer appropriate to expect the taxpayer to cover the cost of solicitors' own neglect of their duty to their clients and their clients' records.

You can probably tell that I'm a bit fed up about all this. For example, we have a collection of over 600 boxes from one solicitor's firm, which has arrived in a disorganised state over several decades, which is unlisted and some of which has suffered terribly from damp and dirt. One of the clients of this firm (the owner of a landed estate) is trying to access his own legal documents from this collection and has been trying to do so for several years; the solicitors' firm themselves takes no responsibility and it falls to us to try and find, within these 600 boxes, the records that might relate to his estate. If I were him, I would be tempted to sue the solicitors for their neglect of his records. The problem we have is that when it comes to the crunch, much though we would like to refuse collections like this, we know that if we don't accept them, the firm will throw them into a skip.

14 The Law Society's Practice Note: *Depositing records and documents with public sector archives*, 15 December 2010.

## Lack of knowledge about how to manage records?

> I was hired to organise the dreadful filing of one very busy solicitor, but also spent two solid months reorganising 800 boxes of closed files into a retention order. These boxes had been sent to external storage three years previously following a flood in the partner's basement where they had been kept. Many were flood-damaged – little attempt had been made to conserve them. They weren't in any real order and there was no way, prior to my project, to know when files were ready to be destroyed. Whilst carrying out this project, I also looked into records management and archiving processes at the firm and found that it was a very confused situation. For example, they had two different retention schedules that no one really knew about and didn't seem to have a great understanding of how to use their external storage. All in all, this firm seemed to have a desire to improve their records management and archiving – for example, they had relatively recently appointed one of their receptionists to manage the closing of files and were pleased to be able to use me for the box reorganisation project. However, it appeared that records management was always going to take a back seat to their other activities, and while they may have liked things to be better, they didn't know how to go about it easily, especially since they were very busy. During my time there, I tried to find as much guidance as possible about managing legal records but found that there was very little.

# 10. Round table discussion topic 1: do the business benefits of preserving legal records outweigh the risks?

### *What are the benefits?*

The group identified the following business benefits:

- Reuse of records for strategic planning, corporate branding, reputational benefits around community engagement, transparency and honesty, speedy and effective service to clients, better compliance with regulatory and legal requirements (especially around the management of client files) and an improved understanding of historical context.
- Business seen as caring about/part of the community, not removed from it.
- Good public relations – honesty, learning from mistakes etc.
- Better understanding by the public of the value of legal services.
- Removal of ongoing management costs if an external archive is used.
- Destroying the rubbish and just keeping the good stuff saves money.

The presentations were cited as clearly demonstrating these benefits. The fact that Barclays had saved upwards of £1 billion through using records in its in-house archives to win a court case was duly noted! It was also agreed that these business benefits apply equally to the proper management of current and semi-current records as well as preserving archives.

### *What are the risks of preserving legal records?*

Risks include potential breaches of confidentiality and security, litigation and reputational damage. It was agreed that these risks are caused primarily by poor information management but that reputational damage could be caused by the publication of records containing politically incorrect content.

It was suggested, however, that being honest and transparent about past mistakes could only benefit an organisation, otherwise rumour will take over ('what have they got to hide?'). Several seminar attendees felt that the legal profession's culture of secrecy unfortunately mitigated against transparency and that the profession at times seemed to be almost afraid of its own records rather than regarding them as a potential asset.

Solutions suggested included educating the profession about the value of its records and of their re-use potential.

# 11. Round table discussion topic 2: does the benefit to legal entities of investing in archival provision for records outweigh the effort involved?

The group agreed that there are three alternatives open to legal entities:

- Store the records in a basement, warehouse or 'archive' server and eventually destroy them.

- Set up an in-house archives for material of value and destroy the rest once it becomes redundant.
- Deposit valuable records in a third-party archives such as a county record office and destroy the rest once it becomes redundant.

Several seminar attendees felt that legal entities, especially law firms, would continue with option 1 as it was a) too difficult to convince the partners and senior administrators of the cost value of records management and archiving of valuable records and b) there was too much nervousness over allowing historic material to enter the public domain.

Option 2: there is no doubt that setting up and managing an in-house archives is costly, but as Barclays has shown, it can certainly be worth the cost. It's interesting that all the major banks in the UK and several large businesses (e.g. Diageo, Marks and Spencers) consider that investing in an in-house archives is financially worthwhile. Why don't the large law firms?

Option 3: transferring records to an external archives such as a county record office costs information owners very little in the larger scheme of things, but some effort and planning on the part of the owners is required to engage with archives. Factors mitigating against such actions include indifference, worry about reputation and confidentiality concerns. This led to some discussion on confidentiality, particularly around client files, where the concept of 'confidentiality in perpetuity' seems engrained, even though it is nowhere expressed in regulatory guidance. 'Confidentiality in perpetuity', however, does not apply to the *business* records of legal bodies.

Some law firms *have* deposited records with archives, often via the rescue service offered by the BRA and usually resulting from an office clear-out or closure of the firm. Records have tended to be passed to the BRA and archives without being listed and often in dreadful condition, yet the BRA and archives have shouldered the cost of doing the essential work necessary to make the records accessible to both the public and the firm's own clients. In the past these firms have, quite frankly, exploited the willingness of the BRA and local record offices to rescue records free of charge and of record offices to house, conserve and catalogue records; however the BRA can no longer provide a warehousing service and it is certainly no longer appropriate in the current economic climate to expect the taxpayer (who funds county record offices) to cover the cost of solicitors' unwillingness to take some responsibility for their own historic records – at least in terms of part payment towards their proper care.

The group all agreed that managing records costs money but that legal entities should be doing this work anyway as part of best practice and regulatory requirements. Archiving valuable material is simply the end of the process.

## 12. Conclusions and options for change

In summary, the group agreed that many institutions specialised to law have:

- Little awareness of information as an asset; therefore records are under-utilised for branding or reuse for strategic planning or to ensure a speedy and effective service to clients or to enhance reputational benefits around community engagement, transparency and honesty.
- Little awareness of the true cost of continuing to keep unmanaged information (unnecessary storage costs, excessive server space slowing down processes, digital obsolescence, time wasting).
- Very low awareness of the value of keeping records of historical value permanently (community engagement, exhibitions, histories) – reputational advantages around being seen as open about an organisation's history – including mistakes and learning from them, demonstrating good practice etc.

The group all felt that educating the legal profession about the importance of managing information responsibly was the key, as without good information management legal entities cannot work efficiently and historical records of value (particularly born-digital records) will become inaccessible. Options suggested included: making information management part of CPD training; more proactive work by the regulators and membership organisations to promote existing best practice guidance; lobbying by researchers and archives on the value of legal records. All agreed that breaking the culture of secrecy was necessary.

Practical solutions suggested for legal bodies:

- Clear accountability and responsibility for managing information and records.
- Active and vocal support of senior managers in enforcing compliance with corporate standards and regulatory requirements.
- Training all staff to recognise their responsibilities for, and improve their competencies in, records management.

- Developing strategies for information management (paper and electronic) over time, including managing records of permanent value. Without this last solution it is not possible to have an end to end records management programme.
- Understanding the true cost of making records accessible and, at the very least, making a donation to archives which are willing to house and care for the records of institutions specialised to law. In relation to this last point the possibility of creating a model along the lines of the Pensions Archive Trust to rescue legal records of value was noted and will be followed up.

# The third LRAR seminar: 'Legal records, confidentiality and access: breaking down the barriers', 27 October 2017

## 1. Seminar introduction: what are the barriers to accessing legal records for research? (Clare Cowling)[15]

The Legal Records at Risk Project seeks to a) broaden the concept of 'legal records' to include records of institutions and individuals specialised to law, mainly in the private sector e.g. the records of law firms and solicitors, barristers' chambers and barristers, legal executives, patent agents, licensed conveyancers, arbitrators and mediators and b) identify – and facilitate the rescue of – 20th-century private sector legal records of potential research value which may be at risk.

Categories of legal records which may have research value include: records of professional legal associations and pressure groups; administrative and policy records of legal service providers; client files and documents and the papers of individual legal practitioners and other professionals. What are the barriers to rescuing these legal records for posterity?

Some legal institutions are quite reluctant to deposit records with archives. Why? Is it:

- A lack of awareness of/just not interested in historical relevance/value of records?
- Not seen as part of the institution's core functions/responsibilities?
- Little sense of the institution as part of the community? and/or....
- Confidentiality concerns.

Are client confidentiality and legal professional privilege real – or just perceived – barriers to rescuing legal records for posterity? In other words, do client confidentiality and legal professional privilege last forever or are they finite? This seminar seeks to find answers to these questions.

## 2. The legal practitioner's perspective: solicitors (Tracey Calvert)[16]

This article discusses confidentiality from the perspective of the solicitor's profession in England and Wales. There are currently just over 142,000 practising solicitors. It is the main tenet of this article that duties of confidentiality do in fact create barriers to solicitors sharing information in their possession with third parties such as archivists.

There are a few things that the public think that they know about the legal profession and which clients expect from their legal advisers. These are that we will do what we say will do (or not), that we will keep money safe, and that we will keep secrets which are told to us. This last expectation is what is meant by confidentiality. Solicitors are trusted advisers and we are trusted to protect client information.

The duty of confidentiality is one of the more onerous and enduring obligations of the solicitors' profession. It relates to all information which the solicitor has in their possession. It is a duty which continues despite the end of the retainer with the client. It will continue despite the death of the client concerned. In practical terms, this duty requires the need for individuals and firms to develop and adhere to systems and controls to manage the risk of loss of confidentiality information. This loss can be accidental, deliberate, caused by ways of working, use of technology and through theft of equipment and cybercrime.

15 The text of this article is based on the author's original Powerpoint presentation at the seminar.

16 The text of this article was compiled by the author from her original seminar notes and is reproduced with her permission.

These expectations about secrets require an understanding of the ethical behaviours which the profession is expected to demonstrate. Here it is important to note that in modern regulation, this reference to profession and professional duties means that not only are solicitors bound to behave in a certain way but also that everyone working in SRA-authorised law firms, regardless of their role or any or no qualification, must also demonstrate. There are approximately 10,000 SRA-authorised businesses and every single owner and employee of each of these entities must uphold the regulatory standards.

An example of the weight of this duty, and the seriousness of breach, is given in the SRA disciplinary ruling against a long-standing member of the profession in 2017. This is the case of Mr Stephen Chittenden who was found to have breached his professional duties by releasing information from a client's file without the client's permission. Mr Chittenden had acted for a client who was acquitted of murder in 1978. A year later he provided his client's file to the solicitors acting for the estate of the murder victim and again, between 1985 and 1987 he provided the file to another law firm and allowed them to make a photocopy of the file. On neither occasion had he obtained his client's permission nor was he complying with any legal duty to disclose. Following an investigation of his conduct, Mr Chittenden was rebuked and made subject to a regulatory settlement agreement in which he admitted breaches of his duties to his client of confidentiality. He undertook to make an application to the SRA to remove his name from the roll of solicitors and not to apply for restoration or to seek employment in any authorised law firm.

It is appropriate to observe that no one, not least the former client, had raised a complaint about these historic disclosures. However, in the regulatory settlement agreement, the following points were made:

> Mr Chittenden accepts and admits that these actions were extremely serious breaches of, in particular, his duty of confidentiality to his client and constituted conduct that is completely unacceptable on the part of a solicitor. He accepts that were the matter to be brought before the Solicitors' Disciplinary Tribunal he might well be struck off.

The regulatory expectations are described in the *SRA Principles* and the *SRA Code of Conduct* 2011. The Principles are the high-level, overarching ethical behaviours required of all members of the profession. Currently, there are ten Principles, of which those most relevant to this discussion are shown below:

- SRA Principle 2 – you must act with integrity
- SRA Principle 4 – you must act in the best interests of each client
- SRA Principle 5 – you must provide a proper standard of service
- SRA Principle 6 – you must behave in a way that maintains the trust the public places in you and in the provision of legal services

Drilling down to the detail, and what compliance looks like in practice, the SRA expects us to demonstrate two specific behaviours in respect of confidentiality. These are expressed as outcomes which must be achieved and they are contained in the SRA *Code of Conduct 2011*:

- You must keep the affairs of clients confidential unless disclosure is required or permitted by law or the client consents.
- You must have effective systems and controls in place to enable you to identify risks to client confidentiality and to mitigate those risks.

Applying this ethical requirement to the issue of access to legal records, where these records are in the possession of the solicitor or law firm because of a retainer with a client, disclosure is only acceptable if this is with client permission or if there is a legal duty which enables this.

The regulatory duty is overlaid with the duty to comply with the law and the knowledge that we must all comply with data protection legislation. The current principal pieces of legislation are the General Data Protection Regulation and the Data Protection Act 2018. These came into force on 25 May 2018. They impose legal duties on data controllers and data processors (of which, solicitors can be either or both) to comply with data protection principles when processing personal data belonging to data subjects.

There are some differences between ethical duties of confidentiality and legal data protection duties. Confidentiality applies only in respect of clients (current and former) but continues until such time as client permission or the law allows a variation. Data protection legislation protects the personal information of a wider group of individuals than a client base but protects only those data subjects who are living.

Breach of data protection legislation can give rise to criminal and civil liability. The Information Commissioner's Office has powers of enforcement and these are often used against the legal profession when personal data is misused, not stored securely, or lost. The headlines from the latest legislation are in respect of the increased fining powers that the ICO has at its disposal. The ICO now has the power to fine a defaulting individual or firm up to €20m, or 4% of annual worldwide turnover, whichever is the greater, for serious breaches.

We are already on notice that the legal profession is of concern to this oversight body. In 2014 the incumbent Information Commissioner issued a warning in which he drew attention to the fact that the Office had received notice of 15 data breaches in three months from the profession. He said of this:

> The number of breaches reported by barristers and solicitors may not seem that high, but given the sensitive information they handle, and the fact that it is often held in paper files rather than secured by any sort of encryption, that number is troubling. It is important that we sound the alarm at an early stage to make sure this problem is addressed before a barrister or solicitor is left counting the financial and reputational damage of a serious data breach.

For these reasons, it is important that solicitors manage the risks arising in connection with the documents and information which they hold. In fact, they are positively encouraged by both their regulator and the law to have storage and destruction policies to minimise the risks of breach of confidentiality and a data legislation offence. They are also expected to identify ownership of documentation in files. The Law Society has recently issued a practice note 'Who owns the file?' which is available on the Society website, http://www.lawsociety.org.uk.

The SRA does not produce such guidance, relying instead on the individuals and firms which it authorises to consider these issues for themselves. It will, as has been seen above, take disciplinary action against anyone in breach of its requirements.

## 3. The legal practitioner's perspective: barristers (Nicholas Le Poidevin)[17]

Two presentations at the seminar were given from the perspective of two legal practitioners, Tracey Calvert and Nicholas Le Poidevin. Tracey Calvert's presentation covered regulatory matters, client expectations and data protection. Nicholas Le Poidevin's presentation, summarised below, covered:

- client confidentiality;
- duties as to documents disclosed in litigation;
- legal professional privilege.

The focus in both talks was on legal requirements affecting the ability of a practitioner to preserve legal records and make them available to researchers. The requirements are much the same for barristers, solicitors and other practitioners and so no distinction was drawn between them by the presenters. Nor is there usually any relevant legal distinction between electronic and hard-copy records.

Nicholas noted that records with which practitioners may be concerned include:

a. client records;
b. records of the practitioner's own practice;
c. litigation records.

It has to be said that the legal environment is not friendly either to the preservation of records or to making them available to researchers. What follows is therefore in large part a list of difficulties with no obvious solutions.

### *Client records*

This category includes:

- documents in the hands of a practitioner because a client has provided them;
- correspondence between the practitioner and the client or a third party;
- attendance notes;
- written advice;
- documents (or drafts of documents) intended to have some legal effect, such as a will, mortgage or contract;
- documents generated in the course of litigation, such as pleadings and witness statements.

### *Ownership and copyright*

In the midst of concerns about confidentiality and data protection, it is easy to forget that documents – or hard-copy documents at least – have owners; that is, the physical paper belongs to someone. Copyright in the contents is also

17 Nicholas Le Poidevin's original ppt presentation and accompanying notes have been paraphrased by Clare Cowling and are reproduced here with his permission. The article contains brief guidance in general terms only. No responsibility is accepted for the accuracy of any statement of law. For the presentation see https://ials.sas.ac.uk/sites/default/files/files/Research/LRAR/LRAR_seminar3_2017_Presentation_N_le_Poidevin.pdf.

owned by someone, not necessarily the same person; the fact that the contents have no literary merit, which is alas true of most legal documents, is immaterial.[18]

Identifying the owner is not always easy. The Law Society publishes a Practice Note on the point, entitled '*Who owns the file?*'.[19] A paraphrase of the guidance is this:

- Original documents sent to the firm by the client will continue to belong to the client.
- Documents sent or received by the firm as the agent of the client belong to the client.
- When the firm is retained to produce a document (e.g. an agreement), the final version belongs to the client.
- Final versions of documents prepared by a third party and paid for by the client also belong to the client (e.g. a barrister's opinion or an expert's report).
- Documents prepared for the firm's own benefit or protection, or prepared as the means by which the firm discharges its function, belong to the firm (e.g. file copies of letters written to the client, drafts and working papers).
- Copies of internal emails and correspondence created while the firm is retained, and all emails and correspondence written by the client to the firm, belong to the firm.
- Accounting records, including vouchers and instructions, belong to the firm.

The question of ownership will arise primarily if the practitioner contemplates depositing records in an archives. The fact that the client has not asked for them to be handed over to him is not of itself a legal protection. It is true that there is a time limit for making a claim, which is six years.[20] Time, however, does not start to run from the date when the practitioner created or received the document but from a wrongful conversion by the practitioner i.e. treating the document as his own; depositing the document in an archives would be a conversion. No one will worry about the actual ownership of really old records but there are contexts in which a long time has to pass before it can be assumed that confidentiality is not a problem, a point picked up below.

Merely allowing inspection of a document is not an infringement of ownership, nor is it a breach of copyright. But it is generally a breach of copyright to allow a copy to be taken, whether a mere photocopy or publishing a document in a book. The author of the document is ordinarily the owner of the copyright, so that the writer of a letter to a practitioner retains the copyright in it. Nonetheless, copying for non-commercial research or private study is specifically permitted by statute[21] and though there are restrictions on the protection it is unlikely, given the nature of legal records, that copyright will be a practical problem.

## *Privilege*

Privilege – more fully, legal professional privilege – is often mentioned in connexion with legal records. It is, however, irrelevant for present purposes.

Privilege arises routinely in the context of civil litigation, though it does so in other contexts too. There is a general rule that parties who are litigating are obliged to disclose to each other documents relevant to any matter in dispute which are or have been in their control and then to allow inspection of those documents (usually by providing a copy).[22] Privilege is an exception to that obligation. It applies to documents by which legal advice is sought or given or which have been brought into being for the purpose of litigation. Such documents do not have to be provided to another party; they are 'privileged'. You need not show your opponent the legal advice you have obtained. The privilege is that of the client, not that of the practitioner, but the practitioner is bound to give effect to it.

The reason why privilege is irrelevant for present purposes is that it is a valid objection to what would otherwise be a legal right in someone else to see a document. Archivists and historians have no legal right against either a practitioner or the client to see any documents. Hence the existence or non-existence of privilege makes no difference.

What makes a difference is the obligation of confidentiality, which comes next.

18 Business letters are the subject of copyright: *Copinger and Skone James on Copyright* (17th ed.), para. 3-41.

19 Authorities relied on are *Leicester County Council* v. *Michael Faraday & Partners* [1941] 2 K.B. 205 (C.A.); *Chantrey Martin* v. *Martin* [1953] 2 Q.B. 286 (C.A.); *Gomba Holdings UK Ltd* v. *Minories Finance Ltd* [1988] 1 W.L.R. 1231 (C.A.).

20 Limitation Act 1980, s. 2.

21 Copyright, Designs and Patents Act 1988, ss. 29(1), (1C), 29A; *Copinger and Skone James*, *op. cit.*, para. 9-36.

22 See Civil Procedures Rules 1998 (CPR), Pt 31. The topic is a large one and the statement in the text is a very brief summary.

## *Confidentiality*

The client has a right against the practitioner to have his affairs kept confidential. The legal rule for solicitors is expressed as follows: 'A solicitor must keep the affairs of clients ... confidential except where disclosure is required or permitted by law or by the client'.[23]

The *Code of Conduct* of the Solicitors Regulation Authority[24] requires the solicitor to '... keep the affairs of clients confidential unless disclosure is required or permitted by law or the client consents.'[25]

Similarly, for barristers the *Code of Conduct* of the Bar Standards Board imposes both a 'core duty' and a rule as follows: 'You must keep the affairs of each client confidential'[26] and 'you must protect the confidentiality of each client's affairs, except for such disclosures as are required or permitted by law or to which your client gives informed consent'.[27]

Those obligations are not confined to material which is obviously sensitive or private, such as commercial negotiations or family secrets, but extends to all information acquired by the practitioner in the course of acting for the client. But for obvious reasons they do not extend to material already in the public domain, such as a planning permission.

The duty to maintain confidentiality does not come to an end merely because the practitioner has ceased to act for the client, so that the latter has become an ex-client.[28] Nor does the duty cease merely because the client is dead. That is part of the general principle that a client's entitlements form part of his estate. The right to insist on confidentiality passes to the executors or administrators; and even when they themselves are dead they can be replaced by others.

It follows that a practitioner would necessarily be in breach of duty by permitting inspection of a client's files or by passing them to an archive, even when the client died some time ago.

There seem to be only two possible solutions:

1. One is to include in the practitioner's agreement with the client, which in the case of a solicitor is set out in a client care letter, a term allowing the practitioner to do those things after the passing of a given period of time. The difficulty with that possibility is that the client is not likely to be willing to agree to a short period and the practitioner has little incentive to press for such agreement. The practitioner's interest in not having to store documents indefinitely is more simply met by obtaining the client's agreement to destroying material after a given period; and that, of course, is the primary choice under the data protection legislation.
2. The other solution is to wait until the practitioner can be confident that no one will care – a practical rather than a legal solution. The difficulty with that possibility is that the wait may be impracticably long. Some legal material may have a lasting relevance – in the case of rights of way, for example, it is sometimes necessary to investigate very elderly material – and it will be unappealing to retain modern records for a lengthy time.

## *Documents received in litigation*

One special case concerns documents received in civil litigation. Given the obligation already mentioned obliging each party to disclose relevant documents to the other, the practitioners on each side will typically end up with a quantity of documents from the other side. In large cases, enormous numbers of documents may be provided. When relevant, even personal documents such as bank statements and tax returns have to be produced, so the obligation can be intrusive. For that reason, it is the subject of a special procedural rule:[29]

1. A party to whom a document has been disclosed may use the document only for the purpose of the proceedings in which it is disclosed, except where –
   (a) the document has been read to or by the court, or referred to, at a hearing which has been held in public;
   (b) the court gives permission; or
   (c) the party who disclosed the document and the person to whom the document belongs agree.
2. The court may make an order restricting or prohibiting the use of a document which has been

23 *Halsbury's Laws of England*, 5th ed., vol. 65, para. 538.

24 Version 21, published 6 December 2018.

25 Para. O(4.1).

26 Core duty 6.

27 Rule C15.5.

28 *Prince Jefri Bolkiah* v. *KPMG* [1999] 2 A.C. 222 at 235-236.

29 C.P.R., r. 31.22.

disclosed, even where the document has been read to or by the court, or referred to, at a hearing which has been held in public.

The restriction is imposed not in favour of the practitioner's own client but in favour of the opposing client. In criminal proceedings, a similar restriction applies to documents disclosed by the prosecution to the defence.[30] Breach of it is a criminal offence.[31]

It would be a breach of one restriction or the other for a practitioner to allow inspection of the documents so disclosed or to lodge them in an archive.

When documents are organised for a trial, both sides' documents are usually copied and then amalgamated into a chronological or topical sequence for use in court. It may therefore be difficult for the practitioner to disentangle one side's documents from the other side's.

## *Records of the practitioner's own practice*

Records under this head include:

- documents constituting the association in which the practitioner practises, such as a partnership deed in the case of solicitors and a chambers constitution in the case of barristers;
- minutes of meetings of the members of the firm or chambers;
- financial records;
- office manuals;
- regulatory documentation;
- records concerned with employees.

Such records would be of historical interest in the future in indicating how contemporary legal practice was carried on. Some material may be in the public domain. Many solicitors, for example, carry on practice as limited liability partnerships and statutory accounts must be filed and available for inspection.[32] But most of it will not be.

It is likely that in the case of a firm of solicitors the partners owe each other an obligation to keep the affairs of the firm confidential. The primary concern will often be to protect the firm against poaching of clients when one of its partners leaves, rather than the sort of material being considered here, and there is a dearth of authority on the other affairs of the firm. Nonetheless it seems obvious that a partner would not be free to disclose such material to others; and partnership agreements will often contain express terms against disclosure.[33] The same will apply to associates and other employees and, if the firm is a corporation, its directors.

It is likely also that barristers, though they do not practise in partnership, will be subject to similar obligations to other members of their chambers.

Hence a practitioner would necessarily be in breach of duty by permitting inspection of such material or by passing it to an archive.

## *Litigation records*

Litigation produces much documentation falling under the rubric 'client's records', already discussed. They include correspondence and written advice. But there are other documents which are produced to be submitted to the court, or are authenticated by the court, and so in some sense destined for the public domain (though they may or may not end up there). In the case of civil litigation, they include:

- the claim form initiating litigation (the old writ);
- statements of case (the old pleadings);
- application notices and similar documents;
- witness statements and affidavits;
- skeleton arguments, containing written summaries of a parties' legal contentions;
- court orders.

Those, or copies of them, will all be held by the practitioner acting for one of the parties.

30 Criminal Procedure and Investigations Act 1996, s. 17.

31 ibid., s. 18.

32 Limited Liability Partnerships Act 2000, s. 15 and regulations made thereunder.

33 *Encyclopaedia of Forms and Precedents*, vol. 31(1), precedent 5, cl. 16.2.5, referring, perhaps circuitously, to 'confidential information'.

It might be thought that since all of them (or all but the last) are intended to be deployed in court or otherwise acted on by the judge (e.g. if read beforehand) and since court hearings have generally to be held in public,[34] all of them would be available to any member of the public – at any rate once a hearing has actually taken place. Their status, however, is more complicated:

1. In ordinary civil proceedings governed by the Civil Procedure Rules, registers of claims can be inspected at the High Court in London but not in other offices of the High Court or in the county court.[35] A non-party may also obtain from the court records a copy of a pleading or an order[36] and may obtain a transcript of any hearing held in public.[37] Access to any other document on the records of the court – a witness statement, for example – may be obtained with the permission of the court.[38] A skeleton argument may not be part of the 'court records' within the relevant provisions (because it is not required to be filed) but there is an inherent jurisdiction to direct its disclosure.[39]
2. Comparable provision, though rather more restrictive, is made in other forms of civil proceedings, such as family[40] and insolvency[41] proceedings.
3. In criminal proceedings, the Criminal Procedure Rules 2013 oblige the court to provide to any member of the public basic information about a case, such as the identity of a defendant, the alleged offence and the outcome of a trial; other information, and access to inspect a document, may be obtained if the court so directs.[42]

In general, any entitlement to access is subject to an order of the court to the contrary.

We are here concerned, of course, with documents held by a practitioner rather than the same documents held by the court. But the fact that mere lodging with the court gives no automatic right to public access or, where it does, that right can be overridden, indicates that the practitioner is not free simply to allow others access to such documents or to deposit them in an archive.[43]

### *General*

Legal practitioners, even if sympathetic to the interests of archivists and historians, therefore face considerable difficulty in permitting the use of documents under their control. The principal difficulty, though not the only one, is the obligation of confidentiality to the client, which is both sweeping in content and indefinite in time. Ideally it would be possible for a practitioner to deposit documents with archivists under some form of arrangement denying access even to researchers for a period but permitting access to the practitioner in the meantime, a solution which would be attractive to practitioners not wishing to be committed to long-term storage. Absent legislative intervention, however, or the negotiation of standard terms to be offered to clients, it is difficult to identify any general solution.

## 4. The researcher's perspective (Lisa Webley)[44]

Archives containing legal records are a rich source of data from a researcher's perspective. These kinds of records often contain details that at the time when the documents were prepared were viewed as common place or even mundane: the occupation, gender, age of those involved in decision-making or disputes; information about time or place. But with hindsight, or a new lens through which to view the document, these kinds of details allow links to be made between people, places and trends, among others. Consequently, some researchers will be very keen to make use of collections of legal records. But the use of archived documents is not unproblematic, and a researcher's engagement with this type of material raises ethical as well as the more obvious practical issues too. This brief article sets out some

34 Convention for the Protection of Human Rights and Fundamental Freedoms, art. 6, enacted by Human Rights Act 1998; *V* v. *T* [2015] W.T.L.R. 173.

35 C.P.R., r. 5.4; Practice Direction 5A – Court documents, para. 4.1.

36 C.P.R., r. 5.4C(1), though by sub-r. (3) only after the case has reached one of certain stages and by sub-r. (4) the court can impose restrictions;

37 Practice Direction 39A – Miscellaneous Provisions Relating to Hearings, paras. 6.3, 6.4.

38 C.P.R., r. 5.4C(2). By C.P.R., r. 32.13, a witness statement standing as evidence in chief is open to inspection during the course of the trial unless the court otherwise orders.

39 *GIO Personal Investment Services Ltd* v. *Liverpool and London Steamship Protection and Indemnity Association Ltd* [1999] 1 W.L.R. 984 (C.A.); *Law Debenture Trust Corpn (Channel Islands) Ltd* v. *Lexington Insurance Co.* [2003] EWHC 2297 (Comm) at [17]; *Dring* v. *Cape Distribution Ltd* [2017] EWHC 3154 (QB).

40 Family Procedure Rules 2010, r. 29.12.

41 Insolvency (England & Wales) Rules 2016, r. 12.39.

42 Criminal Procedure Rules 2015, rr. 5.8, 5.9.

43 Guidance to barristers was given by the Bar Council in June 2015; see https://www.barcouncil.org.uk/media/350196/provision_of_documents_to_journalists__law_reporters_and_other_non-parties.pdf.

44 The text of this article has been compiled by the author using her original seminar notes and is reproduced with her permission.

of the things that researchers need to take into account when proposing to use legal records in their research.

The use of data by researchers is governed by university and professional body codes of ethics and it is very usual for academic researchers to be required to seek research ethics approval before they are permitted to begin their research. Documents are sources of data and so are caught by the codes in similar ways to diaries, interview transcripts etc. Ethical considerations include those that gave rise to the production of the data as well as reflection on the ethical implications and wider effects of their research through the lifecycle of their study and then beyond when the researcher disseminate her findings. Considerations include the way in which the data was originally collected including whether the documents were produced as public documents or private or semi-private ones, and if this is archival research this will include the purpose for which the documents were produced in their original form, by whom, and to what end.

When a researcher is collecting the data herself then the informed consent of all research participants, broadly drawn, would be the expectation. This is not usually possible for data derived from pre-existing archives but that does not negate the need to think about those behind the documents and those affected by their use. Researchers will also need to provide information about what confidentiality and other guarantees or expectations those involved in their original production may have had and how the documents will be used by the researcher, how they are to be selected and analysed and the extent to which this is methodologically and ethically robust. Further, the researchers will be required to set out any risk of harm arising from the use of the documents and any benefit of their use in this way. Harm is considered both backwards and forwards; in other words it is assessed for the totality of the research including any harm and benefit that may arise from the findings being disseminated.

Some of these considerations raise thorny issues for the researcher as she is not able to control the conditions that gave rise to the production of the documents and it may be difficult in advance to foresee the range of interests that may be engaged ahead of consulting the archives. However, by thinking about the study in ethical terms it is often possible for a researcher to gain a greater degree of insight into the likely significance of the research and also to give proper thought to the methods being used and thus to the study's rigour. And further, by considering the context within which the documents were produced, the researcher is often able to provide more nuance in relation to her findings, as data is contextual and findings must thus be contextualized too.

## 5. The archivist's perspective: The National Archives (Philip Gale)

### *Introduction – The National Archives' role*

The Archives Sector Development Department at The National Archives has a general responsibility to support the development and sustainability of archive collections across the country. The National Archives has two spheres of responsibility:

- Our role as national repository for public records and oversight of the public records held by Places of Deposit across the United Kingdom, including the records of courts and inquiries. This flows from the Public Records Act 1958 and subsequent legalisation.
- A wider, more nuanced role of leadership of the archives sector which is essentially focusing on sustaining the preservation, access and value of the nation's archival collections for the present and the future. Legislation is largely absent and much of our role derives from the Historical Manuscripts Commission's (HMC) Royal Warrant and articulated in our recently launched policy document 'Archives Unlocked': http://www.nationalarchives.gov.uk/archives-sector/projects-and-programmes/strategic-vision-for-archives/.

The records of legal businesses generally come under the second element of our work.

### *The National Archives' perspective on legal business records*

The business records, as distinct from court and inquiry records, of the various branches of the legal industry from our perspective form a category of business records; the primary obligation for firms is to meet their legal obligations (e.g. data protection legislation) and hopefully their cultural responsibilities to preserve records of historical significance and those of corporate value e.g. for sustaining a brand; to quote the website of a well-known firm: 'Farrer & Co. is an independent law firm with a rich history'.

It is not The National Archives' role to tell the legal profession how it should manage its records, but we do have a responsibility to encourage good practice and promote the cultural, economic, research and special value of archives.

### *The National Archives' management of archival risk*

The National Archives has developed a system for selecting public records for permanent preservation in accordance with the Public Records Act as amended by other legislation e.g. the Constitutional Reform and Governance Act 2010, amending the legislation to gradually reduce the deadline for transferring records to The National Archives from 30 to 20 years, implemented 2013–22. The framework is largely determined by legislation.

We are responsible for:

- Selection of records for permanent preservation under the guidance and supervision of the Keeper of Public Records.
- Safekeeping of those records.
- Transfer of records to The National Archives or an approved place of deposit by the due date unless they need to be retained, in which case the Secretary of State for Culture, Media and Sport's approval must be obtained.
- Considering formal applications for retention of records by departments are which are reviewed by our Advisory Council.
- Disposal of records not selected for preservation, by destruction or presentation to another institution.

Good practice is supported by the *Code of Practice on the Management of Records*, issued under section 46 of the Freedom of Information Act and the *Civil Service Code for Staff*, issued under the Constitutional Reform and Governance Act 2010, which includes a requirement that civil servants should 'keep accurate official records'.

This elaborate system of appraisal and regulation may not immediately appear to be relevant to the business and clients records of a legal business. However, much of the good practice developed concerning public records can found across the wider archives sector.

## *Managing archival risk outside of The National Archives*

A lot of what follows is a reiteration of good practice cited in the Legal Records at Risk Project *Guideline 4: advice to legal institutions on confidentiality and research access to records.*

### Risk diminishes over time

A basic observation is that that the risk of harm arising from the unauthorised access or inappropriate access to records diminishes with time. The content of relatively few records after 100 years will cause substantial harm or distress. Some public records are closed for longer periods, perhaps notably those of the intelligence services where, for instance, records giving details of informants which might identify their immediate descendants might be protected beyond 100 years.

Similarly business records may include controversial material: Unilever's archives include the archives of the Royal Niger Company; landed families may be sensitive about the activities of their predecessors e.g. in relation to the slave trade or agricultural, clearances and institutions e.g. the Churches over child emigration to the Commonwealth and child abuse.

The other area of risk is of clients, their heirs and personal representatives coming back to make a claim, but experience suggests that this increasingly unlikely with the passage of time. The sensitivities of well established businesses and institutions with long histories generally represent greater levels of risks than small businesses and individuals.

### Deposit or self-curation?

The first fundamental choice facing any business or institution is whether to retain their archives in their own custody and management or deposit them with a reputable archive service. For organisations of a certain critical size retaining archives in their own direct custody under professional management may offer the best solution. One example of such a corporate archive is the Unilever Archives at Port Sunlight (https://www.unilever.co.uk/about/who-we-are/our-history/unilever-archives.html).

Depositing a collection with an established archive service regulated by deposit agreement is the alternative, but archives services are essentially there to facilitate access and generally are less enthusiastic about accepting large collections that cannot be accessed for many years. The acquisitions also need to be aligned with archives' collecting policies. Established archive services include those managed by local authorities and, particularly significantly for business archives, those managed by universities. A good example of a business archives held by a university is the Marks and Spencer archives held at the University of Leeds (https://marksintime.marksandspencer.com/home).

If the decision is to deposit an archive collection, archive services have developed a variety of techniques to protect sensitive information.

### How archivists protect sensitive information

Archivists over the last century have developed a number of measures to manage access to collections which can be used by an in-house archive unit or applied to a collection deposited with an archive service:

- Closure periods – generally these can range from 20–100 years depending on the sensitivity of the material on commercial, data protection and general confidentiality grounds. All catalogues with material subject to restricted access should clearly be marked.
- Confidentiality agreements with researchers; many academic institutions will have their own research codes of ethics to reinforce such agreements.
- Deposit agreements can specify closure periods and specific access arrangements e.g. the Wolfson Foundation archives deposited with the Royal Society Library can only be accessed with the prior permission of Foundation.
- Sensitivity reviews are widely used by government departments to assess the sensitivity of particular classes of records and businesses can develop their own forms of sensitivity reviews.
- Anonymisation and redaction of the data, especially for electronic data.

### Sources of advice

The National Archives's website gives advice on data protection and includes a link to the supporting code of practice for archivists and records managers: http://www.nationalarchives.gov.uk/information-management/legislation/data-protection/

The Information Management pages on The National Archives's website include much that is applicable to business as well as public records: http://www.nationalarchives.gov.uk/information-management/manage-information/planning/records-management-code/implementation-guides/

### *Conclusion*

These techniques and measures are used by archivists to manage access to records while respecting legal requirements and the wishes of depositors and donors. Archival reputations rest on being trusted and any archives that allowed the disclosure of unauthorised information would face a fundamental loss of reputation equivalent to a leaking nuclear reactor!

The various legal professions including the traditional ones of the solicitors and the Bar as well as the newer professions of arbitrators, mediators etc. are increasingly organised on an industrial scale and form a major part of economy and society. The cultural, economic, research and special value of legal archives is important to the wider archival heritage of the country. They also have to navigate changing expectations of accountability and transparency to society as well as to their clients and effective records management and, where appropriate, archival provision is one way of meeting their obligations to both clients and to society at large.

## 6. The archivist's perspective: academic practitioners (Elizabeth Lomas)[45]

### *Navigating Confidentiality, Legal Privilege and GDPR to Maintain Legal Records for Future Generations: the Case for Archiving*

### *Introduction to archival value*

The International Council on Archives defines archives as: 'The documentary by-product of human activity and as such an irreplaceable witness to past events, underpinning democracy, the identity of individuals and communities, and human rights' (http://www.ica.org).

Archival records provide a resource to enable accountability and transparency for the actions of individuals and organisations both immediately at the point of action and through time. They facilitate the evidence for society to reflect on systems of governance and societal activity and change. As such it is key to ensure that a representative sample of legal records is retained for posterity. After all, our laws and interactions within the confines of the law demonstrate the core values of our society at a moment in time.

The value of legal records is recognised in the routine archiving of Acts of Parliament, legal policy from Government files and Court records. However, there is no systematic policy and guidance on the retention of records for solicitors and barristers. Records from such individuals have often survived by happenstance. Since 1932 the British Records Association (BRA) has been one of the key agencies whose efforts have resulted in the deposit of such records. The BRA has acted as a conduit for defunct legal companies' records, processing and then passing these on to suitable archive repositories for permanent preservation.

45 The text of this article was compiled by the author from her original Powerpoint presentation at the seminar and is reproduced with her permission.

Perhaps the most commonly represented legal document sets seen within local record offices are historic deeds which were retained to prove property ownership over long periods and as such reached an age which provided in most minds their status as records with archival significance. When in 2002 the Land Registration Act put in place processes for systematizing the centralization of land sales and purchases, the significance of deeds was to some extent diminished. The Society of Archivists (now the Archives and Records Association (ARA)) took steps to work with the Law Society and Land Registry to flag the significance of deeds to individuals and lawyers in order to try to preserve these important historical records. The Legal Records at Risk project represents a more holistic attempt to address wider concerns about the risks of losing legal records which document our nation's history.

The picture of what survives in terms of a representation of the legal landscape is patchy. Many legal records are of value over the longer term and it is important to ensure that there are more strategic plans to collect and retain these. The value of archives and historical research is legislated for across the globe. This chapter considers the specific context of archiving legal records in England and considerations around access through time. These laws should be navigated in order to consider archival requirements and require the professionals who create records to consider their historical relevance, consulting with those to whom they pertain as appropriate. As we create more digital data this requires active management as digital data may not have the same qualities of endurance as paper records. In addition, it is to be noted that legislation, such as data protection laws, requires us to consider for how long we need specific information and the purposes for retaining that information. Lawyers must navigate recordkeeping legislation in line with other businesses. As pillars of society lawyers should also step up to considering the value of their information for society over the longer term. There are many examples of banks, charities, estates, hospitals, retailers and others taking this next step. This chapter outlines key legislation which archivists consider in terms of holding and providing access to information through time. In addition it draws some initial conclusions for lawyers to take steps to put in place archival frameworks which retain records and make them more widely available at certain points in time.

## *Data protection law*

The General Data Protection Regulation (GDPR) and Data Protection Act 2018 together enshrine into UK law the principles for managing personal data. Under the terms of this legislation personal data is protected for the lifespan of the individual to whom that data, or information, relates. As such these rights do fall away when the individual is deceased. However, the legislation dictates that consideration is given to management frameworks for personal data. Organisations must build systems which build in 'privacy by design'. Under the terms of data protection legislation, data should be kept no longer than necessary but equally there is an expectation to ensure that information is retained in line with legal requirements, best practice and to a certain extent the expectations of the individual and wider society. Law firms do undertake processes to inform clients how long a file will be retained, for example in relation to a house purchase or sale. They are not always systematic in providing such detail in all cases. Under the terms of data protection law this should be reviewed and further consideration should be given to archiving.

GDPR provides a derogation for archival purposes which thus enables Member States to further legislate. Recital 158 of the GDPR sets out:

> public or private bodies that hold records of public interest should be services which, pursuant to Union or Member State law, have a legal obligation to acquire, preserve, appraise, arrange, describe, communicate, promote, disseminate and provide access to records of enduring value for general public interest. Member States should also be authorised to provide for the further processing of personal data for archiving purposes.

This latter sentence establishes the basis for specific localised approaches to archiving to be considered at a national level. In a UK context 'archiving in the public interest' is further set out in the Data Protection Act 2018 which enshrines the GDPR. In addition, it is underpinned by The National Archives' guidance on archiving in the public interest. This guidance illustrates the wide and rich landscape of archives in a UK context including public authority archives, private archives (such as law firms) and community archives (TNA, 2018). Organisations keeping records for permanent preservation in the public interest may claim the right to processing under the archiving terms. It is to be noted that in certain instances organisations may not be able to claim that they are archiving in the public interest. The 'public interest' needs to be defined. An example would be that there is some intention of some potential future public access to the records in some form or public provision of information from the records. If the records are kept solely to support the primary business then a public interest case is hard to make. However, other data protection purposes interrelate with the archiving purpose in the public interest and may be applicable either instead or in addition to this purpose. A key example is the application of processing for historical research purposes, which also provides a basis for retention over the longer term. Key to highlight, in this regard, is that where records are kept for archiving purposes or historical research then the specific consent for this purpose is not required. Nevertheless, archival processing should be provided for in privacy notices and other relevant documentation wherever possible. Farrer & Co. LLP's privacy notice states standard retention periods but in addition that: 'Longer retention periods may be appropriate where, for example, specific legal or public interest archival reasons apply' (available at https://www.farrer.co.uk/footerlinks/legal-regulatory/privacy-policy/ (accessed 31 July 2018)).

Many other law firms have not provided for this purpose in their privacy notices and it is to be hoped that this will be considered and addressed by lawyers more generally. Further guidance on archival processing under the terms of data protection legislation has been published by The National Archives (TNA, 2018) and the ARA (http://www.archives.org.uk).

Records with personal data are carefully managed in archival contexts and normally kept closed from public access during the lifetime of the data subject. Under data protection laws, archivists assume that a personal data subject may likely live no longer than 100 years (unless it can be easily confirmed whether the person is alive or deceased at this time). Assuming that a person was an 'adult' when the records were first created, a record with personal data will be retained closed for 84 years taking the working assumption that the person was 16 years in age or older. If the record relates to a child then depending on the context, the age of the child may be assumed to be less than one year old.

There are some instances under which personal data may be released. In reviewing opening a record this will depend on considerations around its sensitivity and the potential to cause damage or distress to an individual were it to be released. The case in favour of the release would be a key determinant. One person's data might be released were it to have a bearing on another individual's circumstances that were deemed to outweigh the other party. Aligned to this consideration are laws around confidentiality.

## *Confidentiality and legal professional privilege*

In considering archiving client records, lawyers will no doubt wish to consider their contractual and professional obligations. It is normally an expectation that all matters discussed with clients are undertaken under a duty of confidence. Confidentiality law applies in many contexts but is further legislated for in terms of the professional duty of lawyers under section 1(3)(e) of the Legal Services Act 2007 which stipulates that 'the affairs of clients should be kept confidential.'

Similar confidentiality expectations exist with the provision of other professional services, for example in respect of doctor patient consultations. Significant work on the archival considerations for medical and health records has been undertaken as it is well understood that there is a value in keeping and using these records for long periods of time. In addition, National Health Service Trust records are designated as public records under the Public Records Act 1958 and therefore those deemed worthy of permanent preservation must be transferred to TNA. The frameworks in this domain have potential readover to legal contexts and inform an understanding of confidentiality law. Within this context it has become clear that confidentiality laws can be navigated for archival purposes and do not preclude the deposit of records within an archive repository nor their potential to be accessed by researchers and the wider public over time.

It has been the presumption of archivists that confidentiality diminishes through time and this has been confirmed in legal disputes. As such it has become common practice amongst archivists to keep closed information provided under a duty of confidence for 100 years after the date of the actual record rather than any calculation based on a data subject's age. This normally does somewhat extend the closure period of the records beyond those usually applied under data protection law.

Keeping records closed under confidentiality requirements is assessed on the basis:

a. whether the information has the necessary quality of confidence;
b. whether the information was imparted in circumstances importing an obligation of confidence;
c. whether an unauthorised use of the information would result in detriment to the confider;
d. whether the disclosure would constitute a breach of confidence actionable by the person who supplied the information or any other person;
e. whether a breach of confidence may not be actionable when there is an overriding public interest in disclosure.

A 'detriment test' establishes the impact on the confider were the information to be released. Whilst personal data considerations under data protection law relate to living individuals to whom that data relates, under the duty of confidence a wider circle of actors may be captured within the considerations surrounding whether or not to release information. For example, were a person to be an informant then this information is given under a duty of confidence. As such the information will be kept closed whilst that person is alive but also beyond that person's lifetime where there is any potential readover to surviving family members which may include children and grandchildren. This decision is in the public interest as it works to society's benefit to provide enabling mechanisms for informants to feel that the information they provide is closed potentially beyond their own lifetime to protect their families and contacts. In some circumstances it is possible that a decision will be made to retain records closed over very long periods of time.

In the context of confidentiality rights, it is important to understand that commercial exchanges are deemed to have a differing status than a personal duty of confidence although none the less the impact of a release of information would require evaluation and does have legal protection. In TNA's context, 40 years is often seen as a standard maximum closure period for commercial confidentiality but this is not fixed and longer terms may be applied, particularly when a company is still in existence and depending on the 'quality of confidence' residing within that information. In all cases, consideration will be given to what the information reveals and under what circumstances and understandings/ assurances it was imparted.

In addition, in legal contexts underpinning the duty of confidentiality are additional protections relating to legal privilege. In this regard legal privilege protects communications between a lawyer and their client for the purpose of seeking or giving advice. Litigation privilege protects the information or documentation which may be generated in order to deal with litigation. There is a long-standing understanding that this information is protected from disclosure. Nevertheless, as with confidentiality law, archives would deem this protection to diminish through time considering the case and position of the actors to whom it relates.

## *Human Rights legislation*

Related to personal data and confidentiality considerations are certain information rights provided under the terms of human rights legislation. Within the UK, the Human Rights Act 1998 enshrined the European Convention on Human Rights. Key within this legislation are Article 10, which established the right of freedom of expression into UK law and Article 8, which protects the respect of a right to a private family life. In this context family has been interpreted broadly when applied. The legislation covers lifestyle and information considerations including surveillance and third-party scrutiny. Some exemptions do apply; for example national security considerations can override privacy considerations. There have been a number of high profile cases under the terms of these Articles. The press claim their rights under Article 10 for printing stories but those who feel they have had their privacy invaded will often then cite Article 8. Where an individual becomes aware of a story then a privacy injunction may be sought. The application of Human Rights law has a bearing in archival contexts. It will be weighed when considering whether or not papers can be made available in any form.

## *Access to archival information through Freedom of Information and Environmental Information legislation*

Laws on access to information through time have been tested in public authority archival contexts. Under the terms of the UK Freedom of Information Act 2000 individuals may request access to closed information in archives when they are held by organisations which are public authorities. The exemptions from release in these circumstances would most normally relate to considerations as to whether the information is personal data (s.40), whether it is held in circumstances where a case for breach of confidentiality remains possible and depending on the quality of confidence in the material (s.41(1)), whether the information is deemed to be exchanges between a lawyer and a client in which case legal privilege exemptions may apply (s.42), c (s.43), health and safety exemptions (s.38) in terms of the damage or distress to a party which might be caused by its release and s.44 which relates to the application of other relevant legislation such as the Human Rights Act. Whilst some of these exemptions are seemingly absolute, when they have been tested through the related complaints and legal system the legal outcomes have revealed the complexity of the application of the law in practice.

Key cases in regards to each exemption are summarized in the guidance which is provided by the Information Commissioner's Office (ICO) available at https://ico.org.uk/for-organisations/guide-to-freedom-of-information/refusing-a-request/ (accessed 31 July 2018). Some exemptions must be applied through a risk-based approach which:

- identifies the applicable interests within the relevant exemption;
- identifies the nature of the prejudice that would occur if the information was released and shows that the prejudice claimed is real, actual and/or of substance;
- shows that there is a causal link between the disclosure and the prejudice claimed;
- decides on the likelihood of the prejudice occurring.

Within some exemptions the components of the exemption have a different status: section 43(2) of the commercial confidentiality exemption is prejudice based, but the first part section 43(1) is absolute. In regard to what is actually 'absolute' this has been tested in legal cases. The ICO guides review current cases where decisions have been made to release information or retain it closed under the Freedom of Information law. It is under the cases played out in practice that we see that seemingly absolute exemptions from release may not always hold. For example guidance on s.41 which relates to confidentiality law demonstrates how confidentiality may diminish through time (see https://ico.org.uk/media/for-organisations/documents/1432163/information-provided-in-confidence-section-41.pdf (accessed 31 July 2018)). Likewise, the legal privilege exemption has also been seen not always to hold or apply as widely as once assumed. In the cases of Calland v. Information Commissioner & the Financial Services Authority (EA/2007/0136)[46] and Bellamy v. Information Commissioner & Secretary of State for Trade & Industry (EA/2005/0023)[47] what is covered by legal privilege was discussed in detail within both cases. In addition, within the latter case the point was made that:

> Clear, compelling and specific justification for disclosure must be shown, so as to outweigh the obvious interest in protecting communications between lawyer and client, which the client supposes to be confidential.

This makes the point that legal privilege may not always be upheld. In the case of Three Rivers District Council and others v. Governor and Company of the Bank of England [2004] UKHL 48,[48] discussions across the Bank of England were not deemed to be covered by the legal privilege exemption; only discussions within a small centralised team set up to deal with the specific dispute. Further information is available within the ICOs guidance on legal professional privilege at https://ico.org.uk/media/for-organisations/documents/1208/legal_professional_privilege_exemption_s42.pdf (accessed 31 July 2018).

Where lawyers are dealing with environmental information the requests for release may extend beyond the remit of a public authority, as understood under the terms of Freedom of Information legislation, to those undertaking environmental public functions as understood under the terms of the Environmental Information Regulations 2004. Under the terms of these Regulations the public interest in release is given greater weight under the law and the exceptions from release are more limited.

## *Maintaining records for archival purposes*

Where archives are placed with public archive repositories, contracts can put in place as part of the terms of deposit which determine the closure and access terms for the records and as such underpin the confidentiality expectations. These should be agreed ahead of the deposit and would then be weighed were a Freedom of Information request be made to access the closed records. Where records are retained in-house, by for example chambers or a solicitor, then they are not subject to the same rights of access, as whilst data protection rights apply clearly Freedom of Information legislation is not relevant.

Lawyers should consider whether the records of historical/archival value they create are best maintained within in-house archives or stored by a third-party archive. Many organisations will gain value from using their records through time and evidencing their long-term values and stability. This is a factor for consideration in determining whether an in-house archive is a valid option and can be resourced properly. However, for many an alternative option will be to make arrangements for a local archival repository to store records. It is to be noted that most public archives will expect records to be gifted rather than loaned given the public resources that will then be invested in their care. Either route is valid but, in both instances, properly considered processes should be put in place. Guidance on managing business archives is available at https://managingbusinessarchives.co.uk.

Lawyers should have a responsible agreed approach to archiving which includes:

- Retention/disposal and archiving strategies for all records.
- Formats, storage and digital management procedures.
- Information on archiving policies for legal clients and other parties where possible. In some instances, it is perfectly possible to discuss archiving records with a client. Where appropriate there should be agreed client consent processes which are transparent about destruction and/or archival deposit. In other instances, this may not be practical but central documentation and privacy notices can set out archiving policies and procedures.

At a higher level it would be possible to produce:

- Sample policies and procedures for a range of legal contexts.
- A sample retention and access schedule which provides transparency about different record sets' value through time. At present retention and disposition periods may be set but there are few public facing schedules detailing records of permanent value and the timeframes from which access can be reviewed. Much can be learnt from wider work which has been undertaken by the business archives community and the medical profession.

46 Calland v. Information Commissioner and The Financial Services Authority [2008] UKIT EA_2007_0136 (8 August 2008) URL: http://www.bailii.org/uk/cases/UKIT/2008/EA_2007_0136.html [2008] UKIT EA_2007_0136.

47 Bellamy v. The Information Commissioner [2006] UKIT EA_2005_0023 (04 April 2006): http://www.bailii.org/uk/cases/UKIT/2006/EA_2005_0023.html [2006] UKIT EA_2005_0023.

48 Three Rivers District Council & Ors v. Bank of England [2004] UKHL 48 (11 November 2004): http://www.bailii.org/uk/cases/UKHL/2004/48.html [2004] UKHL 48, [2005] 1 AC 610, [2005] AC 610, [2004] 3 WLR 1274.

- Sample client consent processes which are transparent about destruction and/or archival deposit.
- A templated deposit contract for deposits with archive repositories. This needs to agree ownership, access/confidentiality expectations and legal costs e.g. for dealing with access disputes if the status of records as closed need to be defended.

Where possible the above can be agreed with key parties; examples may include the ICO, TLS/SRA, BSB, ARA and BRA.

### *Conclusions*

In conclusion, information rights laws are placing an expectation on organisations and individuals to better manage the information they hold. These laws specifically legislate for archiving records, thus recognising the significance of historical information to inform society. This chapter is not a substitute for legal guidance as who better to set out archiving guidance than lawyers!

### *References*

The National Archives. (2018) *Guide to archiving personal data*. London: OPSI. This guide is currently in draft at http://www.nationalarchives.gov.uk/documents/information-management/guide-for-public-comment.pdf (accessed 31 July 2018) but is in the process of being finalised.

## 7. Information pack attachment I: The National Archives guideline on data protection and personal information 2016

http://www.nationalarchives.gov.uk/information-management/browse-guidance-standards/?letter=p

### *Introduction*

The purpose of data protection legislation is to ensure the proper use of personal information about living individuals. The legislation imposes obligations on those who hold such personal information, while giving rights to those the information is about – data subjects.

Archivists have a different role in relation to personal data from those who collected the personal data in the first place. Firstly, they do not control the type of data collected, because they were not involved in why, when and how it was originally collected and used for business purposes; secondly, their interest in the personal information lies in its value as a record of its time that can be used in future research, and its current accuracy is therefore not of concern; and thirdly, they have no interest in the future of the individual data subject, only their past.

This means that the activities of archivists can sit uneasily within the data protection legislative field, as at times they are obliged to comply with provisions which were designed for a different purpose. However the Data Protection Act 1998 (DPA), which came into force in March 2000 (amended by the Freedom of Information Act (FOIA) in 2005), does recognise the importance of data being kept for historical purposes, and contains provisions for this to be achieved within the framework of the legislation.

The DPA imposes a duty on those holding personal data to register such data with the Information Commissioner, to comply with eight data protection principles, and to allow individuals to access and, in certain circumstances, to correct data that relates to them. With the implementation of the FOIA, the DPA has been extended in scope so it that it applies to all information about living individuals held by public authorities, whatever the format or structure of the records.

The National Archives, Society of Archivists, Records Management Society and National Association for Information Management produced a Code of practice for records managers and archivists under s 51(4) of the Data Protection Act 1998 which may be of interest.

### *Archiving personal data for research purposes, s33*

The definition of research purposes in the DPA includes processing for historical research purposes. This is an important section for records managers and archivists, as it lays down the conditions with which the data controller of an archive should comply if the archive is to be exempt from compliance with various other requirements of the act.

Without the benefit of such provisions, archiving data could be in breach of the second and fifth data protection principles. The second data protection principle requires that personal data shall only be obtained for one or more specified and lawful purposes and shall not be further processed in a manner which is incompatible with such purpose(s). The fifth data protection principle requires that personal data shall not be kept for longer than is necessary for such purpose(s).

Section 33 provides that processing for research purposes is compatible with the purposes for which the data were collected, and the data may be kept indefinitely if the relevant conditions apply. These are:

- that the data are not processed to support decisions about individuals, and
- that substantial damage or substantial distress is not likely to be caused to any data subject

Personal data can be selected for permanent preservation, and stored, if these two conditions apply, on condition that the other data protection principles are complied with.

Note that TNA has registered personal data in transferred records to the Information Commissioner with the special purpose of processing for the purposes of archival preservation.

### *Closure of personal information*

The most common reason for records at archives services to be closed is that they contain personal information about an identifiable living individual and disclosure would breach one of the Data Protection Principles (and consequently is exempt under FOI exemption 40).

Note that the name of a person may not in itself be enough to make the person identifiable and it usually depends on the context in which it appears or the presence of supplementary information enabling a person to be identified.

Usually such information falls within the DPA's definition of sensitive personal data, namely information on a data subject's:

- racial or ethnic origin
- political opinions
- religious, or other, beliefs
- trade union membership
- health (physical or mental)
- sex life
- offences, committed or allegedly committed
- details of proceedings for offences

The Information Commissioner's Office has issued guidance on what personal information should be considered exempt. Note that not all sensitive personal information must be withheld for the full lifetime of the data subject. The particular content and context of the information may allow earlier access. Guidance on closure periods should be applied on a case-by-case basis.

One difficulty is establishing whether the person to whom the information relates is still alive. In practice, it is usually impossible for a department or archives service to know if an individual is still living and impracticable for them to find out. The Advisory Council has recommended that a lifetime of 100 years should be assumed. Thus if a person is aged 30 in a 1950 record and the information should not be released during their lifetime, the closure period would last until the end of 2020 (open on 1 January 2021).

If a person's age is unknown, estimate the closure period. If it is obvious the person is an adult then the estimated age at the time of the record should be 16. If it is not obvious what age a person is from contextual evidence then the full 100-year closure period should be used, for example, a child who is the victim of crime.

It may be possible from contextual evidence to reduce the closure period, for example, if it is known a person has a professional qualification that requires several years of training or where a person is applying for a benefit such as a pension that has a minimum age. In these circumstances the closure period should be reduced accordingly.

## 8. Information pack attachment II: Research exemptions under the Data Protection Act and the General Data Protection Regulation (GDPR)[49]

### *Data Protection Act 1998 S.33 Research, history and statistics*

1. In this section—
   - "research purposes" includes statistical or historical purposes;
   - "the relevant conditions", in relation to any processing of personal data, means

49 Information Commissioner's Office: *Guide to the General Data Protection Regulation* (GDPR) https://ico.org.uk/for-organisations/guide-to-the-general-data-protection-regulation-gdpr/

(a) that the data are not processed to support measures or decisions with respect to particular individuals, and

(b) that the data are not processed in such a way that substantial damage or substantial distress is, or is likely to be, caused to any data subject.

2. For the purposes of the second data protection principle, the further processing of personal data only for research purposes in compliance with the relevant conditions is not to be regarded as incompatible with the purposes for which they were obtained.

3. Personal data which are processed only for research purposes in compliance with the relevant conditions may, notwithstanding the fifth data protection principle, be kept indefinitely.

4. Personal data which are processed only for research purposes are exempt from section 7 if—

(a) they are processed in compliance with the relevant conditions, and

(b) the results of the research or any resulting statistics are not made available in a form which identifies data subjects or any of them.

5. (5) For the purposes of subsections (2) to (4) personal data are not to be treated as processed otherwise than for research purposes merely because the data are disclosed—

(a) to any person, for research purposes only,

(b) to the data subject or a person acting on his behalf,

(c) at the request, or with the consent, of the data subject or a person acting on his behalf, or

(d) in circumstances in which the person making the disclosure has reasonable grounds for believing that the disclosure falls within paragraph (a), (b) or (c).

### *General Data Protection Regulation (GDPR):*

Article 5 of the GDPR requires that 'personal data shall be collected for specified, explicit and legitimate purposes and not further processed in a manner that is incompatible with those purposes; further processing for archiving purposes in the public interest, scientific or historical research purposes or statistical purposes shall not be considered to be incompatible with the initial purposes'.

## 9. Information pack attachment III: Code of Practice for archivists and records managers under Section 51(4) of the Data Protection Act 1998

**Excerpts from s.4 Responsibilities of archivists** (for the full text of the Code see: http://www.nationalarchives.gov.uk/documents/information-management/dp-code-of-practice.pdf)

### *Responsibilities of Archivists*

The purpose of this chapter is to complement chapter 2 by summarising the particular responsibilities of archivists for personal data held by them. Responsibilities common to records managers and archivists have been described in chapter 3.

### *4.1 Responsibilities*

4.1.1 While ultimate responsibility for compliance with the Act is at the corporate level (see 2.1 above) it is likely that the archivist will play a key role in ensuring organisational compliance with the Act. The archivist, like the records manager (see 3.1), should ensure policies and procedures are compatible with the Act, particularly in relation to storage and access.

4.1.2 Archivists will be concerned with two types of personal data: personal data in their own administrative records, such as staff and reader records and correspondence with depositors, and personal data in the archives within their repository.

4.1.3 Archivists often manage the collections of many different organisations and individuals within their repository, and the nature of the agreement made with the depositor or donor will determine the role of the archivist in relation to each collection. The responsibilities of each party in relation to data protection must be clear.

4.1.4 As a general rule archives received by an archives repository can fall into any of three categories:

- Records transferred from within the organisation, which may be a public authority or a private sector body such as a business. Corporate policy should set out the basis on which archives containing personal data will be passed to the archivist and the level of control and responsibilities that will be passed with them. Like the records manager, the archivist may be acting in a "local data manager" capacity (see Annex A) in relation to transferred records

- Gifts, legacies or purchases, the common factor being that ownership of the archives passes to the archives repository or its parent organisation. The data controller will be the organisation of which the archives repository is a part, with the archivist as "local data manager" unless there is explicit provision to the contrary
- Deposits on loan from external sources, whereby custody passes to the archives repository but ownership remains with the depositor or another party, such as a Trust. In such cases the organisation of which the archives repository is a part may become sole data controller or may share that responsibility with the owner as joint data controllers, or may act merely as a data processor, leaving control wholly in the hands of the owner. Which applies will depend on the terms of the deposit. As a general rule, the more control over access and use passed to the archives repository, the more likely it will be that its parent organisation has acquired data controller responsibilities. A variant of this last option occurs when control passes to the archives repository in whole or in part, but storage is contracted out to a third party which is a data processor. What is vital is that the owner's continuing interest in the records and the obligations of all parties are set out clearly in the deposit agreement. If the terms of deposit are unclear and the current owner is unknown or cannot be contacted, the organisation of which the archives repository is a part should be regarded as data controller by default.

4.1.5 Given the large number of individuals commonly featuring in archive collections, archivists will not be in a position to ascertain whether they are still alive and hence protected by the Act. If it is not known whether a data subject is alive or dead, the following working assumptions can be used:

- Assume a lifespan of 100 years.
- If the age of an adult data subject is not known, assume that he was 16 at the time of the records
- If the age of a child data subject is not known, assume he was less than 1 at the time of the records

4.1.6 When researchers obtain copies of personal data from an archives repository they become the data controllers in respect of those copies and must observe the data protection principles, unless they can claim an exemption, for example because their processing is for domestic purposes only, i.e. personal, family or household use. However, archivists cannot control subsequent use of personal data and it is advisable to assume that researchers will be subject to the Act and make them aware of their responsibilities.

## 4.2 Acquisition and processing of personal data (Principles 1 and 2)

4.2.1 According to Principle 2, personal data should only be collected for one or more specified lawful purposes and further processing should be compatible with those purposes. As a general rule, processing for the purposes of archival preservation can be considered a compatible further use of the data and the special purpose set out at 2.3.7 will apply.

4.2.2 Processing for the purposes of archival preservation is undertaken by reference to the "research exemptions" set out in section 33 of the Act (outlined in Annex B, B4). Personal data may be stored indefinitely as archives for research purposes provided that the "relevant conditions" are observed, namely:

- The data is not processed to support measures or decisions relating to particular individuals, and
- The data is not processed in such a way that substantial damage or substantial distress is, or is likely to be, caused to any data subject The meaning of "substantial damage and distress" is discussed further at 4.9

4.2.3 When personal data categories (a)-(d) are being processed in accordance with these conditions, there is also an exemption from Principle 5 but the other Principles must be observed unless the personal data is "eligible data" (see Annex A), in which case further exemptions apply (see Annex B). The data may be disclosed to third parties for research purposes in accordance with section 33 or to the data subject without the exemption from Principle 5 being lost. (See also 4.9.) Category (e) personal data is exempted from Principles 1–3, 5, 7 and 8. (See Annex A for an explanation of the different categories of personal data.)

4.2.4 All archives repositories acquiring personal data falling into categories (a) to (d) and wishing to undertake further processing must be able to show that there is a "fair" and "lawful" basis for doing so, in accordance with Principle 1 (See 2.2.5–2.2.6). This means looking at the conditions in Schedule 2 and, for sensitive personal data, Schedule 3.

4.2.5 For schedule 2, archivists dealing with public records will be exercising statutory functions under the Public Records Act and so can refer to paragraph 5(b), which relates to processing for the 'exercise of functions … conferred by an enactment'. Archivists dealing with other public sector records can refer to paragraph 3, which relates to processing 'in compliance with any legal obligation' (other than a contract), paragraph 5(c) which relates to processing for 'the exercise of any functions of ... a government department' or paragraph 5(d) which relates to processing for 'functions of a public nature exercised in the public interest'. Archivists in the private sector can refer to paragraph 5(d) also, particularly if the organisation admits visitors seeking to undertake research. Another possibility for private sector archivists is paragraph 6(1), which relates to processing that is necessary 'for the purposes of the legitimate interests of the data controller' or by third parties to whom the data is disclosed, except where processing would be unwarranted because of 'prejudice to the rights and freedoms or legitimate interests of the data subjects'.

4.2.6 One of the conditions in Schedule 3 must also be identified for sensitive personal data. Archivists processing sensitive personal data who are unable to comply with any of the conditions specified in Schedule 3 may benefit from SI 2000 No. 417 Data Protection (Processing of Sensitive Personal Data) Order 2000. This sets out additional circumstances in which sensitive personal data may be processed and thereby provides supplementary Schedule 3 conditions. Paragraph 9 of the Order makes lawful any processing which, in addition to satisfying the general requirements that sensitive data are processed lawfully and fairly: "(a) is in the substantial public interest; (b) is necessary for "research purposes" (which expression shall have the same meaning as in section 33 of the Act); (c) does not support measures or decisions with respect to any particular data subject otherwise than with the explicit consent of that data subject; and (d) does not cause, nor is likely to cause, substantial damage or distress to the data subject or any other person."

4.2.7 Except when they themselves collect data for the purposes of administering their offices, archivists will generally not be expected to inform data subjects of processing they undertake for research purposes because to do so would involve disproportionate effort. The unfairness of not so informing data subjects is minimal where the relevant conditions are observed and records either kept closed for an appropriate period or used only for research which will be anonymised.

## 4.3 Appraisal (Principle 5)

4.3.1 Archivists involved in the appraisal of records prior to their transfer should ensure that personal data worthy of permanent preservation is identified as soon after creation as possible and scheduled for retention accordingly (Principle 5).

4.3.2 There is a danger that over-cautious interpretation of the Act may lead to the weeding, anonymising or destruction of files containing personal data that would otherwise be passed to the archives repository. An archivist's ability within the Act permanently to retain personal and sensitive personal data for the purposes of research (see 4.2.1) should therefore be made clear to potential depositors. The legislation contains the necessary safeguards for depositors.

4.3.3 When considering the permanent preservation of sensitive personal data for the purposes of research, archivists should give serious consideration to how far this will be in "the substantial public interest". This will mean weighing up whether society as a whole, and the research community in particular, will benefit from preservation of the data for research purposes. All appraisal decisions should be documented as a matter of good professional practice.

## 4.4 Accessioning

4.4.1 All newly received archives, whether manual or electronic, should be checked to ascertain whether they include personal data covered by the Act, for example a database or a series of case files about named living individuals. Bodies that are not subject to the FOI Acts will find that some manual archives fall outside the Act because they are neither accessible records (category (d) personal data) nor records from a relevant filing system (category (c) personal data).

4.4.2 Bodies subject to the FOI Act should assume that all archives containing personal data about identifiable living individuals are subject to the Act. Archivists in public authorities should note that category (e) personal data in archive collections of private origin may fall within the Act by virtue of being held by a body subject to the UK FOI Act. The position is different for bodies subject to the Scottish FOI Act; personal data of private origin will fall within the scope of the Act only if ownership has passed to the archive repository or its parent body.

4.4.3 When arranging the transfer of archives, archivists should ascertain from the donor or depositor whether they contain data already covered by a notification, whether the data is already exempt from subject access and whether measures have been taken to confirm its accuracy. Transfer documentation should incorporate questions that confirm these points (see examples at Annex C). 4 Assessment of private archive collections to determine whether they fall under the FOI Act is the subject of guidance issued by The National Archives in 2005 – see http://www.nationalarchives.gov.uk/documents/guidance_private_archives.pdf

4.4.4 Transfer and deposit agreements should clarify the responsibilities of the archivist, stating whether the originating person or body is retaining or transferring data controller responsibilities as outlined at 4.1.3. It may be necessary to obtain legal advice to ensure that the wording of these agreements is accurate.

4.4.5 As a general rule, it is simpler to accept only those sets of personal data that are no longer required for current business and hence can be retained for the sole purpose of archival preservation. This is because it will be clear that they are a contemporary not up to date record. However, this may not always be practicable and continued use may prove necessary (see 4.11 for further guidance on this). Notification should accommodate expected use of the data. It should also be clear to someone consulting the data whether the records are still in active use and have been kept up-to-date, or instead reflect a historical position.

## *4.9 Third-party access to personal data*

4.9.1 The Freedom of Information Acts have made significant changes to provision of third-party access where bodies subject to those Acts are concerned. The text that follows deals first with access in accordance with the Data Protection Act (4.9.2 – 4.9.6) and then with the effect of the FOI Acts on access to personal data (4.9.7 – 4.9.12). Access in accordance with the Data Protection Act

4.9.2 The Act does not give third parties rights of access to personal data. Access to personal data in archives by someone other than the data subject or the data controller (or his employees) will normally be permitted for historical or statistical research under the relevant conditions (see 4.2). Such access will be subject to closure periods up to a maximum of 100 years, the assumed lifetime of the individual. In administering shorter closure periods or otherwise authorising disclosure of data, archivists should be able to cite conditions in Schedules 2 and 3 as applicable and should consider the following two criteria:

4.9.3 (a) Access must be lawful Principle 1 requires data to be processed lawfully and so, even if the Act seems to provide no impediment to access, other aspects of lawfulness must be considered:

- Statutes protecting the confidentiality of personal information must be respected. For example, the Sexual Offences (Amendment) Act 1992 protects the identity of victims and alleged perpetrators of rape and some other sexual offences during their lifetime. Archivists should check whether any statutory bars to access apply to personal data they propose to release. The former Department for Constitutional Affairs published a report which identifies the main statutory bars that apply. It can be seen at http://www.foi.gov.uk/reference/ReviewOfStatBars.htm
- A duty of confidence may attach to particular records, such as health records, where the consent of the individual is required unless there is an overriding public interest in disclosure. This will necessitate consideration of the way in which the information was first acquired, its nature and age (see 4.9.4), and whether research will make possible the identification of individuals:
- The information made available must not be libellous or obscene

If the information is held by a public body, the Human Rights Act may make access impossible (see 4.9.12).

4.9.4 (b) Access must be fair Principle 1 also requires data to be processed fairly. Fairness to people about whom personal data are held is the overriding concern of the Act and the guiding principle is when in doubt, withhold the data. The impact of disclosure, including whether it would cause substantial damage or substantial distress, should be assessed, taking into account the following factors:

- The nature of the information must be considered. Some personal information, including some 'sensitive personal data', is comparatively innocuous, some is not. To take medical information as an example: information about hospitalisation for a broken leg 20 years ago is not something people feel a need to keep secret whereas information about treatment for a mental illness 40 years ago is still considered to carry a stigma and hence is not for disclosure. In both cases the information is 'sensitive personal data' under the Act but different judgements as to whether substantial damage or distress are likely to be caused by disclosure can be formed. Another example, not relating to "sensitive personal data", is information about receipt of public funds. When the funds are received as of right (such as the old age pension or housing repair grants) there are no implications about the income of recipients and hence it is unlikely to be considered embarrassing, whereas when the funds depend on means testing (such as supplementary pensions or social fund payments) receipt is associated with low income and disclosure could be regarded as invasion of privacy and hence unfair to the individual.
- The age of the information may be relevant. The need to provide protection diminishes over time. For example, the report deals with statutory bars within UK legislation. Some of them may apply to information held by Scottish public authorities but any Order under the UK Act to repeal or amend these statutory bars can apply only to bodies subject to that Act. Note that the review did not look at statutory bars in legislation passed by the Scottish Parliament. Membership of an extreme political group or party may be of little interest after 20 years and none after

40 and disclosure therefore may not damage the data subject's reputation or standing in the community. The age and status of the data subject should also be considered as this can affect the extent of distress they might feel.

- Genuine information (as opposed to speculation) already in the public domain because it is a matter of public record should normally be accessible. An example would be conviction for an offence in a court where no restrictions on naming the person apply (although note that a court case file may contain a mixture of information placed in the public domain at the time of the trial and information that was not made public). Potentially distressing information deliberately made public by the data subject should also be made accessible
- The credibility of the data, i.e. its likely accuracy and comprehensiveness, should be considered as this affects whether the good name of the individual is likely to be put at risk by disclosure
- It is impossible to anticipate what research may be done on any particular set of data but, if substantial damage or substantial distress to any individual would be a likely consequence of any research, the data should remain closed. (Note that processing for medical purposes and racial equality monitoring is allowed, see Schedule 3, paragraphs 8–9) 4.9.5 Steps to safeguard the fair and lawful use of data include:
- Explaining to intending researchers the "relevant conditions" that apply to the research use of particular data, including sensitive personal data (see 4.2)
- Requiring researchers to sign a declaration that, as a condition of access to data that might otherwise be closed, they will comply with the relevant conditions and Data Protection Principles (1, 3–4 and 6–8). Application forms to consult specific personal data subject to these conditions should be signed and kept as an audit trail
- Informing researchers that they are responsible under the Act for any processing by them of personal data disclosed to them, including copying, realignment, transmission abroad and publication (see 4.1.6)
- If researchers are bound by a sectoral code of practice or particular employer requirements, e.g. guidelines produced by a university ethics committee, making access conditional on the researcher undertaking to comply with that as well as with any special conditions applying to specific sets of personal data. This is particularly relevant if he intends to publish or to make use of the data for purposes other than private research

4.9.6 Note that if researchers breach the terms of any access conditions and publish name-identifiable information, the exemption from section 7 will be lost but not the general exemption for processing for research purposes.

## 10. Information pack attachment IV: Legal Records at Risk Guideline 4: advice to legal institutions on confidentiality and research access to records

### Legal records and historical research

Private sector 'legal' records have never been collected systematically in the UK other than by a very small number of specialist archives. Collecting in the public archives sector has tended to be ad hoc (i.e. as and when individuals or legal bodies such as law firms decide to clear out some of their records). As a result research using legal records is inevitably weighted towards the pre-20th-century study of government policy, legislation and the courts, producing a historical picture of the UK's legal framework and legal services which is skewed towards the policies and actions of central government. One reason for this dearth of private sector legal records may be the legal profession's legitimate concerns about record confidentiality and a mistrust of or misunderstanding about how archive repositories respect and manage this, plus the reluctance of archives to accept deposits of records with unfeasibly long closure periods. These issues, and how to resolve them, are discussed below.

### Legal records and confidentiality

The Legal Records at Risk project seeks to broaden the concept of 'legal' records from the traditional definition of them as court records or formal documents such as deeds to the business records of private sector institutions with a connection to the law such as law firms, barristers chambers, regulators, membership bodies, pressure groups and educational bodies as well as to legal records created and held by businesses, companies, charities etc. 'Business records' will include corporate governance records, policy and procedures files, marketing, public relations and accounting records; as such they will be bound by the usual conditions of commercial confidentiality and the Data Protection Act. In this respect the records of a legal institution should not be treated any differently to the records of other private sector organisations when seeking to make them available for research and so there should be no particular confidentiality problems in depositing them in archives. There is, however, one exception to this rule as follows:

## Legal professional privilege and client confidentiality

All client information is held by legal institutions under a long-term obligation of confidentiality.[50] Legal service providers are bound by their professional codes of conduct to keep client and complaints information confidential (see **Appendix** to this Guideline). This may be the primary reason both for the reluctance of legal providers to make *any* information about their work available for research despite the fact that many of their records will not be subject to client confidentiality. It may also explain why archive repositories may not wish to collect and store such records where unfeasibly (in archival terms) lengthy closure periods are demanded.

## How long does client confidentiality last?

The question is whether this guarantee of confidentiality is in perpetuity or for a limited (in archival terms) period. None of the Codes of Conduct listed in the **Appendix** specify a length of time, so the next question is whether there is a tacit assumption of confidentiality in perpetuity, and whether this has ever been challenged.

'Actionable Breach of Confidence' is a useful baseline for discussion. An action for breach of confidence can only be brought by a deceased person's personal representative i.e. executor or administrator. Once that person can be proved or presumed dead (say 82 years after death of the data subject, if we assume that a personal representative must be at least 18 – though 16 might be safer), there is no legal risk in releasing the information. This may be useful in dealing with the confidentiality for individual clients but is more problematic for companies, which do not 'die' unless they are wound up or dissolved. It is not an insuperable barrier to eventual release of client information but it may well be an obstacle too far for archive repositories, which as a rule simply cannot afford to sit on material for hundreds of years until they can make it available.

Legal bodies presumably have a responsibility not to transfer client information to a third party unless and until the files are no longer subject to an obligation of confidence (i.e. the client has died and the time limit for all legal actions has expired or the company has been dissolved/wound up), when they can legally be destroyed or sent to an archive repository.

It appears to be easier to say that this responsibility implies confidentiality in perpetuity than to make decisions as to when client files become redundant and can safely be disposed of. Yet client files cannot be held indefinitely, not least because where individual clients are concerned such retention would be in breach of the Data Protection Act.[51] We suggest, therefore, that legal institutions and practitioners look afresh at the way in which they manage their client files and make carefully considered decisions as to disposal.

### *Archives and confidentiality*

All archive repositories[52] have well developed techniques for dealing with 'sensitive' records, including closure periods and conditions on access and use; they operate under strict confidentiality guidelines and follow The National Archives' advice to close all records for at least 20 years and personal data for 100 years.[53]

Deposit agreements: any legal institution or individual depositing records with an archives can also stipulate their own confidentiality requirements (though the archives, equally, can refuse to accept records with an unfeasibly long closure period). Where a private sector organisation deposits records in an archives an agreement is always drawn up specifying the length of time the records should be closed to public access unless the depositor is happy with the archives' own standard access rules.

Standard closure periods based on confidentiality applied by archive repositories, after which records may be made available for research, are as follows:

- Records in general: all records held by an archives are closed for 20–30 years other than material already in the public domain or for which permission for earlier access has been given by the depositing organisation/individual.

50 The 2004 Clementi Report *Review of the regulatory framework for legal services in England and Wales* describes confidentiality thus (p.23): 'The codes of conduct of the legal professional bodies generally require lawyers to keep clients' affairs confidential. Communications between a client and his lawyer may be subject to Legal Professional Privilege (i.e. certain communications between a client and legal adviser in the context of obtaining legal advice or assistance are protected from disclosure, even in legal proceedings).'

51 See Schedule 1 and the 8 Data Principles, in particular Principle 5: 'Personal data processed for any purpose or purposes shall not be kept for longer than is necessary for that purpose or those purposes'.

52 The term 'Archive repositories' in this guideline refers to places where archival records (i.e. collections of records selected for long-term preservation as evidence of the activities of organisations or individuals) are stored, preserved and made accessible. The term does not refer to the mass storage of information in third-party records stores, basements or lower tier servers pending disposal.

53 TNA Code of practice for archivists and records managers under Section 51(4) of the Data Protection Act

- Commercial confidentiality: usually assumed to expire after 20–40 years, unless a specific stipulation is made by the depositing body that it should be closed for a longer period.
- Personal data: the Data Protection Act specifies that the term 'personal data' only applies to the data of living individuals, so archives close such data for 75–100 years as recommended by The National Archives. Once the data subject is deceased or presumed deceased the Act no longer applies. In certain circumstances personal data may also be examined for bona fide research purposes provide a legally binding guarantee of anonymisation is signed, or research bodies may redact personal data to make it available.[54] In other words, client confidentiality is not an insuperable barrier to making client data available for research.

There is, therefore, no reason for any legal institution to be concerned that an archive repository will not professionally manage access to deposited records.

## *Appendix to Guideline 4: Institutions specialised to law: Confidentiality Codes of Conduct and Practice Guidelines*

**The Bar:** the BSB *Handbook* states in S.12:

> 'The regulatory objectives of the Bar Standards Board derive from the Legal Services Act 2007 and can be summarised as follows... "that the affairs of clients are kept confidential" and rC106: "All communications and documents relating to complaints must be kept confidential"'.

**Solicitors**: the SRA *Code of Conduct 2011* states in Ch. 4 Client confidentiality:

> 'Firms are required to have effective systems and controls in place to identify risks to client confidentiality and to mitigate those risks..... Protection of confidential information is a fundamental feature of your relationship with clients. It exists as a concept both as a matter of law and as a matter of conduct. This duty continues despite the end of the retainer and even after the death of the client.'

**Arbitrators:** institutions have their own rules e.g. Article 30(1) of the *Rules* of the London Court of International Arbitration states:

> Unless the parties expressly agree in writing to the contrary, the parties undertake as a general principle to keep confidential all awards in their arbitration, together with all materials in the proceedings created for the purpose of the arbitration and all other documents produced by another party in the proceedings not otherwise in the public domain – save and to the extent that disclosure may be required of a party by legal duty, to protect or pursue a legal right or to enforce or challenge an award in bona fide legal proceedings before a state court or other judicial authority.

**Mediators:** the Chartered Institute of Arbitrators' Practice Guideline 1: Confidentiality in Mediation states:

> Save as required or permitted by law... the Institute, the parties, their representatives, their advisors and the mediator(s) shall keep confidential all information (whether given orally, in writing or otherwise) produced for, or arising out of or in connection with, the mediation passing between any of the participants and between any of them and the mediator made for the purposes of the mediation, including the fact that the mediation is taking place or has taken place...The mediator's duty to protect the confidentiality of the mediation proceedings commences with the first communication to the mediator, is continuous in nature, and does not expire upon the termination, for whatever reason, of the mediation under Rule 11. The mediator's duty extends to all information relating to the mediation proceedings, even indirectly, such as previous invitations and/or negotiations leading to mediation, terms of the agreement to mediate, appointment of mediators and performance, or non performance, of the settlement agreement. All records, reports, or other documents received by a mediator, as well as all notes taken by the mediator during, with reference to, or for the purposes of, the mediation should be returned to the parties or kept secure until no longer needed for any purpose relating to the mediation and then destroyed.

**Conveyancers**: Outcome 3.6 of the Council for Licensed Conveyancers' *Code of Conduct* requires that: 'Clients' affairs are treated confidentially (except as required or permitted by law or with the Client's consent)'.

54 Section 33 of the Data Protection Act 1998 refers.

**Notaries:** Ch. 17 Recordkeeping and file storage of the Master of Faculties *Code of Practice* states: 'A notary's records are as a general principle confidential' [Practice Rule 23.6].

**Patent and Trade Mark Attorneys**: the Chartered Institutes of Patent Attorneys and Trade Mark Attorneys have produced joint Business practice guidance containing many references to the need to safeguard clients' confidential information, including information of clients for whom the attorney no longer acts.

**Will writers:** the **Institute of Professional Will Writers'** Code of Practice **states:** 'Members shall act with independence and integrity, maintain proper standards of work and keep the affairs of the Client confidential' **[S.5.1].**

## 11. Questions for the expert panel

The following questions were put to the panel, with responses also invited from seminar attendees:

**Expert panel question 1**: a barrister present at the seminar noted that if the legal profession were to make client files available for research it runs the risk of being sued for breach of confidentiality, or at the very least suffering reputational damage, even after the clients are deceased. Admittedly this risk does diminish over time, but even so *what is the benefit to the legal profession in depositing records in archives for future access?*

*Panel response*: there may be a public interest in releasing some material. Examples included case files relating to historic child abuse. The point was also made that aggregated or anonymised medical data is often released for research, though admittedly this is not so easy to do with legal records. Another point was made that the history of how the legal profession works is under-represented in archives and therefore in our national history and that it should be in the profession's interest to correct this imbalance. Attendees asked how the emphasis on client confidentiality and concerns over reputational risk square with the historic practice of many law firms and some individuals to offload records en masse to archives without any idea of what they contain; with leaving client files for decades in third-party repositories without any provision for appropriate disposal; and with auctioning records off to the highest bidder. Solutions for the future suggested better records management processes; including consent notices on how their data will be used and disposed of in agreements to be signed by clients; clearer guidance by the regulators on ownership, storage and disposal of data; the reissue of The Law Society's practice note on depositing records in archives.

**Expert panel question 2**: an archivist whose repository has accepted deposits of client files from law firms wrote to ask: 'Of course there are issues with preserving client files for historical purposes as I doubt any clients have given their consent to that and there are issues with solicitors not understanding the ownership of the material that they send us'. *Should the permission of clients be sought prior to deposit of client files? Would this be feasible in practice?*

*Panel response*: two questions to answer: a) who owns the documents and b) do they contain confidential information? In an ideal world law firms would have a process in place whereby the client was asked (e.g. at the end of the relationship) if they were happy to have their records deposited in an archives on terms specified by the firm. Many clients may not be comfortable disclosing confidential information if they thought it may be shared, even at after a long closure period. In the past once records arrived at an archives the terms of the firm/client relationship had been lost, so this is really a question for future potential deposits. The legal regulator (i.e. the SRA) should be providing guidance on these issues.

**Expert panel question 3**: a firm which has already deposited records in a local authority archives is having second thoughts about eventually allowing access to researchers. There were two separate concerns from the firm a) complaint to legal ombudsman for breach of confidentiality from the descendent of a client and b) bad publicity from the impression that they would advise clients then make details public later on. *Are their concerns founded? if yes can they be allayed and if so how?*

*Panel response*: this law firm should have sorted out these questions before deposit. As above, all law firms should have a process in place to ensure that these questions have been dealt with. The SRA should also be providing guidance on these issues.

**Expert panel question 4**: the archivist of a large in-house business archive wrote:

> We've encountered nervous resistance from the legal team when it comes to the transfer of certain types of records and, having slightly unexpectedly secured a few minutes of the senior lawyer's time tomorrow, I wondered if you might have any best practice examples to hand that I could use to reassure her? She is particularly concerned about the transfer of material that could be of assistance in legal proceedings, that discloses confidential sources or which may waive privilege having been transferred to the archive. We have of course clarified that records in the archive are not automatically open to researchers, and offered to take advice on appropriate closure periods, but because transfer to the archive affects the legal ownership of the records her concerns remain. For example, we are struggling to get permission to take in any records from the

> [-] legal team except statements of case and judgments (available elsewhere) and standard advice sheets (e.g. on libel, data protection etc.) produced for journalists in-house. We would like to take correspondence documenting key decisions in significant legal cases (e.g. those attempting to set precedents or make challenges for [-] rights), but there is concern that these records ought never to be transferred or made available to researchers, which seems a shame to me in terms of their potential interest and significance in future.

*How would the Panel suggest that the archivist alleviate the concerns of this legal team?*

*Panel response*: the law firm should have a retention schedule in place which would specify which records should and should not go to the archives. The SRA should be providing guidance on retention, destruction and deposit of records in archives, as the Law Society once did with its practice note on disposal of solicitors' records (no longer available on the TLS website). Additionally an in-house archives is primarily there for the use of the law firm itself and can close records to the public for as long as it wishes. Setting up an in-house archives may in fact be the answer to many of the problems larger law firms face in managing their records appropriately.

**Expert panel question 5**: a barrister has offered his personal papers (which include notes on cases he has been involved in) to an archives. *Are they subject to legal professional privilege and if so for how long must they be closed to public access?*

*Panel response*: ownership is a major issue here. Are the papers copies of material held by other parties e.g. the court; the organisations or individuals involved in the cases; the firm of solicitors employed? Or the barrister's own papers? Do they contain confidential material/personal data? If so just passing these papers to an archives could be seen as a breach of confidentiality, although the new Data Protection Bill will provide an archival derogation. The first action for a potential archival recipient is to obtain a detailed list of the papers. The regulators (i.e. the Bar Standards Board) should be providing guidance to practitioners on disposal of their case notes and related papers.

**Expert panel question 6**: the Chartered Institute of Arbitrators' Practice Guideline 1: Confidentiality in Mediation states:

> Save as required or permitted by law… the Institute, the parties, their representatives, their advisors and the mediator(s) shall keep confidential all information (whether given orally, in writing or otherwise) produced for, or arising out of or in connection with, the mediation passing between any of the participants and between any of them and the mediator made for the purposes of the mediation, including the fact that the mediation is taking place or has taken place…The mediator's duty to protect the confidentiality of the mediation proceedings commences with the first communication to the mediator, is continuous in nature, and does not expire upon the termination, for whatever reason, of the mediation under Rule 11. The mediator's duty extends to all information relating to the mediation proceedings, even indirectly, such as previous invitations and/or negotiations leading to mediation, terms of the agreement to mediate, appointment of mediators and performance, or non performance, of the settlement agreement. All records, reports, or other documents received by a mediator, as well as all notes taken by the mediator during, with reference to, or for the purposes of, the mediation should be returned to the parties or kept secure until no longer needed for any purpose relating to the mediation and then destroyed.

*Is this a direct instruction to individual arbitrators and mediators NOT to deposit their case notes and papers in archives or could* 'any purpose relating to the mediation' *also be interpreted as including research?*

*Panel response*: possible research value cannot be used as a justification for keeping these records.

**Expert panel question 7**: the ILA – ICA Committee Report, The Hague 2010 *Confidentiality in International Commercial Arbitration* has stated:

> The duration of confidentiality obligations, as regards both the moment when it arises and when it ends, is equally the subject of uncertainty and is not dealt with in the sources. The answer will probably vary to a large extent depending on the nature of the information and, obviously, on the source of the duty. If the source is contractual, the duration might be stated in the contract (which may be prior to the beginning of the arbitration or subsequent) or should be able to be derived through the interpretation of the contract. The fact that the duty of confidentiality usually covers the award seems to point to an expectation that the regime of confidentiality should outlive the arbitral proceedings and that the obligations will not cease after the end of the arbitration. It is less clear whether the obligations are perpetual or whether at some point they lapse, and if so at what point. It is reasonable to assume that the obligations cease where it can be established that confidentiality is no longer relevant.

*Can the Panel suggest scenarios where confidentiality is 'no longer relevant'?*

*Panel response*: confidentiality is no longer relevant if the information comes into the public domain. It may also no longer be relevant if both parties are companies or businesses which have dissolved. The legal regulators should be providing advice on whether confidentiality obligations are perpetual or, if not, when they may lapse.

## 12. General discussion and points raised

The following points were raised by attendees during the seminar:

- There are legal and ethics issues around the management of client files, in particular the duty to keep client records confidential.
- The Data Protection Act and the GDPR also require personal data to be kept confidential.
- Confidentiality of client records is, according to the members of the legal profession present, infinite, so a risk-based approach to releasing material for research is required.
- There are also issues over document ownership which must be dealt with before records are made available for research.
- Research ethics require rules around: collection of data; use of data; storage of data and disclosure of data.
- Collection of data requires informed consent (why is it being collected; who will see it; how it will be used; how it will be confidentially destroyed). If the rules are relaxed what is the potential for harm? Informed consent of course can't be obtained from the dead, so a risk-based approach is needed.
- Storage and destruction of data: researchers usually have an end date in mind, but how many of them do actually destroy the data? Where are the checks on confidential storage and destruction? The same questions on storage and destruction of the information they hold about and on behalf of clients should be asked of the legal profession.
- There is a need for clear guidance from the legal regulators on records ownership, records management and records disposal. At present there is very little.
- There is a need for better guidance from the legal regulators on confidentiality and legal professional privilege – in particular definitive statements as to whether confidentiality obligations are in fact perpetual or, if not, when they lapse.
- The legal regulators should define client consent processes which are transparent about destruction and/or archival deposit of client documentation.
- There is a need for generic templates to be made available to the legal profession when depositing records in archives e.g. a templated deposit contract agreed with the ICO, SRA, ARA and BRA which includes access terms. This template ideally needs to agree legal costs for dealing with access disputes.
- The changes imminent as a result of the GDPR (e.g. the requirement for legal institutions to draft and implement retention schedules) need to be more widely circulated within the legal profession.
- There is a mismatch between the public and private sectors over transparency. The public sector and some parts of the business sectors are leaning heavily towards being more open and transparent; the legal sector is still leaning towards secretiveness. This is a major issue because the legal profession is an important part of our national heritage but is still under-represented in archives.
- Information risk diminishes over time. TNA usually imposes closure periods of 75–100 years on personal or confidential data.
- The legal profession is risk averse and out of step with recent trends in both government and business towards transparency, public accountability and community engagement.
- The legal profession needs to be more aware of its responsibilities around good recordkeeping and to stop viewing information and records management as a separate overhead to be undertaken as an afterthought, if at all, instead of as an intrinsic part of running an organisation in the same way as Finance or HR.
- If the legal profession does not facilitate the preservation of records of value we will be left with a major gap in our historical record, undermining the understanding of the importance of legal developments to our nation's history.

# LRAR seminar at the Centre for Socio-Legal Studies on 25 April 2016: 'Legal Records at Risk 1914–2014: the use of unpublished data in socio-legal research'

## 1. Seminar introduction (William Twining)

The purpose of this seminar is:

- To attempt to understand the users' points of view from those who have had access to and used (or not used) documentary material, whether archived or not, in their research, whether they encountered any difficulties in obtaining access, what restrictions (if any) were placed on use.
- To find ways of making judgements about what kinds of records/institutions are likely to be of interest to potential users of different kinds; for most institutions the main external use will usually be from outside the legal academic community. One exception to this is socio-legal scholars. In our 1994 publication, *Legal Records in the Commonwealth*, Neil Rickman (then at CSLS) wrote a very useful chapter on this topic. We are interested in finding someone to update this, but also to seek suggestions from current socio-legal scholars who have used, or might use, certain kinds of records that are not at present accessible.

The aims of the LRAR project are as follows:

- To broaden the concept of 'legal' records from their traditional definition as court records or deeds to the business records of private sector institutions specialised to law (ISLs), including arbitration and mediation services, barristers, insolvency practitioners, legal executives, licensed conveyancers, multi-disciplinary practices, notaries, patent attorneys, pro bono legal services, scriveners, solicitors, trade mark attorneys and providers of ancillary services such as law publishers and law stationers.
- To identify and rescue historically significant legal records of private sector institutions that are at risk of destruction or loss because of indifference, apathy, lack of resources or concerns over confidentiality or reputational damage and to raise awareness of creators/holders of their potential value.

All private sector institutions in the UK face similar information management challenges, but modern legal records (20th–21st century) are particularly vulnerable due to recent developments which are transforming the nature, organisation, regulation and economics of legal services. If these changes are not captured for posterity by the systematic collection and preservation of relevant records our more recent legal history will continue to be government-centric, with obvious implications for the study of legal, social and cultural change.

The project is currently undertaking three major investigations into:

- Arbitration records
- The Intervention Archives managed by the Solicitors Regulation Authority
- Digital legal records

## 2. The use of unpublished data in socio-legal research and the Legal Records at Risk project (Clare Cowling)[55]

What do we mean by 'unpublished legal data'? We mean:

- Business records created by legal practitioners.
- Legal records created in the course of their work by businesses.
- Research data collected by legal scholars.
- Legal records held and made accessible by archive repositories.

The 20th and 21st centuries have seen enormous changes in the UK's legal framework. These changes are documented both in government records and in the business records of private sector ISLs. The records of these ISLs are not currently being systematically (if at all) preserved for research, so we may have a lopsided (i.e. government-centric) view of our legal history over the past two centuries. This has implications for the study of social and cultural change.

LRAR hopes to achieve its objectives by:

- Publishing examples of best practice – and horror stories.
- Raising awareness among legal information owners of their recordkeeping responsibilities.
- Working with ISLs to encourage better management of legal records.
- Working with the research community to identify their needs plus gaps in provision.
- Working with the archives community to seek practical solutions to resourcing issues.

We will not collect records but will act as a conduit through which legal records of value (in all formats and media) are identified, preserved and made available for research

LRAR has contacted three major categories of stakeholder institutions as follows:

- Research institutions.
- Archival institutions and pressure groups.
- Institutions specialised to law (ISLs).

The response from the first two groups has been overwhelmingly positive, with offers to publicise, actively assist and/or co-operate with the project. The response from ISLs has been overwhelmingly non-existent or negative, the only exceptions being where personal acquaintance with individuals could be called upon as an entry point. The project would value active lobbying from research institutions to help break this deadlock.

The project has also undertaken extensive investigation into the existence of modern legal records (using our definition above) already held in archival institutions, using The National Archives' Discovery portal and has recently completed a case study of 20th-century alternative dispute resolution (ADR) records held in the Transport for London Corporate Archives. These investigations show that there are many, varied and detailed legal records available for research, though there is no systematic process of collecting legal records other than by an extremely limited number of specialist repositories. This leaves a gap which the project hopes to work towards reducing.

Why might this be of interest to socio-legal scholars? Helping ISLs to identify and better manage their records so that they will survive for posterity and bringing ISLs with records of value together with archive repositories will result in enhanced research access to legal records of value.

Would these records be of interest, assuming they were available for research? Records of: ADR bodies, ADR cases, legal membership organisations, legal regulatory bodies, legal pressure groups and campaigns, law firms, legal advice groups. We need socio-legal scholars to us know about records which are *not* available i.e.:

- Problems locating and accessing relevant records.
- Do these issues constrain your research or alter your choice of study?
- Do secrecy and confidentiality issues hinder your research?

And about records which *are* available ie already in archives:

- Difficulties encountered in finding relevant entries in archives catalogues.
- Difficulties encountered in accessing material in archives.
- Issues around accessing digital records for research.

55 Paraphrased by the author from the original Powerpoint presentation.

## 3. Research undertaken by CSLS (Denis Galligan)[56]

Denis Galligan described the research undertaken as follows: 90% are empirical studies; conducting interviews and evaluating current data (e.g. case files, media releases, public domain reports, position papers, submissions) are the preferred methods of research. There is no particular pattern to the subject matter chosen for study, but something around alternative dispute resolution could be a useful topic, provided research material were available. Students to date have encountered no issues around accessing relevant material, but they may not be fully aware of the existence of much accessible – and relatively modern – information already available in archives.

CSLS theses themselves are clearly of archival research value; they are stored in the Bodleian Library and are therefore not at risk.

## 4. Using unpublished and published data for researching regulatory histories (Bettina Lange)[57]

Using unpublished records and archival data for researching regulatory histories has both advantages and disadvantages. Two examples, drawing on DPhil research I have supervised and my own research are:

- *European Union Archives* formed one data source for a DPhil research project that addressed the question 'How do "social" and "economic" views of risk become entrenched and thus inform regulatory standard setting in the European Union?'. Access to the EU Archives enabled the graduate researcher to develop an innovative account of risk regulation that questions 'exceptionalism' i.e. the idea that a particular regulatory failure – in this case the breach of the 60% public debt standard which the Maastricht Treaty established for EU Member State governments – should be considered as an extraordinary, entirely irregular and abnormal event. Instead, the research showed that there were structural reasons for the regulatory failure. Among these were a lack of balance between various Member States in the negotiation of the 60% public debt standard, and a view by some of the professionals involved in the negotiations, including economists, that taking economic risks could also translate into creating economic opportunities. These structural reasons point to a specific historical trajectory of developing standards for macroeconomic management in the EU that can help to explain contemporary regulatory failures in the management of the eurozone.
- *Hansard*: Extracts from *Hansard* were a source of data in a research project[58] that examines continuity and change in the institutions that govern water resources in England. More specifically, access to *Hansard* informed socio-legal research about the historical evolution of drought and its legal regulation in England, with reference to five key historic drought episodes, 1976, 1984, 1995, 2003–6 and 2010–12. Analysis of parliamentary debate during these drought episodes shows that over time there is significant continuity in what are considered as the key regulatory issues that need to be addressed for preventing water scarcity and drought. Among these are debates about how centralised or decentralised water resource management should be, and whether it is possible to achieve greater integration of the water supply infrastructure across the UK.

Hence, as the two examples show, archival data are very valuable for socio-legal research. The particular significance of the EU archives was to enable an analysis of the publicly not visible aspects of developing regulatory standards for the eurozone. While archival data are thus undoubtedly very important for socio-legal researchers seeking to understand legal regulation, it can also be necessary to enhance the validity of archival data by complementing them with oral histories or semi-structured interviews.

No issues were encountered in relation to accessing these archival data. It is, however, important for researchers to have some understanding of how the archival record was created in order to assess the validity and reliability of the data.

Further advantages for socio-legal researchers of accessing archival data are:

1. Unpublished records can provide interesting insights into 'image management' undertaken by the organisation that created the record. Understanding what the organisation – as a regulator or as being subject to regulation itself – thought was important to record constitutes very

56 The text produced here is a version compiled from the author's seminar notes and is reproduced with Denis Galligan's permission.

57 The text of this article is an amended version compiled by the author from her original seminar presentation and is reproduced with her permission.

58 I gratefully acknowledge funding for this project from the UK Government Natural Environment Research Council (NERC), grant number NE/L010356/1.

valuable socio-legal data, e.g. for the purpose of writing regulatory histories.

2. More specifically, unpublished records can be a source of both public institutions' and private organisational histories.

Challenges for socio-legal researchers in using archival data include that it is often not straightforward to identify what constitutes a 'record', though this matters for being able to formulate queries that are specific enough to make an access request. Moreover, smaller regulatory agencies may not have sufficient resources to establish archives.

There are two possible responses:

1. Private organisations with a public service mandate may be required by government archiving policies to establish archives and to gain access to some public funding in support of this.
2. Socio-legal research organisations, such as the UK Socio-Legal Studies Association and the Centre for Socio-Legal Studies, should be – as a matter of principle – informed before archives, in particular those of public institutions, are destroyed. This would enable research organisations to ascertain the value of these archives for socio-legal and legal research. This principle should be included in the recordkeeping policies of regulatory agencies.

## 5. Notes on socio-legal projects and sources used (Peter Bartlett)[59]

Peter Bartlett outlined two projects of relevance, both in a sense very standard socio-legal: the first looking at implementation of law; the second looking at how crime happens and how it's responded to. In both cases, an interest in the voice of non-legal actors (a big issue in the field of mental disability law) was a major factor.

**Project 1**: (PhD 1993, University of London, Published as *Poor Law of Lunacy*, Continuum, 1999) on Poor Law (PL) administration of lunacy in mid 19th-century Leicestershire. This was a branch of 19th-century poor law, effectively run by poor law officials, caught up in poor law debates (c.f. academic views at that time that this was all about medical debates).

Sources used were:

- Published Parliamentary papers at the British Library.
- Period (and more recent) published sources – journal articles, treatises etc.
- Records of Leicestershire County Asylum, 1837–70 held in Leicestershire County Records Office, including:
  - Admission orders (medical report from PL doctor, PL relieving officer comment).
  - Case book – including notes at time of admission; some material on time in the asylum; some notes on discharge/death (often slight).
  - Admission registers – providing basic demographic information [throughout period].

Usage of the records: to get a reasonable sense of dynamic of relationships, how events occur e.g.:

- Poor law ideologies as affecting administration of people.
- Complexities of the poor law: some people wanted in; some people really didn't. How people manipulated the poor law (both administrators and patients/inmates).
- Descriptive statistics – n.b. for example that women were not particularly over-confined, statistically (ideologies more complex – but still a hard case to make out that this was about women, in classic feminist sense) (big issue in the background – 20th century statistically different!)

Problems: fairly standard for administrative records: they are what they are (and nothing else). NOT as much from Parliament as I would have liked – no letters, transcripts – what we have is what is repeated in the documents, and that is for specific administrative purposes (getting the person in, diagnosis…). Obvious question: would Parliament have understood the situation the same way it's recorded? (Similarly, would administrators have written down different things/perceived the situation differently if in a different context?)

**Project 2**: gay murders – how do gay men end up dead in short relationships (one-night stands and the like) 1976–2001. 47 *BJ Criminology* (2007) 573

Starts as interest in 'homosexual panic' – A comes on to B, B freaks out, and bludgeons A to death. For lawyers: provocation defence ('Portsmouth Defence'). Became clear that a focus on the situation rather than the defence would make a more interesting paper.

59 The text of this article is an amended version compiled from the author's original seminar presentation and is reproduced with his permission.

The start date was chosen because that's when the Crown Prosecution Service (CPS) computerises case records: 'homosexual: casual' is a category within their classification. 78 accused/convicted (no one acquitted) and 77 deceased (accident – while most one-on-one, some multiple killers, some multiple accused for one deceased)

Records: PB had access to CPS files – key documents included:

- Witness statements (lots of them, most notably, with accused, since he will usually be the only witness)
- Forensic statements
- Pictures of the crime scene
- Trial note by counsel (often)
- If appeal, sometimes some transcript evidence, but that's fairly rare.

Usage

- Descriptive stats. A lot not surprising – poor and drunk. Horrible pasts – c.½ at special school or borstal. Almost everybody had a history of offending; roughly half for violence. Some interesting findings – overwhelmingly young (median age 23; cf median age of 30 for heterosexual comparators in Thomsen study); c. half – two-thirds had had sex with men before without payment. Important finding: this is in part about my community's violence against itself. (interesting question whether that will have changed in the last decade)
- Qualitative analysis – contexts (robbery, rent boys, power issues).

Problems of documents

- Again, context of documents: these are not detached views; these are people being interviewed by the police, with a view to a murder/manslaughter trial. What do the accused (or police) say to their mates?
- Note that a significant number of accused in the murder study were subject to probably flawed psychology reports.

## 6. To publish or not to publish? (Michael Reynolds)[60]

One of the key advantages of arbitration over litigation is said to be confidentiality. Confidentiality (the nondisclosure of commercial information held in the private domain of the parties) is critical to the success of arbitration. Arbitrators indeed are bound to keep the course of the proceedings confidential. If, however, the parties consent to the release of certain information and they waive their rights of confidentiality, that is another matter. Many students of attrition and others would welcome the publication of awards which would give considerable assistance to those seeking to become arbitrators and also to parties who may want to consider the quality of the arbitrators' work. Indeed, others go so far as to suggest that there will be benefit in building up a body of commercial arbitration jurisprudence.

International arbitration rules, however, militate against publication save and except the International Centre for Settlement of Investment Disputes (ICSID), which by tradition publishes its awards. Also, the China International Economic and Trade Arbitration Commission (CIETAC) *Arbitration Rules* Article 38 Confidentiality, provide that hearing shall be held in camera, but also significantly provide that both parties may request an open hearing. It is for the Arbitral Tribunal then to decide whether to direct such a hearing.

Arbitrators are not allowed to disclose any details or names without party consent.[61] There is a duty of confidentiality as a matter of law under various rules, for example: The London Court of International Arbitration *Rules* Article 30.2; American Arbitration Association (AAA) *Rules* Article 3; Geneva Arbitration Rule 5; International Bar Association *Rules of Ethics* Rule 9.

Parties may in limited circumstances be allowed to publish awards.[62]

Confidentiality according to Lew and Mistelis requires that what proceeds during the arbitration is kept absolutely confidential.[63] This extends to the existence of the arbitration, the subject matter of the arbitration, the evidence produced during the arbitration and all documents and awards which cannot be divulged to third parties. But it is also

60 The text of this article is an amended version compiled in August 2018 by the author from his original seminar notes and is reproduced with his permission.

61 ICC *Bulletin* 27 (1996) 30.

62 See for example: Associated Electronic and Gas Insurance Services Ltd v. European Reinsurance Company. Zürich. [2003] HKPC II and Belgium Foreign-Trade Bank Limited v. A1 Trade Finance Inc 13 (1) WTAM.

63 Lew, Mistelis and Kroll, *Comparative International Commercial Arbitration* (Kluwer 2003) 1–26.

suggested that in the absence of explicit agreement there is no binding obligation of confidentiality.[64]

In his work Mauro Rubino-Sammartano[65] says that publishing an award is a delicate issue because the parties prima facie have a right to confidentiality, although this seems to militate against the interests of scholars, lawyers and arbitrators and also clients having an interest in knowing of developments. A knowledge of such matters will undoubtedly assist others who may be contemplating arbitration.

ICC Rule 26.3 respects the parties' right to confidentiality. The Statute of the International Court provides that the work of the court is confidential and this is also the case in Article 6 of the ICC Court of Arbitration. The Inter-American Commercial Arbitration Commission provides that under Article 25(4) hearings are held in camera unless the parties otherwise agree. The AAA provides that under Article 20.4 hearings are private unless otherwise agreed.

However, some institutions as above indicated publish awards protecting the identity of the parties which is helpful to scholars and arbitrators and collectively combines to facilitate an arbitral jurisprudence. The International Council for Commercial Arbitration's *Yearbook Commercial Arbitration*, which is published annually, provides a useful compendium of important awards with the assistance of the Permanent Court of Arbitration on key developments including: institutional and ad hoc arbitral awards, court decisions on arbitration in a variety of jurisdictions including decisions on major multilateral arbitration conventions, commentary on the court decisions on the New York Convention 1958, updates on developments in arbitration law and practice, investment treaty awards and a decisions digest and a bibliography of the latest texts. These are of high-quality and considerable assistance to scholars and researchers.

Certain Eastern European countries publish awards in periodicals or special collections subject to the interests of the parties excluding names, enterprises, commodities and prices in particular the rules of the Court of Arbitration of the USSR Chamber of Commerce and Industry published in 1987. The Polish arbitration rules similarly provided such disclosures in the publication of their rules in Warsaw in 2003.[66] In several socialist countries hearings were held in public as for example in *Czechoslovakia v. Bulgaria.* As a footnote to history the author of this note when an assistant solicitor in the Legal and Parliamentary Department of the Greater London Council took part in the first and longest public arbitration in local government history, namely the arbitration between Test Valley Borough Council and The Greater London Council. Although there was some immediate public interest most of the proceedings went unnoticed by the public as after two days the reporters for the national newspapers left the public gallery.

There may be an argument that where the public/national interest is involved such tribunals should be open to the public. The greatest public arbitration was the Geneva Arbitration in 1871 between Great Britain and the United States to resolve the latter's compensation claims in respect of losses and damages caused to the United States by the deployment of cruisers built in England and manned by British sailors for the insurgent southern states in the civil war of 1861–65. In such cases where an issue of hostilities may arise there is an overwhelming public interest. But in general, subject to such exceptional circumstances as arose in the Geneva Arbitration, the Common Law and the Civil Law are generally against publicity.

Whilst the above is a snippet of a few of the arbitral institutions' approach it does seem that in general as between private parties or business organisations confidentiality is a sensitive subject as privacy and secrecy, especially regarding trade secrets is a critical consideration. Since Roman times, and possibly before, traders have shied away from the state courts where some commercial and trading interests are concerned. On the other hand, it may be that in the case of states where there are serious international disputes then publicity and openness may be required as in ICSID cases. In other cases it must be a matter for the parties' consent rather than a mandatory law to freely consent to publication if deemed appropriate, and even if the parties want to have an open hearing the tribunal may have to consider the appropriateness of it and whether it serves the needs of justice and fairness.

## 7. Information pack attachment I: LRAR: aims and objectives

The Legal Records at Risk project, based at the Institute of Advanced Legal Studies, University of London, commenced in September 2015 to:

- Broaden the concept of 'legal' records from their traditional definition as court records or deeds to the business records of private sector institutions specialised to law (ISLs), including arbitration and mediation services, barristers, insolvency practitioners, legal executives, licensed conveyancers, multi-disciplinary practices, notaries, patent attorneys, pro bono legal services, scriveners, solicitors, trade mark attorneys and providers of ancillary services such as law publishers and legal stationers.

64 Ibid. 8–45.

65 *International Arbitration Law and Practice* (Kluwer, 2001) 624–5.

66 City of Moscow v. Bakus Trust [2003]EWHC 1377 (Com) 70 Arbitration3,234.

- Identify and facilitate the rescue of legal records of potential value which may be at risk through globalisation, digital obsolescence, physical neglect, lack of interest on the part of information owners or reduced archival resources to rescue records.
- All private sector institutions in the UK face similar information management challenges, but modern legal records (20th–21st century) are particularly vulnerable due to recent developments which are transforming the nature, organisation, regulation and economics of legal services. If these changes are not captured for posterity by the systematic collection and preservation of relevant records our more recent legal history will continue to be government-centric, with obvious implications for the study of legal, social and cultural change.

The project will not collect records but will act as a conduit through which legal records of value (in all formats and media) are identified, preserved and made available for research. In doing so we hope to raise the awareness of the information owners of legal records as to the value of their records and assist them to unlock the potential of the records for both internal business reference and external research use. We will achieve this aim by:

- Creating a census of private sector ISLs in England and Wales, with details of what, if any, provision has been made to preserve their archives.
- Identifying legal records of research value and relevant repositories.
- Providing generic recordkeeping advice to information owners.
- Working with the archives community on a co-ordinated strategy for the identification and preservation of legal records of value.
- Working with research communities to understand their needs and to bring to their attention modern legal records of potential research value which may hitherto have been overlooked.

The project is being led by Clare Cowling, an experienced archivist and records manager; contact her at clare.cowling@sas.ac.uk. For the latest project news see our website: http://ials.sas.ac.uk/research/lrar/lrar.htm, which includes a questionnaire for researchers – please contact us with your thoughts/suggestions.

## 8. Information pack attachment II: examples of unpublished sources in socio-legal research

### *Unpublished sources:*

1. Postal, interview, and online surveys (including email and website surveys)
2. Participant observation data sets
3. Documentary and records evidence
4. Statistical evidence
5. Other archival material
6. Items from TNA and other public records offices
7. Papers of notable persons (e.g. diaries of persons of interest)
8. Doctoral and masters' theses
9. National archives (including minutes of meetings)
10. Minutes of private meetings
11. Letters and unpublished memoirs
12. Proceedings of public institutions (e.g. the British Medical Association)
13. Internal records of NGOs (e.g. Amnesty International)
14. Court records
15. Medical records (including hospital records)
16. Police records (including interviews)
17. Prison records
18. Legal practitioner records (documents of law chambers)
19. Corporate records (including factory records)
20. Local authority registers
21. Union records
22. Government department records (e.g. Department of Employment register of disabled persons)

23. Academic notes (from instructors and students)
24. Radio records (including archived recordings)
25. Parliamentary/senate/house/council minutes (i.e. minutes and records of public office holders)
26. Archive of weather reports
27. Stock market data
28. University and college records (including staff meetings, student union minutes, congressional minutes, etc.)
29. Records of small businesses
30. Family records
31. Artist notes and scraps (e.g. manuscript drafts, sketches, etc)
32. Constitutional committee notes and minutes (e.g. from formal or informal bodies that drafted constitutions)
33. Legal aid records (including invoices).

### *Categories (working list):*

1. Public entities
    a. Political
        i. Records of the executive branch
        ii. Records of the legislative branch
    b. Legal
        i. Records of the judicial branch
    c. Administrative
        i. Governmental departments
    d. Medical
        i. All public medical entities (e.g. hospitals)
    e. Charitable
        i. NGOs
        ii. Public universities and colleges
        iii. Public schools
2. Private entities
    a. Corporations
    b. Law firms
    c. Private universities and colleges
    d. Private schools
    e. Small businesses.

# LRAR seminar on 22 February 2017 for postgraduate students at the CSLS: 'Use of unpublished documents in socio-legal research'

Andrii Kondiuk/Shutterstock.com

## 1. Exploring the recent past in socio-legal research: the use of unpublished legal documents (Clare Cowling)[67]

What do we mean by 'unpublished legal documents'? LRAR defines them as: private sector business records created by legal practitioners and institutions; client documents held by legal practitioners; legal records created in the course of their work by businesses and research data collected by legal scholars. Currently researchers can access these documents either by contacting the legal institution or individual practitioner or by using the research facilities of archive repositories to find relevant records, such as TNA's *Discovery* portal (http://discovery.nationalarchives.gov.uk).

What legal documents do archives collect? There are a few dedicated 'legal' archives collecting records (including the Records of Legal Education Archives at IALS, the Inns of Court Archives and The Law Society Archives). Most legal documents turn up in unexpected places, such as in business archives like Transport for London Corporate Archives, which holds TfL's own legal case files and arbitration records; the London School of Economics Archives, which currently holds records of mediation organisations; the London Metropolitan Archives, with records of the London Court of Arbitration and a number of London law firms; and local authority archives with many records of law firms, individual practitioners, local law centres and citizens' advice bureaux.

How do researchers find the records they need? We suggest starting with *Discovery*; it lists all archive repositories and one can search for individual record creators and records by keyword, date or location provided the repository has a digital catalogue and has sent TNA the link. If not, the individual repository should be contacted for help.

Who is using unpublished legal documents and for what purpose?[68]

- Records of Legal Education Archives: primarily academic research such as records of famous legal practitioners (e.g. examination results of Nehru); changes to professional legal roles; history of intellectual property; role of Associations in legal development (e.g. International Law Association and international law). Some research is genealogical, such as relatives seeking information about individual solicitors.
- The Law Society Archives: most research is by members or is genealogical but there is also a growing number of law firms seeking information from TLS about their firm which they cannot find in their own records.
- Inns of Court archives: the primary use is internal, mostly relating to property, from the legal profession concerning membership and chambers' records and by genealogists.
- Local authority archives: most research is genealogical, with particular reference to deeds or for compiling biographies of prominent practitioners.

What is the Legal Records at Risk project's role? It is threefold:

67 Paraphrased by the author from the original Powerpoint presentation.

68 Information gleaned during conversations with the respective archivists/librarians.

1. To raise awareness of the variety and extent of modern private sector legal records in the UK – not just the records of law firms but of barristers' chambers, legal executives, patent agents, licensed conveyancers, court interpreters, arbitrators and ancillary bodies such as law stationers and law publishers.
2. To work towards a national strategy to systematically rescue those of value which are at risk through globalisation, digital obsolescence, neglect, lack of interest or lack of resources to preserve and provide research access to the records.
3. To ensure, by doing so, that that the socio-legal (and other) researchers of the future are given a balanced picture of the developments in legal services and processes over the past two centuries.

How can we help researchers? We need to know about:

1. Problems locating and accessing relevant records not yet in archives. Do these issues constrain your research or alter your choice of study? Do secrecy and confidentiality issues hinder your research?
2. Problems locating and accessing relevant records which are already in archives, such as difficulties you encounter in finding relevant entries in archives catalogues, difficulties you encounter in accessing material in archives and issues around accessing digital records for research.

## 2. Thoughts on archives by a user (Derek Roebuck)[69]

My work, past and future, on the history of dispute resolution, relies on archives of one sort or another. Good history depends on finding and interpreting the best evidence; primary sources rather than discussions of other historians, however distinguished.

A process which included mediation and arbitration has been generally practised in England and Wales from time immemorial. Litigation came later, with the state, as a particular alternative. There is ample evidence to show that, at least until the end of the 18th century, the state, as well as other communities, relied on mediation or arbitration to deal routinely with most kinds of disputes, e.g. in the 16th century Elizabeth I's legal aid schemes, especially for widows; in the 17th Nathaniel Bacon, who accepted all kinds of referrals from the Government and the courts; in the 18th Justices of the Peace's notebooks.[70]

If legal history were about no more than development of law, it might be found in the law reports, as a process of constant refinement, each case building on precedent and leaving it better. That fits nicely the assumptions of social Darwinism, society evolving as species do. Whig history, even Marx, got that wrong. The evidence is against their assumption that we organise ourselves better now than they did in the past. Sometimes they did it better then – fairer, faster, cheaper, more accessible, inquisitorial and, most important, peacemaking, and with provision for the poor and women.

What do legal historians have to say about developments in dispute resolution in the last four centuries? Where better to start than with Holdsworth's *History of English Law (HEL)*, still the first place even non-legal historians go to; e.g. XII p. 187: 'In medieval England the courts did not look very favourably on a practice which tended to diminish their jurisdiction'. That misled non-historian Konrad Zweigert and has become gospel: 2nd edn p. 412: 'The Common Law has always been very suspicious of arbitration clauses'. My 'Myth of Judicial Jealousy' (1994) 10 *Arbn Intnl* 395–406 showed that to be simply wrong. *HEL* p. 188: 'YBB say an award could not operate as a conveyance'. True. But two pages later that has become: 'the rule that there could be no arbitration as to the title to real property'. I could produce hundreds such arbitrations, which the parties knew would give as good a title as any. *HEL* sinks deeper into error, p. 189: 'as a general rule criminal cases could not be referred'. I could produce thousands which were from earliest times to the end of the 18th century: routine, private and public mediation and arbitration. The law was clear and regularly repeated in the law reports and the texts which relied on them: no award could decide who owned land. But that was not what the parties expected. It was enough that the award should resolve the dispute and require the parties to do whatever was necessary to give a good title. Arbitrators ordered the parties to execute whatever conveyances and quitclaims were required. Failure to abide by the award would lead to imprisonment if the award had been made an order of the court, as it commonly was. That was cheaper, faster, and more comprehensible than the artificialities of the current legal practice, based on the action of ejectment.

69 The text is a slightly amended version by the author of his original seminar handout and is reproduced with his permission.

70 The story is told in my *Early English Arbitration* 2008, *Mediation and Arbitration in the Middle Ages* 2013, *The Golden Age of Arbitration: Dispute Resolution under Elizabeth I* 2015, *Arbitration and Mediation in Seventeenth-Century England* 2017 and *Arbitration and Mediation in Eighteenth-Century England* due 2019.

The best example of a land dispute is from a negative exception, rather than the positive thousands. Lady Anne Clifford, born c.1590, was the only surviving child of the earl of Cumberland, who died when she was 15, leaving all his land to his brother, or so he thought. But he had only a life interest and was succeeded by his heir, Anne, who never gave up the fight to keep what was hers by Common Law, confirmed by a judgment of the Court of Common Pleas. At 19 she married the earl of Dorset. From the start her family and her husband tried to get her to transfer her rights to her uncle. James I did all he could to force her to accept his arbitration. He browbeat her and the archbishop of Canterbury called down the wrath of heaven. But Lady Anne Clifford – she always kept her own name – faced them down, as she did Cromwell in his turn. Every move is recorded in her diaries and a mass of other surviving documents. What a story! Unnoticed by Holdsworth or any other 'legal historian'. Even Antonia Fraser can claim that a married woman could not at Common Law own land – or even give her husband a birthday present. Tell that to little Annie Clifford who died at 86 enjoying legal ownership of most of Cumbria and half of North Yorkshire!

History shows what has been done, not that any of it is replicable. It can say nothing about what should be done. But if something can be shown to have worked well in the past, lessons may be learned. So historians must get it right, relying on the best evidence – usually documents in archives, of which I am a fortunate and grateful consumer.

I try to ignore the ringing jibe which Plautus has a soldier throw at a banker – and bankers were good for a laugh even 2,200 years ago: Plautus *Curculio* 551, *Stultior stulto fuisti si tabellis crederes,* 'You've been stupider than stupid, if you intend to rely on written documents'!

## 3. Information pack attachment I: theory and method in socio-legal research seminars: note by the CSLS, 2017

The course is intended to develop an appreciation of law as a social phenomenon, to introduce influential theoretical perspectives, and to consider the variety of methods by which socio-legal research questions might be addressed. The course does not seek to provide a comprehensive coverage of the whole field of social-legal inquiry but focuses instead on selected issues as an introduction to and way of illustrating the approaches taken by a variety of scholars. Each of the seminars is a self-contained, stand-alone two-hour interactive session. In these seminars you will discuss the practical techniques available to carry out socio-legal research and the ways in which they relate to whatever theoretical approach you might take. You will consider which questions you can ask and answer through which methods.

*WEEK 6, Wednesday, 22 February, 1.30 – 3.30, Professor William Twining and Clare Cowling: exploring the recent past in socio-legal research: the use of unpublished documents*

This session will demonstrate the importance of using primary source material in socio-legal studies. Records were not usually created for the purpose of research, so they often provide a less biased account of events than secondary sources. The session will show how the study of the recent past (using 20th- and 21st-century legal records held in archives) informs our analysis of the relationship between present day law and society, provides evidence of activities, tells us more about individuals, institutions and cultures and can even ensure justice.

The session will give practical examples of how to locate and use archival records and dispel some of the myths around the selection, extent, subject matter, availability and accessibility of legal records in archives. It will also briefly describe the work of the Legal Records at Risk project, the main aims of which are a) to raise awareness of the variety and extent of modern private sector legal records in the UK and b) to rescue those of value which are at risk, ensuring that the socio-legal researchers of the future are given a balanced picture of the developments in legal services and processes over the past two centuries.

**Read:** Neil Rickman, 'The Use of Unpublished Data in Socio-Legal Research', in W. Twining and E. Varnden Quick (eds.), *Legal Records in the Commonwealth*, Dartmouth Publishing Co., Aldershot (1994)

Attendees are also expected to briefly familiarise themselves with the following:

- The National Archives' Discovery portal: http://discovery.nationalarchives.gov.uk. Look under 'Pupillage'; 'barrister' – filter by date and record creator. Sometimes need an individual's name e.g. Jean Henderson barrister (in LSE archives).
- The Archives in London and the M25 area (AIM25) website: http://www.aim25.ac.uk. AIM25 has no 'legal' subject category. Under 'Gender Studies' – Abortion Law Reform Association.
- The Archives Hub website: http://archiveshub.ac.uk. Go to 'Contributors' (e.g. Barclays Group Archives).
- The UK Data Archive website: http://www.data-archive.ac.uk/home. Click on UK Data Service e.g. Human Rights Atlas or 'data by theme' e.g. crime or type 'legal' into keyword search.

- The Legal Records at Risk project website: http://ials.sas.ac.uk/research/areas-research/legal-records-risk-lrar-project.

## 4. Information pack attachment II: Legal Records at Risk Project – case study into alternative dispute resolution records in the Transport for London Corporate Archives, 23 May 2016

Below is a truncated version of the report. For the full report circulated to seminar attendees see **Appendix X Case study 3: Alternative dispute resolution records held in the Transport for London Corporate Archives**

The case study looked at a specific category of legal records, alternative dispute resolution (ADR) records, which had been created and later selected for archival preservation within a major transport company, Transport for London (TfL). The particular aims were as follows:

1. To look at the business context within which ADR records sit and achieve a brief overview of the dispute resolution process in a large business.
2. To gain an idea of the extent, content and value of such records.
3. To determine how ADR records are selected by the Archives for preservation.
4. To understand how ADR records are classified and indexed by the Archives.
5. To support the hypothesis that ADR archives are primarily located within business archives and must therefore be searched for under their business context.

Case Study conclusions:

1. TfL holds a wealth of legal records in its Archives, including numerous records relating to alternative dispute resolution. This supports our thesis that the bulk of surviving archival ADR – and other legal – records will at present be found within business archives.
2. ADR records will be found under a variety of series titles, which are based on either functions or departmental structures at the time the records were created. 'Arbitration' or 'mediation' is rarely (though occasionally) included in series titles. Researchers therefore need to be careful not only to think widely about keyword terms, but also not to narrow their fields of search to series titles or the records of 'Legal' departments.
3. ADR records in TfL are not only numerous, but often very detailed and comprehensive, containing not only the minutes of the case itself and the findings, but solicitors' shorthand notes, correspondence, summaries and copies of original documents used as evidence.
4. Concerns that confidentiality of proceedings might be a barrier to accessing modern ADR records appear to be unfounded, at least as far as TfL is concerned. It is probable that a similarly liberal approach to access to ADR records will be found in other business archives, though we have yet to investigate whether they have the same commitment to transparency and openness as TfL.

## 5. Information pack attachment III: Neil Rickman, 'The Use of Unpublished Data in Socio-Legal Research'

Published in W. Twining and E. Varnden Quick (eds.), *Legal Records in the Commonwealth*, Dartmouth Publishing Co., Aldershot (1994).

### *Introduction*[71]

A common perception of legal research (and practice) is of a fairly narrow concentration on detail, definition and consistency. This view is understandable but (certainly in the case of research) not wholly accurate. For a number of years now, academics on both sides of the Atlantic have been analysing legal issues from a wide variety of perspectives under the auspices of an emerging academic discipline called' socio-legal studies'. In the UK, this approach has been pioneered (and, indeed, unified) by the Centre for Socio-Legal Studies at Oxford. The objective of the present essay is to explain the extent and nature of the use of unpublished material in these 'socio-legal studies' by way of illustration with some examples from the Centre's work. It is hoped that, by explaining this research, attention will be drawn to a broader interpretation of what material is required for studying the law and its effects on individuals and society.

It is not new to observe that law can be viewed legitimately from a number of disciplinary perspectives. Neither is it new to suggest that this observation should enlighten archival policy (e.g. see Hay, 1987). Nevertheless, I have felt the need to approach my objective via a slightly circuitous route, spending some time discussing the nature of socio-legal studies on the way. Thus, the present contribution is of a case study, both explaining how such a broad perspective works (in theory and practice) and the variety of (in particular, unpublished) data upon which it must, necessarily, draw.

To achieve this, the following section starts with a general discussion of what socio-legal studies are and where their focus lies. Stressing the empirical nature of the focus will enable archivists and records managers to understand what is generating the demand for unpublished material discussed later. It also allows me to draw some general conclusions about the types of data required by socio-legal researchers. The third section provides a broad introduction to the work of the Centre for Socio-Legal Studies by briefly describing its recent research programmes. In this way, I hope to 'bridge the gap' between the theory and specific examples.

This fourth section contains the main body of the essay. By looking at some specific pieces of the Centre's work, it highlights the types of unpublished material used therein and how they were employed. It also describes the main research methods used at the Centre and explains why some of these involve the creation of new data sets, rather than the use of existing records. One implication of this section is that, on reading some of the Centre's output, a heavier reliance on unpublished material emerges than might initially be suggested by its research techniques. Whilst this analysis could have been performed by surveying the whole of the Centre's publication list, I have chosen instead to look at a small, representative sample from it. The main reason for this is one of practicality: the extent and scope of the Centre's output since its establishment in 1972 are such that a complete analysis would be unmanageable.[72] However, I think that there are some clear trends in its choice and use of unpublished material which the research presented points up; producing more examples might only have clouded the issues.

A brief summary and conclusion end the paper.

Before progressing, a word about my working definition of unpublished material. In Chapter two [of *Legal Records in the Commonwealth*], Twining has defined criteria for categorizing archival material as 'legal records'. The present essay, however, takes a broader view than this and considers the use of all forms of unpublished material in the Centre's work.[73] This is because it focuses on the diversity of material that can be relevant to such legal research. One implication of this is that much of the discussion will be of interest to records managers in organisations that generate their own records (e.g. local authorities, solicitors' firms, etc.) and will not always be relevant to archivists as they are traditionally perceived. Given the limited policy that exists towards archives in these organisations, this seems a legitimate fact for a policy-oriented study like the Commonwealth Legal Records Project to highlight.

71 I am grateful to the members of the Centre for Socio-Legal Studies for discussing some of the issues in this essay with me. Unattributed opinions are my own.

72 For example, during the period 1985–91 alone, Centre staff (solely or jointly) authored 48 books and reports, 324 chapters in books or articles in academic journals and edited 15 other books.

73 I am excluding from this statistical sources published by the government etc. and also the unpublished data that the Centre generates itself. I am concentrating on unpublished material that could have been created by any process other than the Centre's research (and therefore could have been properly recorded).

## *Socio-legal studies in theory*[74]

Socio-legal studies have become increasingly influential in the way law has been viewed and studied over recent years.[75] One might trace this back (in the UK) to the establishment of the Centre for Socio-Legal Studies by the Social Science Research Council (now the Economic and Social Research Council) at Oxford in 1972. This would be justifiable though it should be remembered that the move was

> 'in response to the growing interest from many academic lawyers and some social scientists for an institution which could explore by empirical research aspects of the relationship between law and society' (Hawkins and Harris, 1988, p. 272).

Subsequent evidence of influence can be gleaned from the growing text book references to socio-legal research findings (e.g. Hepple and Matthews, 1985; Haggett and Pearl, 1991), the level of policy debate they have informed, and the numerous university law departments now offering socio-legal course options. Despite this rising profile, however, the purpose and methods of socio-legal studies are often misunderstood. In the context of archives policy, this runs the risk of causing valuable information to be destroyed (because of ignorance as to its potential uses) or inconveniently stored (perhaps because of unawareness as to its relevance to a wide variety of disciplines). The present section addresses the question of 'purpose' in an attempt to indicate generally the types of data requirements that socio-legal studies have. A broad view of 'socio-legal studies' would deem them as the study of law in its social context. Harris (1989, p. I), however, provides a more specific definition: socio-legal studies are

> 'The study of law and legal institutions from the perspectives of all the social sciences (meaning all the social sciences, not just sociology)'.[76]

The parenthesis is important because it stresses the breadth of social science inputs used in socio-legal studies, thus preventing the frequent misinterpretation of 'socio' as referring uniquely to the application of sociological techniques (to legal issues). The 'social science approach' allows a combination of the different perceptions that different disciplines can provide of the same social problem. Accordingly, socio-legal studies are well placed to produce policy-relevant research insights.

The socio-legal approach may be contrasted with traditional legal scholarship. The latter focuses attention on the internal consistency of the law and the inter-relationship between legal rules in different areas of the law. The former, however, examines the way that law works in practice and the social consequences it may have. It views legal institutions as only:

> 'one of many social institutions (albeit an important one) ... [and argues that]... legal rules can be properly understood only through detailed study of their actual operation in their social and economic setting' (Hawkins and Harris, 1988, p. 270).

Accordingly, it lends itself to a wider set of questions raised by the social sciences. These include:

> 'How are legal rules made? Are they in fact complied with in the real world? If not, why not? Who tries to enforce the rules against rulebreakers? How do they set about their task, and with what results? What are the indirect and secondary effects of the law? Do those subject to the law make efforts to avoid the impact of the law? With what results?' (Harris, 1989, p. I).

Such questions have two clear implications for the types of research material needed in order to address them. First, the questions are primarily empirical. As Hawkins and Harris note,

> 'We are committed to the development of empirical research on the realities of law. its institutions, actors, rules, and processes with a view to furthering the development of theory' (p. 270).

This empirical approach is not typical of traditional legal scholarship. Second, there are implications for the types of empirical data required. The questions necessarily generate a complex view of the law and its effects which, in turn, obviously calls for a richer, wider variety of data sources than does the traditional approach. In the case of unpublished data, this might include data obtained via interviews or internal documents describing an organisation's regulatory procedures. Such 'hands-on' data allow researchers to evaluate the empirical workings of a legal rule and

74 Apart from the specific references in the text, see the special issue of *Law and Policy* edited by Gessner and Thomas (1988) for a variety of perspectives on socio-legal studies.

75 See Harris (1983) for a more detailed account of this development than is presented here.

76 This definition suggests clear similarities between socio-legal studies and the 'law-jobs' perspective taken by the Commonwealth Legal Records Project (see Twining, op cit., ch. 2).

the organisations enforcing it, as well as how these differ both from the situation before it was introduced and the aims (stated or otherwise!) of policy-makers.[77]

The numerous types of material used in research at the Centre for Socio-Legal Studies bear these conclusions out. Included here are postal and interview surveys, 'on-the-job' (or participant) observation of how laws and regulations affect behaviour, documentary and records evidence and statistical evidence. It is clear that many of these categories do not fall easily within the framework of perceived archival practice (some, for example, involve the creation of data sets by researchers themselves, either because the relevant material is not available or because it is felt that archive material would not capture the behavioural issues in question). However, they do indicate the richness of the material that can be brought to bear on analysis of the law; their illustration in the penultimate section will, hopefully, stimulate some thought as to whether perceived practice cannot be broadened to incorporate such diversity.

## *Socio-legal studies in practice: research topics*

In this section, I provide some broad practical examples of the research topics pursued at the Centre for Socio-Legal Studies since 1972. This will not only allow a more concrete understanding of the purpose of socio-legal studies but will also help explain why the Centre has used the types of research methods and data that are illustrated later.

The Social Science Research Council's provision of funding continuity to socio-legal studies was intended to stimulate full-time, long term research in this nascent field. This it has done, all of the Centre's work being organised around research programmes of (at least) two or three years' duration. This work is best seen in terms of these research programmes. Not only do they provide a structure for viewing the work, but also stress the diversity of topics upon which the Centre has focused. To make this brief sketch more manageable, I have chosen to look primarily at research programmes since 1985. It should be noted, however, that this does not completely ignore work carried out previously as several of the programmes originated at earlier dates.[78]

Since 1985, the Centre has been running four major research programmes. In keeping with the eclectic social science approach outlined in the last section, these have combined the inputs of lawyers, economists, sociologists, psychologists, historians and anthropologists. The first programme, 'Regulation and Discretion', analyses occupational health and safety regulations in the UK. The aim is to follow a wide-ranging set of regulatory rules through their stages from inception to results. Study of this 'regulatory cycle' involves considering the way problems are determined and defined, and how this feeds into the policy and legislation which follow. It then examines how this legislation is implemented and enforced by those concerned, and its effects on/reception by these parties. Studies within the programme have examined, inter alia, the history of health and safety regulation (e.g. Bartrip, 1992),[79] the role of field-level inspectors in generating compliance with the legislation (Hutter, 1988; Hawkins, 1989) and the way the enforcement of one particular set of regulations (the Control of Lead and Work Regulations, 1980) has influenced the affected firms' behaviour. The research has provided insights into the degree of discretion enjoyed by those implementing and enforcing the law and the effects of this discretion. This, in turn, has important implications for the effectiveness of this area of legislation and the livelihoods of those at which it aims.

Some similar themes can be discerned in the Centre's 'Business, Finance and the Law' research programme. For example, compliance with legislation has been examined in the contexts of tax avoidance and evasion, corporate finance and accounting (McBarnet, 1991; 1992), city regulation (Fenn, McGuire and Prentice, 1990, on insider trading) and insolvency (Wheeler, 1991). Another important aspect of business behaviour concerns relationships between different sectors of a given industry (e.g. between suppliers and retail outlets). Many such relationships are long-term and contractual in nature. The Centre has been conducting research into these in the context of the motor industry, including a comparative Anglo-French study of the ways contract law is used to govern them on both sides of the English Channel (Harris and Tallon, eds., 1989). A major difference highlighted here is the more frequent recourse to formal law when contractual conditions are breached in France than in the UK.

A recurrently important policy issue in Britain is the provision of health care. In this area, legal rules affect practitioners, administrators, patients and their families. There are clear socio-legal issues here and the Centre for Socio-Legal Studies has been conducting research into some of these under its 'Law and Health Care' programme. This has focused on how the above parties are affected by medical negligence law and claims, and by National Health Service (NHS) complaints procedures. Results here have drawn attention to the motivations for making complaints and legal claims and to deficiencies in the processes that have been established for doing so. Other areas of research in this programme are examining wider issues in health sector regulation: the implementation of recently instituted NHS contracting; also the effects of statutory regulation (e.g. patent law) on pharmaceutical product innovation.

77 One might add that it can also have implications for the format in which data are usefully kept (for example, economists often find it convenient to work with tabulated data).

78 Also, in the fourth section I discuss the 'Compensation for Illness and Injury' research programme, started in 1973–74.

79 All of the citations given in this section are examples of the outputs produced by the research programmes. There are many others to choose from.

The final research programme that the Centre has been running since 1985 is that in 'Law and Family Policy'.[80] The impact of law on family life is clearly enormous. The Centre is studying its role in divorce and child abuse cases, and in encouraging the elderly to use their property as a means of financial support (on the latter, see Eekelaar and Pearl, eds., 1989). Research into the effects of matrimonial (divorce) law has tackled such crucial issues as how the divorce mediation process affects the parties and outcome of proceedings (Greatbatch and Dingwall, 1989), the role of registrars in this outcome (Eekelaar, 1991), the financial consequences of divorce for those involved (Maclean, 1991) and long-term consequences of divorce for children (Eekelaar and Maclean, 1986). As an example of findings from their work on children and divorce, Eekelaar and Maclean (1986) found that, from a sample of 5,000 children born in 1946, those who experienced parental divorce before they reached the age of 15 were likely to leave school with lower educational qualifications than children from continuing two-parent families. Other findings are too numerous to mention, but this example will give a flavour of their relevance to any serious policy debate concerning matrimonial law.

Apart from their diversity and inter-disciplinary nature, there are several notable themes to these research topics. First, they all are (at least partly) concerned with the way law is implemented. In this, they implicitly examine the questions posed by Elmore for analysing the implementation of a legal rule:

> 'why the legal action should be enforced (authority), the way responsibility for enforcement is allocated, and factors which affect the capacity to enforce [competence]' (in Gessner and Thomas, 1988, p.86).

Second, they are very much concerned with who is affected: the regulator, the enforcer and the parties at whom the law is aimed. Finally, they clearly depict the breadth of the definition of law used in socio-legal studies. 'Law' does not refer only to statutory and case law, but also considers rules and regulations that may be put in place to fulfil a wider statutory obligation (e.g. NHS complaints procedures).

These themes are clearly those exhibited by the description of socio-legal studies. Further, having seen there the questions upon which those studies focus, it is easy to see how the research topics described in the present section were arrived at. All can be recognised as addressing crucial issues in policy debates that have taken place in the UK in recent years; indeed, in many cases, they demonstrate how policy-makers have responded to them. For this reason (and their own inherent interest), they seem to me comfortably to illustrate the value of a broad perspective on the law and its consequences.

## *Socio-legal studies in practice: use of unpublished data*

The section on 'socio-legal studies in theory' demonstrated that the focus of socio-legal studies has clear implications for the research material they require. Further, in general, it appears that this material can differ quite substantially from that used in traditional legal research. To substantiate this point, I now turn to some practical examples of socio-legal work; in particular, I review some of the Centre for Socio-Legal Studies' projects in recent years. It will be clear from this that the main focus of the Centre's research is on explaining how a chosen area of law actually operates, for instance by studying the behaviour of the people (e.g. lawyers, officials, business advisers, etc.) who translate a legal mandate or rule into action.

Two points should be made about what follows. First, I have chosen to group the work in this section according to type of research. This in turn determines the data used. The implication is not that research reported under one heading does not contain data and methods reported under others (indeed, I have tried to highlight some linkages). Instead, the method of presentation is chosen purely for reasons of simplicity and clarity. Second, as explained in the Introduction, I have used a small sample of the Centre's output to make my points below. This has been chosen according to three criteria: (i) its representativeness; (ii) to cover several of the Centre's research programmes and (iii) to span a reasonably long history of its publications. The latter enables a general pattern of continuity to be observed in the research material required.

### Uses of archive and library material

The clearest use of unpublished records (as they might traditionally be defined[81]) in Centre research is in its analyses of the social history and effects of legislation. To consider this, I choose two books (Bartrip and Burman, 1983; Bartrip, 1987) and one article (Bartrip, 1982). These works have contributed to issues in both the 'Regulation and Discretion' and 'Compensation for illness and injury'[82] research programmes. It has been noted elsewhere (Hay, 1987) that records (including legal ones) are of immense value to social historians. However, though the examples below confirm this,

80 Space does not permit descriptions of the Centre's other research projects in 'Law and Psychology' and ' Law and Economics'. However, an example of work in the latter occurs in the account of 'socio-legal studies in practice' given below (see the discussion of Gray and Fenn, 1991).

81 In other words, public archives, libraries, collections of papers, etc.

82 See below.

they also demonstrate the variety of sources that necessarily are required if a full evaluation of the consequences of legislation is to be made.

Bartrip and Burman analyse the evolution of law and government policy in the area of industrial safety and compensation between 1833 and 1897. In so doing, they pick up the earliest British provisions in this area. Using historical documents and statistics, they describe the legal and financial position of workers prior to reform, when industrial accident compensation came only through public and private charity. In this way, they are better able to assess the effects of reform proposals (which first surfaced in the 1860s) and legislation (Employers' Liability Act, 1880; Workmen's Compensation Act, 1897) on workers' conditions. Consideration is given to the role of inspectorates in implementing this legislation and to the parallel development of common law on employers' liability. Unsurprisingly, the research draws on a number of unpublished materials and library archives.[83] The easiest way to illustrate this is to check the bibliography and chapter endnotes. These reveal the following use of sources (figures in brackets indicate the number of references): Public Record Office (HO and LAB series, 38); university libraries (12, including the Joseph Chamberlain Papers at Birmingham and the Asquith Papers at Oxford, also four doctoral theses and one master's); the Howell Collection (Trades Union Congress – TUC – Papers, 8); National Register of Archives (Broadland Manuscripts, Shaftesbury Diaries, I). This extensive variety of political minutes, comments, letters, memoirs, etc. are essential to the rich analysis of the introduction and effects of industrial safety legislation that Bartrip and Burman present.

A similar array of sources can be found in Bartrip's (1987) follow-up study on 'Workmen's Compensation in the Twentieth Century'.[84] This traces the development of the Workmen's Compensation Scheme after its 19th-century origins, finishing (as did the scheme) with the National Insurance (Industrial) Injuries Act, 1946. Once again, the socio-legal analysis stresses not only the context and background to the legislation, but also its effectiveness in attaining its goals and any unintended consequences for firms, workers, etc. Here the use of unpublished data is as follows: Public Record Office (PIN, CAB, HO series, 72 references); Warwick Modern Records Centre (especially its CBI predecessor materials, 43); the Middleton Papers (Labour Party headquarters, 15); various TUC files (8); PhD theses (3) and one reference each to the National Register of Archives (Broadland Mss.), university libraries and the proceedings of the International Labour Organisation's conference (Geneva, 1925).

Finally, I turn here to Bartrip (1982). An important feature of industrial safety legislation as it developed in the 19th century was the introduction of central government inspection as a means of ensuring compliance. In the absence of prior empirical research, Bartrip concentrates on the specific role of these inspectorates. He assesses

> The nature and extent of central government inspection between 1832 and 1875 in terms of departments formed, officials employed and budgets deployed ... [he examines] two particular inspectorates, ...factories and mines. to evaluate inspection as a means of enforcing statute law and furthering both social reform and government intervention ... [and], again by taking factory and mines inspection, ... [he considers] the controversial question of inspectors' attitudes to reform and regulation both before and after appointment (p.605).

He concludes that inspectorates' importance has been exaggerated; for example they were in fact provided with insufficient resources to fulfil their objectives. The paper makes use of unpublished material at the Public Record Office (HO and LAB series, 23 and I references respectively) to highlight, inter alia, the government's motivations for introducing inspection. It is also used to show that, even after this introduction, workers still had cause to complain to the government about accidents whose ultimate causes had been missed by inspectors.

It is perhaps instructive to provide an example of social history where archival material was of no help. Bartrip has been researching the introduction of regulations to counter arsenic-related diseases (these were one of the first four industrial diseases to be scheduled by the Home Secretary in 1895). As part of this work, it was considered necessary to take a longer historical perspective on arsenic regulation, and Bartrip (1992) discusses the introduction to the Arsenic Act, 1851. On reading this paper, it is apparent that no reference is made to unpublished material. The reason is that the Public Record Office apparently has no record of the political background to the legislation. This, of course, need not be a criticism of the PRO, but it is nonetheless surprising. For my purposes, it confirms that archival policies (decisions about destruction, cataloguing, storage or what records to keep) do have important effects on the work that researchers are able to perform.[85]

These examples evince the value of traditional archive material to socio-legal studies, providing a richer understanding of what legal rules have been intended to do and how they have fared. Thus, as seen, Bartrip is able to apply such data to make an original assessment of the effectiveness of the early factories inspectorates. However. as noted at the

83 Of course, much published material available in such places is also used, e.g., parliamentary papers and newspaper reports.

84 For a journal article discussing related issues and making use of similar unpublished material, see Bartrip (1985).

85 Bartrip informs me that, since completing his research, his attention has been drawn to recent PRO recataloguing activities, which may bring relevant material to light.

head of this sub-section, the range of material relevant to legal issues might be larger than expected. In particular, because the research analyses aspects of political context in the relevant legislation, it draws upon a number of political papers. Further, its simultaneous focus on the social consequences of that legislation brings the unpublished material of workers' institutions into play as well.

## Participant observation and interview studies

A substantial amount of the Centre's research has not used unpublished material available in public archives. The reason for this should be apparent from the discussions in the previous two sections: many of the questions in which socio-legal studies are interested involve analysing behaviour before any formal record would have been started.[86] Thus, it is of just as much interest to know why one road accident victim did not start legal proceedings (and thus not initiate a case file or statistic) as why another did; both provide us with insights about the way the law is working and is perceived to be working. Similarly, many of the questions that socio-legal studies ask are contemporary legal ones (with, therefore, contemporary policy relevance). The result is that the Centre for Socio-Legal Studies engages much of its time in creating data sets through postal surveys, interviews and 'on-the-job' (or participant) observation in the research area concerned. Below, I provide some illustrations of these techniques at work. In many of the examples, however, it is important to note that unpublished material is nevertheless essential to the subsequent research. I start with a discussion of the Centre's most popular research technique (often known as an 'ethnographic' technique) and why it is so frequently used. Following its establishment in 1972, the Centre instituted a research programme on 'Compensation for Illness and Injury'. The findings are reported in Harris et al. (1984) and follow-up work based on these still continues (e.g., see Genn, 1987; Bartrip, 1987). The objective of the programme was a large-scale evaluation of the tort system as a support and compensation mechanism for those injured, disabled or made seriously ill in accidents (on the road or at work, for example). The Centre felt such a study to be needed, believing

> 'that discussion of compensation systems seriously lacked reliable information on the experience of those affected by existing arrangements, and that there was a clear need for a comprehensive investigation of all systems of compensation and support, which studies not only the victims of all accidents wherever they occur, but also that of those who suffered similar kinds of incapacity through illness or congenital defects' (Harris et al., p. xviii).

Issues covered therefore included the factors associated with claiming and obtaining damages, the legal procedure for negotiating out-of-court settlements in accident cases, a psychological assessment of accident victims' views of fault and liability, alternative means of compensation available (social security, etc.) and the effects of accidents on victims' earnings and future earning power. The results (see Harris et al.) have been highly influential, both in the spheres of government policy and research methodology.[87] The analysis of the issues was carried out using all of the research techniques discussed in the present section. However, it was performed on one main database which the Centre constructed between 1974 and 1979. I now turn to this database and the reasons for the Centre's belief that such a base was not available elsewhere.

The database was constructed via a two-stage information process (see Maclean and Genn, 1979, for a full account). First a nationally representative sample of 15,000 households was questioned by post to generate a sample of individuals who had suffered some incapacity of at least two weeks' duration, arising from injury or illness. Then a 2,000-strong subsample of individuals was re-interviewed in depth (in person and by subsequent questionnaire) at a later stage, both to determine the circumstances of their incapacity and to follow the progress of any claim for damages made. All of this had been preceded by a pilot study to discover any difficulties with the questions and methods used (e.g. any implicit bias introduced). The result was a thorough data set, as required by the research.

Though in presenting the results generated by this data set, Harris et al. make little reference to unpublished data,[88] Maclean and Genn (Chapter 2) discuss the use to which such data were put and why they were found wanting. This discussion also highlights the potential value of unpublished data, even in what is ostensibly a piece of 'survey research'. A priori, the types of information required by the compensation study might have been found in the records of the police, hospitals, general practices, and factories and other inspectorates. Other potential sources might have been industrial injury and disablement records, war injury benefit records, sickness and invalidity disablement benefit records, records of the Criminal Injuries Compensation Board, local authority registers of the disabled, blind and chronically sick, court records and the Department of Employment register of disabled persons. Apart from indicating a wide range of sources to which socio-legal studies might turn, Maclean and Genn's discussion of these demonstrates the potential assistance they may provide to researchers in the field. They note that

86 A common observation concerning socio-legal studies is that they analyse the workings of the law from 'the bottom up'.

87 In policy, several studies (including the Centre's) contributed to the government's institution of the Civil Justice Review (e.g. 'Personal Injuries Litigation' Consultation Paper, Feb. 1986) to overview the English personal injury litigation system. In research, the recent Rand study of personal injury litigation in the United States (Hensler et al., 1991) adopted the Centre's approach.

88 To be precise, four conference papers and four working papers.

> In the process of aiming at a strategy for research which would meet the demands of experience, economy and methodological logic, it was necessary to explore all the possibilities of data collection ... It was ... conceivable that a sample of victims could be constructed from the records of ... agencies, from whom information about the consequences of accidents and illness could be obtained at a later stage either by personal interview or postal questionnaire (p. 6).

In other words, even if interview techniques are brought in at a later stage, records may be used to determine the characteristics that a representative sample might display. However, Maclean and Genn continue to explain why such an approach was not taken in this case. The reasons given are the types of data collected by these agencies and their accuracy. The former can be broken down into two parts. First, an organisation's data will tend to reflect its criteria for collection. These, in turn, will be determined by the functions of the organisation rather than an individual's circumstances. They are

> 'primarily a record of the activities of the agency or organisation, a record of clients seen, treatment given or cases reported. They are subject to the same limitations as the organisation itself and embody the bias determined by the terms of reference of the organisation' (p. II).

Second, there are individual or group factors involved:

> 'The path which an individual must follow to reach the final stage of inclusion in official records can be characterised as a series of steps consisting of actions which follow from perceptions and definitions of given situations. Failure at any stage in this process will result in the individual not appearing in such situations' (p. 12).

Thus, both over- and under-reporting of cases may occur in agency statistics because reporting involves a subjective process on the part of the reporter. The 'internal accuracy' (p.14) of agency records is also discussed by Maclean and Genn. In particular they ask whether, if successful contact has been made between agency and client, the subsequent record reflects what took place. They give several examples of why this might not be the case (pp. 14–17). It would thus appear that the most useful agency records, from the perspective of a socio-legal researcher, would be ones that were consistent, accurately kept and economical to access (possibly computerised).

Such issues can be further illustrated by other Centre work using this ethnographic technique. Hawkins (1984) and Hutter (1988) both contribute to the 'Regulation and Discretion ' programme. Both analyse government inspectors in their role as enforcers of particular legal rules and regulations. Hawkins considers water pollution control, using a combination of participant observation, tape-recorded interviews and internal water authority documents. In particular, he looks at the work of staff at two regional water authorities to determine the role played by the criminal law in the daily routine of protecting water quality. He also enquires into the level of discretion they enjoy. By doing this, Hawkins is able to describe how abstract statutory statements are translated into administrative action and how differences between legal word and legal deed can provide valuable enforcement strategies. The bibliography refers to the use of only ten pieces of unpublished material[89] but the appendix, 'A Note on Research Method', confines the use of unpublished documents internal to the water authorities concerned. Apart from his interview and observation data, Hawkins says 'I also made use of published agency materials and those internal agency documents to which I was given access: notes, minutes of meetings, reports, and statements of policy' (p. 226).

The limited extent of this use is made clear in that only five references are made to them in various chapter endnotes.

Hutter's study considers the work of Environmental Health Officers. Again, combining observation and informal discussion (to learn about the officers' work) with a second phase of more specific (taped) interviews, she examines issues similar to those explored by Hawkins in this different context. Once again, the bibliography contains few references to unpublished material[90] but the 'Research Methods' appendix (Appendix I) does:

> 'The second phase of field-work comprised more formal methodological techniques than the first, namely examination of the records of the environmental health departments in the sample and semi-structured interviews with officers' (p. II).

In discussing this use of unpublished internal documents, Hutter confirms the problems and potential uses as noted in Maclean and Genn. As she says, 'the documentary survey proved less helpful than had originally been anticipated' (p. 211).

89 Four conference papers, four PhD dissertations and two working papers.

90 Two Master's dissertations, one doctoral, one conference paper and one internal report (on 'Staffing in Environmental Health ', a report for the Association of District Councils, Association of Metropolitan Councils, Local Authorities Conditions of Service Advisory Board and the Local Government Training Board, 1978).

This was because records varied in their content (due to differing attitudes to recording within departments) and in their quality and quantity (due to financial constraints). Though access was easily obtained, many case files were hard to locate because of administrative staff shortages. In consequence. the ones examined were those that were centrally available and centrally collated – those whose contents were most efficiently available. The information in these varied and was usually brief; many of the decisions to which they referred were taken in conversation and the departments required only the outcomes of such decisions to be recorded.

However, Hutter continues (and here she is worth quoting in full):

> Despite these problems with the documentary sources they did provide a valuable check on some of the assertions made by officers, most particularly claims about the stringency with which the law is enforced by the various departments [under examination]. For instance, they gave some idea of the proportion of cases which resulted in prosecution, formal warnings, and informal action. And gave some indication of how environmental health cases were treated by the courts (p.212).

Thus, as well as their usefulness on matters of detail, internal documents were valuable in providing 'a feel' for the departments analysed, comparability across the (four) departments and a benchmark against which other information could be assessed. These are exactly the points identified in Maclean and Genn.

A whole series of other Centre work uses interview and observation analysis, reinforced by unpublished organisational data. I briefly add another to further indicate the range of data sources that have been used.[91] In the 'Law and Health Care' programme, researchers have been granted access to two NHS districts' patient complaints processes from patients', practitioners' and administrators' perspectives. Subsequent interviews (with patients and NHS staff) have followed up on the findings here. This work is (at time of writing) being prepared for publication so cannot be quoted. However, when discussing the project with the researchers, it is interesting to note the importance they placed on initial analysis of the files. Once again, this unpublished material provided a stock of information upon which to better 'target' the interviews and against which to check findings, as well as helping to determine the representativeness of the interview sample. In short, it provided a foundation for the subsequent research.

What of the records of those regularly involved in litigation themselves? During its research, the Centre has studied solicitors, barristers, court registrars, insurance companies, trade unions and medical defence unions. Gaining access to case files can often be difficult, the problem, of course, being one of confidentiality. Nonetheless the Centre has been able, on occasions, to gain direct access to case files, or at least indirect access through interviews with the relevant lawyers. Genn (1987), for example, studies out-of-court settlement negotiations in personal injury litigation to determine how plaintiffs and defendants use to their advantage the various legal rules at their disposal. Using a combination of observation and interview/questionnaire surveys, she gains a fascinating insight into the negotiation process involved. This includes a substantial amount of material from negotiators' discussions of specific cases (kept anonymous) and, in chapter 8, the outcomes of two cases which could not have been published.[92] Harris (in Harris et al, chapter 3) did not receive direct access to solicitors' confidential documents but reports that solicitors were generally willing to respond to a questionnaire (with client consent) about cases that the Centre was following. However, interestingly, nine solicitors (out of 98) reported that the relevant file had been destroyed (something which must have occurred within five years) and five could not trace it (p. 134, note 2).

As noted above, on some occasions, the Centre has gained access to litigated files. In such cases (as in all matters of confidentiality) it offers anonymity and confidentiality, as well as some opportunity for the provider of the data to see a draft of any publishable findings. An instance of case file access, that the Centre has at present, involves its current research into the operation of the tort system in medical cases.[93] This is being undertaken with excellent access to the case files of medical defence unions. Yet again it is the breadth of knowledge that these provide and the insights they offer into settlement strategies that have enabled very fruitful interviews and postal surveys to be constructed and carried out with lawyers, doctors and patients. The analysis has been able to highlight the stressful nature of medical litigation (for doctors and patients) as well as the strategies that plaintiff and defendant lawyers use in negotiating pre-trial settlements.

It is clear that legal actors and their files are of much import to aspects of the Centre's work, whether this is through direct access or via the opportunity they give lawyers to refresh their memories on cases in question (as Harris's example demonstrates). Staff to whom I have spoken about access to confidential documents have generally been happy with

91 As further examples: a piece of research currently being written up uses the internal (unpublished) manuals of compliance officers in London financial firms in order to be better informed when preparing and conducting interviews; McBarnet (1991; 1992) uses internal company documents along with interview data to consider tax evasion and avoidance together with 'creative accounting'.

92 One was settled, the other went to trial but was not reported.

93 See also the discussion of Fenn and Dingwall, in Dingwall & Fenn (1993), below. Another example of such access is Wheeler (1991).

that which the Centre has received. A key point that comes across is the need (on both sides) to negotiate this access and to be flexible in doing so. A corollary of the access issue, however, is that the data destruction policies of those generating files etc., might take a broader view of the use to which such files can be put (in particular, once closed).

A final (though tangential) example of the importance of unpublished legal records to research has been provided to me in conversation by the Centre's Peter Bartrip. He is presently conducting some research for the British Medical Association (BMA), who has apparently not operated a consistent archives policy but has recently appointed an archivist to establish a collection of past and future BMA material. The lack of past recordkeeping has obviously added to the difficulty of this task. Fortunately, the BMA has retained the services of the same solicitors over the years and is currently enquiring as to which files they have kept that might provide a more thorough account of its work in the past.

What conclusions can be drawn from this sub-section? I have described a research technique (participant observation and interview) which is extremely important to the Centre's work. The reasons for using this have been given as the contemporary nature of its research, its desire to capture the influence of the law at the earliest stage (which often pre-dates records) and a recognition that much unpublished data are not suitable (for legitimate reasons) for its needs. Accordingly, it has sought its own data. However, unpublished material has frequently performed a crucial role in defining the parameters for these ethnographic studies and has provided essential breadth, depth and background. It seems clear to me that this is particularly so where research has focused on the contribution of a specific organisation to some socio-legal phenomenon, rather than the wider phenomenon itself.[94] This strongly suggests that all manner of agencies involved in work that requires the policing or operation of legal rules should be aware of the rich research potential of the unpublished material they generate (everything from minutes of meetings to internal monitoring statistics to files concerning finished work).

## Statistical work

Statistical methods are frequently employed at the Centre to draw results from sets of data. In this sub-section, I shall illustrate the use of unpublished data in relation to two types of statistical work. The first is econometrics while the second involves more descriptive statistical techniques. In both cases, the data are often from the internal material of an organisation under study, as in the previous sub-section. The following examples therefore provide more illustrations of the uses of such data. However, the data are now being used' in their own right', as opposed to providing breadth and background for the subsequent construction of interviews and questionnaires.

A particularly common approach adopted at the Centre is econometrics (a set of computer techniques often used by economists to quantify and test hypotheses). Plenty of examples of the Centre's work exist in this area. I choose to consider Gray and Fenn (1991), a contribution to the Centre's 'Law and Economics' research project.[95] This draws on work commissioned by the Legal Aid Board to examine the factors behind the recent increase in the unit cost of legally-aided criminal cases in England and Wales. It finds that the court-determined length of case is the main explanation of regional and temporal variations in unit costs. The unpublished data in this research involve a random sample of 2,914 legal aid bills drawn from all legal aid areas and covering the period 1988–1990. These were supplied by the Legal Aid Board.

Two important features of Gray and Fenn's data set are of note. First, these bills were originally constructed to help determine the payment due to the lawyer in each case. Thus, a lengthy initial part of the research involved inspection of bills to determine the richness of the data available, followed by the processing of the sample to distil out the relevant information (coded in a style suitable for computer analysis). This supports an observation made in the last sub-section: that the form in which data are initially stored can have a great impact on the duration (and cost) of a research project. Second, as the researchers say, 'the timescale [of the survey] could not be longer [than 1988–1990] because the destruction policies of [Legal Aid] offices result in no bill being kept for more than three years' (pp. I, 622). As a result of this observation, the Legal Aid Board is reviewing this policy, with the aim of extending the destruction deadline. This provides a valuable example of the discrepancy that may emerge between archive and research needs, and the way in which it can be solved by making archivists aware of their collections' research potential.

Whilst econometrics can provide valuable quantitative data, it is often sufficient to analyse figures by comparison of tables, etc. An example of this 'descriptive' method is Fenn and Dingwall (in Dingwall and Fenn, eds., 1993).[96] This compares medical negligence litigation experience in the UK and the USA. The UK data were taken from:

> 'an extensive series of case files when Oxford Regional Health Authority commissioned [the authors] to review all the records available in the region of closed claims alleging negligence by

94 For instance, much of the work in the 'Law and Family Policy' programme is conducted without recourse to internal documents which very rarely exist in this field.

95 As another example, see Fenn and Vlachonikolis (1990).

96 Other good examples of such work are Lloyd-Bostock (1988) and Whelan, ed. (1990).

> hospital or community medical staff to see what could be learnt from the aggregate picture' (p. 14).

The authors' comments on these files are interesting and provide further evidence of the themes that have permeated the discussion until now. Some districts maintained complete records, while others were more 'fragmentary' (p .14). These latter were often dispersed across locations, as opposed to centrally kept. However, procedures had been tightened in 1980–1981, enabling Fenn and Dingwall to have 'much greater confidence in the data from that period onwards' (p. 14). They continue:

> 'This picture of disarray... sends its own message about the importance with which these files were regarded as a source of information ... As we learned from the staff involved, claims were managed on a case-by-case basis. Each was treated as a one-off event, resisted or settled or closed. Only one district produced any kind of statistical summary, although another was in the process of creating a small computerised database which would allow it to do the same' (pp. 14–15).

They continue to maintain that the benefits to the districts from collecting such data were not obvious (an example of Maclean and Genn's 'organisation' point). However, given the size of the resulting data set, the authors conclude

> 'if tort claims are to be used in medical risk management, and to contribute effectively to the process of quality assurance in the NHS, arrangements will have to be made to collect reports on a much larger scale' (p. 15).

The implication is clear: it is in the interests of agencies to maintain effective records if they wish to improve the quality of their output through research findings.

Fenn and Dingwall's reference to computer databases leads me to a final anecdote with which to conclude this sub-section. I have already argued that computerisation is an obvious way in which some material could be made more 'researcher-friendly' (as well as more useful to the organisation concerned). Not only can this make data easier to access and analyse, it can also make it more transportable (the Centre regularly receives computerised databases through the post). However, one must be careful here as some computers store data in ways that are incompatible with other machines. This observation was confirmed at some cost when the Centre was given access to the Health and Safety Executive's large computerised database in the 1980s. Incompatibility of computers meant that the whole set had to be printed out in London, transported to Oxford, then re-input.[97] Such an exercise, costly in both time and money, reminds researchers and archivists alike of the need to be mindful when considering a choice of computer hardware and software.

## Conclusion

Socio-legal studies provide a perspective on legal issues that traditional legal scholarship does not aim for. By focusing on the social consequences of legal rules, they aim to assess how these rules are working and to isolate any contributory factors in their success or failure. The results that such research yields are becoming increasingly important in policy debate, as well as being of interest in their own right. Should archivists and records managers take note of this?

It seems to me that the answer to this question should be 'yes'. In this essay, I have made clear that the emphasis of socio-legal studies is on empirical issues. In fact, though, the interdisciplinary nature of socio-legal research generates demands for complex combinations of data. This complexity and the contemporary focus of much socio-legal research would seem to render large quantities of archival material useless to answering these empirical questions. I have tried to suggest, however, that this is not so; from a reading of some of the ethnographic research performed by the Centre for Socio-Legal Studies, it is clear that unpublished data provide valuable (and often crucial) foundational material upon which subsequent research is based. This is particularly so of work which examines the role of a particular organisation in, for example, the implementation of, and compliance with, a given legal rule. However, it is also clear that the unpublished data to which I refer carry a much broader definition than simply traditional archive collections. I am also talking of records held by authorities and private firms (like solicitors). None of this should diminish the fact that traditional archive material is still invaluable to socio-legal studies, particularly those involving the social historian's perspective. However, the earlier discussion of these materials has demonstrated that even here, socio-legal studies necessarily require that the definition of what records are relevant for 'legal research' is a broad one. This is because they adopt a broad view of how the law should be assessed.

What should the archivist or records manager take away from this essay? The point of the paper has been very much one of 'consciousness raising'. A recognition and awareness, therefore, that a broader perspective on legal issues exists, is valuable and has its own empirical needs would certainly be a good start. From here, a number of questions seem to

97 For an account of some of the work performed on this data set, see Lloyd-Bostock (1988).

be raised: what is a legal record (an 'old chestnut')? If socio-legal studies rely so heavily on participant observation, will video-recorded data adopt a higher profile (e.g. court cases)? If so, how might they be kept? Similar issues arise with tape-recorded material (police interviews). Should archivists be familiarizing themselves with the data sets being created by institutions such as the Centre for Socio-Legal Studies (so that, at least, they might help direct other researchers to them)? Should firms in possession of unpublished data (case files) ever be willing to relax their access restrictions in return for anonymity/confidentiality (as the Centre always provides)? How might archivists in organisations and firms be made more aware of the research potential of their records? Indeed, if there are important decisions to be made with regard to records collection in organisations, it seems that they should first ensure that they have archivists in place to take these (this is clearly not always the case, as in the BMA example above). I certainly do not have answers to these (and many other similar) questions. However, it seems to me that they are the kinds of question necessarily raised by an acceptance of the need to address the types of question addressed by socio-legal studies. If the essay stimulates such thoughts, it will have succeeded.

## Bibliography


Bartrip, P.W.J. (1982), 'British Government Inspection, 1832–1873: Some Observations', *The Historical Journal*, vol. 23.

— (1985), 'Beveridge, Workmen's Compensation and the Alternative Remedy', *Journal of Social Policy*, vol. 14.

— (1987), *Workmen's Compensation in the Twentieth Century*, Gower Publishing Group, Aldershot

— (1992), '"A Pennurth of Arsenic for Rat Poison": The Arsenic Act 1851 and the Prevention of Secret Poisoning', *Medical History*, vol. 36.

Bartrip, P.W.J. & Burman, S.B. (1983), *The Wounded Soldiers of Industry: Industrial Compensation Policy, 1833–1897*, OUP, Oxford.

Dingwall, R., ed. (1989), *Socio-Legal Aspects of Medical Malpractice*, Royal College of Physicians of London, London.

Dingwall, R., Fenn. P. & Bernhart, M.H., eds. (1993), *Quality and Regulation in Health Care: International Experiences*, Routledge. London.

Eekelaar, J.M. (1991). *Regulating Divorce*, OUP, Oxford.

Eekelaar, J.M. & Maclean, M. (1986), *Maintenance After Divorce*, OUP, Oxford.

Eekelaar, J.M. & Pearl, D., eds. (1989), *An Ageing World: Dilemmas and Challenges for Law and Social Policy*, OUP, Oxford.

Fenn, P.T. & Vlachonikolis, I.G. (1990). 'Bargaining Behaviour by Defendant Insurers: An Economic Model', *Geneva Papers on Risk and Insurance*. vol. 54.

Fenn, P.T., McGuire, A. & Prentice. D. (1990), 'Information Asymmetry and the Securities Market', in Hopt, K. & Wymeersch, E. eds., *European Insider Law*, Butterworths. London.

Genn, H. (1987), *Hard Bargaining: Out-of-Court Settlement in Personal Injury Actions*, OUP, Oxford.

Gessner, V. & Thomas, J.M. (1988). 'Special Issue: Socio-Legal Research and Policy Studies', *Law and Policy*, vol.10

Gray, A. & Fenn, P.T. (1991). 'The Rising Cost of Legally Aided Criminal Cases', *New Law Journal*, vol. 141.

Greatbatch, D. & Dingwall, R. (1989), 'Selective Facilitation: Some Preliminary Observations on a Strategy Used by Divorce Mediators', *Law and Society Review*. vol. 23.

Harris, D.R. (1983), 'The Development of Socio-Legal Studies in the United Kingdom', *Legal Studies*. vol. 3.

— (1989), 'An Introduction to Socio-Legal Studies', in Dingwall, ed. (1989).

Harris, D.R. et al. (1984), *Compensation and Support for Illness and Injury*, OUP, Oxford.

Harris, D.R. & Tallon, D., eds. (1989), *Contract Law Today: Anglo-French Comparisons*, OUP, Oxford.

Hawkins, K. (1984), *Environment and Enforcement: Regulation and the Social Definition of Pollution*, OUP, Oxford.

— (1989), 'Rule and Discretion in Comparative Perspective: The Case of Social Regulation', *Ohio State Law Journal*, vol. 50.

Hawkins, K. & Harris, D.R. (1988), 'Policy Research and Funding: Socio-Legal Studies in a Changed Political Climate' in Gessner & Thomas (1988).

Hay, D. (1987), 'Archival Records in the History of the Law: A User's Perspective', *Archivaria*, vol. 24.

Hensler, D.R. et al. (1991), *Compensation/or Accidental Injuries in the United States*, Rand Publication: R-3999–HHS/ICJ, California, USA.

Hepple, B.A. & Matthews, M.H. (1985), *Tort: Cases and Materials*, 3rd ed., Butterworths, London.

Hoggett, B. & Pearl. D. (1991), *The Family, Law and Society: Cases and Materials*, 3rd ed., Butterworths, London.

Hutter, B.M. (1988), *The Reasonable Arm of the Law? The Law Enforcement Procedures of Environmental Health Officers*, OUP, Oxford.

Lloyd-Bostock. S. (1988), *Legalism and Discretion*, Centre for Socio-Legal Studies, Oxford.

Maclean, M. (1991), *Surviving Divorce: Women's Resources After Separation*, Macmillan. London.

Maclean, M. & Genn, H. (1979), *Methodological Issues in Social Surveys*. Macmillan. London.

McBarnet, D. (1991), 'Whiter Than White Collar Crime: Tax, Fraud Insurance and the Management of Stigma', *British Journal of Sociology*, vol. 42.

— (1992), 'Legitimate Rackets: Corporate Tax Evasion and Avoidance', *Journal of Human Justice*, vol. 3.

Wheeler, S. (1991), *Retention of Title Clauses: Impact and Implications*, OUP, Oxford.

Whelan, C.J., ed. (1990), *Small Claims Courts: A Comparative Study*, OUP, Oxford.

# Stakeholder group seminars

AlexLMX/Shutterstock.com

During the course of the project, the LRAR Director gave a number of presentations at seminars held by stakeholder groups (archives and records management membership/pressure groups, research groups and legal bodies) as follows:[98]

- 3 November 2015 Presentation to AIM25 (Archives in London and the M25 area) Group: 'The Legal Records at Risk project'.
- 30 November 2015 Presentation to the London Archives Partnership: 'The Legal Records at Risk project'.
- 10 February 2016 Presentation to The National Archives Collections Rescue Strategy Workshop: 'Legal Records at Risk'.
- 25 February 2016 Presentation to the Centre for Archives and Records Research (ICARUS) – UCL: 'Legal Records at Risk'.
- 19 April 2016 Presentation to the Archives and Society Group – UCL: 'Legal Records at Risk'.
- 1 December 2016: Iron Mountain Legal Forum for law firms. Participation in a discussion on LRAR in general and TfL's Corporate Archives in particular.
- 2 March 2017 Presentation to the Legal Regulators' Research Forum: 'Rescuing Regulators' records – how and why'.
- 23 March 2017 Joint presentation with the BRA to the IRMS Property group: 'Legal Records at Risk'.
- 20 October 2017 Presentation to UCL Archives and Records Management students: 'Collections at risk: legal records'.
- 21 May 2018 Presentation to the Information and Records Management Society annual conference: 'Who cares? Legal records and poor records management'.

Two articles have been compiled by the author using the original seminar presentations to give a flavour of issues raised which were particular to the three main categories of stakeholder: archival/research and legal. They are reproduced below.

## 1. Legal records at risk: issues for the archival and research sectors

The LRAR project seeks solutions to the lack of diversity of legal records available for research. Currently large numbers of court records and central/local government legal records are available and accessible in TNA and local authority record offices but there are far fewer private sector legal records readily available (other than deeds and wills), leading to an unbalanced view of the history and development of the UK's legal framework and its impact on social and cultural change.

LRAR has concentrated on 20th- and 21st-century legal records, since these are especially at risk due to:

- Reduced collecting and management resources on the part of archive repositories – or no repositories at all.
- Unsustainability of traditional arrangements to save legal records.

98 For the original presentations see http://ials.sas.ac.uk/research/areas-research/legal-records-risk-lrar-project/lrar-seminars

- Digital records accessibility and obsolescence.
- Distinct lack of interest on the part of institutions specialised to law.

Sustainability: local authority archives can no longer afford to take in and manage badly arranged and physically damaged collections of records, particularly from law firms.[99] Similarly, the BRA can no longer afford to act as a free warehouse facility for the unwanted records of law firms pending transfer to a repository. All archives, additionally, face spending cuts and a narrowing of their collections policies, meaning that most can no longer proactively collect private sector records.

Accessibility and digital obsolescence: all institutions face the issue of digital obsolescence and all archives face the prospect of a digital black hole in their collections. Without proactive records management of born-digital records from the point of creation to disposal there will, in the future, be few records for archives to collect.

Lack of interest: the legal sector appears to be unusual among business organisations in the UK in that many of its constituents see no benefit – commercial, reputational or in terms of community engagement – in preserving its records for posterity. There are, for example, very few dedicated legal archives, no major London law firm (as far as we know) maintains an in-house archive available to the public and the records of barristers' chambers, most alternative dispute resolution bodies, legal executives, patent agents, trade mark attorneys and will writers remain a mystery. The majority of legal institutions contacted by LRAR appeared to be uninterested in preserving their records for posterity. In contrast most of the major UK banks, many commercial enterprises and membership organisations have set up in-house archives, viewing them as a business benefit.[100]

Limited research use: historians still seem wedded to traditional 'legal' research and are often unaware of what is already available. The impression received from seminars, meetings and email exchanges with academic researchers, primarily in the legal field, was that they were not always aware of just what legal records are available in archives or how to search for them.[101] Two seminars held at the CSLS tended to confirm this impression, with students conducting empirical studies using interviews and current data (such as case files, media releases, public domain reports, position papers, submissions) as their preferred research methodology. The findings from the seminars were that students to date have encountered no issues around accessing relevant material, but they may not be fully aware of the existence of much accessible – and relatively modern – information already available in archives.

Anecdotal evidence from archivists suggests that the primary use of legal records such as deeds, wills, examination and membership records is genealogical, but LRAR considers that legal records – in particular the business records of legal institutions – could be of immense value for any and all categories of research as well as legal – social, gender, race, diversity, geographical, local etc.[102]

## *What is being done about all this?*

LRAR will not collect records but will act as a conduit through which legal records of value (in all formats and media) are identified, preserved and made available for research, by:

- Liaising with potential repositories about legal records of research value.
- Facilitating the process by which information owners reach agreement to deposit with or donate records to those repositories.
- Providing generic advice and guidance on recordkeeping to information owners.
- Disseminating guidance on the location and content of legal records of value to research communities.

How will it achieve its objectives?

- By publishing case studies of best – or worst – practice.
- By lobbying legal information owners about their information management responsibilities and the demonstrating benefits of good recordkeeping.
- By working with research communities to identify their needs plus gaps in provision.

99 Nor should they, incidentally – this is a dereliction of responsibility on the part of the depositing organisations. We suggest that archives charge private sector organisations for management services such as repair, listing and cataloguing.

100 The Bank of England, Barclays Bank, Lloyds Bank, Rothschild, Santander Group, BBC, BP, British Telecom, British Airways, Diageo, Glaxo Smith Klein, The Guardian, Harrods, ITV, Marks and Spencers, Nestle, Network Rail, Pfizer, Prudential Group, Rolls Royce, Sainsbury, Transport for London and Unilever, to name just a few. The Royal Medical Colleges also have in-house archives.

101 'I doubt whether any textbook writers ever heard of any of these e-cases', quoted by a senior law lecturer and arbitrator in an email response on 9 May 2016 to the author's forwarding from TNA's *Discovery* a list of 20th-century arbitration cases and related legal records available in archives.

102 Legal records will, of course, provide evidence of the diversity (or lack of same) of the profession and of changes in practitioner and organisational attitudes to race, gender, class etc.

- By working with the archives community to seek practical solutions to resourcing issues e.g. a charging model for depositors, standardised forms.

In particular LRAR, along with the BRA and other stakeholders, is working as part of the Records at Risk group to identify, and find solutions to, the issues around rescuing private sector records, including legal. Drawing on the expertise of legal practitioners and charities whose remit is to rescue records,[103] LRAR is also undertaking a study on the feasibility of creating a Legal Archives Trust to rescue legal records.

We are also asking the archive and records management sectors to work with us on an advocacy programme to proactively lobby the private sector to manage its records in a cost-effective way, to employ professional archivists and records managers and to safeguard records of value by depositing them in archives or setting up in-house archives.

## 2. Legal records at risk: issues for the legal sector

From the horse's mouth (with apologies to the Legal Standards Board)

> 'For many people, an initial barrier [to engagement with legal professionals] is lack of awareness and understanding of lawyers and the law…understanding is further clouded by the amount of legal jargon…Greater visibility and understanding of the role of the legal services regulatory and complaints bodies will provide reassurance and ultimately lead to greater trust.'[104]

Not only would more transparency through making historic records available to researchers lead to greater trust but doing so would underwrite the legal sector's broader contribution to history. The legal sector is often unaware of the importance of its heritage, the benefits of good recordkeeping and the legacy value of its archives within the community. Appraising the potential research value of records is rarely a top priority when running a business, yet good business records management can bring benefits in reduction of costs and improved service provision to clients. Records establish a corporate memory which can be mined to tackle current or recurring business problems; determining and saving what is of archival value is the end result of this process.

Lack of awareness in the legal sector of the value of archives and their management leads to their under-utilisation by legal institutions as a marketing and client relations tool and in wider corporate social responsibility projects. Records that could be used to provide legal protection or safeguard intellectual property rights and trademarks are not identified and preserved. Business records are particularly vulnerable at periods of change, such as mergers, acquisition and buy-outs, when historically important records can be either unwittingly or purposely destroyed. Misinterpretation of the Data Protection Act, the GDPR and other information legislation can also result in premature destruction of records.

The primary goal of the LRAR project is to change the culture surrounding the perception of what legal records actually are, to facilitate their use in academic research, and to enhance the relationship between legal practitioners, researchers and archivists. This work is being undertaken in collaboration with the BRA, TNA and others. Our first priority will be to identify and save private sector records at risk by devising a co-ordinated strategy for the identification and preservation of private sector records of value, including legal records. This strategic work will be supported by practical advice and guidance to the legal sector on how to lessen the cost and improve the efficiency of information management practices, both to remove the burden of managing archival records and to reduce ongoing management and storage costs for both paper and digital records.

The project will not collect records but will act as a conduit through which legal records of value in all formats and media are identified, preserved and made available for research. It is conducting a census of private sector legal institutions in England and Wales, with details of what, if any, provision has been made to preserve their archives. It has commissioned a number of case studies[105] to demonstrate best practice and models for the legal sector to follow.

### *What particular issues apply to legal records?*

What are legal institutions doing about their records? Most seem to use external storage indefinitely. Many seem to have little idea of just what's in storage, leading to unnecessary costs due to not having destruction programmes for

103 Notably the Pensions Archive Trust http://www.pensionsarchive.org.uk.

104 LSB, *Lowering barriers to accessing services report* 13 March 2016: http://www.legalservicesboard.org.uk/news_publications/publications/pdf/2016/20160331_Lowering_Barriers_Final_Report.pdf.

105 They include: a study of dispute resolution records held in the Transport for London Corporate Archives , which has demonstrated the scope and content of legal records within business archives and the business context within which they sit; a case study of the records of a prominent legal publisher which showed the breadth of records potentially available for research; and case studies of Chadwick Lawrence, a solicitor's firm outside London with a professional archivist and the records of the Council for Licensed Conveyancers, both of which have provided examples of how instituting best practice in managing information reduces costs, improves efficiency and assists in preserving our legal heritage.. All published case studies are available on our website: http://ials.sas.ac.uk/research/areas-research/legal-records-risk-lrar-project/lrar-case-studies.

redundant records and no concept of potential historical value. There is a huge emphasis on reputation and client confidentiality, but a lack of consciousness in the information owners that their archives are an asset to be valued.

While TNA, local authority record offices, HE and specialist repositories work tirelessly, despite ever-reducing resources, to preserve our heritage and some private sector bodies understand the value to themselves and the wider community of preserving key records and destroying redundant material, the legal sector (with some notable exceptions[106]) simply does not seem to be aware of – or is indifferent to – the risk of losing records documenting the changes to legal services over the past two centuries.

Cost can be a major factor behind any legal institution, large or small, deciding not to create and maintain an in-house archives. Yet this does not explain why legal institutions may be reluctant to deposit records in an archive repository such as a local authority record office which generally does not charge for its services, though it may seek a donation or fee towards ongoing expenses such as conservation or cataloguing and ask the organisation to pay for the cost of transporting material to the archives. These expenses are negligible compared to the year-on-year costs of storing information in third-party records stores pending eventual destruction, yet many legal organisations seem unaware of this service and choose instead to pay for indefinite storage of their records.

Confidentiality and access: there appears to be a basic misapprehension that records deposited in an archives are somehow open to all. Established archives, on the contrary, have well developed techniques for dealing with 'sensitive' records, including closure periods and conditions on access and use; they operate under strict confidentiality guidelines and follow TNA's advice on access to personal data.[107] Any institution or individual depositing records with an archives can also ask that more stringent confidentiality requirements are applied where appropriate.

Another concern is reputational damage, as past records might reveal former mistakes or contain statements or notes which seem politically incorrect by today's standards. But denying access to archives does not stop stories and rumour; access to the archives can help draw a line under a distasteful aspect of the company history. A statement by The Barclays Group Archivist sums this up perfectly:

> Decisions made 40 years ago which seemed right at the time turned out to be the wrong choice with the benefit of hindsight. And sometimes, as we all now know, people have been downright dishonest…But if we deny access to the archives, we deny access to the other side of the story too. And there is always the danger that by not letting people in, they will automatically assume the worst. The stories will always be there, regardless of whether we allow people in to the Bank's archives or not. At least by allowing access we are demonstrating our transparency, our desire to share our history we are enabling people to seek out the facts and draw their own conclusions. While the archive is used only internally, there is always the risk that we will be charged with using it for propaganda, for only sharing the good bits. If we truly want to be good corporate citizens, we have to share our archives. They need to be seen as a reliable and objective resource.[108]

Institutions, including legal institutions, must be encouraged to see their archives as business assets rather than liabilities. Most companies recognise that they need to be good corporate citizens and be transparent. Part of that is allowing access to their archives and the history of their business, even if it does mean revealing links to practices which are now disapproved of.[109]

We understand that legal practitioners are busy people and that appraising the potential value of records is rarely a top priority when running a business. Yet managing one's business records efficiently to reduce costs, provide a good service to clients and reduce the need to constantly reinvent the wheel is, or should be, a high priority. Determining and saving what is of archival value, while getting rid of the dross, is simply the end of that process.

### *Are the records of the legal sector more at risk than those of other private sector bodies?*

Certainly those of law firms are. The Law Society, working with the Selden Society, has for many years encouraged solicitors to seek options for the preservation of their firms' historically significant legal documents. TLS until recently published a practice note *Depositing records and documents with public sector archives* (15 December 2010) which gave advice on depositing old client documents or records documenting a firm's history with the appropriate local authority record office. Many record offices, however, are now operating on severely reduced resources, compromising their

106 Such as the Archives of the Inns of Court, the Law Society, the Institute and Faculty of Advocates and the Records of Legal Education Archives at IALS. Not to be confused with the almost universal practice of depositing non-current records en masse in a warehouse for indefinite storage!

107 TNA Code of practice for archivists and records managers under Section 51(4) of the Data Protection Act, 2007.

108 Maria Sienkiewicz (Group Archivist, Barclays Group Archives): 'Take the 109 bus and bring a packed lunch': Confidentiality, reputation and logistics – the challenges and opportunities of opening up business archives. Presentation at the BAC conference 2014.

109 BAC Access Guidance Note: 'Let the right one in? Challenging perceptions of access to business archives' 2015.

ability to accept private sector records. Solicitors' records of value are, therefore, more at risk now than in the past.[110] To these records at risk we must add the millions of records of defunct law firms in the Intervention Archives, managed by Capita on behalf of the Solicitors Regulation Authority (SRA). The SRA is currently making valiant efforts to locate relevant archive repositories willing to accept some of these records.

Legal records may also be at risk through auctioning to the highest bidder. TNA monitors the auctioning of documents with a UK provenance, both here and abroad and has maintained a database since the 1990s. TNA keeps an eye on all auctions and notifies the relevant record office when something comes up in which it might be interested. The record office will then bid, but only if it has sufficient funds or time to apply for a grant before the auction. TNA also advises the Department for Business, Innovation & Skills where an item is being sold overseas which by law can't leave the country without an export licence.[111]

Some transactions are perfectly legitimate, for example the sale of personal correspondence of someone who happens to be identified by their job title; some are of solicitors' business papers which are not legally protected, though it is highly likely that a record office would accept them if offered; and some transactions recorded on TNA's database certainly show dispersal of client papers, contrary to TLS's own advice.[112]

The closing down or merger of a law firm with another firm also adds to the risks to records. The Legal Ombudsman has summarised this issue succinctly as follows:

> We investigated a number of cases where firms had either closed down or merged, so customers were unable to access files kept in storage. This highlights the need for firms to ensure that documents in storage are managed correctly, and to put in place clear audited systems to ensure documents can be retrieved when firms close down or merge.[113]

## *What is LRAR actually doing about all this?*

We have developed generic guidance for legal bodies wishing to deposit records with archives which will also assist them in reducing the costs of managing their current information, particularly in digital format. The guidance includes generic retention schedules which provide transparency about different record sets and allow a debate around the future of these records. We are also asking TLS to allow an update of its current guidance on disposal of solicitors' records to be published.

In particular LRAR, along with the BRA and other stakeholders, is working as part of the Records at Risk group to identify, and find solutions to, the issues around rescuing private sector records, including legal. Drawing on the expertise of legal practitioners and charities whose remit is to rescue records,[114] LRAR is also undertaking a study on the feasibility of creating a Legal Archives Trust to rescue legal records.

## *What's in it for the legal sector?*

- Cost savings: archives don't charge for preserving your records of value.
- Great PR: demonstrating how you have protected the rights of the public – and of the legal profession – and are continuing to do so.
- Transparency: helping to get rid of the perceived culture of secrecy around the workings of the legal profession.
- The broader contribution to history.
- Documenting the development of an important service industry.
- Documenting the development of the legal profession.
- Records relevant to significant legal, political and social changes.
- Contributions to social, legal, economic and family history.

A plan for the future: for legal records, there needs to be:

110 This is a resource issue; in the past law firms have, quite frankly, exploited the willingness of the BRA and local record offices to rescue records free of charge; however it is no longer appropriate in the current economic climate to expect the taxpayer to cover the cost of solicitors' unwillingness to take some responsibility for their own historic records.

111 Auction information gathered during a meeting with personnel from TNA's Manuscript Sales Monitoring Service, 17 Nov 2015. Any document which is not the property of the exporter and is over 50 years old must have an export licence.

112 TLS's Practice Note *Depositing records and documents with public sector archives* S.3.1 Client documents specifies that 'Documents such as wills, deeds, property transactions and agreements do not belong to the firm as they remain the property of the client for whom they were drawn up or his successor in title. These documents should not be sold or destroyed.' The practice note is no longer on TLS's website.

113 Legal Ombudsman, Learning from complaints: case study publication, March 2016.

114 Notably the Pensions Archive Trust http://www.pensionsarchive.org.uk.

- A responsible approach agreed between the legal sector, records managers and archivists which acknowledges complexities and challenges.
- Greater clarity from the regulators on confidentiality, how long it lasts and management of risk.
- Agreed client consent processes which are transparent about destruction and/or archival deposit.
- Standardised deposit processes for records in archives and clarification about access to archives.

# Appendix X: Case studies and sub-projects

## Generic case study proposal by LRAR to legal institutions[1]

### The *Legal Records at Risk* project: case studies

The project is concerned with identifying records of archival value in the private sector created by institutions specialised to law (ISLs). Saving significant collections, stimulating changes of practice, avoiding duplication, and raising awareness of the value of legal records at risk are prioritised. We will not collect records but will be a conduit through which legal records of value (in all formats and media) are identified, preserved and made available for research.

Undertaking case studies of selected ISLs will form a key platform of the project. Case studies will demonstrate areas of best practice and community of practice, identify key issues common to all or most ISLs and suggest potential solutions, including liaison with archive repositories relating to the deposit of records of permanent value.

Methodology: each case study will differ, but the methodology is essentially as follows:

1. Initial contact with key persons in selected ISLs.
2. Management agreement to collaborate in the project (i.e. to allocate the time of key personnel – there will be no other costs to the ISLs).
3. A survey of the records (both paper and digital) created and managed by the ISL.
4. Creation of a records retention and disposal schedule for the ISL.
5. Identification of records of permanent research value and interested repositories.
6. A report to the ISL on findings and, if relevant, recommendations for more cost-effective recordkeeping practices. The report will be published with permission of the ISL, anonymised if required.

There are numerous benefits for ISLs to participating in case studies:

- A survey of records and recordkeeping practices by a qualified archivist and records manager.
- Production of a retention and disposal schedule for immediate use, adaptable for future needs. This will identify existing records and recommend how long each category needs to be kept, with those of archival value highlighted for permanent preservation. Electronic records will also be surveyed and included.
- Advice on recordkeeping, which assists efficient business practice and compliance.
- Reduced need for storage space as records are systematically disposed of.
- Identification of a possible repository for records of permanent value *or* advice on how to manage one in-house so as to unlock the research potential of the ISL's records.
- Identification of ISLs with similar practices and issues, developing a community of practice.
- An enhanced reputation for openness and transparency plus a better understanding of importance of the ISL in the development of the United Kingdom's legal framework.

1 A total of ten legal institutions were specifically approached by LRAR for permission to undertake a case study of all or some of their records; five agreed. four are reproduced below; one has not given permission to publish at the time of writing.

# Case study 1: Records and recordkeeping in a legal publishing house

Compiled by Lindsay McCormack, Pilot Project Archivist

Completed November 2015

alejandro dans neergaard/Shutterstock.com

## *Introduction*

The Legal Records at Risk project at the Institute of Advanced Legal Studies, University of London sets out to identify a broad range of records relating to institutions specialised to law (ISLs) which are at risk, particularly in relation to gaps in provision for their long-term preservation. This pilot project set out to survey the paper and born-digital records of a legal publishing house based in the south-east of England. It sought to identify records of archival value and to make recommendations about their permanent retention. It aimed to create a bespoke records retention and disposal schedule including current, semi-current, hard copy and electronic records, based on legal retention periods and current best practice.

## *Methodology*

Two initial meetings took place between the founder and current Managing Director of the organisation, the project archivist and Professor William Twining, Emeritus Professor of Jurisprudence at UCL, to understand the development of the publishers and their current business situation. The project archivist then undertook a survey of the current, semi-current and historic records in paper form, along with a sample of electronic records on the business's shared drives and databases. The survey findings were recorded in a retention schedule (see **Annex I** below), along with a specific retention period for each series of records. The retention guidance was based on current legislation, best practice in other similar organisations, and/or current administration use in the business.

The retention schedule was sent to the MD of the organisation in advance of a meeting to discuss the findings. The retention schedule was presented along with guidance on managing electronic records on shared or network drives and email, which was tailored for their business needs with space for further customization by including job titles for delegating specific responsibilities in managing records (see **Annex II** below). Though a local repository for transfer of the company's historic records had been identified, this was not desired by the business at present. Categories of records for historic and legal permanent preservation were discussed and advice on preserving records was given. The MD is to enquire about records designated for permanent preservation at the end of the records cycle in the commercial records store and the possibility of their transfer to a local archive service at that point.

## *Time spent*

This case study took 10 working days, broken down as follows:

- Proposal: 0.5 day
- Records survey: 2 days
- Preparation of retention schedule: 2.5 days
- Drafting *Essential Electronic Records* guide: 2 days
- Interview and meeting with business staff: 1 day
- Correspondence and meetings with project staff: 2 days

## Outcomes

In total, approximately 17.5 linear meters of paper records were surveyed in addition to a sample of 2.35 terabytes of electronic records.

The survey methodology and the retention schedule template were tested and amended during the process. Guidelines for the good management of records on shared drives and email were drafted and delivered to the publishers. The organisation felt that the survey and recommendations were useful and the positive will built up should result in an improvement of recordkeeping practices, especially around electronic records. There is an increased understanding in the organisation of the historic importance of its early and accruing record series. An office move will prompt a transfer of some of the semi-current records to external storage, but there is an awareness of the eventual aim to transfer the historic records to an appropriate local archive repository which has already been identified.

This ISL proved a useful case study as it is a small publishing house with a short history, yet significant within the industry and thus of research interest. In terms of recordkeeping, the firm benefits from a stable administration since its foundation and a catalogue of interesting titles and authors. This enabled the project archivist to carry out a full survey of its paper records in a reasonably short time, with a further sampling of digital records. Having an in-depth overview of the administrative history following the interview with the business's founder plus full access to the records and project support for the project by the current MD, were essential. These factors (administrative context, high-level support, open access) were important to the success of the case study as they allowed the project archivist to rapidly identify key record series. Understanding the business helped target the retention schedule and e-records guidance to its current business situation. An appropriate local archive repository was identified from the outset should the business wish to transfer its historic records there in the future.

••••••••••••••••••••••

## Annex I: Law publisher (anonymised): retention schedule

### Paper records:

| Business function | Record type | Retention sentence | Guiding legislation / practice |
|---|---|---|---|
| Editorial | Author's files: including Publishing Agreements (contract), product profiles including cost of sales and book proposal, correspondence | Permanent: core business records | Good practice |
| Production | Published works | Permanent: core business records | Good practice |
| Production/Finance | Service Level Agreements with external companies | Appraise for historical value. If not selected, destroy last date + 6 years | |
| Editorial | Proof correction marks, publishing style guidelines | Permanent: historical and evidential value | |
| Editorial/Marketing | Book reviews | Retain during administrative use then appraise | |
| Editorial/Marketing / Customer Services | Subject files: including Agents, Bookshops, E-books, Advertising, Mailing List Rental, Subject Mailings, Agents' Commission, Catalogue files with mailing list contacts; catalogues; flyers, London Book Fair; Marketing Strategy; Printers; Scrapbooks; news clippings | Appraise: weed + retain majority | |
| Finance | Credit notes | Destroy end of financial year + 6 years | Financial Services Act 1986, Limitation Act 1980 |
| Customer Services | Order forms in numbered series | Destroy end of financial year + 6 years | Financial Services Act 1986, Limitation Act 1980 |

| Business function | Record type | Retention sentence | Guiding legislation / practice |
|---|---|---|---|
| Editorial | Journal files incl correspondence, agreements, sales figures, editorial meeting papers, marketing strategies | Retain Journal files | |
| Finance | Budget reports on sales, marketing, and yearly financial summary information | Permanent: core business record – top level financial information | |
| Finance | Payment transaction reports | Destroy end of financial year + 6 years | Financial Services Act 1986, Limitation Act 1980 |
| Finance | Invoices and credit notes | Destroy end of financial year + 6 years | Financial Services Act 1986, Limitation Act 1980 |
| Finance | E-books: invoices & royalty reports | Destroy end of financial year + 6 years | Financial Services Act 1986, Limitation Act 1980 |
| Finance | Agents' journal reports | Destroy end of administrative use + 3 years | |
| Finance | Paying-in slips | Destroy end of financial year + 6 years | |
| Finance | Bank statements | Destroy end of financial year + 6 years if this information is kept at a higher level, ie annual accounts | |
| Finance | Credit cards: account statements and payment receipts | Destroy end of financial year + 6 years | |
| Finance | Bank statements | Destroy end of financial year + 6 years if this information is kept at a higher level, i.e. in annual accounts | |
| Finance | Batch remittance advices | Destroy end of financial year + 6 years | Financial Services Act 1986, Limitation Act 1980 |
| Finance | Author reprint royalties: aggregate report printouts | Destroy end of financial year + 6 years | Financial Services Act 1986, Limitation Act 1980 |
| Finance | VAT manual returns | Preserve sales list reports if not kept elsewhere. Weed + destroy VAT material end of financial year + 6 years | Value Added Tax Act 1994 |
| Finance | Tax & NI [National Insurance]: New starter applications, corporation tax return copies. | Destroy applications and other information subject to data protectionlegislation | Data Protection Act 1998 |
| Finance | Purchase ledger (P/L) invoices | Destroy end of financial year+ 6 years | Financial Services Act 1986, Limitation Act 1980 |
| Finance | Budget reports on sales, marketing, and yearly financial summary information. | Permanent | |
| Finance | Expenses: business credit card statements | Destroy end of financial year + 6 years | Financial Services Act 1986, Limitation Act 1980 |
| Finance | Printed/Published year end Financial Statements | Preserve 1–2 copies each year | |

## 2. E-records

| Business function | Record type | Format | Location | Retention sentence | Guiding legislation / practice/ notes |
|---|---|---|---|---|---|
| Editorial/ Production/ Marketing/ Customer Services/Finance | Database including functions for customers, sales enquiry profiles, orders, orders enquiries, supplier register, journal [financial], stock, marketing, returns, production and rights | Specialist publishing software database | Server via desktop icon | Permanent | |
| Editorial/ Production/ Marketing/ Customer Services/Finance | Network shared drive of more current work. Includes titles submitted for prizes 2006–2010, speeches and articles 2003–2015, student prizes, sales conference, car and expenses information, premises information including 'scrapbook' photographs, staff and administrative folders including logos, scholarship images; exhibition images | Word; PDF; JPEG | Shared network drive | Permanent | |
| Editorial | Files and folders pertaining to Journal publications, containing manuscripts; journal tables of contents, abstracts and articles; copyright license agreements | Word, PDF, WinZip, | Shared network drive | Appraise with view to retaining most, weed | |
| Editorial/ Production | Files containing images of journal covers | JPEGs | Shared network drive | Duplicated elsewhere? Preserve if not retained elsewhere | |
| Marketing/ Customer Services | 1 folder and files on book sales for 2013–14, authors and other contact details. | Excel, 1 Access | Shared network drive | Preserve if not duplicated elsewhere | Some is subject to financial sentencing, some contains personal data |
| Non-business function – computer programme files | Adobe: system files | PDF, PFB, OpenType font, LST file, True Type 1 Font file, XML, Application extension, HTML document | Shared network drive | Current + 3 years | |
| Editorial/ Production / Marketing | Agents Reports: Agency agreements, summary of terms, distributors lists, comparison reports [sales reports], instructions on how to create reports in specialist software | Word, PowerPoint, Excel | Shared network drive | Appraise with view to retaining most, weed | |
| Editorial/ Production / Marketing/ Finance | Contributor copies, license agreements for particular individuals, invoices 2015, Autonomy of Labour Law page images, templates for e-book PDF download. | Word, PDF, Excel | Shared network drive | Current + 5 year, then appraise. Weed duplicates. Destroy invoices end of financial year + 6 years. Preserve license agreements if not duplicated elsewhere | |

| Business function | Record type | Format | Location | Retention sentence | Guiding legislation / practice/ notes |
|---|---|---|---|---|---|
| Production/ Marketing | Amazon Image Upload: cover images | WinZipped JPEGs | Shared network drive | Preserve if not duplicated elsewhere | |
| Financial | Amazon Invoicing: excel spreadsheets of titles and costs | Excel | Shared network drive | Sample for preservation if not duplicated elsewhere | |
| Production | Production schedule 20 Jul [2015], new acquisition form (book title), professional division price table, Biblio workflow 2014 | Word, Excel | Shared network drive | Preserve if not duplicated elsewhere | |
| Financial | Audit of Completion Accounts: bank statements, reports on: stock, purchases, journals, cashbook, cost of books published, returns, distributors, dividends, directors loan, by ISBN publication period et al. | Word, Excel | Shared network drive | Preserve if not duplicated elsewhere | |
| Marketing | Author Questionnaires: folders 2003–16 containing questionnaires by author completed to help market book based on readership, contacts, ideas and resources | Word, Att file, text document | Shared network drive | Permanent | |
| Marketing/ Finance | Batch: folders incl music files, templates, letters, journal subscribers lists; E-books including publisher's metadata 2010, E-books v. book costs, flyer, sample agreements, discounts; Global list of bookshops selling publisher's titles 2009 | PDF, JPEG, Word, Excel, PS file, P65, WinZip files | Shared network drive | Appraise with view to retaining most, weed low-level admin files and music | |
| Finance | Sales reports by country, stock transition reports, cost calculator; Chinese business law contents | Excel | Shared network drive | Preserve if not duplicated elsewhere. Likely to be duplicated | |
| Editorial/ Production / Marketing | Files by author showing tables of contents | PDF, Word | Shared network drive | Preserve if not duplicated elsewhere | |
| Editorial/ Production | Biblio: reports from software by ISBN, title, author, anthology, type of publication, binding, edition data, imprint and other publication data; contracts for territorial rights | Word, Exc, WinZip files | Shared network drive | Appraise. Preserve if not duplicated elsewhere | |
| Production/ Marketing/ Customer Services/ Finance | Biblio instructions: guidance on using software | Word, Outlook, PDF | Shared network drive | Destroy current + 3 years | |
| Production/ Marketing / Customer Services/ Finance | Bill: administrative files on sales, expenses, Biblio software reports, author care, author materials, cover concepts, journal contracts, manuscripts, presentations, production schedules et al. | Word, Excel, JPEG | Shared network drive | Preserve if not dublicated elsewhere | |

| Business function | Record type | Format | Location | Retention sentence | Guiding legislation / practice/ notes |
|---|---|---|---|---|---|
| Marketing | Book Citation Index: Collections incl 2014/15 publication list | PDF | Shared network drive | Preserve Collections catalogue if not preserved elsewhere. Destroy Book Citation Index Current + 3 years | |
| Marketing | Book Examples: one manuscript exemplar for categories Edited Collection, monograph 1–2, Practitioner 1–3, textbook and Unusual 1–2. | PDF | Shared network drive | Preserve if not duplicated elsewhere. Likely duplication | |
| Marketing/ Finance | Book Info: folders on Book History, book list templates, marketing Schedules, Nielsen data check, Price changes, short excel sheets, weekly book information. Files on BIC codes and dimensions, book blurbs & info, (software) data, series information, series list, et al. | Excel, Access, Word, WinZip | Shared network drive | Preserve if not duplicated elsewhere | |
| Editorial | Book Proposals: folders on dormant, rejected, accepted books, proposal documents, then folders by author containing a variety of proposals, reviews, thesis reports, manuscripts, chapter lists. Files on current book proposals (2014), proposals web page, several single author files | Excel, Word, RTF, PDF, | Shared network drive | Preserve. Appraise + weed | links to series of paper author files, but by surname rather than ISBN |
| | Network drive (\\Datastore1). Shared drive for less current work including Conference 2009-12 papers. Manuscripts A-Z by author, Marketing, Page design – Royalty Payments, Text Design Templates, Word files and Work in Progress by Author | Word; pdf; WinZip etc | Shared network drive | | Some duplication in folders on this drive. A search from one ISBN returned 3 files of the cover image in different folders |
| Editorial/ Production | 29 Individual PDF files of book titles tables of contents 2014, likely named by ISBN | PDF | Shared network drive | Preserve if not duplicated elsewhere | |
| Editorial/ Production | 7 individual administrative files on Biblio, workflow, processes plus cover of a publication | shortcut, PDF, Excel | Shared network drive | Current + 3 years then destroy Biblio items; move publication cover + preserve | |
| Production / Marketing | Images of published covers | PDF | Shared network drive | Permanent | |
| Marketing | 3D Cover Templates: images of titles showing cover and sides, plus 3D image of blank paperback | J, PSD (inaccessible) | Shared network drive | Duplicated elsewhere? Preserve if not retained elsewhere | |

| Business function | Record type | Format | Location | Retention sentence | Guiding legislation / practice/ notes |
|---|---|---|---|---|---|
| Marketing | 13 Digit ISBN Contents PDFs: 3D covers, templates, boxset images, publisher's banner, Journal cover images, Tables of contents filed by ISBN number 1999–15. | PDF, JPEG | Shared network drive | Permanent | |
| Editorial/ Marketing | Folders by year 2009–16 containing advance information from publisher, changes to book information, reports from Biblio/Focus software, pertaining to USA, Canada, UK and website. Also Templates, Canada data feeds | Word, PDF | Shared network drive | Preserve if not duplicated elsewhere | |
| Financial | Access Temp Files: financial reports 2013 – balance sheet, amazon stock, management accounts, ISBN transfers et al. | Excel, Access | Shared network drive | Destroy 2021 if duplicated a a higher level | |
| Financial | Accounts: folders Management Accounts 2000–13 including forecasts 2013/14 and financial review 2001/2, 2002/3, To Pay [creditors list 2013]. Files on creditors and debtors 2011–13 | Excel | Shared network drive | Preserve management accounts. Destroy creditors / debtors reports current financial year + 6 | |
| Production/ Marketing | Adobe E-book files by ISBN: cover images, manuscripts by ISBN, OP books | JPEG, PDF | Shared network drive | Preserve if not duplicated elsewhere | |
| Production/ Marketing | Adobe Press Ready Files by ISBN: manuscripts by ISBN | JPEG, PDF | Shared network drive | Preserve if not duplicated elsewhere | |
| Production/ Marketing | Amazon: manuscript files by ISBN | JPEG | Shared network drive | Preserve if not duplicated elsewhere | |
| Marketing/ Customer Services | Backup: printer file drivers, backup containing contact lists, email backup | Setup files, Excel, Access, Word | Shared network drive | Likely complete duplication of shared network drive. Current + 3 years | |
| Personnel | Photographs of a member of staff's retirement cake and buffet | JPEG | Shared network drive | Transfer to 'scrapbook' or destroy end of administrative use (no people or premises featured in photographs) | |
| Non-business function – computer programme files | Biblio Access Files: access database setup – transfer from Focus | Access, Excel | Shared network drive | Destroy current + 3 years | Information duplicated on Biblio |

| Business function | Record type | Format | Location | Retention sentence | Guiding legislation / practice/ notes |
|---|---|---|---|---|---|
| Finance | Folders for accounts (reports 2013–14), budget [20]14–[20]15, daily sales, forecast, 'info' journal phasing of issues, journal transfers to MDL, monitor, PL [profit + loss] transfer, royalty transfer , SL [sales ledger] transfer. Other files including contacts, bank payments, logo, holidays | Excel, JPEG, PDF | Shared network drive | Destroy financial records end of financial year + 6. Destroy administrative records current + 3 years | |
| Production/ Finance | Book costs: anniversaries, book costs including accrual versus planned costs, book cost reports by month 2006–13, dues 2011, estimates 2010–11, manuscripts delivered 2012, overstock at 6/7/2011, cost charts 2007–11, production cost reports 2010–11 including typesetting | Excel | Shared network drive | Preserve if not dublicated elsewhere or at a higher level | |
| Marketing/ Customer Services | Catalogue 2010: UK price list, cover image of catalogue, full PDF of catalogue, list of out of print titles | Excel, Word, PDF | Shared network drive | Permanent. Weed duplicates | |
| Marketing/ Customer Services | Catalogue 2011: UK and US cover images of catalogue, full PDF of catalogue, journals, mailings, titles for catalogue, print run and costs 2011 | JPEG, Excel, Word | Shared network drive | Permanent. Weed duplicates and low-level administrative files | |
| Marketing/ Customer Services | Catalogue 2012: cover images (of all imprints to go in catalogue), price list, contents list, covers new [cover images by author], journal cover images, catalogue mailing list, invoices for catalogues, print run and costs | JPEG, Excel | Shared network drive | Permanent. Weed duplicates and low-level administrative files | |
| Marketing/ Customer Services | Catalogue 2013: catalogue images, price list, contents, cover images of books and journals, mailing lists, cover designs, print run and costs, proofs, web ready PDFs | JPEG, PDF, Excel | Shared network drive | Permanent. Weed duplicates and low-level administrative files | |
| Production | CIP [cataloging in production] tagging: 2x/model texts, tagged manuscripts in folders by author | Word | Shared network drive | Appraise | |
| Production | Copied from Server: Migrate folder – Accounts, April; staff work folders | Word, Excel, shortcuts, PDF, OPT file, Applications, text documents | Shared network drive | Destroy current + 3 years. Duplicate information | |
| Editorial | Journal PDFs and WinZip files | PDF, WinZipped PDF's | Shared network drive | Permanent | |

## *Annex II: Essential Electronic Records: Guidance for Email and the Network Drives*

The records created, received and used by [the law publisher] are essential to its effective functioning. They provide evidence of its activities and important information about its status, rights of its members and its relationships with other individuals and organisations. In order to realise the true value of this asset, it is essential that records in all formats are managed appropriately.

This guidance is intended to support good practice in creating, storing, managing and disposing of records held digitally for business efficiency and compliance with legislation. Much time is wasted when documents can't be found quickly and easily. This could be because of how they are named or where they are stored. Good practice can help speed up finding documents, eliminate duplication, and save space, while at the same time adhering to relevant security precautions.

The purpose of this guidance is to help you and your colleagues rationalise the documents in shared network drives and on email. Such work can be both tedious and time-consuming, but it is crucial if we are to save time and minimise frustration in the future. It will also help us to comply with legislation such as the Data Protection Act 1998. Where possible, one member of staff in each department should have responsibility for the file structure of digital records storage. This ensures consistent folder naming, minimal duplication or overlap between folders, and an up-to-date record available for all staff to use.

In the course of your work, please consider:

### Location and security

Keep documents on the S:/ Drive and images on the I:/ Drive. Please do not keep open business records on the H:/ Drive, as they will not be accessible to colleagues. Do not store records on the C:/ drive where they may not be backed up or not retrievable in the event of a disaster. If there are particularly sensitive documents, store them in your H:/ drive on the server. Alternatively, to set up user permissions, please contact the IT manager.

### Structure

Organise the folders for which you are responsible in a clear and simple format. Use appropriate titles based on business functions which reflect the contents. Classify folders according to the functions/activities of the department, not individual members of staff. Department structures, team names, and individuals may change but functions and work activities will remain the same, or similar, over time. The retention schedule available from [-] can form a basis of a file scheme.

Please limit the number of folder and subfolder levels to promote clarity. Try not to exceed 5 levels of hierarchy. For example: Undergraduate Admissions/Policies/Approved/Financial Assistance Policy.doc. For email, 2 levels should be sufficient.

### Naming conventions

Concise titles which avoid repetition in the path are preferable. File titles should be self-explanatory and meaningful: avoid 'general' or 'misc'. Dates, if used, should take the format YYYY-MM-DD at the start of the file name to ensure records will sort chronologically.

### Version Control

Delete any duplicates or superseded documents which do not require further retention or permanent preservation. The status (draft/final) should be included along with the version of the document. Associate digital records with paper ones where appropriate, by adding paper file location information into the digital record, and a cross reference in the paper file. Email drafts can be immediately deleted once no longer required.

### Retention:

Since electronic records do not have a physical presence they are often kept indefinitely. However, they should be retained along with all other records in line with the retention schedule, available from[-]. It can be useful to create sub-folders which identify which records will be destroyed, e.g. if some financial records are destroyed 7 years from creation, create a folder named 'Financial Year 2008–09' and transfer appropriate records to this file, then at the end of 2016 the file can be deleted in its entirety.

Most emails only need to be kept for administrative use for 3 years and weeded/deleted after that time. Keep those for permanent preservation which have historic value or evidence of business activities which does not exist elsewhere. The **originator** is responsible for retaining and filing the email when the email is created internally. The **recipient** is responsible for retaining and filing the email where the email is received from an external source, and where that information does not exist elsewhere and forms part of the official business record. See also **Annex I**.

A regular spring-clean will stop the file structure becoming too unwieldy. Deleting data that is no longer required is one way of keeping the folder structure manageable. Staff are encouraged to undertake a review of their records on the H:/, S:/ and I:/ drives and on email. See also **Annex I**.

When you are spring-cleaning the folders make sure all relevant staff are informed first. The retention schedule gives details of when records can be destroyed, and it can be modified to suit each department. If the shared drive or emails contains information which is not described in the model retention schedule, contact [-] for advice. Records no longer in active business use should be review for historical significance before destruction.

## *Flowchart for managing and disposing of email*

Every email transaction falls into one of the following categories during its lifecycle:

| | | |
|---|---|---|
| Business | Has business, evidential, legal or historical value | Keep until value expires |
| Informational | Has informational, reference or historical value | Keep until value expires |
| Redundant | Business, evidential, legal or reference value has expired | Delete promptly |
| Irrelevant | Spam, unsolicited messages of no value | Delete promptly |
| Personal | Not work-related thus of no administrative value | Delete promptly |

How to store emails consistently while they are active

| | |
|---|---|
| Hold the message in your inbox/ sent items if you are: | Not yet sure what the email is about |
| | Not yet sure what activity is developing |
| | Not yet sure if it will develop into an ongoing transaction or is transitory |
| | Not yet sure if it will turn out to be important |
| Move messages into mailbox folders which mirror the folders you use in your shared network drive so that you can: | See all related emails together |
| | Quickly view the chain of transactions/delete earlier transactions in the chain |
| | Easily decide on their importance i.e. whether/when to move them into your shared storage area or delete them |
| Once a transaction is complete, decide whether or not the associated emails are still required for business use: | If yes, they should be moved to the relevant shared storage area as soon as possible and deleted from your mailbox. They will then be retained in their relevant business context for as long as required for business, legal or reference purposes and disposed of in accordance with the retention schedule |
| | If no, the email should be deleted. Why fill mailboxes or shared storage areas with information which is no longer needed? |

When to delete or move emails to shared storage area

| | |
|---|---|
| Delete messages from your mailbox within 15 days if... | You are not responsible for completing the transaction and: |
| | • It is a message sent/initiated by someone else |
| | • It is a string of messages (originally initiated by someone else) to which you have not contributed |
| | • It is just for your information ('Cc:', 'FYI', 'All staff' etc) |
| | You are responsible for completing the transaction but: |
| | • There's no business, operational, statutory, regulatory or historical need to retain it |
| | • There's no ongoing reference value to work |
| | • Not sure? Consult the retention schedule or line manager |
| Move to the shared drive if... | You either initiated the email or received an external email to action and: |
| | • There's a business need for others to access the information |
| | • The action is completed and there is a requirement to retain for a period of time as evidence of a business transaction |
| | • The action is completed and there is ongoing reference or historical value for the company |

| | |
|---|---|
| Move emails to the shared drive without too much effort by... | Ensuring your email folders mirror the folders in your shared network drive; this makes moving important emails from Outlook to the relevant shared folder quick and easy |
| | Waiting to file a string of messages until the email topic has been completed or there is a natural break in the 'conversation' |
| | Making sure the email has a meaningful title, including the date, as follows: YYYY-MM-DD (e.g. 2009-07-18) |
| | Saving emails into the shared drive in '.msg' format (File/Save as/Message format) to enhance evidential weight |
| | Remembering that deletion does **not** happen automatically even if you cut and paste; you must manually delete transferred emails from Outlook |

## *Adopting best practice day-to-day*

**Remember:** emails which have to be kept for business, evidential or statutory reasons must be moved, as soon as is practical, into your shared drive.

| Do | Don't |
|---|---|
| Delete irrelevant or redundant emails and move others into your mailbox folders daily or at a set time which suits you each week (e.g. Friday afternoons) | Let a backlog of unmanaged emails build up |
| Keep emails in mirror folders in your mailbox until you know whether to delete or move them | Leave emails in your inbox/sent items |
| Say yes to deletion of deleted items every day | Use your deleted items folder as a storage area |
| If possible send hyperlinks to documents in shared drives | Circulate attachments without thinking |
| Check that there's no alternative location to access an attached document before you save yet another copy | Save attachments unnecessarily |
| Save business emails into the shared drive as soon as possible so that they will be accessible within their business context for as long as needed | Rely on Outlook to store business emails |
| Contact the IT department or line manager for help | Struggle on alone if you really don't know how to manage your email or have a question about a particular issue |

## *Rules of email etiquette*

To ensure efficiency, professionalism and protection from liability, all staff should follow these rules of etiquette when sending, or replying to, email:

| Do | Don't |
|---|---|
| Think about whether it is necessary to send the email at all! | Email if a telephone call or quick chat will do instead |
| Include name, job title and contact details in all emails | Overuse the reply to all or the 'Cc:' field |
| Include an appropriate and meaningful subject heading | Forward chain letters or emails |
| Be concise and to the point | Copy or forward email messages or attachments without the sender's agreement |
| Try to answer all questions and pre-empt further questions | Send or forward emails containing libellous, defamatory, offensive, racist, sexist or obscene remarks |
| Use URGENT, IMPORTANT or HIGH PRIORITY sparingly | Request delivery and read receipts unless you really must know if something has arrived |
| Use correct spelling, grammar and punctuation | Reply to spam |
| Always adopt a polite and professional tone | Send emails when angry – wait until you have cooled down! |

## *Shared folders rationalisation checklist*

| **Action required** | **Completed** |
|---|---|
| Get together with all the users of your section of the shared network drives to assess what's working and what isn't. Use mind maps where possible to give you a visual picture of the various folders and sub-folder contents | |
| Undertake an initial clear-out to remove obvious duplicates and redundant documents and folders. Use the retention schedule [insert network location] to assist | |
| Are there documents which should only be accessed by line managers, a limited number of team members, or personal documents which should not be shared? Delete or move personal material into your personal folders (H:) and set up new folders for restricted material with clear access permissions | |
| Now look at what's left. What works and what doesn't? How easy would it be for a new member of staff to find specific documents? Do folder and document titles make sense? Is the folder as it stands capable of being tidied up or would it be easier to set up a new folder and simply move business critical information into it? | |
| Consult the rest of the team to validate your proposed structure. Move all relevant documents into new sub-folders and delete the existing folders (or, if there are already appropriate folders, change their names to the updated titles) | |
| Aim to make access to your shared folder as open as possible within your office. If your folder is open to all potential users you will be able to collaborate with them more efficiently by sending them hyperlinks to documents saved within the shared network drive, instead of having to send multiple or duplicated attachments | |
| If you are moving documents into a new folder make sure access permissions are the same as for the old one. If you move documents and folders from one folder to another they will take their current access permissions with them | |
| Look again at what is left – these should be folders which reflect the office's unique core functions e.g. student files, technical documents, project material. Create sub-folders which reflect these core functions and give them meaningful titles. Again, remember to discuss and agree with all users. For a fresh perspective, why not get a colleague from another department to see if they understand your proposed folder structure? | |
| Avoid ambiguity, acronyms, abbreviations and team jargon, too many folders and folder layers which make it difficult to find and store information. If you must use acronyms or abbreviations then keep a key to what they mean and store the key where all team members can easily find it (preferably in the office's 'Administration' or 'Office management' folder) | |
| To protect the security of information folders, owners need to remember to keep a log of who has access to the folders they manage | |
| Owners should regularly monitor their folders to check on the appearance of odd titles or duplicate documents/sub-folders and conduct periodic housekeeping exercises | |
| Regularly review, discuss and agree any required amendments/additions at departmental meetings | |
| Finally – always be consistent and look at the bigger picture – what works for you may not work for another user or department | |

# Case study 2: The records of Chadwick Lawrence Solicitors

Chadwick Lawrence
Yorkshire's Legal People

*Logo reproduced by permission of Chadwick Lawrence*

Compiled by Clare Cowling

Completed December 2016

## *Acknowledgements*

The Legal Records at Risk project Director and Executive Committee wish to express our thanks to Chadwick Lawrence LLP for its co-operation in this case study and in particular the active support and detailed information given by Emma Ferguson, the Archivist and Records Manager.

## *Definitions*

- Archive/archives: in the traditional definition the term 'archive' or 'archives' refers both to the repository where records of permanent value are stored and made available for research and to the records stored in it.
- Archiving: in Chadwick Lawrence and most businesses, the process of transferring records to cheaper storage to reduce costs.
- Records: information, in any form, created, received and maintained as evidence and information by an organisation in pursuance of legal obligations or in the transaction of business.
- Records disposal: the process of *either* destroying records once they no longer have any business or legal value *or* depositing them in an archives.
- Records store: in some large organisations (e.g. government departments) the records store, as distinct from the archives, is a secure repository for semi-current records pending their disposal as opposed to records of permanent value which are stored separately in an archives. In a number of organisations however, including Chadwick Lawrence, the two functions of semi-current records store and archives are combined for economy of effort and the term 'archives' is used to refer to both.
- Semi-current records: records which are no longer needed for day to day use but are still required for occasional business reference.

## *Purpose of the case study*

The Legal Records at Risk (LRAR) project is concerned with identifying, and rescuing for posterity, legal records of archival value in the private sector. Saving significant collections, stimulating changes of practice and raising awareness of the value of LRAR are prioritised. Our definition of legal records is wider than their traditional classification as court records or formal documents such as deeds; we include records of institutions and individuals specialised to law (e.g. law firms, arbitrators, barristers, legal executives, patent agents, licensed conveyancers, court interpreters and ancillary bodies such as law stationers and legal publishers). We also include legal records produced in the course of their business by private sector companies (such as policy and procedure records and the individual case files produced by legal, property and governance departments).

Undertaking case studies of selected institutions which create legal records and of particular categories of legal records of value which may hitherto have been overlooked by researchers forms a key platform of the project. Our case studies will demonstrate areas of best practice and community of practice (or lack thereof), identify key issues common to all or most institutions and recommend potential solutions, including liaison with archive repositories relating to the deposit of records of permanent value.

The case study which follows looks at the creation, management and disposal (by destruction or transfer to an archive) by a prominent law firm, Chadwick Lawrence LLP, based in the north of England and offering a wide range of legal services. The specific aims were as follows:

- To survey the firm's records and recordkeeping practices.
- To understand the business drivers behind the firm's management of its records.
- To evaluate the business benefits of employing professionally qualified persons to manage records.
- To demonstrate the benefits to law firms of maintaining an archives.

For a copy of the case study proposal made to the firm see **Annex I.**

## *Methodology*

- Interviews and emails: face to face and email discussions were held between the LRAR project Director and the firm's Archivist and Records Manager. The purpose was to obtain an overview of the business reasons behind her appointment, the work she has done in streamlining Chadwick Lawrence's recordkeeping and the use by the business of the records held in the records store/ archives.
- Chadwick Lawrence's website was examined in detail to gain an insight into its core functions and values.
- Questionnaires: two questionnaires were sent to the Archivist requesting details of the firm's records, its recordkeeping practices, its disposal policy and the use (internal and external) of records in the archives. For the questionnaires see **Annex II**.

## *Administrative background*

### The business context

Based in Yorkshire, the firm of Chadwick Lawrence LLP dates back to the 1840s and offers a wide range of traditional legal services for both personal and business matters (family law, conveyancing, employment, commercial property and dispute resolution). Chadwick Lawrence also has specialist medical negligence and sports law capabilities. It has seven offices throughout Yorkshire and the practice is one of the twenty largest firms in the region.

### The community context

Chadwick Lawrence actively supports regional initiatives and is involved in the local community. It organises business and employment seminars, both in its own right and in partnership with other business organisations, taking a keen interest in promoting efforts to foster economic growth in the region. In recognition of this Chadwick Lawrence has received a number of awards, including 'Business of the Year' at the Wakefield District Business Awards, 'Employment Law Award' and 'Residential Property Award' at the Yorkshire Legal Awards 2015 and been nominated for many more. In other words, the firm sees itself as part of, and contributing to, the local community.

## *The records*

In common with most large law firms, Chadwick Lawrence holds the following categories of business and client records:

- Governance: e.g. Board and committee papers, partners' papers, policy and strategy records.
- Regulatory and statutory compliance: e.g. records relating to compliance with legislation (Courts and Legal Services Act, Data Protection Act) and with The Law Society and Solicitors Regulation Authority rules and regulations.
- Business: e.g. finance, human resources, office management, information management, facilities and premises records, public relations records.
- Clients: e.g. matter files, complaints, deeds, leases, wills, grants of probate.

## *Records management*

- Chadwick Lawrence runs a hybrid records management system i.e. a combination of paper and electronic records.
- Paper records: the firm is attempting to go paper-less, but legacy records are still in paper as are some current records; a digitisation programme is in the planning stages. Legacy paper records are covered by a records retention and disposal schedule, but the schedule's provisions have not as yet been extended to electronic records. The schedule is also used to weed paper records regularly.

- Electronic records: the firm uses the Microsoft Office Management (OMS) suite and Proclaim Legal Case Management Software (endorsed by The Law Society) for its current and archived matter files. The Archivist worked with the IT department to develop catalogues on both systems; prior to this control records were held on access databases and index cards/ledger books. Proclaim will eventually replace OMS.

### *The Archives and Records Store*

In common with a number of private organisations, Chadwick Lawrence manages a combined off-site archives and semi-current records store for its hard copy records and refers to this repository as its Archives.

### The role of the Archivist

Until the appointment of a professional archivist (now the Head Archivist) on 31 October 2011, an 'archivist' at the Huddersfield office looked after the records, but found it more and more difficult to cope with the increasing work load. Each of the seven office sites also managed and stored its own records in a different way, making it difficult and frustrating to locate files and documents.

The Archivist's appointment resulted from the realisation by the Management Team that, with the regular increase in the size of the firm and consequent acquisition of more original documents and files to be managed, stored and located when needed, a more streamlined and consistent process for archiving records was required.

The Archivist's first task was to develop this new process by:

- Visiting each office site and establishing what was held where/what types of records were held.
- Creating an 'archives' inbox, so that all requests to retrieve items from storage were sent to a central email account, rather than to individual email addresses or written on post-it notes!
- Streamlining the archive process so that each office site archived documents in the same way.
- Creating a standardised procedure across the firm for sending new items to be archived, returning items to storage and requesting something from storage.
- Going through the huge backlog of files that had been stored in various basements to establish what needed to be kept and archived and what could be shredded.

### The role of the Archives

The Head Archivist is supported by a team of three archivists (based at Huddersfield, Leeds and Wakefield). They are responsible for archiving files and dealing with requests for retrieval at their individual offices. An office assistant/ archives assistant retrieves items from the off-site storage units and weeds files. Front of house staff also archive files for one hour a day (five staff members in total). The Archives, therefore, also doubles as a semi-current records management facility, undertaking retrievals of records for business use by staff. There may be as many as 250 document requests per month.

The Archives itself controls the storage and management of the financial records of the organisation and its client files, including wills, deeds, leases, powers of attorney, grants of probate and accounts. It deals with some external enquiries about these records from former clients, but rarely receives any requests to look at material from the general public. This is no doubt due to lack of publicity; the Archives has not sent any details of its holdings to The National Archives, so there is no information about the firm in *Discovery.*[2] The Archives would be willing to publicise its holdings or to consider transferring non-confidential archival records such as pre-19th-century title deeds to a public repository where they could be more readily made available.

The archives catalogue of client files is detailed and comprehensive, listing documents by client, type (will, grant of probate, lease etc), date of creation, area created, storage location and whether checked in or out.

The firm's business records (other than Finance) are archived separately from the client files and are managed by the Managing Partner and Human Resources.

### *The role of the Archivist in strategic records management*

From January 2015 the Head Archivist's role officially incorporated strategic records management duties in addition to managing the records stores; prior to this time she was unofficially carrying out these tasks. One of the strategic initiatives is the digitisation of all files going forward from a certain point in time. The digitisation will be carried out to

2 *Discovery* (http://discovery.nationalarchives.gov.uk) is a searchable archives database managed by The National Archives. It holds more than 32 million descriptions of records held by The National Archives and more than 2,500 archives across the country.

BS 10008 standard[3] by a third-party scanning company. This, it is hoped, will eventually reduce the need to store paper files and therefore reduce costs.

The Head Archivist hopes in future to have, in collaboration with the IT department, input into developing information management rules for the document management systems, Sharepoint, shared network drives and email. She also intends to extend the retention and disposal schedule to cover digital records.

The schedule was recently redrafted to include a more streamlined process for managing destructions, including requiring fee earners to record the proposed destruction date for each file when it is sent to be archived; this will then be recorded on a central system by the Archivists with a flag set up that will alert them when the file is ready to be destroyed. The schedule specifies minimum retention periods for business records and each category of client files. For a copy of the schedule see **Annex III**.

## *Case study conclusions and recommendations*

Chadwick Lawrence provides an excellent model for the management of both current and non-current client files by law firms through the following activities:

- It has invested in a professional archivist/records manager to rationalise and streamline its recordkeeping processes for the bulk of its records. The business and financial benefits of this appointment are already obvious in the improved efficiency of the records management and retrieval processes.
- In undertaking the above it is recognising the importance of good records management when seeking to provide an excellent service to clients. It is already better able to manage external enquiries from former clients and to provide them with assurances that their information is held securely and can be accessed by them as needed.
- In recognising the need to involve the Archivist in strategic decisions around the management of current records the firm will soon see further efficiency benefits e.g. in the systematic disposal of unneeded records and in forward scanning. It has made the sensible decision not to invest in back-scanning, which most organisations quickly discover not to be cost-effective.[4]

For economies of scale it would be logical in future for the archiving process for all business records to be managed by the Archivist/Records Manager rather than having split responsibilities.

The Archivist already intends to extend the records retention and disposal schedule to electronic records. If Chadwick Lawrence decides to retain some records permanently to preserve its corporate history then this requirement should also be added to the schedule. It could also consider providing greater external access to its historical records. Although the first duty of a business archive is always to service its organisation, LRAR considers that by demonstrating greater transparency through making non-confidential historical material available for research, Chadwick Lawrence would enhance its already strong reputation for providing an excellent service to its clients and for community involvement. LRAR would be happy to help facilitate any such efforts by, for example, liaison with TNA in relation to putting links on *Discovery*.

Going forward, Chadwick Lawrence may, however, prefer to consider making its non-confidential historical records more readily available to the general public by depositing them in a local archive repository. LRAR would be happy to help facilitate this process by brokering an agreement to transfer archival records to a local archive repository to enhance accessibility. Such an activity would of course reduce Chadwick Lawrence's own records storage and management costs, since local archives do not charge organisations for storing and caring for historical material, though a one-off donation towards physical transfer expenses would be welcomed.

Confidentiality was not raised as a major issue in the case study, since the primary purpose of the Chadwick Lawrence archives is to serve the business. If, however, the firm decides to enhance its profile as described above then it may wish to set rules for the opening of its records to the public. Most business records held in archives, for example, are open for research after 20 years, while records containing personal data are closed for up to 100 years. Client records are usually seen as confidential for as long as the family or firm has a relationship with the solicitor and for some years afterwards or indeed in perpetuity, but in practice this is not always observed, as evidenced by the existence in local county archives of client documents deposited by solicitors such as deeds and wills and even historical case files of named clients. If Chadwick Lawrence does decide to transfer any of its records to a public sector archives then The Law Society's guidance[5] should be followed.

3 British Standards Institution, BS 10008:2014 *Evidential weight and legal admissibility of electronic information: specification*

4 Scanning itself may be relatively cheap but the business effort involved in the sorting and prepping files, indexing each item, quality assurance, purchase and ongoing management of a document management system in which to store scanned images and digital migration is expensive.

5 The Law Society Practice Note: Depositing records and documents with public sector archives.

# Annex I: Case study proposal to Chadwick Lawrence

## *Proposed case study: records of Chadwick Lawrence Solicitors*

*Summary note*: dating back to the 1840s and specialising in medical negligence and sports law, Chadwick Lawrence employs a records manager/archivist to care for its records, many of which are clearly of long-term business value to the firm and some of which may be of potential value to external researchers.

*Objective*: the Legal Records at Risk project wishes to survey the firm's records and recordkeeping practices. From preliminary discussions with Chadwick Lawrence's archivist, we anticipate that this exercise will confirm our thesis that the firm is a model of good practice which could and should be followed by other law firms to reduce costs, enhance efficiency and protect records of value.

*Scope*: the project will seek to briefly identify the main categories of Chadwick Lawrence's records and their management, particularly the benefits gained by employing a professionally qualified person to undertake the task and manage the records. It will ask for information concerning a) the initial programme to rationalise records and recordkeeping processes and b) the ongoing management of the firm's information.

*Methodology*: the LRAR archivist will undertake a series of discussions, primarily via email and using questionnaires, with the Chadwick Lawrence archivist. The discussions will include questions about the firm's initial project to sort, list and preserve its records, on the establishment of the archive, on the business use of archived records by the firm and on current records management guidelines and practices. The firm's archivist will be asked to provide a list of the main categories of records held by the firm and their anticipated retention periods. Ongoing issues such as digital continuity and storage constraints for paper records will be identified. It may be necessary for the LRAR archivist to pay one visit.

*Quality*: the survey will be carried out by the LRAR's qualified archivist/records manager. The archivist will give an undertaking (in writing if required) to abide by the firm's own conditions of confidentiality and to comply with the provisions of the Data Protection Act when surveying the records and making her report.

*Resources and costs*: there will be no costs to the firm other than in the allocation of time to assist the LRAR archivist.

*Constraints*: agreement of the firm to permit the LRAR archivist to discuss current procedures and processes with key members of staff, primarily the Chadwick Lawrence archivist.

*Issues and risks*: not being allowed access to the required information or to publish the findings.

*Projected outcomes*: a report to Chadwick Lawrence on its records and recordkeeping (the report will be published with the permission of the firm); enhanced publicity for the firm as a model of good practice; following publication of the report, a better understanding by law firms generally of the potential value of their records both to their own organisations and to the external research community; beginnings of a community of practice in the management of information by law firms.

# Annex II: Legal Records at Risk questionnaires

Two questionnaires were sent to Chadwick Lawrence. The first was a preliminary set of questions to gain an overview of the firm. The second was a more detailed number of questions directed specifically to the Archivist/Records Manager to identify historical, current and planned information management practice and procedure.

**Questionnaire 1:** (answers removed to protect confidentiality)

| Organisation details: questions asked |
|---|
| • Organisation name |
| • Organisation address |
| • Governing/parent body (if relevant) |
| • Email |
| • Telephone |
| • Function/purpose of organisation |
| **Organisation's records** |
| • Main categories of records |
| • Do you have a retention/disposal policy for your records? |
| • Who is responsible for managing your records? |

| | |
|---|---|
| • | % paper records |
| • | % digital records |
| Paper records storage: | |
| • | On-site in offices (current records) |
| • | In-house records store (for non-current records) |
| • | Third-party records store (for non-current records) |
| Digital records storage: | |
| • | Document management system (current records) |
| • | Sharepoint/shared drives/email (current records) |
| • | On premise lower-tier storage (non-current records) |
| • | Cloud storage (non-current records) |
| Archival storage (paper records of permanent historical value) | |
| • | In-house archives |
| • | Deposited with a third-party archives repository (give name of repository) |
| • | List/inventory sent to The National Archives |
| • | No paper archives have survived |
| Archival storage (born-digital records of permanent historical value) | |
| • | In-house digital archive |
| • | Third-party digital archive |
| • | List/inventory sent to The National Archives |
| • | No plans for a digital archive |

**Questionnaire 2** (answers removed to protect confidentiality):

| No. | Question | Explanatory notes |
|---|---|---|
| **1. The role of the archivist/records manager** | | |
| 1.1 | Why did the firm decide to employ a records manager/ archivist? Is it possible to see a summary of the business case? | |
| 1.2 | Prior to this appointment, how and by whom were the records managed? | |
| 1.3 | For how long has the firm had a records manager/ archivist? Have you been in post long enough to show a clear cost benefit or is it too soon? | The immediate benefit is usually a reduction in the quantity of paper stored. Other business benefits include increased efficiency and speed of information retrieval, but these are harder to quantify |
| 1.4 | Do you have support staff? If yes, how many and what are their roles? | |
| 1.5 | What was the first thing you did when appointed? | Such as compiling a records survey; drafting a retention schedule; destroying redundant records, creating a location list, archival value records |
| 1.6 | Does management see your role as primarily that of archivist or records manager or both? | In other words, is your role seen as primarily dealing with records *after* they cease to be current or are you involved in current and forward information management planning? |
| **2. Hard copy records management** | | |
| 2.1 | Does the firm have a records retention and disposal schedule? | |
| 2.2 | Are you able to monitor/control when and whether paper records are destroyed or archived according to the schedule? | |

| No. | Question | Explanatory notes |
|---|---|---|
| 2.3 | How frequently are semi-current records referred to by staff? | Once these records are no longer needed they could be either destroyed or added to the archives. In many businesses the line is very blurred and semi-current records are often stored in the archives in a hybrid mix of permanent and semi-current material |
| 2.4 | Can staff retrieve semi-current records from the store? If yes, how do you manage this process? | |
| 2.5 | Is the semi-current records store in the same location as the archives or are they physically separate? | |
| **3. Digital records management** | | |
| 3.1 | What document management system does the firm use? Were you able to have input into its selection? | Such as an electronic document and records management system (EDRMS); legal case management system; shared network drives; Sharepoint; email used as a case management system |
| 3.2 | Have you had input into management and disposal rules (if any) for the case management system, Sharepoint, email, shared drives? If yes, is it possible to have copies of your guidance? | |
| 3.3 | If you have a records retention and disposal schedule, does it cover digital records? If no, are you intending to extend it to cover them? | |
| 3.4 | If you have on premise lower-tier storage for non-current digital records can you provide details? | |
| 3.5 | Are you able to monitor/control when and whether digital records are destroyed or archived or is this work done by the IT department? | |
| **4. Archives** | | |
| 4.1 | Who decides what records go into the archives? | |
| 4.2 | What are the primary categories of records in the archives? | Examples:<br>• Governance records: e.g. Board and committee papers, partners' papers, policy and strategy records<br>• Regulatory and statutory compliance records: e.g. records relating to compliance with legislation (e.g. Courts and Legal Services Act, Data Protection Act) and with The Law Society and Solicitors Regulation Authority rules and regulations<br>• Business records: e.g. finance, human resources, office management, information management, facilities and premises records<br>• Client records: e.g. matter files, complaints, deeds, leases, wills, grants of probate |
| 4.3 | How frequently is the archives used by staff? | |
| 4.4 | Is it used by external researchers? How do they know about it? | |
| 4.5 | Is the firm worried about the confidentiality of records in the archives? | In other words, how long does it think some material such as client files should remain confidential? |
| 4.6 | Would you be interested in a reference to the firm's archives being included in TNA's register of business archives? | |
| 4.7 | Do you have an archives catalogue? | |
| 4.8 | If yes, do you intend to put your archival catalogue online at some future date? | |
| 4.9 | If yes, would you be interested in providing a link to your catalogue to The National Archives? | |

| No. | Question | Explanatory notes |
|---|---|---|
| 4.10 | Would you like LRAR to broker an arrangement with a public archive repository for depositing your historical records to make them more readily accessible? | |

## Annex III: Chadwick Lawrence File Storage, Retention and Disposal Policy 2016

| | |
|---|---|
| Date of effect | October 2016 |
| Date of last revision | October 2015 |
| Date due for review | October 2017 |
| Contact | Compliance Officer for Legal Practice<br>Head Archivist |

### *1. File closure*

Fee earners are to ensure that:

- all work has been completed on the matter, that there are no undertakings outstanding and no money is owed to or by the client;
- Risk Assessment forms are fully completed and saved in the correct format to either OMS or Proclaim;
- the file is well organised with any unnecessary or duplicate documents removed, including unannotated duplicates of originals, drafts of letters or informal notes that do not represent significant steps or decisions in the preparation of an official record;
- any original documents which should not be destroyed are removed from the file. Original documents should be sent to the Archives department separately from the file.

### *2. Storage and Retention*

Each type of matter file has a specific retention period (see table 4.2).

Fee earners are to:

- record the proposed destruction date for each file when it is sent to be archived. This is then recorded on a central system by the Archivist.
- indicate if there are any factors relating to the file that might make it necessary to extend the standard retention period.

A central record of the file is created and maintained by the Archivist to include details of:

- the file(s) stored, including client and matter number, client name and description of matter;
- location of the file(s), including box number and site;
- the date the file was sent to be archived;
- the provisional destruction/review date;
- the date of the eventual destruction (as appropriate).

### *3. Retrieving items from storage*

To retrieve a file or original document from storage:

- complete a Request form (found on Precedent Manager under Archive 002) with details of the items that you require.
- email the form to archives@chadlaw.co.uk or archiveswakefield@chadlaw.co.uk depending on your location.
- the items will then be retrieved by an Archivist and either hand delivered or sent to the requestor via tracked DX.

### *4. Destruction*

The destruction of documents should be an authorised, appropriate, secure, timely and documented process. Appropriate legislation and guidance should be consulted before destruction takes place.

## 4.1 Procedure

- The fee earner/Head of Department will be informed that the file is ready for destruction by the Archivist.
- Staff with authority to do so will then review the file. If the file is deemed to be of ongoing important business value then it will remain in storage; otherwise it will be confidentially destroyed.
- A central record of all destroyed files is retained by the Head Archivist, including the date of destruction, the name of the person who authorised the destruction and the reason for destruction.

## 4.2 File Retention Periods

| **Type of matter** | **Minimum retention period** | **Exceptions/reasons for storing the file for longer** |
|---|---|---|
| Business, including company/partnership formation, insolvency, trademark/copyright/patent | 6 years | |
| Employment | 6 years | |
| Family, including divorce, separation, custody and contact, injunctions, child protection and court of protection | 6 years | |
| General litigation e.g. tribunals, mental health, prison matters, harassment | 6 years | |
| Leasehold and tenancy | 6 years | |
| Medical Negligence | 6 years | If the client is a minor, then retain until 6 years after the client turns 18 years old |
| Personal Injury | 6 years | If the client is a minor, then retain until 6 years after the client turns 18 years old |
| Powers of Attorney and Probate | 6 years | |
| Private client non-litigation advice e.g. employment, pensions, change of name, debt, personal insolvency, housing disrepair | 6 years | |
| Property purchase and mortgage | 6 years | |
| Property sale | 6 years | |
| Trusts | 6 years | |
| Wills | 80 years | |

## 4.3 Confidential Waste

- Any documents that have been identified to be destroyed are collected by a contracted confidential waste company from either the office site or off-site storage unit.

## 4.4 Certificates of Destruction

- Certificates of Destruction are provided on a monthly basis by a confidential waste company and are stored in the Accounts department at the Wakefield office.

# Case study 3: Alternative dispute resolution records held by the Transport for London Corporate Archives

*Photograph of a collection of their legal records reproduced courtesy of the TfL Corporate Archives*

Compiled by Clare Cowling

Completed May 2016

## *Acknowledgements*

The Legal Records at Risk project Director and Executive Committee wish to express our thanks to Transport for London (TfL) for its active, open and supportive co-operation in this case study; the TfL Corporate Archives in particular could not have been more helpful and we were highly impressed with the quality of the online catalogue and the extent and detailed nature of the records we viewed. Our special thanks to the following individuals:

- Melissa McGreechan, Assistant Archivist, TfL Corporate Archives, for her patience and courtesy in dealing with fragmented and vague requests for assistance, often at short notice.
- Jonathan Morris, Head of TfL Legal's Commercial Dispute Resolution team, for taking the time to provide us with a detailed explanation of TfL's dispute resolution process and of the Legal team's recordkeeping procedures.
- Simon Guild, Head of the Information Access team, for clarifying TfL's commitment to transparency and openness and for guiding us to the location and content of contract information on the TfL website.

## *Purpose of the case study*

The Legal Records at Risk (LRAR) project is concerned with identifying legal records of archival value in the private sector. Saving significant collections, stimulating changes of practice, avoiding duplication, and raising awareness of the value of LRAR are prioritised. Our definition of legal records is wider than their traditional classification as court records or formal documents such as deeds; we include records of institutions specialised to law (e.g. law firms, arbitrators, barristers, legal executives, patent agents, licensed conveyancers, court interpreters and ancillary bodies such as law stationers and legal publishers). We also include legal records produced in the course of their business by private sector companies (e.g. policy and procedure records and the individual case files produced by legal, property and governance departments).

Undertaking case studies of selected institutions which create legal records and of particular categories of legal records of value which may hitherto have been overlooked by researchers form a key platform of the project. Our case studies will demonstrate areas of best practice and community of practice (or lack thereof), identify key issues common to all or most institutions and recommend potential solutions, including liaison with archive repositories relating to the deposit of records of permanent value.

The case study which follows looks at a specific category of legal records, alternative dispute resolution (ADR) records, which have been created and later selected for archival preservation within a major transport company, TfL. The particular aims were as follows:

- To look at the business context within which ADR records sit and achieve a brief overview of the dispute resolution process in a large business.
- To gain an idea of the extent, content and value of such records.
- To determine how ADR records are selected by the Archives for preservation.
- To understand how ADR records are classified and indexed by the Archives.

- To support the hypothesis that ADR archives are primarily located within business archives and must therefore be searched for under their business context.

The case study was undertaken over a period of time from December 2015 – April 2016 by the LRAR project team, comprising project Director, Clare Cowling (an archivist and records manager) and the inspiration behind the project, William Twining (Quain Professor of Jurisprudence Emeritus, UCL).

## *Methodology*

1. Interviews: as part of the case study we conducted interviews with Jonathan Morris, Head of Commercial Dispute Resolution in TfL Legal, Simon Guild, Head of Information Access in Information Governance and Melissa McGreechan, Assistant Archivist, TfL Corporate Archives in Information Governance. The purpose was to obtain an overview of the business context of ADR records, the dispute resolution process within TfL and the policies around selection and preservation of, and internal/external access to, ADR records.
2. Searching the catalogue: the TfL Corporate Archives online catalogue was examined in detail to identify relevant records and understand the process by which researchers would locate them.
3. Examining the records: sample records were selected and examined in detail by the project team to understand their context, content and value in reflecting the development of the ADR process in the UK. Four visits in all were made to TfL to search the records and talk to stakeholders.

## *Administrative background*

### The business context

TfL is a statutory body created by the Greater London Authority Act 1999. This Act gives the Mayor of London a general duty to develop and apply policies to promote and encourage safe, integrated, efficient and economic transport facilities and services to, from and within London. TfL's role is to implement the Mayor's Transport Strategy and to manage those services across the capital for which the Mayor is responsible. TfL gained most of its functions from its predecessor London Regional Transport, but only took over responsibility for the Underground in 2003.

TfL has three subsidiary companies incorporated under the Companies Act 2006:

- London Transport Insurance (Guernsey) Limited
- TfL Trustee Company Limited
- Transport Trading Limited

The Commissioner reports to the TfL Board and leads a management team which is accountable for the daily running of the organisation and the work of more than 25,000 employees. There are three operational units, each with responsibility for different aspects of the organisation:

- Surface Transport
- Rail and Underground
- Crossrail

### *The legal context*

We interviewed Jonathan Morris, Head of TfL Legal's Commercial Dispute Resolution team, about the dispute resolution process at TfL. The team deals with any claims or disputes under TfL's infrastructure/construction contracts; additionally it manages disputes over intellectual property, operational and commercial property and debts owed.

TfL is quite unique in its merging of transport infrastructure and (currently) the size of budget for capital works. It has a strong focus on project delivery and implementation and as a result, whilst ensuring proper use of public funds, is less likely than many companies to engage in intransigent and lengthy litigation.

Having said that, TFL has in the past been involved in a number of high profile arbitrations, notably the 1910–11 arbitration between Westinghouse Electric and Manufacturing Company Ltd and the Underground Electric Railways Company of London Ltd. There are 89 records covering the dispute, dated 1901–30, available for research in the TfL Corporate Archives.

### TfL's dispute resolution process

- External law firms are employed for any significant disputes and always for large arbitration cases. The main category of dispute relates to construction contracts and costs can run into millions. TfL's construction contracts prior to 1996 sometimes included a standard arbitration clause to facilitate the process.

- Arbitrators are selected by mutual consent between the parties. Some contracts include lists of pre-agreed adjudicators/arbitrators. If the parties can't agree a nominating authority (e.g. London Court of International Arbitration, Centre for Effective Dispute Resolution (CEDR), Institute of Civil Engineers) is asked. The team has only ever used single arbitrators.
- Arbitrators' terms of appointment usually comprise standard forms proposed by the arbitrator and subject to negotiation and agreement by the parties. Some suites of standard form contracts contain model adjudication/arbitration terms. TfL's commercial lawyers draw up contracts and regularly review provisions e.g. for New Engineering Contract contracts. Contracts specify that arbitrations are confidential between the two parties, though the period of confidentiality is not specified. It is likely in any case that a liberal view would be taken to providing access due to the Freedom of Information Act and TfL's commitment to transparency (see below under **Compliance Context**); in other words TfL would approach the decision on the basis of 'why wouldn't we disclose' rather than 'why should we disclose'.
- Domestic arbitration has declined in recent years as a result of S.108 of the Construction Act (Housing Grants, Construction and Regeneration Act 1996), which gives an automatic right to refer a dispute to adjudication (meaning there's now no need to provide for this mechanism in contracts). Adjudication provides a relatively quick decision which is immediately implementable; adjudications are quicker and cheaper. Contracts will still provide for a full dispute resolution procedure (either arbitration or court) which a party dissatisfied with the adjudication decision may pursue, but the adjudication decision stands unless and until overturned. Arbitrations have therefore reduced from about two to three per year a few years ago to one a year at present and that figure will probably reduce further in the future.
- Additionally, following procedural changes within the Technology and Construction Court c. six–eight years ago, TfL reviewed its standard dispute resolution provisions and decided it would go to court as the final stage in a dispute instead of arbitration. TfL's greater commitment to transparency has also reduced the perception of the need to use arbitration to protect confidentiality. The standard procedure now is adjudication – court.
- Mediation is usually discussed pre-adjudication but is a mechanism that parties will keep in mind at any stage through to full trial in court or arbitration. Mediation offers greater flexibility to the parties to be innovative in reaching a settlement. In general less documentation is needed than in adjudication or arbitration – most mediations only last one day.

## The team's recordkeeping processes

- The team maintains a hybrid system of paper and digital case files. The digital material is stored in a case management system (currently in the process of being replaced by a new system). Cases are indexed in by case number and name of contractor or company, and/or project and location; no deletion of case files has taken place. Paper files are removed to the TfL Records Store when no longer current and stored pending disposal, either by destruction or transfer to the TfL Corporate Archives for permanent retention.
- Retention requirements: the business and legal life span of a case file can be very long indeed. Contracts executed as a deed have to be kept for 14 years after end of contract (given the terms of the Limitation Act), while Public Private Partnership contracts have a current life of 30 years. Once the legally specified retention period expires, however, there is no value to TfL Legal in keeping the records and the decision on what to preserve permanently is left to the Archives, which keeps major dispute resolution cases and contracts over £500,000.
- Retention of records by arbitrators themselves: most arbitrators TfL has dealt with are barristers and solicitors and they are instructed to return the papers to the parties at the conclusion of the case. In the case of appeals it is the awards and records of the parties to the hearing which are used as evidence, not the arbitrators' notes. According to Jonathan, arbitrators' own notes should be destroyed after the case is over, but TfL does not mandate or monitor this.

## *The compliance context*

We interviewed Simon Guild, Head of the Information Access team. The team manages Freedom of Information requests and facilitates the development of TfL's Transparency Strategy. Simon advised that all current contracts and tenders over £5,000 are listed, in accordance with the Strategy, on the Government contract finder site or the TfL website at the Invitation to Tender stage. All contracts over OJEU (Official Journal of the European Community) level are published on the government contract finder website; retention is not under the control of TfL. Where dispute resolution or confidentiality clauses are included, therefore, it will be possible to view them, although not all contracts will include such clauses.

TfL's commitment to transparency and FOI means that, as noted above, requests to view records not yet in the public domain (including legal records) will be treated positively unless it is clear that release would result in a breach of commercial confidentiality, legal professional privilege, personal privacy or public safety.

## The archives context

We interviewed the Assistant Archivist, Melissa McGreechan. The *TfL Corporate Archives* is the repository for those business and operational records of TfL which have been assessed as being of permanent research value and, as such, is responsible for safeguarding TfL's corporate memory. The Archives holds over 100,000 items (in both paper and digital format) dating from the 17th century to the present day. The Archives actively collects records which document the principal business functions and actions of Transport for London, its predecessor and subsidiary companies, particularly engineering, infrastructure, property records or records which demonstrate TfL's interaction with the wider community. The Archives' catalogue is now available online but is not yet linked to TNA's *Discovery* portal.

The Archives sits within TfL's General Counsel Directorate, composed of the following departments:

- Secretariat
- Internal Audit
- TfL Legal, comprising:
  - Commercial Dispute Resolution
  - Public Litigation Dept
  - Employment Relations
- Information Governance, comprising:
  - Privacy and Data Protection
  - Information Access (Freedom of Information)
  - Information and Records Management
  - TfL Corporate Archives

*The Archives collections policy:* the Archives collects records covering the history and legacy of TfL and predecessors, especially engineering, infrastructure and property records or records which demonstrate TfL's interaction with the wider community.

*Records retention and disposal rules and process:* the Records Manager and Archivist work closely when developing schedules to determine which records should be destroyed and which preserved permanently in the Archives. TfL has developed a number of generic schedules applicable to all departments plus business area-specific schedules. The schedules reference records by function rather than subject, so arbitration records would not be specifically mentioned but be tacitly included in Legal case files selected for preservation due to the importance of the case to TfL or the wider community.

For paper records the Archives undertakes an appraisal process three times a year of records signed off for destruction by the business (c.40,000 cartons per annum). An initial trawl is made using the descriptions of the records made by the information owners. If items look as though they may be archivally valuable they are physically examined by the Archives staff and a selection made (c.1000 cartons per annum). A lot of sampling is also undertaken. For digital records a process is still being developed – currently, other than for records of the 2012 Games (collected and listed immediately after the Games were over) and Secretariat records (an ongoing agreement has been made for digital transfers), there is no consistent collections process. The Records Manager seeks to identify such records in consultation with the Archivist when drafting disposal schedule rules, but the Archives has as yet no means of monitoring whether the business follows the rules.

*Archive storage*: paper records are held in a salt mine in Cheshire managed by Deepstore, a third-party provider. Digital records are stored in a Cloud-based system managed by a third-party company, Preservica. It is approved by TNA. The main benefits of using Preservica are that a) file format conversion is part of the contract b) system upgrades are automatic c) storage is secure d) the company has expertise in digital preservation, which the Archives does not yet have and e) the system is very affordable.

*Access rules*: the Archives operates a 20 year closure rule in line with TNA, though this would be subject to review and if a request was considered under FOI. The only records embargoed for more than 20 years are those containing personal data (84 years) or which may constitute a security risk (100 years). Bona fide academic researchers may be allowed access to closed records provided they sign the usual undertakings.

*Legal records*: the Archives collects legal records if they are relevant to the business context of a department and/or reflect a major dispute or cause celebre. It also holds numerous legal documents such as contracts and deeds. It does not deliberately target legal records – if they are relevant to the business context or reflect a major dispute or cause celebre they will be kept.

*Use of legal records*: the main customer base is the business itself; internal use has increased by 500% in the last five years. There is not a lot of external reference use, though this is expected to increase now that the catalogue is online. Few lawyers or legal researchers have approached the Archives. Statistics for 2015–16 to date (prior to the catalogue being widely available) on categories of researchers show that of 158 enquiries 12 were categorized as legal; seven of these were from internal clients and five were external of which four were enquiries about copyright and reproduction. Of internal clients not all enquiries submitted by TfL Legal have been defined as legal in nature – often they relate to property history, organisation history etc. And not all internal enquiries defined as legal have come from TfL Legal e.g. the Heritage Advisor and Property Programmes Director have made enquiries into legal records.

## *Finding the records*

*Search:* using the catalogue to find legal records: if a word appears in the title or description a catalogue search will pick it up, but records may not necessarily be defined in the descriptions in the way researchers expect, as files tend to be classified and described by function rather than subject matter. For example, TfL Legal lists and indexes construction disputes by contract number or company name, and this process will be followed by the Archives when cataloguing, so for 'mediation' or 'arbitration' records it might also be necessary to search on 'settlement', 'award', 'dispute' or 'contract' or by the name of the company, project or location.

Word searches of the catalogue by the LRAR team produced the following results:

- A search for 'legal' records produced 1074 hits for records dating from 1620–2014. Records listed included lands tribunal records, property agreements, deeds, wills, indentures, contracts, court cases, legal advice and the corporate records of TfL's various legal departments.
- The biggest number of hits came from a search on 'contracts', with 4,636 results listing major and minor contracts and leases dating from 1798–2015 and including contractual disputes.
- A search on 'deeds' yielded 532 results dating from 1620–2002.
- Searching under 'arbitration' in the catalogue yielded 291 file level entries, ranging from 1856–2000 as follows: individual arbitration cases relating primarily to construction or employment disputes and, post 1933, TfL's own records of proceedings and awards of the London Passenger Transport Arbitration Tribunal (the official records of the Tribunal are held by TNA).
- Searching on 'disputes' gave 99 results dating from 1855–1995 and comprising mostly industrial and construction contract issues.
- 'Conciliation' searches yielded 360 results, primarily in relation to conciliation staff, but with some records of industrial disputes.
- 'Mediation' only gave seven results dating from 1986–95; these were of particular interest as they related to construction disputes.
- 'Adjudication' yielded only one result, relating to a tender for the Northern Line Adjudication: Depot Enabling Works in 1995.
- 'Court case' gave 46 results from 1865–1995 and comprised both court and tribunal cases.
- 'Tribunal' yielded 349 results from 1910–96 and primarily comprised records of transport tribunals both in the UK and abroad.

Many entries will of course be duplicated. The wide variations in catalogue search results indicate the need for researchers to think beyond obvious keywords when seeking relevant material. 'Disputes', for example, could refer to arbitration, mediation, conciliation or a court case.

*The records:* for details of records physically examined see **Annex I**.

We found detailed records relating to arbitration and mediation cases. Most were either industrial or construction disputes; files relating to the latter sometimes, but not always, included the relevant sections of the contracts under dispute. Typical examples of construction disputes examined in detail included:

- An arbitration case in 1903–10 between The British Westinghouse Electric and Manufacturing Company Limited and The Underground Electric Railways Company of London Limited (89 folders, ref: LT000195), including points of claim; briefs to respondents; notes on hearings; correspondence; evidence; summary.
- An arbitration (compensation) dispute in 1932–34 between the Metropolitan Railway Line and

the Edgeware Golf Club over the diversion of the club (two bound volumes, ref: LT001541) contained correspondence, maps and papers (including valuations submitted to hearing) concerning arbitration between Foster Brothers Company Limited and the London Passenger Transport Board (LPTB) over claims of disturbance and damage to the Foster Brothers' business caused by LPTB works at Uxbridge. It also included presumably extraneous material such as the handicaps of golf members!

- International mediation records also feature, such as a 1986–87 contract mediation case between London Transport International Services Ltd and the Singapore Mass Rapid Transit Corporation relating to construction of a tunnel (one box, ref: LT001434). Records include correspondence, memoranda, reports, working and legal papers concerning consultancy work provided by London Transport International Services Ltd.
- The records of a 1992–96 contract dispute which went to mediation (ten folders, ref: LT000577) include correspondence, summary of dispute, contract summary, legal advice, attendance notes, proceedings, synopsis of matters referred for mediation, site visit notes, contractor's response, London Underground's instructions to counsel, lists of documents submitted and correspondence with CEDR re appointment of mediator and agreement (terms of mediation) drafted by CEDR (but no copy of the agreement, alas).

## *Case study conclusions*

1. TfL holds a wealth of legal records in its Archives, including numerous records relating to alternative dispute resolution. This supports our thesis that the bulk of surviving archival ADR – and other legal – records will at present be found within business archives.
2. ADR records will be found under a variety of series titles, which are based on either functions or departmental structures at the time the records were created. 'Arbitration' or 'mediation' is rarely (though occasionally) included in series titles. Researchers therefore need to be careful not only to think widely about keyword terms, but also not to narrow their fields of search to series titles or the records of 'Legal' departments.
3. ADR records in TfL are not only numerous, but often very detailed and comprehensive, containing not only the minutes of the case itself and the findings, but solicitors' shorthand notes, correspondence, summaries and copies of original documents used as evidence.
4. Concerns that confidentiality of proceedings might be a barrier to accessing modern records appear to be unfounded, at least as far as TfL is concerned. It is probable that a similarly liberal approach to access to ADR records will be found in other business archives, though we have yet to investigate whether they have the same commitment to transparency and openness as TfL.

## *Annex I: sample records examined*

A selection of records within series originating from the following departments was examined.

| Series | Series title and dates | Item description/notes on viewing |
|---|---|---|
| LT000102 | Staff: Local Working Party Meetings 1984–1987 | Minutes of the meetings of Machinery Attendants Local Working Party 1–18, including details of discussions on the Jubilee Line works, escalator chain lubricating equipment and proposed incentive schemes for attendants. Also included are notes of meeting with SC9 representatives and the Conciliation Committee, with references to fire hazards. |
| LT000155 | London Transport Executive (LTE): Chief Establishment Office: Staff Administration Office: Sponsorship Housing Arrangements for Staff: Minutes, Correspondence and Memoranda, 1919–1950 | Includes staff arbitration tribunal papers |
| LT000195 | Underground Electric Railways Company of London Limited: Power Department: Reports of Proceedings between Westinghouse Electric and Manufacturing Company Limited and the Underground Electric Railways Company of London Limited, 1903–1910 | Arbitration Case between The British Westinghouse Electric and Manufacturing Company Limited and The Underground Electric Railways Company of London Limited: Points of claim; briefs to respondents; notes on hearings; correspondence; evidence; summary |
| LT000232 | London Passenger Transport Board (LPTB) and Successors: Office of the Executive: Arthur Herbert Grainger: Correspondence, Minutes of Meetings and Reports, 1934–1965 | Minutes of the proceedings of a tribunal concerning differences between the London Transport Executive and the Transport and General Workers' Union regarding the proposed payment of extra rates to road operating and garage and depot staffs for duties after 1pm on Saturday, 1949 |
| LT000302 | London Passenger Transport Board (LPTB): Office of the Comptroller and Accountant: London Passenger Pooling Scheme Papers, 1931–1936 | London Passenger Pooling Scheme: Arbitration Proceedings Counsel's Brief, 1934–1935 |
| LT000343 | Metropolitan and Great Central Joint Committee: Secretary's Records, 1889–1947 | Metropolitan and Great Central Joint Committee: standing arbitration correspondence 1923 |
| LT000577 | London Underground Ltd (LUL): LUL Department: Litigation section – reports and papers, 1992–1996 | Costain Building and Civil Engineering Ltd: Earl's Court Station: Platform Reconstruction and Interim Refurbishment Contract BCE 0236: Mediation Papers 21 Feb 1994–31 Aug 1995 between Costain and LUL. Includes correspondence, summary of dispute, contract summary, legal advice, attendance notes, proceedings, synopsis of matters referred for mediation, site visit notes, contractor's response, LUL instructions to counsel, lists of documents. Corr with CEDR re appointment of mediator and agreement drafted by CEDR |
| LT000594 | London Passenger Transport Board (LPTB): Parliamentary Office: Correspondence and Papers on the Independent Undertakings Arbitration Tribunals, 1926–1946 | The London Passenger Transport Arbitration Tribunal – The London Passenger Transport Board (LPTB) and The independent Undertakings – Brief to Counsel, 1929–1933 |
| LT000644 | London Passenger Transport Board (LPTB): Secretary: East London Railway Joint Committee: Papers, Minutes and Correspondence, 1880–1947 | East London Railway Joint Committee: arbitration – 2 cases 1886–1887. Includes proceedings; selection of members; solicitor's shorthand notes |
| LT000665 | London Transport and predecessors: Labour Relations Office, 1925–1984 | Control Grade Staff – arbitration. Correspondence, minutes and papers 1960–1970 |
| LT000694 | London Passenger Transport Board (LPTB): Parliamentary Office and Solicitor: Correspondence, Notes and Memoranda regarding London Passenger Transport Bills, 1913–1971 | London Passenger Transport Act 1933 – arbitration under Section 23 between the London Passenger Transport Board (LPTB) and the Council of the Metropolitan Borough of Fulham, 1938 |

| Series | Series title and dates | Item description/notes on viewing |
|---|---|---|
| LT000783 | London Passenger Transport Board (LPTB) and Successors: Solicitor: Papers, Correspondence and Memoranda concerning Staff Arbitration Cases with regards to the London Passenger Transport Act 1933, 1924–1960 | London Passenger Transport Act 1933: Individual Arbitration Cases, 1934–1938 |
| LT000799 | London Passenger Transport Board (LPTB): Office of the Executive: Correspondence, Minutes and Reports, 1928–1964 | Report by the Board of Conciliation entitled 'The Proposal of the London Transport Executive in an Endeavour to Overcome the Shortage of Bus Drivers and Conductors'. Includes details of a history of negotiations and an explanation of London Transport's proposal 1955 |
| LT001176 | London General Omnibus Company (LGOC): Office of the Operating Manager: Correspondence and Memoranda, 1914–1933 | Correspondence and minutes of meetings concerning a conciliation scheme between representatives of the Railway Executive Committee and Railway Staff Union representatives. Also contains details of proposals for the creation of a trainmen's committee in place of existing conciliation boards 1914–1920 |
| LT001434 | London Transport International Services Ltd: Singapore – correspondence and reports, 1968–1991 | Mass Rapid Transit (MRT) Mediation: Contract 105: Correspondence, memoranda, reports, working and legal papers re consultancy work provided by London Transport International Services Ltd for the tunnel mediation between the Singapore Mass Rapid Transit Corporation and John King Management Services 11 Jun 1986–10 Dec 1987 |
| LT001541 | London Passenger Transport Board Estate Office: Railway Acts, 1880–1974 | Arbitration (compensation) dispute between the Metropolitan Railway Line and the Edgeware Golf Club over the diversion of the club; Correspondence, maps and papers (including valuations submitted to hearing) concerning arbitration between Foster Brothers Company Limited and the London Passenger Transport Board (LPTB) over claims of disturbance and damage to the Foster Brothers' business caused by LPTB works at Uxbridge. 1936–1937 |
| LT001670 | London Regional Transport (LRT) and Predecessors: Bus Operations: Correspondence, Memoranda and Minutes of Meetings, 1913–1992 | Arbitration award – Difference of interpretation between the London Transport Board and the Transport and General Workers' Union of certain clauses in the Central Bus Drivers and Conductors Agreement – June 1966. Includes correspondence, background papers, verbatim notes of Board's proceedings, award. |
| LT001907 | London Regional Transport (LRT): London Underground Limited (LUL): Central Line Project (CLP): Correspondence, Reports, Meetings and Engineering Drawings, 1988–2001 | Reports and information from the legal department; consists of time and money claims, case laws, time and damages in construction contracts, delay analysis, construction disputes, claims and resolutions, building contract claims and extracts from legal documents |
| LT001934 | London Regional Transport (LRT): London Underground Limited (LUL): Northern Line Renewal Project, 1967–1999 | Northern Line Adjudication: Depot Enabling Works – budget/tender cost comparison and proposed changes to schedule 6 part one of the usage contract, 1995 |
| LT000172 | London Passenger Transport Board (LPTB) and Successors: Chief Engineer: Contracts, Agreements and Tenders, 1931–1952 | Contracts nos 1–99 [some (not all) include a standard arbitration clause (see Annex II)] |

## *Annex II: Standard arbitration clauses in TfL contracts*

The clause below was found in a number of contracts in the London Passenger Transport Board (LPTB) and Successors' Chief Engineer's records, 1931–52, ref: LT000172:

> Every certificate in writing by the Engineer and every decision, requirement or order given or made by him in accordance with the provisions of this Contract with regard to any matter left to the control, approval or decision of the Engineer shall be binding and conclusive on the parties. Save and subject as aforesaid if and when any question shall arise between the Contractors and the Board or the Contractors and the Engineer in connection with this Contract or as to the construction or meaning of this Contract, the question at issue shall be referred to the decision of an Engineer to be agreed upon by the Board and the Contractors or failing agreement to be nominated by the President for the time being of the Institute of Civil Engineers and the decision of such arbitrator shall be final and binding upon both parties and the cost of the Reference shall be in his discretion and the submission in this clause contained shall be deemed a submission to arbitration within the Arbitration Act 1889, or any statutory modification thereof for the time being in force. Provided always that the pendency of any dispute, difference or arbitration shall not entitle the Contractors to suspend work or exempt them from the consequence of a suspension of work unless it be ultimately decided that such suspension was reasonable.

## *Annex III: TfL Corporate Archives categories of users*

Requestor category:

- Internal (for all internal customers the business area in which they work is recorded)
- Academic
- Genealogist
- London Transport Museum
- Museum/Archive
- External Legal
- Government
- Student
- Media
- Public other
- Religious Order
- Volunteer Enquiry
- Author
- Transport Enthusiast

Subject category:

- Genealogy
- Architecture History
- Property History
- Transport History
- Organisational History
- History of Art and Design
- Social History
- Technology
- Public Policy
- Environment
- History of London
- Legal
- Economic History
- Prominent People
- Other
- Website

Statistics on 'legal' categories of researchers and research:

2015–16

- Of 158 defined enquiries received 12 were categorised as legal; seven internal and five external of which four were enquiries about copyright and reproduction.
- Of 225 defined enquirers only one was categorized as Legal External (the LRAR project).

2014–15

- Of 273 enquirers only five were defined as (internal) legal; there were no legal external.
- Of internal clients not all enquiries submitted by the Legal department were defined as legal in nature – they often related to property history, organisation history etc. And not all internal enquiries defined as legal came from the Legal department; the Heritage Advisor and Property Programmes Director amongst others have made 'legal' enquiries.

## *Annex IV: TfL Corporate Archives Reader Registration Form*

*Please provide proof of your identity, for example passport or photocard driving licence;* AND *proof of your address, for example a photocopy of a recent bank statement, council tax bill or utility bill.*

**Name:**
**Address:**
**Email:**
**Telephone:**

DATA PROTECTION STATEMENT

- I will ensure that my use of any personal data contained within records held by the TfL Corporate Archives complies with the Data Protection Act 1998
- I will not pass personal data to any third parties
- I will use personal data contained in the collections only for the purposes of my research as detailed in my initial enquiries
- I understand that I must not produce research, or any other form of communication, that identifies a living data subject or descendents(s) whose personal information is contained within the TfL Corporate Archives unless express permission from the Corporate Archives has been obtained
- I will ensure that any personal data obtained by me from the Corporate Archives is kept secure, and that it is securely disposed of when no longer required for the purposes of my research

SIGNATURE*:

DATE:

NAME:

*This must be the personal signature of the person making the request. A stamped or typewritten signature or the signature of an agent is not acceptable. Anyone ordering copies on behalf of another person must obtain that person's signature on this form.

COPYRIGHT DECLARATION

I declare that:

a. I shall not use the Work/s except for research for a non-commercial purpose or for private study;
b. I shall not copy, publish or distribute the whole or any part of the Work/s for any reason whatsoever;
c. to the best of my knowledge the copyright owner has not prohibited copying of the Work/s.

I agree to indemnify and hold TfL and/or the rights owner(s) of the Work/s, harmless from any and all claims, liabilities, damages, costs and expenses, including reasonable legal expenses, arising from the use of the Work/s or any breach of the above.

I acknowledge that the use of copies in TfL copyright for publication (including web-site publication), exhibition or broadcast or any other purpose requires permission from the TfL Corporate Archives.

I acknowledge that the use of copies for publication (including web-site publication), exhibition or broadcast or any other purpose requires permission from the current owner(s) of copyright in the original document. Researchers are responsible for identifying the current copyright owners and obtaining permission.

SIGNATURE*:

DATE:

NAME:

*This must be the personal signature of the person making the request. A stamped or typewritten signature or the signature of an agent is not acceptable. Anyone ordering copies on behalf of another person must obtain that person's signature on this form.

I have read and understood both the Reading Room rules and the Record Handling Guidelines of the TfL Corporate Archives.

*Signed:*

*Dated:*

*Data provided on this form will be used for visitor monitoring and statistical collation. TfL Corporate Archives will not share personal data with any third party.*

# Case study 4: The records of the Council for Licensed Conveyancers

*Logo reproduced by permission of the Council for Licensed Conveyancers*

Complied by Clare Cowling

Case study completed March 2017

Report vetted and amended by the CLC, November 2018

## *Acknowledgements*

The Legal Records at Risk Project Director and Executive Committee wish to express our thanks to the Council for Licensed Conveyancers (CLC) for its co-operation in this case study and in particular the active support of Simon Thomson (Information and Intelligence Officer) and Stephen Ward (Director of Strategy and External Relations).

## *Definitions*

- Archive/archives: in the traditional definition the term 'archive/archives' refers both to the repository where records of permanent value are stored and made available for research and to the records stored in it.
- Archiving: in the CLC and most institutions specialised to law, the process of transferring records to cheaper storage to reduce costs.
- Records: information, in any form, created, received and maintained as evidence and information by an organisation in pursuance of legal obligations or in the transaction of business.
- Records disposal: the process of *either* destroying records once they no longer have any business or legal value *or* depositing them in an archives for permanent retention.
- Records store: in some large organisations (e.g. government departments) the records store, as distinct from the archives, is a secure repository for semi-current records pending their disposal as opposed to records of permanent value which are stored separately in an archives. In a number of organisations however, the two functions of semi-current records store and archives are combined for economy of effort and the term 'archives' is used to refer to both.
- Semi-current records: records which are no longer needed for day to day use but are still required for occasional business reference or to be kept for a period of time by law before being destroyed.

## *Purpose of the case study*

The Legal Records at Risk (LRAR) project is concerned with identifying, and rescuing for posterity, legal records of archival value in the private sector. Saving significant collections, stimulating changes of practice and raising awareness of the value of legal records are prioritised. Our definition of legal records is wider than their traditional classification as court records or formal documents such as deeds; we include the records of institutions and individuals specialised to law (e.g. law firms, arbitrators, barristers, legal executives, patent agents, licensed conveyancers, court interpreters and ancillary bodies such as legal stationers and law publishers). We also include legal records produced in the course of their business by private sector companies (such as policy, procedure and compliance records and the individual case files produced by legal, property and governance departments).

Undertaking case studies of selected institutions which create legal records and of categories of legal records of value which may hitherto have been overlooked by researchers forms a key platform of the project. Our case studies will demonstrate areas of best practice and community of practice (or lack thereof), identify key issues common to all or most institutions and recommend potential solutions, including liaison with archival repositories relating to the deposit of records of permanent value.

The case study which follows looks at the creation, management and disposal of its records (by destruction or transfer to an archive) by the CLC. The specific aims were as follows:

1. To survey the CLC's records and recordkeeping practices.
2. To understand the business drivers behind the CLC's management of its records.
3. To demonstrate the business benefits to the CLC of making provision for the preservation of its archives.
4. To seek an archival home for historically valuable records of the CLC.

For a copy of the detailed case study proposal made to the CLC see **Annex I.**

## *Methodology*

1. The provisions of the Legal Services Act 2007 were scrutinised to gain a general understanding of regulatory functions and responsibilities.
2. The CLC's website was examined in detail to gain an insight into its core functions and values and to note records already in the public domain (e.g. Council minutes 2013–16).
3. CLC publications, including the Handbook and Factsheets, were examined for references to records created and recordkeeping requirements.
4. Interviews and emails: face to face and email discussions were held between the LRAR project Director and key personnel in the CLC, including the heads of the following departments:
   - Education
   - External Relations
   - Operations
   - Regulatory Standards
5. Questionnaires: questionnaires were circulated at the time of interview to the departmental representatives requesting details of the department's records, its recordkeeping practices, its disposal policy and the use (internal and external) of non-current records. See **Annex II** for the questionnaires.

## *Changes since the time of writing*

The CLC have asked us to point out as we publish this case study that there have been a range of developments since it was completed. Most notably, the GDPR has come into force and the CLC has taken steps to ensure that its generation and retention of records is compliant with that. Also, the staffing structure of the CLC and the responsibilities of directors have both evolved.

## *Administrative background*

### The legislative context

The CLC was established under the Administration of Justice Act 1985 as a regulatory body for conveyancers. Unusually in the sector, it is not a membership organisation,[6] but it is itself both an Approved Regulator and Licensing Authority with its activities overseen by the Legal Services Board. It is bound by the provisions of the Legal Services Act 2007 to include in its regulatory activities:

- setting educational and training standards for entry to the profession;
- issuing licences to practise to those qualified to provide conveyancing and probate services and to alternative business structures (ABS's);
- maintaining a register of all licensed conveyancers and regulated bodies;
- setting standards to regulate the professional practice, conduct and discipline of licensed conveyancers and regulated bodies;
- setting standards to maintain adequate professional indemnity insurance and a compensation fund to protect consumers;
- monitoring the work and conduct of regulated bodies;

6 Representation of CLC-regulated lawyers is undertaken by a number of organisations including the Conveyancing Association and the Society of Licensed Conveyancers.

- providing guidance and advice to regulated bodies to maintain compliance with its regulatory requirements;
- investigating allegations of misconduct and, where appropriate, taking disciplinary action;
- collaborating with key stakeholders in the legal services market to monitor and shape future policy.

## The business context

The CLC currently licenses over 1,300 individuals and 210 institutions, accounting respectively in 2011 (the CLC estimates) for about 4% of authorised persons and 5% of all institutions in the legal sector. It services 10–15% of the market for conveyancing – transactions with a value of around £11bn–£15bn each year – and more than 20% of all re-mortgaging activity. More recently the CLC has extended its regulatory expertise to cover probate and, following the Legal Services Act, alternative business structures, although the CLC was already regulating ABS firms under another name thanks to its founding legislation.

The CLC considers that conveyancers require business acumen in addition to legal expertise. It requires those applying for licences to include a 3-year business plan with their application and monitors the progress of that business plan.

## The community context

The Introduction to the CLC's *Handbook* makes it clear that the CLC considers that it has the following obligations

> 'protecting and promoting the public interest as follows;
> a) supporting the constitutional principle of the rule of law;
> b) improving access to justice;
> c) protecting and promoting the interests of consumers;
> d) promoting competition in the provision of legal services;
> e) encouraging an independent, strong, diverse and effective legal profession;
> f) increasing public understanding of the citizen's legal rights and duties;
> g) promoting and maintaining adherence to the professional principles'.[7]

According to its website, the CLC's

> 'mission is to protect the public interest, provide consumer choice and to promote effective competition in the legal services market. We do so by setting entry standards and regulating providers to deliver high quality, accessible legal services'.

The organisation is keen to demonstrate the transparency and openness of its procedures and policies to the public and would like to see conveyancing become more of a focus for academic research. Its Publication Policy reinforces this proactive approach as follows:

> 'Unless otherwise stated, information will be published on the CLC's website. Where information is not published because it is not proportionate to do so, it will still be available on request.We make this commitment in the public and consumer interest and in line with the principles of good regulation.'[8]

## *The records*

CLC is governed by a non-executive Council and its operations are managed by a Senior Management Team (SMT). The following categories of records are created, acquired and managed:

1. Governance: e.g. Council and committee papers, policy and strategy records.
2. Education and training: e.g. training policy, CLC and CPD training records, examination papers, student files.
3. Marketing and external relations: e.g. website, consultations, surveys, conferences, press releases, speeches.
4. Regulatory: e.g. *Handbook*, *Code of Conduct*, Register of all licenced conveyancers and regulated bodies, licensing applications, appeals and adjudication records, accountants' reports, complaints, monitoring records, investigations records, Compensation Fund records and the records of intervened firms.

7 CLC *Handbook* 2011 Introduction https://www.clc-uk.org/handbook/the-handbook/#Introduction.
8 Publication Policy 2014 s.2 & 5 http://www.conveyancer.org.uk/About-Us-(1)/Publication-Policy.aspx.

5. Administration: e.g. finance, human resources, office management, management information, facilities and premises records.

This case study will concern itself with the first four categories of records.

### *Who does what*

In common with most organisations, the CLC moves its functions between departments, abolishes and merges departments and creates new ones from time to time. To undertake its work the CLC was at the time of writing structured into the following departments in addition to the usual administrative areas.

- Education
- External Relations
- Operations
- Regulatory Standards

At the time of writing the departments carried out the following functions:

### Education:

Responsible for the education and training of conveyancing students. The department was part of Operations until May 2016. Its training role was passed to the Scottish Qualification Authority as an awarding body in 2017. It now concentrates on education and training policy and standards development.

It holds paper student files from 1985; until 2009 these were held in paper format. In 2009 records began to be entered into a digital database managed by a third-party company (the database has since been brought in-house). There are currently c.13,550 student records in the database. Input has been inconsistent and the amount of information entered has been reduced e.g. until 2016 licensing details were included in the database.

The department also holds material such as examination papers, records of training providers and consultants and policy material such as training framework records. Much of the material contains personal data. For details see **Annex III**.

### External Relations:

Responsible for the CLC's media and government relations and communications with the regulated community as well as licensing and complaints handling as follows.

1. Licensing: the department oversees the process. It inherited an IT project to move licensing data to a new database and now manages the database and the records in it.
2. Complaints. The CLC deals with two categories: complaints about lawyers and complaints about organisations. The department is responsible for managing complaints about organisations.
3. Communications with conveyancers about particular issues.
4. Publicity/marketing/surveys/research. Surveys and research comprise raw data and reports; the latter are usually published. The department also writes articles, press releases, press statements, press comments etc and guidance notes on, e.g., cybersecurity.
5. The department creates the CLC *Newsletter* and manages the website and Twitter account. It moderates all content. The website is not regularly archived although a version of its website was archived in early 2018.
6. Government/regulatory liaison/consultations, including consultations and responses to legal regulators and lobbying government departments.
7. Twice-yearly conferences and graduation ceremonies. The department organises the conferences, including marketing, presentations, attendees.
8. It contributes to Legal Choices, a consumer-facing website jointly funded by all the regulators and managed by the SRA.
9. The department produces papers for Council and briefing papers for the Senior Management Team.

### Operations:

Undertakes the regulation and monitoring process, covering 235 practices (c.13,500 conveyancers) at the time of writing as follows:

1. Licensing records: the department carries out due diligence for the first licence as an employee;

to be a partner or director in a firm a Manager Licence is required. The records include practice details, new licences and applications for a CPD licence, Experian checks, costs, complaints and Compensation Fund information.

2. Monitoring and inspections – the team is overseen by Operations. In 2016 there were 62 inspections; they are carried out for the following reasons: complaint or intelligence received, unsatisfactory previous inspection or simply because there has been no inspection for some years. Two Regulation Supervision managers are allocated certain firms and develop a relationship with them. Inspections are face to face, checks are made for non-compliance, efforts made to help resolve the issues and reports compiled. The department is now measuring patterns of non-compliance to provide better guidance to the regulated community.
3. Interventions. The department carries out the intervention process and is responsible for the intervention files, though the process as a whole is overseen by Regulatory Standards.
4. Compensation Fund management.
5. Responsible for the annual Accountants' reports. Included in the monitoring files.
6. Records on individual practices e.g. a new practice has to provide bank reconciliations and attend workshops.
7. Thematic reviews and desktop reviews around issues affecting all practices e.g. anti-money laundering reviews; ICO reviews; cybercrime to help determine which issues need addressing next.
8. Responsible for the legacy Education records

## Regulatory Standards:

Responsible for legal and regulatory functions including CLC Policy, Standards, Disciplinary Action and Legal Affairs as follows:

1. Policy development: consultations, wider issues, changing role of regulation; relationship with Legal Standards Board, the CLC's oversight regulator.
2. Regulatory guidance – *Handbook*, *Code of Conduct*, Client Charter etc.
3. Maintenance of the Register of licensed conveyancers (a regulatory requirement).
4. Database of licensees: dates of registration, when relationship terminated (similar to, but contains more information than, the Register).
5. Conduct complaints – there are two categories; service complaints and conduct complaints. The former are referred back to the firm and/or the Legal Ombudsman; the latter are managed by Regulatory Standards, which contacts the practice with a request for an explanation.
6. Records of intervened firms: matter files are destroyed after six years (sale files) or 15 years (purchase files). Original documents are currently kept indefinitely.

## *Records management*

In common with most businesses, the CLC runs a hybrid records management system i.e. a combination of paper and electronic records. A relocation in 2014 resulted in some scanning, destruction and rationalisation of records in line with the destruction and retention policy.

*1. Paper records*:

- Scanning: the CLC is attempting to go paperless, but some legacy records are still in paper as are a small amount of current records; a scanning programme for legacy records has been completed and incoming hard copy material is being digitised going forward. Only paper records which have been scanned have been destroyed to date – the CLC would welcome advice on disposal of the remainder.
- Storage: semi-current hard copy records, both of the CLC and of the firms in which it intervenes, are held by an off-site third-party storage provider. Storage costs are low but retrieval costs are high. The 2015 Business Plan (p.10) included an objective to complete the removal of and client files collected during interventions into CLC-regulated firms to third-party storage in order to reduce costs which was completed.

*2. Electronic records*: the majority of records created by the CLC are now born digital and the intention is that they be managed digitally. CLC would appreciate suggestions on how to facilitate the more efficient use and management of born-digital records.

*3. Records of intervened firms*: when a firm closes or is intervened in (e.g. due to competency or misconduct issues) the CLC takes in the firm's records. The records may be in digital or paper format or both. Firms' use of born-digital records has also changed the relationship with clients as there may now be no physical meeting; it is therefore even more important that accurate records of client relationships are maintained. There can be challenges with digital records created by firms that have subsequently been intervened into where they are stored on bespoke IT systems which could be more difficult to access than widely used case management or data storage tools. There may also problems accessing records stored in the Cloud or protected by identity verification checking systems, but the CLC has not yet encountered resistance from firms to providing that information.

*4. Disposal of records*: the CLC has rules for the disposal of the matter files of intervened firms, whether paper or digital. It has destroyed many of its own paper files following scanning. There are, however, no rules in place for the disposal of the CLC's own digital records and there is a need to decide when and how the CLC's own paper records should be disposed of.

*5. Use of records*: the potential value of semi-current paper records as an asset has not really been considered. The CLC has not received any external requests (other than from conveyancers) for information about its records but would be happy to respond to such requests. With born-digital records, the CLC's outward-facing modern digital records are made publicly available on the website in accordance with its Publication Policy[9] but there is no policy as yet of routinely ensuring the continued public accessibility of these records once they have been removed from the website. Snapshots of the website would help, but CLC is aware that it also needs to devise a procedure to log material on the website, including all published versions, plus a record of where documentation is stored after removal.

## *Case study findings*

*The CLC and records as an asset*: the CLC clearly recognises the value of its current records as an asset, making a great many of them publicly accessible via its website. It is also aware of the PR value of making its older records available to the public via an archive repository but does not appear to be reusing its older records for its own business purposes such as marketing, house histories or exhibitions. This may be due to the fact that staff do not have a detailed knowledge of the older paper records and that the current arrangement of digital records is not conducive to this type of internal research, or it may simply be that the potential value of older records as a business asset has not yet been considered.

*The CLC and confidentiality*: the exception rather than the rule? Confidentiality was not raised as an issue during this case study since the CLC is confident in the security of its records storage systems. Client confidentiality is therefore protected and is not seen in any way as a barrier to making other CLC records (i.e. its business records) available for research.[10] The CLC clearly sets out its position on confidentiality in its Publication Policy, which includes clear definitions of absolute and qualified exemptions, as follows:

> 'Our approach to considering exemptions to our general commitment to openness takes account of general freedom of information practice, the public interest and the principles of good regulation (proportionality, accountability, consistency, transparency, targeting)'.[11]

The CLC therefore bucks the trend LRAR has come up against in many legal institutions, which is to be unnecessarily secretive and nervous about letting the public know how it works and has worked in the past; indeed, respecting client confidentiality is sometimes used as the justification for not wishing to make *any* records available. The CLC, on the other hand, has a commitment to openness and transparency and to act according to the principles of Freedom of Information, even though it is not subject to FOI. This is a model which should be studied and, preferably, followed by, other institutions specialised to law if they wish to challenge the public's perception that legal practitioners work in arcane and secretive ways.

*The CLC and archives*: several legal institutions contacted by LRAR advised that their organisation, and therefore their records, were 'too recent' to require any action or even consideration towards saving them for posterity. It is refreshing to engage with an organisation like the CLC which considers that there is value in developing procedures now to ensure modern records too (especially born-digital records) are rescued for eventual research.

LRAR is already in discussions with the London Metropolitan Archives regarding an ongoing arrangement for the deposit of CLC records of value. This will of course reduce the CLC's own records storage and management costs,[12] since archive repositories do not charge organisations for storing and caring for historical material, though donations

9 http://www.conveyancer.org.uk/About-Us-(1)/Publication-Policy.aspx

10 For example, all individual cases (such as interventions) discussed in Council are anonymised, so making Council papers available for research would not breach confidentiality.

11 Publication Policy section on Exemptions http://www.conveyancer.org.uk/About-Us-(1)/Publication-Policy.aspx.

12 Not only to reduce the cost of storing paper. The ongoing costs of digital storage and of accessing older digital records are often overlooked when organisations are seeking to reduce information management overheads.

towards physical transfer expenses are welcomed.

The bulk of CLC's records, including those of archival value, are now born-digital; many of them are published on the CLC's website but there is no digital 'archive' as such which can easily be searched for material which has been removed from the website. An arrangement with LMA to transfer digital records will remove any business need to keep an in-house digital 'archive' of records formerly available on the website, though it is recommended that CLC seek expert advice, such as that offered by the British Library, on regularly archiving snapshots of its website.

*The CLC and records management*: the CLC has requested practical advice and guidance on the management of modern records. In response to this and similar requests from other organisations, LRAR is creating a set of best practice guidelines on records management which will be made available on the LRAR website. The guidance will include advice on, e.g., managing born-digital records, email, documents in shared network drives and scanning.

The CLC is also seeking advice on records disposal. A retention and disposal schedule for its business records has been drafted for comment and will be found at **Annex III**. The schedule does not include recommendations for administrative records as advice on disposal of such records is readily available elsewhere.[13]

*Interventions records: a special case*: the CLC has made the risk-based decision to regularly destroy the bulk of records of intervened firms, while retaining client documents (deeds, birth certificates etc.) and records relevant to the intervention into the regulated entity.[14] It has therefore largely avoided the issues faced by the SRA, which has until recently stored enormous quantities of records of intervened firms indefinitely.[15] The records of interventions held by the CLC are, admittedly, less complex than those held by the SRA in that most of the matter files held by CLC are straightforward conveyancing records which require little in the way of appraisal, but the disposal of client documents is still an issue. The CLC might like to examine the relevant sections of the draft file retention schedule[16] published by the SRA to see if some of its provisions could be a good fit for the CLC. It might also like to follow the recommendation of The Law Society to offer client documents to local authority record offices if efforts to return the documents to the client are unsuccessful.[17]

The CLC has advised that intervened firms sometimes are not easily able to hand over intervention records where they are in digital format and have been stored with external providers (particularly in the Cloud). It would benefit the CLC in particular and the conveyancing profession in general if all conveyancers were required to include a contractual clause with Cloud providers (and indeed with any external information storage provider) specifying that, on contract expiry or firm closure (including intervention), the firm's records must be returned to the firm or, in the case of an intervention, passed to the CLC.

The CLC recognises that it needs expert advice on the management of its modern records and the disposal of its legacy material. LRAR can provide generic advice on the former and will broker the arrangement with LMA for transfer of the latter, but neither activity should be viewed as a one-off exercise (see **Recommendations** below).

## Case study recommendations

*Archiving records*: the CLC should liaise with LMA as soon as practicable to arrange the transfer of legacy material of research value as defined by the retention and disposal schedule at **Annex III**. LRAR will be happy to broker this arrangement. An ongoing agreement should be made with LMA for the regular transfer of born digital records of value (e.g. annually) via a secure file transfer protocol or other means as agreed. The agreement should include the CLC's access requirements for its records (e.g. open to the public, closed for 20 years, closed for 100 years where personal data is included). Although the LMA does not charge for its services, the CLC should consider making a donation to LMA in recognition of the cost of maintaining its records of value permanently, cataloguing them and making them available to the public.

Concerning client documents held by the CLC following interventions, the CLC should consider transferring unclaimed documents to local authority archives. The British Records Association has been brokering such transfers from law firms to archives for decades and will be happy to offer advice on how to go about this activity.

*Ongoing records management*: the CLC has benefitted from the enthusiasm and experience of individual members of staff with an interest in records management and archiving. It does, however, have an ongoing requirement to manage its records more efficiently on a day-to-day basis. While generic guidance provided by LRAR and other organisations

13 See, for example, the National Archives' guidance at http://www.nationalarchives.gov.uk/information-management/browse-guidance-standards/?letter=r&keyword=retention.

14 See S.7.4 of the draft retention and disposal schedule at **Appendix III**.

15 LRAR is currently undertaking a separate case study into selected records held in the SRA's Intervention Archives.

16 SRA, *Records retention schedule* https://www.sra.org.uk/sra/how-we-work/records-management.page.

17 As advised in The Law Society *Practice Note: Depositing records and documents with public sector archives* (no longer available on TLS's website).

(notably The National Archives) may be beneficial, it should be recognised that without a centrally managed and supported information and records management programme to implement best practice such guidance will not have any long-term effect. It must be understood that information does not manage itself and that expecting untrained individuals to do information management work on top of the day job is inefficient, unnecessarily costly and can result in compliance breaches.

LRAR therefore recommends that the CLC institutes a centrally managed programme, supported by the Senior Management Team, to institute best practice in the management and disposal of all information held.[18] The programme should include: training all staff in basic best practice in recordkeeping; implementation of disposal rules for all the CLC's information, including deletion of redundant electronic data and backup tapes and decommissioning of redundant IT systems; management of the relationship with external records storage providers, archive repositories and scanning companies; the inclusion of records management requirements in all IT contracts[19] and the creation, monitoring and enforcement of rules for managing documents and emails, including naming and dating conventions, addition of relevant metadata, security classifications, version control and guidance on file formats, digital continuity and scanning.

The only significant cost of a records management programme is the employment of a part-or full-time permanent records management professional to a) establish and b) run the programme. It cannot be emphasised too strongly that this kind of programme requires professionally qualified people in just the same way as managing IT systems or providing legal services to clients; it should also be recognised that an ongoing programme will produce a greater return on onvestment than a one-off project.[20] The benefits in terms of reduced cost, increased efficiency and faster access to records which may be used by the CLC to enhance its public image will speedily outweigh the cost.

### *Case study conclusion*

LRAR considers that the CLC should be seen as a role model for other legal institutions, regulatory or otherwise, in its commitment to openness and transparency, its willingness to make its records available to the public as early as possible and its understanding that today's business record may be tomorrow's historical record and therefore needs to be managed and preserved.

## *Annex I: Case study proposal to the CLC*

### The Legal Records at Risk (LRAR) project: case studies

The project is concerned with identifying records of archival value in the private sector created by institutions specialised to law (ISLs). Saving significant collections, stimulating changes of practice, avoiding duplication, and raising awareness of the value of LRAR are prioritised. We will not collect records but will be a conduit through which legal records of value (in all formats and media) are identified, preserved and made available for research.

Undertaking case studies of selected ISLs will form a key platform of the project. Case studies will demonstrate areas of best practice and community of practice, identify key issues common to all or most ISLs and suggest potential solutions, including liaison with archival repositories relating to the deposit of records of permanent value.

Methodology: each case study will differ, but the methodology is essentially as follows:

- Initial contact with key persons in selected ISLs.
- Management agreement to collaborate in the project (i.e. to allocate the time of key personnel – there will be no other costs to the ISLs).
- A survey of the records (both paper and digital) created and managed by the ISL.
- Creation of a records retention and disposal schedule for the ISL.
- Identification of records of permanent research value and interested repositories.
- A report to the ISL on findings and, if relevant, recommendations for more cost-effective recordkeeping practices. The report will be published with permission of the ISL and anonymised if required.

18 The LRAR case study of Chadwick Lawrence Solicitors demonstrated the benefits to an organisation of implementing an ongoing records management programme managed by an information and records management professional; see http://ials.sas.ac.uk/research/areas-research/legal-records-risk-lrar-project/lrar-case-studies

19 Such as the recommendation earlier that contracts with all Cloud providers should include a provision to return all data at the conclusion of the contract.

20 It is currently common for organisations to institute a one-off records management project to set up a best practice framework for managing information. While useful in the short term (e.g. by reducing physical storage costs), such a project will ultimately fail to have any long-term beneficial effect if there is no designated individual or team in place to update, monitor and enforce its recommendations on a permanent basis.

There are numerous benefits for ISLs to participating in a LRAR case study:

- A survey of records and recordkeeping practices by a qualified archivist and records manager.
- Production of a retention and disposal schedule for immediate use, adaptable for future needs. This will identify existing records and recommend how long each category needs to be kept, with those of archival value highlighted for permanent preservation. Electronic records will also be surveyed and included.
- Advice on recordkeeping, which assists efficient business practice and compliance.
- Reduced need for storage space as records are systematically disposed of.
- Identification of a possible repository for records of permanent value *or* advice on how to manage one in-house so as to unlock the potential of the ISL's records for both internal business reference and external research use.
- Identification of ISLs with similar practices and issues, developing a community of practice.
- An enhanced reputation for openness and transparency plus a better understanding of importance of the ISL in the development of the UK's legal framework.

## Proposed case study: records of the Council for Licensed Conveyancers (CLC)

*Summary note*: established in 1985, the CLC is a regulatory body with records spanning 30 years, many of which are clearly of long-term business value to the organisation and some of which may be of potential value to external researchers.

*Objective*: the Legal Records at Risk project wishes to survey the records of the CLC with a view to identifying records of archival value and making recommendations about their permanent retention. In doing so the project may also identify recordkeeping issues and make recommendations as to the management of the CLC's current and semi-current records.

*Scope*: the project will survey the current, semi-current and historic records of the CLC in both hard copy and digital format. The survey will identify the main categories of records, the purpose for which they have been created/held, storage locations and how long the CLC requires them for business use. It is understood that the CLC has made provision for a) digitisation and b) off-site storage of paper records.

*Methodology*: the archivist will undertake a survey of CLC records and note all findings in an information assets register which will double as a records disposal schedule recommending a specific retention period for each class/series of records. Governing legislation for specific series will be recorded. The assets register/disposal schedule will be presented to the organisation with an opportunity to discuss the findings. Recommendations for transfer of records of permanent research value to an archival repository will be made, along with recordkeeping advice on the management of current and semi-current records as appropriate.

*Quality*: the survey will be carried out by a qualified archivist and records manager. The archivist will give an undertaking (in writing if required) to abide by the CLC's own conditions of confidentiality and to comply with the provisions of the Data Protection Act when surveying the records and making his/her report.

*Resources and costs*: there will be no costs to the CLC other than in the allocation of time to assist the archivist.

*Constraints*: agreement of the CLC to allow access to its records and storage systems and to permit the archivist to discuss current procedures and processes with key members of staff.

*Issues and risks*: not being allowed access to the records; finding that historical records are not accessible due to destruction, digital obsolescence or physical neglect; not taking up the recommendations put forward by the survey; not being able to find a suitable repository.

*Projected outcomes*: a report to the CLC on its records and recordkeeping (the report will be published with the permission of the CLC); transfer of records of research value in both hard copy and digital formats to a professionally managed archive repository; better understanding of the value of its records both to the CLC itself and to the external research community; cost and efficiency savings in the management of the CLC's records.

## *Annex II: Legal Records at Risk questionnaire*

### Council for Licensed Conveyancers: records survey – notes for respondents

1. **What is the Legal Records at Risk project?** It's a project to identify and save records which document recent developments in legal services so that they can, eventually, be made available to researchers in many fields (e.g. legal, social, geographic). CLC's records are highly important in demonstrating one major area of change to the UK's legal framework.
2. **What is a records survey?** It's an inventory of the records your Department creates and maintains to carry out its core functions. It will help us to assess which records are of permanent research value, but it also has practical benefits for CLC (see next point).
3. **Why should you take part in the survey?** Knowing just what records are held, where they are and when to dispose of them will help everyone at CLC to:
   - Reduce space and storage costs by getting rid of duplicate material and by systematic destruction/deletion or transfer of records to an appropriate archive repository where they will be securely stored and made available for research once all CLC's and legal confidentiality requirements have expired.
   - Ensure legislative compliance e.g. with the Data Protection Act.
   - Improve services to customers through cost savings and quicker information retrieval.
   - Support implementation of better IT systems to store and retrieve content. It's not possible to successfully upgrade existing systems or implement new ones to manage information until we identify what we have and how we currently deal with it.
4. **How do you fill in the records survey questionnaire?** Just ask yourself these questions…
   - What does our Department do within CLC i.e. what activities/functions are our particular responsibility?
   - How do we document each activity/function i.e. what information/records do we create or collect?
   - What do we do with the information (action it, pass it to other departments for action, keep it for internal or external use, for legal reasons or statistical or reference purposes)?
   - Do we keep it electronically, in paper or both? How many duplicates do we circulate? Do we know?
   - Do we know what to do with it when the Department doesn't need it for day to day business anymore?

   ….and then fill in the form overleaf, using the explanatory notes attached if necessary. Don't worry if you don't know all the answers.
5. **What will the long term advantages of the survey be?** After the survey is completed, we will:
   - Arrange for material of permanent value which CLC no longer needs to be taken off its hands and sent to a professionally managed archives.
   - Draw up an information assets register/records disposal schedule for CLC which will tell you exactly how, when and why to dispose of records once they are no longer needed.

| CLC: RECORDS SURVEY QUESTIONNAIRE | |
|---|---|
| Name and function of department: | |
| Date survey completed: | |
| Contact name and job title: | |
| **Records created/maintained by department** (see notes overleaf for guidance)**:** | |
| 1. Records category/description | |
| 2. Date range | |
| 3. Format/medium | |
| 4. Security classification:<br>Not confidential<br>Confidential (not personal data)<br>Confidential (personal data) | |
| 5. Arrangement | |
| 6. Retrieval/finding aids | |
| 7. Storage location/s | |
| 8. Business retention requirements | |
| 9. Information management procedures | |
| 10. Particular information management issues | |
| 11. Notes | |

## *CLC RECORDS SURVEY: EXPLANATORY NOTES*

1. **Records category/description**: a records category is a collection of records having a common subject or theme or function e.g. interventions case files, enquiries, accountants' reports, training records, personnel files, annual accounts, Council minutes, registers of licensed conveyancers. A category can comprise any number of items, from one document (e.g. Publication Policy) to several hundred files (e.g. complaints files).
2. **Date range of records category**: e.g. 1988–2000, Jan-June 2001, 2005–[still current].
3. **Format/medium**: e.g. paper files, databases, word documents, e-mail, excel spreadsheets, microfilm, photographs, videos, CDs, DVDs, publications or promotional material e.g. leaflets.
4. **Security classification**:
   - Not confidential (e.g. policies and strategies, consultation responses, most minutes, annual reports, publications).
   - Confidential: not personal data (e.g. contracts, financial information);

- Confidential: personal data (e.g. personnel files, some enquiries files).

5. **Arrangement**: e.g. alphabetical, chronological, numeric, arranged by subject, no arrangement.
6. **Retrieval/finding aids**: e.g. is there an index to the files or a file classification scheme, either manual or automated, to help locate relevant files or retrieve information?
7. **Storage location/s**: e.g. filing cabinet, open shelves, basement, internal or external records store (paper); email accounts, personal drive, shared drive/s, Sharepoint, document management system, case file management system, database (electronic).
8. **Business retention requirements**: how long are the records needed for the current business of the office (e.g. six months, two years, seven years, 20 years) or for legal compliance (e.g. contracts) or under Finance Regulations (e.g. accounting records)? If you don't know just say so – this isn't a test.
9. **Information management procedures:** are there office rules for naming or numbering folders and documents, version control, security classifications, scanning, where to store records (paper and electronic), what to do with them when they are no longer needed? Are your department's records covered by a records retention and disposal schedule?
10. **Specific information management issues:** e.g. difficulty or delays in finding records when they are required for clients, litigation, surveys, subject access requests; multiple locations of records; version control issues; loss of important records.
11. **Notes**: any additional information not covered by the above which you think may be relevant.

## *Annex III: Council for Licensed Conveyancers: Draft records retention and disposal schedule*

### Schedule Contents

1. Corporate governance
2. Education and training
3. External relations
4. Regulatory policy and procedures
5. Regulatory practice
6. Regulatory monitoring
7. Regulatory interventions

Note 1: general administration records – finance, human resources, office management, information management, facilities and premises records – are not included in this schedule as advice on their retention and disposal is readily available elsewhere. See, for example, the National Archives' guidance at http://www.nationalarchives.gov.uk/information-management/browse-guidance-standards/?letter=r&keyword=retention

Note 2: where records are designated as 'retain permanently' they should be transferred in their original format (ie either paper or born digital) to the London Metropolitan Archives (LMA). LMA will liaise with CLC as to the method and frequency of transfer.

| | **Record category** | **Disposal rule** | **Legislative, regulatory or business retention requirement** | **Notes** |
|---|---|---|---|---|
| 1. | Corporate governance | | | |
| 1.1 | Minutes of Council meetings:<br>• Published<br>• In camera | Retain permanently | | |
| 1.2 | Minutes of Senior Management Team meetings | Retain permanently | | |
| 1.3 | Memoranda of Understanding | Retain permanently | | |
| 1.4 | Corporate Strategies and Policies | Retain permanently | | |
| 1.5 | Annual Reports | Retain permanently | | |

| | Record category | Disposal rule | Legislative, regulatory or business retention requirement | Notes |
|---|---|---|---|---|
| 1.6 | Annual financial statements | Retain permanently | | |
| 1.7 | Business plans | Retain permanently | | |
| *2.* | *Education and training* | | | |
| 2.1 | Training policy files | Retain permanently | | |
| 2.2 | Database/register of students | Retain annual snapshots permanently | | |
| 2.3 | Student files | Retain for lifetime of individual | May be required to provide academic transcripts or for licensing or fraud checks | Assume 75 years from creation.<br>May be possible in future to weed to only retain academic transcripts for lifetime of individual |
| 2.4 | Record of achievement | Retain permanently | | |
| 2.5 | CLC and CPD training records | Destroy after 2 years | | |
| 2.6 | Reasonable adjustment records | Destroy 6 years after termination of relationship with student | Data Protection Act | Contain sensitive personal data |
| 2.7 | Criminal convictions | Destroy 6 years after termination of relationship with student | Data Protection Act | Contain sensitive personal data |
| 2.8 | Examination papers | Destroy after 2 years | | |
| 2.9 | Examination reports, twice yearly | Destroy after 2 years | | |
| 2.10 | Training providers' records | Destroy 6 years after termination of relationship with student | Data Protection Act | Contain personal data |
| 2.11 | Apprenticeship standards records | Retain permanently where kept separately from policy files | | There are strict government criteria for apprenticeships |
| 2.12 | Consultants | Destroy 6 years after termination of relationship | Data Protection Act | Contain personal data |
| *3.* | *External relations* | | | |
| 3.1 | Design and control of CLC's corporate identity | Retain permanently | | |
| 3.2 | Speeches and presentations by CLC Council Members and Staff | Retain permanently | | |
| 3.3 | Consultation papers | Retain permanently | | |
| 3.4 | Surveys | Retain published surveys permanently; destroy supporting records as convenient | | |
| 3.5 | Research outputs | Retain permanently | | |
| 3.6 | Articles, press releases, press statements, press comments, blogs | Retain permanently | | |

| | Record category | Disposal rule | Legislative, regulatory or business retention requirement | Notes |
|---|---|---|---|---|
| 3.7 | Seminars, conventions and graduation ceremonies organised by CLC | Retain final programmes permanently; destroy supporting records as convenient | | |
| 3.8 | Website | Retain regular snapshots | | LRAR will approach the British Library on behalf of CLC |
| 3.9 | Social media records (e.g. Twitter) | Delete as convenient | | All information of importance will be included in policy files |
| 3.10 | CLC *Newsletter* | Retain one copy of each issue permanently | | |
| *4.* | *Regulatory policy and procedures* | | | |
| 4.1 | CLC Client Charter | Retain permanently | | |
| 4.2 | CLC Handbook | Retain permanently (one copy of each version) | | |
| 4.3 | CLC Code of Conduct | Retain permanently (one copy of each version) | | |
| 4.4 | CLC Regulatory guidance | Retain permanently | | |
| 4.5 | Reviews around issues affecting all practices | Retain permanently | | |
| 4.6 | Annual regulatory return | Retain permanently | | Produced since 2015 |
| *5.* | *Regulatory practice* | | | |
| 5.1 | Licensing files | Destroy 7 years after termination of relationship with firm/ firm closure | | |
| 5.2 | Register of licensed conveyancers and regulatory bodies | Retain permanently | Licensing authorities are required to create, maintain and make a register publicly available by the Legal Services Act 2007 (S.87) | |
| 5.3 | Accountants' Reports (annual) | Not determined | | |
| 5.4 | Correspondence with licensed conveyancers | Not determined | | |
| *6.* | *Regulatory monitoring* | | | |
| 6.1 | Conduct complaints:<br>Unfounded<br>Further investigation | <br>Destroy 2 years after last action<br>Destroy 7 years after investigation closed | | |
| 6.2 | Service complaints | Destroy 2 years after last action | | Referred to firm or Legal Ombudsman |
| 6.3 | Register/database of complaints | | | Created? |

| | Record category | Disposal rule | Legislative, regulatory or business retention requirement | Notes |
|---|---|---|---|---|
| 6.4 | Monitoring files | Destroy after 7 years unless further investigation required | | |
| 6.5 | Investigations files | Destroy 7 years after investigation closed unless investigation results in an intervention | | |
| 6.6 | Adjudication Panel hearings | Retain permanently | | Panel hearings are open to the public |
| 6.7 | General Regulatory Chamber appeals | Retain permanently | | No appeals have been heard at the time of writing |
| *7.* | *Regulatory interventions* | | | |
| 7.1 | Lists/database of interventions | Retain permanently | | |
| 7.2 | Interventions case files | Keep for duration of retention of the records of intervened firms | | |
| 7.3 | Interventions case files of historical significance e.g. high profile cases; cases which resulted in policy changes or amendment to regulations | Retain permanently | | CLC will determine whether files are of sufficient interest to retain |
| 7.4 | Records of intervened firms:<br>Matter files<br>Client documents (e.g. deeds) | Destroy sales files after 6 years<br>Destroy purchase files after 15 years<br>Offer client documents to a local record office after 15 years if unable to return to client | As per current practice for matter files | |
| 7.5 | Records of intervened firms: matter files where the intervention has been designated as of historical significance | Retain permanently with interventions case file | | CLC will determine whether files are of sufficient interest to retain |
| 7.6 | Compensation Fund records: enquiries, fund accounts documentation; grants and claims | Destroy 7 years after action completed/ claim closed | Finance Act 1998; Limitation Act 1980; Value Added Tax Act 1994 | |

# Case study 5: Pilot project on construction arbitration records (England and Wales)

Andrey_Popov/Shutterstock.com

## *A preliminary feasibility study for a project on records of arbitration*

Compiled by Alan Shipman, LRAR Research Assistant

Completed July 2017

Edited and with additional material by Clare Cowling, August 2017

## *Executive summary*

The project brief was to consider arbitration records with special reference to construction records for the following reasons:

1. The Business Archives Council 2013 report on the records of construction firms[21] which noted that construction companies in general 'demonstrated a lack of awareness of archives and the archival profession'. This lack of awareness presumably also applies to construction arbitration.
2. The decline in construction arbitration means that most relevant records will be 20 years old, meaning that sensitivity/confidentiality should be less of an issue than with more recent arbitration records.
3. The existence of potential contacts in institutions such as King's College London Centre of Construction Law.

Surveys were undertaken as follows:

- An examination of arbitral rules and guidance affecting recordkeeping.
- Identification of existing construction arbitration records in archives and of potential repositories.
- A case study of the records of one arbitrator.

The findings and recommendations were as follows:

1. There are construction – and other – arbitration records in archives which may be at risk.
2. A wider survey needs to be undertaken of arbitral organisations' and individual arbitrators' records and archival homes identified for them.

## *Introduction*

This project is a preliminary exploration and feasibility study for a major project in respect of arbitration records located in Great Britain/England and Wales. This will be achieved by:

1. Identifying and analysing current guidance to arbitrators and other stakeholders relating to management and disposal of arbitration records, evaluating its efficacy and seeking models of guidance from other jurisdictions.

21 *Architecture, Building and Construction Records Survey 2011–13*, a partnership project between The National Archives and the Business Archives Council, April 2013.

2. Identifying arbitration records that do not form part of existing external or in-house archives of organisations and pinpointing categories of special value that may be at risk.
3. Identifying potential repositories that would welcome discrete collections of arbitration records of potential archival value and assisting such repositories by facilitating the collection of arbitration records.
4. Providing a detailed report which will assist the larger LRAR project to assess the feasibility of and, if appropriate, to design a major study of records of domestic arbitration including recommending whether this should be extended to cover international commercial arbitration.

## Operational Plan

To achieve the above, the following plan was adopted to:

1. Survey the records and the records management processes of selected organisations actively involved in construction dispute resolution (e.g. the Royal Institution of Chartered Surveyors and the Chartered Institute of Arbitrators).
2. Identify priority categories of construction arbitration records of potential practical and scholarly significance.
3. Undertake a preliminary analysis of special issues (e.g. digitisation, sensitivity, access).
4. Survey arbitration records held in businesses and other private sector institutions that are listed on The National Archives' *Discovery* resource.
5. Conduct informal interviews with stakeholders.
6. Undertake a small number of case studies of:
   (a) arbitration in UK construction companies (Mowlem archive, at least one other construction company); and
   (b) the records of one or two individual arbitration practitioners.
7. Produce a report on the above.

## People

Patron: Professor William Twining

Project Director: Clare Cowling

Research Assistant: Alan Shipman

## Key to abbreviations and acronyms

| | |
|---|---|
| ACAS | Advisory, Conciliation and Arbitration Service |
| BAC | Business Archives Council |
| BRA | British Records Association |
| CHS | Construction History Society |
| CIARb | Chartered Institute of Arbitrators |
| CMC | Civil Mediation Council |
| CSLS | Centre for Socio-Legal Studies |
| HE | Higher education |
| IALS | Institute of Advanced Legal Studies |
| ICA | International Court of Arbitration |
| ICC | International Chamber of Commerce |
| IRDC | International Dispute Resolution Centre Limited |
| KCL | King's College London |
| LMA | London Metropolitan Archives |
| LRAR | Legal Records at Risk |
| PCA | Permanent Court of Arbitration (Netherlands) |
| RICS | Royal Institution of Chartered Surveyors |
| SCA | Society of Construction Arbitrators |

| | |
|---|---|
| TCC | Technology and Construction Court |
| TNA | The National Archives |

## *Actions undertaken*

1. Briefing between William Twining and Alan Shipman.
2. Briefing between Clare Cowling and Alan Shipman.
3. Attended conference at IALS on 'Legal Records at Risk'.
4. Administration (Recruitment services, payroll).
5. Technology set-up (access to IALS SharePoint folder + email server).
6. Desk research.
7. Visit to Michael Reynolds on 24 March 2017.
8. Draft report writing.
9. Further research.
10. Final report writing.

## *Why was construction arbitration chosen?*

### Business Archives Council report on the records of construction firms[22]

The BAC has an objective to 'promote the preservation of business records of historical importance'. This report, undertaken in partnership with TNA (but apparently no longer available on either website) sought (p.2) 'to establish the nature and location of collections of records produced by architectural practices and construction firms in England and Wales which had not been deposited'. The report highlighted (pp 2–3):

> that encouragement should be given to businesses within the architectural and construction sectors to strengthen record keeping practices and raise awareness of the importance of their archives. The greatest focus should be on the construction industry, which proved more difficult to persuade to participate than the architectural sector and demonstrated a lack of awareness of archives and the archival profession.

This report was the starting point for the project.

### Institute of Advanced Legal Studies (http://ials.sas.ac.uk)

The Institute has long been involved in the study of law and practice relating to arbitration and alternative dispute resolution. The current project is part of this work. The IALS has made available a number of guidance notes, including the 'Legal Records at Risk Guideline 1: current advice available to legal institutions on managing and disposing of records'. It notes that most of the available guidance covers confidentiality. Further details of the available guidance are available in this report.

### The decline of construction arbitration and records sensitivity over time

LRAR is well aware that there is a lot of sensitivity within the arbitration community about confidentiality and privacy. In recent years construction arbitration has tended to be replaced by adjudication, as arbitration is now seen as too costly and cumbersome. Construction arbitrations have therefore declined in recent years, so the project would be focusing on records that are at least twenty years old which might allay some concerns about sensitivity.

## *What is arbitration?*

Definitions include:

> 'The hearing and determining of a dispute or the settling of differences between parties by a person or persons chosen or agreed to by them' (http://www.dictionary.com)

> 'The hearing and determination of a dispute, esp. an industrial dispute, by an impartial referee selected or agreed upon by the parties concerned. The procedure laid down for the settlement of international disputes' (Collins English Dictionary)

22 Ibid

## The Arbitration Act 1996 (http://www.legislation.gov.uk/ukpga/1996/23/contents)

There are no rules or guidance in the Arbitration Act on retention and disposal. Thomson Reuters have produced a guidance note on the Act https://uk.practicallaw.thomsonreuters.com/5-204-0030?transitionType=Default&contextData=(sc.Default)&firstPage=true&bhcp=1. Access to this guidance note was requested via their web site but no response was forthcoming.

### *Arbitral organisations, guidance and rules*

The websites of the organisations listed below were examined to a) clarify the role of each organisation b) note if any case files or awards have been published on the websites and c) to find whether any records management and retention rules or guidelines have been laid down for arbitrators to follow.

*Advisory, Conciliation and Arbitration Service* http://www.acas.org.uk/index.aspx?articleid=1711: ACAS provides arbitration services (as can be seen in public disputes between trades unions and employers). A review of guidance available did not identify any retention recommendations.

*Chartered Institute of Arbitrators* http://www.ciarb.org: the CIArb is an international centre of excellence for the practice and profession of alternative dispute resolution (ADR). It has 14,000 members across 133 countries. It runs a course on domestic arbitration (one day) – there are no entry requirements. The published syllabus does not include any records management topics (but these may be hidden under arbitration rules and procedures).

The CIArb published a survey of domestic construction arbitration in the UK in 1999. It also provides guidance on including arbitration clauses in construction contracts. These are only available to members.

The CIArb publishes guidance on mediation, and in particular on confidentiality in mediation http://www.ciarb.org/guidelines-and-ethics/guidelines/mediation-guidelines (note that these guidelines were published in 2007, and are under review, due to be republished in 2017). *Practice Guideline 1: Confidentiality in Mediation* recommends (p.1) that:

> 'All records, reports, or other documents received by a mediator, as well as all notes taken by the mediator during, with reference to, or for the purposes of, the mediation should be returned to the parties or kept secure until no longer needed for any purpose relating to the mediation and then destroyed.'

The key phrase from an archiving point of view is 'for any purpose'; could this purpose include archiving in the long term for research into mediation?

*Civil Mediation Council*: http://www.civilmediation.org/ the CMC is the UK's recognised authority for all matters relating to civil, commercial, workplace and other non-family mediation. It has issued a guidance note http://www.civilmediation.org/downloads.php?f=46 on mediation confidentiality (2009). This states that mediation agreements should make it clear that all proceedings should be confidential.

*International Chamber of Commerce* https://iccwbo.org/about-us/who-we-are/dispute-resolution/: the ICC administers the International Court of Arbitration (ICA). A recent report states that the ICA had received a record number of new cases files under ICC rules in 2016 – 966 cases involving 3,099 parties from 137 countries.

The ICC has a set of rules for use in cases submitted to the ICA. These rules regulate the filing of claims, the constitution of arbitral tribunals, the conduct of proceedings, the rendering of decisions and the determination of costs. While offering security and predictability, the ICC Rules also accommodate any preferences parties in dispute might have with respect to certain aspects of the proceedings, such as the choice of arbitrators, the place, and the language of arbitration. In all matters that are not expressly provided for in the ICC Rules, the Court and Arbitral Tribunal act in the spirit of the Rules and make every effort to have an enforceable Award.

This organisation has published their *2017 Arbitration Rules and 2014 Mediation Rules (English version)* – freely available from https://iccwbo.org/publication/arbitration-rules-and-mediation-rules/. The publication details 'two discrete but complementary dispute resolution procedures'. Amongst the guidance, it requires copies of all pleadings and other communications to be supplied (in any media/format) to all parties involved. Email or other forms of telecommunication can be used 'provided that a record of the sending is retained'. The guidance also requires the settlement to be 'recorded in the form of an award made by consent of the parties'.

No guidance is given to parties on how long records need to be retained, or who should retain them. There is a requirement to: 'retain in the archives of the Court all awards, terms of reference and decisions of the court, plus copies of pertinent correspondence of the Secretariat'.

Article 6 of Appendix 1 of the Arbitration Rules relates to the confidentiality of court proceedings and to the access to materials related to the court or its secretariat.

*International Dispute Resolution Centre Limited (London)* https://www.idrc.co.uk: based in Fleet Street, the IDRC provides accommodation for arbitration cases. It provides rooms of many sizes for hiring, including all necessary IT and administration resources and staff to assist with meeting management.

*Kluwer Arbitration:*

Thanks to Michael Reynolds for information about this resource. For details see http://www.kluwerarbitration.com. This is claimed to be 'The world's largest commercial collection of arbitral awards from various leading arbitral institutions, including the ICC'. It is a commercial undertaking, with a subscription process in place. It is unclear whether IALS has a subscription – there is an IALS subscription to some of the other resources (not arbitration). An online demonstration of Kluwer Arbitration is apparently available on request on the web site. This was requested but was not made available.

*Permanent Court of Arbitration (Netherlands)* https://pca-cpa.org/en/home/: the PCA is 'an intergovernmental organisation providing a variety of dispute resolution services'. Its website advises that it: 'identifies the parties and publishes awards or other information in proceedings under PCA auspices where the parties have so agreed'.

The PCA is also gradually making its historic arbitral awards and related documents available electronically. It has published a couple of case files which relate to construction arbitration. One concerns the Eurotunnel project and alleged breaches of the concession agreement. Records of the award and opinions are available.

*Royal Institution of Chartered Surveyors* http://rics.org.uk: the RICS is 'a global professional body promoting and enforcing the highest international standards' in the construction industry. It offers a couple of training options for arbitration in the construction industry:

- Diploma in Adjudication in the Construction Industry (distance learning);
- Arbitration Masterclass (1-day workshop).

The RICS also runs a dispute resolution professional group which has produced a series of guidance notes related to construction arbitration. Details are at http://www.rics.org/uk/knowledge/professional-guidance/professional-guidance-search?sq=arbitration&so=Relevance

*Society of Construction Arbitrators*: (SCA) https://www.constructionarbitrators.org: the SCA is:

> 'dedicated to the pursuit of excellence in Construction Dispute Resolution...The principal object of the Society is to lay down and secure the maintenance of standards to be observed by members in connection with their work as arbitrators or other tribunal members in disputes in the Construction Industry.'

The SCA has a number of publications available, mainly are papers and presentations by members – none appear to relate to records management issues.

## Research paths

*The National Archives*: TNA publishes a set of retention schedules. The one relating to building records has one entry for 'Claim and arbitration files' which recommends 'review 25 years after settlement'. See http://www.nationalarchives.gov.uk/documents/information-management/sched_buildings.pdf for further information. It is unclear whether this advice has been picked up by the construction industry.

In 2009 TNA published *A National Strategy for Business Archives (England and Wales)*. This has an objective to 'raise the profile of (business) archives, ensuring that they are utilised by businesses and researchers alike and that future collections are more representative of the UK's diverse economic activity.'

*London Metropolitan Archives (Richard Wiltshire)*: Richard Wiltshire is the LMA's Senior Archivist – Business Archives and mainly deals with acquisitions and cataloguing of business archives. The project director emailed Richard in November 2016; Richard confirmed that they held Mowlem arbitration records and were happy to respond to questions. These were forwarded to the LMA enquiry team who provided detailed information with regards to the Mowlem collection (see p.10 below for a report on the Mowlem holdings).

*Centre for Socio-Legal Studies (Dr Michael Reynolds)*: Michael is an arbitrator of long standing and a member of the CSLS. In 2014 the CSLS published his Overview of Arbitration in England[23] which, among other recommendations, suggested (p.33) that: 'whilst Arbitration has a place in the disputes process, to better promote itself it requires stricter rules and timescales'. He is planning to interview some of the Technology and Construction Court (TCC) judges for his next CSLS report.

23 https://www.law.ox.ac.uk/sites/files/oxlaw/a_report_by_dr_michael_reynolds_of_december_2014.pdf.

Michael advised that construction arbitration records usually comprise:

- Claims for contractors' loss and expense (damages) for breach of contract.
- Contractors' claims resulting from variations to design.
- Contractors' claims for extension of time in which to complete the contract works.
- Money claims arising from late payment on interim or final certificates.
- Money claims from non-payment on such certificates.
- Tortious claims arising from breach of duty to design, quantify, measure the works involving architects, engineers, quantity surveyors and project managers.
- Various claims as to interpretation of the contract.

Most of the money claims now go to adjudication and after the decision of the adjudicator is given enforcement is by virtue of summary judgement in the Technology and Construction Court. Possibly one of the reasons why arbitration is not popular is because it widely believed that the process is too cumbersome and costly. A reason for this may well be the lack of proper education in arbitration.

A visit was made to Michael's home to view arbitration material held by him (see p.9 below).

*Kings College London (Professor Renato Nazzini)*: Renato leads on the MSc programme on construction arbitration and met with the project director in July 2016 to discuss the proposed case study into construction arbitration records. Renato confirmed that they do not hold any archives of arbitration awards; as an academic institution they have no remit to hold such an archive. King's College London manages a library for student research. No construction arbitration records were identified in this library.

It is understood that the Kings College Archivist has indicated that KCL Archives would take in records of the Centre of Construction Law.

*Construction History Society (Michael Driver)*: Michael Driver is the Honorary Secretary of the CHS. The research assistant asked a question about any holdings of construction arbitration records.

Michael attended a CHS trustees meeting on 3 July 2017 and reported back on an agenda item 'Construction Arbitration'. He confirmed that the CHS does not hold any construction arbitration records (they have one store in Stroud but this is not ordered). The trustees thought it unlikely that any arbitration records are being held. And as their only store is unordered, the records are not available for research purposes. However, Michael reported that trustees were keen to confirm their interest in the IALS work and hoped at some stage they could make a positive contribution.

## Records of an arbitrator (Michael Reynolds) – report

Like many arbitrators, Michael Reynolds works (and stores his case files) mainly from home. As well as the essential IT equipment, Michael has an extensive book library for research purposes, as well as paper and electronic files from arbitration cases with which he has been involved. Michael's paper filing system is well organised, with case folders and managed content. He retains information based on personal requirements. There is no overall file index, as this is not necessary for a very small organisation. In practice, much of the information is also held by others (organisations and individuals), so any individual loss could (in theory) be replaced.

Michael was unaware of any published rules or guidance on the management and disposal of arbitration records.[24] Disposal of records is rarely undertaken. Michael does 'weed' files before they are stored, typically once a case is closed.

## Construction arbitration records in archives – report

*The National Archives*: TNA has a *Discovery* portal through which researchers can seek records via keywords, names of individuals or organisations or function: http://discovery.nationalarchives.gov.uk/. A keyword search for 'arbitration' returned 25,364 hits, which then linked to a number of national and local repositories. A specific search for 'construction arbitration' yielded 182 records; see **Annex I** for an extract from the search results. The results of other keyword searches were as follows:

- Arbitration tribunal 1,788
- Contract dispute 699
- Dispute 52,049
- Dispute resolution 15
- Mediation 2,536

24 The only 'general' advisory document on legal retention rules is the *ICSA Guide on Document Retention*; there is no mention of arbitration (or dispute resolution) records in this publication.

In other words, arbitration records should be searched for and may be found under many categories.

*King's College London Archives*: online catalogue https://www.kcl.ac.uk/library/archivespec/archives/access.aspx. A search for 'arbitration' brings ten results, and 'dispute resolution' brings four results. A review of the selected items indicates that those relevant to the IALS project relate to overseas cases. No further research was undertaken into the contents of this archive.

*Transport for London Corporate Archives*: see the LRAR Case study into alternative dispute resolution records held by Transport for London for details of construction arbitration records available for research relating to disputes involving TfL and its predecessors. The case study appeared to confirm the thesis that many arbitration records will be found within business archives.

*London Metropolitan Archives: a* search for 'arbitration' on the LMA online catalogue returns 539 hits – reduced to eight when 'construction' added (but they are all many years old). It is worth bearing in mind that the search results obtained depended upon the information held in the LMA catalogue. Often such information is limited (particularly when cataloguing was carried out a number of years ago) – the modern 'free text' search processes are only typically available on digital archives.

The results of some other searches were:

- dispute (1602 hits)
- construction dispute (8 hits)
- building dispute (61 hits)
- contract dispute (14 hits)
- building arbitration (8 hits)
- contract arbitration (14 hits).

See **Annex II** for details of some of the case files available on request.

*Mowlem Group archive*: the LMA holds records of the Mowlem group of companies. This company has been involved in a number of large scale arbitrations (see below for an example). Searching the LMA catalogue for 'mowlem arbitration', however, resulted in no hits. A review of the catalogue shows that the LMA's Mowlem archive contains mainly financial reports and minutes from over 50 separate companies.

A 'Mowlem arbitration' Google search, however, results in the following case study:

> *15Jun90 Mowlem and Carlton Gate find arbitration* https://www.constructionnews.co.uk/news/15jun90-uk-mowlem-and-carlton-gate-find-arbitration-best-route-for-settling-dispute-1-of-3/1694588.article
>
> Where a construction contract provides for interim payments it is usually for the very good reason that the people doing the work need the money to continue the project. 'The sums involved are so large that even the large construction companies feel the pinch when payment is withheld. In appropriate cases, the court should not shrink from dealing with an Order 14 summons even if the evidence is bulky. But if the inappropriate cases can be discouraged, those cases in which it is appropriate to give summary relief will receive earlier attention. 'The words are those of His Honour Judge Bowsher, Official Referee, taken from his ruling on John Mowlem's application last month for summary judgement against Carlton Gate Development Company for £1,113,469, being the balance unpaid on two interim certificates issued by the architect, Phippen, Randall and Parkes. Mowlem's contract, determined by Carlton Gate just before Christmas (Construction News, January 4), though not in standard form, contained a clause providing for arbitration in case of contractual dispute. Readers will recall that the matters now at issue came to a head when Carlton Gate, developer of the former St Mary's Hospital site at Paddington, claimed that two sections of the works were in delay and others, in the architect's opinion, were likely to be delayed. On these grounds the client withheld the sum in question under clauses 4.3 and 21.1 of the contract. Deprived of the cash, Mowlem in its turn was unable to make payments due to subcontractors under a pay-when-paid clause. As a result, the management contractor is being sued by several of the subcontractors. Since the contract with Mowlem was brought to an end, the Declan Kelly part of the former Carlton Gate joint venture has gone into voluntary liquidation with debts estimated at around £200 million (Construction News, March 1).With a new management contractor in place – Costain Management and Design – the development is continuing as an operation funded jointly by Eagle Star Group and a consortium of banks led by Security Pacific Euro Finance. Prior to being told to quit the site, Mowlem had already served notice of arbitration.

> The contract was determined on December 27. The contractor has said he will be contesting the notice of determination on the grounds that it was issued 'unreasonably and/or vexatiously'. The issue before the Official Referee was however Mowlem's claim for payment. As Peter Bowsher[25] noted in his judgement, due to pressures on court time, regrettably five months passed before the matter came before him. 'The evidence sits on the desk in a pile over six inches high,' he said. For Mowlem Colin Reese, Q.C., put the arguments for summary judgement under the RSC Order 14 procedure to secure the money deducted. For Carlton Gate, Howard Palmer contended that, since his client had applied for a stay of proceedings pursuant to Section 4 of the 1950 Arbitration Act, the matter was not suitable for resolution by this means. Carlton Gate argued strongly that all the issues raised by Mowlem should be decided by an arbitrator as provided in the contract. The contractor's case was firstly that the two letters issued by the architect seeking to justify the deductions did not comply with the terms of the management contract pursuant to which they were said to have been issued. These letters were issued on October 18 1989, the last day when payment of the disputed certificates should have been made. Mowlem also alleges that Carlton Gate's asserted counterclaims arose after the date when the money due on the certificates should have been paid. For that reason, as a matter of law, the contractor submitted that these sums should not be set off against the developer's liability to pay on the interim certificates. Because the Judge felt that this point was a matter of importance to other litigants, he decided to adjourn his decisions on this into open court for judgement. He did so having heard submissions from Mowlem and having decided that submissions from Carlton Gate were not necessary to his judgement. His conclusion was that the whole matter should be sent to arbitration in accordance with the agreement. In his summary of the facts, the Judge said that last September the architect issued two interim certificates, together certifying that a total of £2,290,702 was payable. That sum should have been paid by Carlton Gate on or before October 18. On the last day for payment, he said, the architect sent letters to the contractor purporting to be notices authorising deductions from the certified interim payments. One of those letters purported to be written pursuant to clause 4.3 and the other pursuant to clause 21.1.

*Records of other construction companies*: TNA's *Discovery* lists 54 construction companies which have deposited records in archives (http://discovery.nationalarchives.gov.uk/results/c?_q=construction&_naet=B. The BAC report also listed 15 construction firms which apparently maintained their own in-house archives at the time of writing. A wider project could examine the records of some of these companies to see if any arbitration records (which may not necessarily have been classified as such) are included.

## Construction arbitration records: potential repositories

*Archive repositories*: one of the objectives of this research was to identify potential repositories for discrete collections of construction arbitration records of value. During discussions with the various research resources (see above), questions relating to existing and potential repositories were posed. Details of their responses are included above. It is apparent that most arbitration records are retained by the parties involved, in business archives[26] if they exist and by the arbitrators themselves. Other arbitration records will be collected by archive repositories such as TNA, LMA, local authority archives or HE repositories like KCL Archives if they form part of the records of the depositing individual, organisation or faculty. Occasionally these will comprise the records of arbitration bodies themselves e.g. the LMA holds the archive of the London Court of Arbitration while the Library, Archives and Special Collections department of the London School of Economics collects records of mediation organisations.[27]

See **Annex II** for records of arbitral organisations known to be held in archive repositories and **Annex IV** for the small number of individuals classified as arbitrators whose papers are known to have been deposited in archives.

The LRAR project director had previously tried (see **Annex V**) to engage with arbitral organisations such as CIARb, the SCA and the Arbitration Club to encourage them to deposit their records with LMA, which has expressed an interest in accepting deposits of records of London-based institutions specialised to law. Responses received were not encouraging; a future project should recontact these organisations to put the business case for depositing records in archives more forcefully.

25 His Honour Peter Bowsher QC is a former judge of the Technology and Construction Court who practices from Keating Chambers as an arbitrator, adjudicator and mediator. Keating Chambers state that they have 'unparalleled expertise and experience in construction law'. They have been involved in many construction industry arbitration cases – further details are at http://www.keatingchambers.com/expertise/construction-engineering/

26 See, for example, the LRAR case study of construction (and other) arbitration record held in the Transport for London Corporate Archives.

27 E.g. the records of Mediation UK.

## *Research using arbitration records*

### Sensitivity

It is likely that some construction arbitration records will contain personal information, so privacy legislation (currently the Data Protection Act 1998 in the UK) may be applicable. Where arbitration records are already in the public domain (as may be the case with the final arbitration report) then there is no issue. In other cases, particularly where the arbitration case is recent, there may be a need to obtain consent of the individuals concerned or apply redaction processes to the records prior to making them available for research.

### Confidentiality

**Arbitrators:** institutions have their own rules eg Article 30(1) of the *Rules* of the London Court of International Arbitration states:

> Unless the parties expressly agree in writing to the contrary, the parties undertake as a general principle to keep confidential all awards in their arbitration, together with all materials in the proceedings created for the purpose of the arbitration and all other documents produced by another party in the proceedings not otherwise in the public domain – save and to the extent that disclosure may be required of a party by legal duty, to protect or pursue a legal right or to enforce or challenge an award in bona fide legal proceedings before a state court or other judicial authority.

**Mediators:** the CIARb's Practice Guideline 1: Confidentiality in Mediation states

> Save as required or permitted by law… the Institute, the parties, their representatives, their advisors and the mediator(s) shall keep confidential all information (whether given orally, in writing or otherwise) produced for, or arising out of or in connection with, the mediation passing between any of the participants and between any of them and the mediator made for the purposes of the mediation, including the fact that the mediation is taking place or has taken place…The mediator's duty to protect the confidentiality of the mediation proceedings commences with the first communication to the mediator, is continuous in nature, and does not expire upon the termination, for whatever reason, of the mediation under Rule 11. The mediator's duty extends to all information relating to the mediation proceedings, even indirectly, such as previous invitations and/or negotiations leading to mediation, terms of the agreement to mediate, appointment of mediators and performance, or non performance, of the settlement agreement. All records, reports, or other documents received by a mediator, as well as all notes taken by the mediator during, with reference to, or for the purposes of, the mediation should be returned to the parties or kept secure until no longer needed for any purpose relating to the mediation and then destroyed.

**The European Union:** the *European Code of Conduct for Mediators* (http://ec.europa.eu/civiljustice/adr/adr_ec_code_conduct_en.pdf) has a confidentiality clause (section 4) which requires all information arising from a mediation to be kept confidential unless compelled by law or public policy to disclose it.

There may be issues related to access to construction arbitration records where courts (for example the International Court of Arbitration) have been involved. The ICA's rules states that

> 'documents submitted to the Court, or drawn up by it or the Secretariat in the course of the Court's proceedings, are communicated only to the members of the Court and to the Secretariat and to persons authorized by the President to attend Court sessions.'

However, researchers may be authorised to undertake work of an academic nature, and thus have access to some documents, by the ICA. The public interest test also applies (see next paragraph).

**The ICA:** a recent ICA report has some interesting comments to make on arbitration records and confidentiality in England as follows:

> England, where the Arbitration Act 1996 is silent on confidentiality, is the country where the courts have been the most eloquent in articulating the existence of a broad duty of confidentiality, starting from a decision of 1880. Over time, English courts have formulated three relatively clear rules. The first is that arbitration proceedings are held in private, which implies that, in the absence of the parties' consent, arbitrators have no power to order the concurrent hearing of two arbitrations in which the arbitrators but not the parties were identical and the disputes closely

associated. The second rule, expressed by the Court of Appeal in 1990, is that an implied obligation of confidentiality, binding on the parties, arises from the very nature of arbitration. However, in a more recent case, the Privy Council expressed reservations about the desirability or merit of adopting a general duty of confidentiality as an implied term of arbitration and then formulating exceptions to which such a duty would be subject. The third rule is that the duty of confidentiality is subject to the following specific exceptions (i) consent; (ii) order of the court; (iii) leave of the court; (iv) reasonable necessity; and (v) public interest .....The lifespan of confidentiality obligations: the duration of confidentiality obligations, as regards both the moment when it arises and when it ends, is equally the subject of uncertainty and is not dealt with in the sources. The answer will probably vary to a large extent depending on the nature of the information and, obviously, on the source of the duty. If the source is contractual, the duration might be stated in the contract (which may be prior to the beginning of the arbitration or subsequent) or should be able to be derived through the interpretation of the contract. The fact that the duty of confidentiality usually covers the award seems to point to an expectation that the regime of confidentiality should outlive the arbitral proceedings and that the obligations will not cease after the end of the arbitration. It is less clear whether the obligations are perpetual or whether at some point they lapse, and if so at what point. It is reasonable to assume that the obligations cease where it can be established that confidentiality is no longer relevant. One such case is where the information in question has become of public domain.[28]

## *Conclusions*

The following is a list of the main conclusions to date, based on the 4 points identified in the introduction to this report:

1. *Current guidance:*

- There is guidance available in the construction arbitration sector from the RICS, which offers some guidance notes managed by their dispute resolution professional group. IALS has also published guidelines on managing and disposing of records.
- There is no guidance on retention and destruction in the Arbitration Act 1996.
- TNA recommends 'review 25 years after settlement' of arbitration records.

2. *Records held outside archival institutions:* if we may assume that Michael Reynolds is typical of most arbitrators, then there are a number of records held by individuals, typically at their offices or homes. They are of particular value to the individual arbitrators concerned, for example for further research, the writing of biographies or for personal interest. They may be of value to researchers, but knowledge of their existence in relation to particular cases may be hard to obtain. These records are typically 'personal copies' of research, reports and arbitration decisions which should normally be held by the organisation involved. Any personal notes are likely to be held by the arbitrator.

Records held by individuals are at risk, particularly in the areas of security and retention.

A potential future research project in this area would be to contact a professional institute and set up a questionnaire/ guidance note to send to their members who are arbitrators. It is understood that the CIArb was contacted with this suggestion but no response was received.

3. *Potential repositories:* it is understood that the LMA might be willing to hold archived arbitration files, but only if they relate to individuals or organisations based in Greater London, while local authority archives may be able to provide such a resource for arbitrations and arbitral organisations relevant to their own areas. This does leave a gap for records of national significance created and held by organisations and individuals located outside the Greater London area. LRAR is already discussing this gap with TNA, as finding a strategic solution to the lack of repositories for all records in this category (i.e. not just arbitration records) is assumed to be their responsibility.

4. *A wider LRAR project into arbitration records*: the following would need to be included in a larger LRAR project:

- Identification of more archives which will accept arbitration records.
- Identification of, and engagement with, arbitrators (especially individuals) and arbitral organisations which are willing to send their files to archives.
- Development of more detailed guidance on retention and data protection requirements (in addition to what is already available on the LRAR website http://ials.sas.ac.uk/research/areas-research/legal-records-risk-lrar-project/lrar-information-and-records-management).
- Resources to create lists of potential deposits to reduce the burden on archives.

28 Confidentiality in International Commercial Arbitration – ILA – ICA COMMITTEE REPORT, THE HAGUE 2010 pp 8 & 18.

- Development of submission procedures and protocols for future deposits.[29]
- Investigations into the viability of a setting up a dedicated archive for discrete collections of arbitration records.
- As much arbitration information is now created electronically (and there is a slow transition to full electronic working), the issues around electronic arbitration information and its archival requirements should be included in the full LRAR project, including the viability of including a digital repository in any dedicated archive.

## *Next steps: a new project looking into alternative dispute resolution records with special reference to arbitration and mediation?*

With the help of two well-qualified researchers we have canvassed problems of preserving records relating to arbitration and more generally alternative dispute resolution. Our original hypotheses were broadly conformed i.e. that such records have not been a focus of archival attention; that they contain a vast amount of material of potential value to a wide range of researchers as well as the arbitration community; that some material has been preserved, notably in the archives of larger institutions and businesses that have been parties to particular arbitrations, but the very existence of these, let alone their content and significance is not widely known; and that the vast majority of such records are at risk. Despite the secrecy surrounding most kinds of arbitration, we have concluded that standard archival best practice relating to 'sensitive' records (e.g. confidentiality, data protection, privilege etc) can deal with such problems and that there are no insuperable obstacles to collecting records relating to arbitration.

Arbitration is an immense, various and fragmented field and to undertake a thorough study would involve a major project and special funding beyond the current resources and capacity of LRAR. It would need a well-defined, selective project, fundraising and a timescale of at least three years. LRAR is due to finish in September 2018. However, we have collected a lot of material and learned enough to do a general analysis of the significance, extent and problems of arbitration records.

## *Annex I: Construction arbitration records in archives*

Source: TNA's *Discovery* portal – keyword search on 'construction arbitration' (182 hits):

| **Context Description** | **Title** |
|---|---|
| Small Collections | ARBITRATION AWARD |
| TOWN CLERK'S MISCELLANEOUS PAPERS. TRAMWAYS. VALUATIONS, ARBITRATION | Measurement of line (details of construction and dates) |
| WHITSTABLE URBAN DISTRICT COUNCIL. Offices. Clerk. Post 1958 filing system. Sewers and drainage | Gorrell Drainage Scheme – Phase III – Kenmac Construction Co Ltd – Arbitration |
| Miscellaneous Papers and Records. Vale of Glamorgan Railway. Capital | Arbitration re Contract for construction. Company's claim against Messrs. Pethick |
| Ministry of Labour and successors: Arbitration Tribunals, Registered Files | Award No. 449 Constructional Engineering Union v Sir Robert McAlpine and Sons (London) Ltd: claim ... |
| Ministry of Labour and successors: Arbitration Tribunals, Registered Files | Award No. 2455 Constructional Engineering Union, Amalgamated Engineering Union, United Society of Boilermakers and Iron ... |
| Ministry of Labour and successors: Arbitration Tribunals, Registered Files | Award No. 1622 Constructional Engineering Union and Engineering and Allied Employers National Federation: claim regarding... |
| Ministry of Labour and successors: Arbitration Tribunals, Registered Files | Award No. 1502 Construction of Engineering Union and Messrs Charles R Price: question regarding recognised... |
| Ministry of Labour and successors: Arbitration Tribunals, Registered Files | Award No. 880 Constructional Engineering Union and Engineering and Allied Employers' National Federation: claim by... |
| Ministry of Labour and successors: Arbitration Tribunals, Registered Files | Award No. 871 Constructional Engineering Union and Engineering and Allied Employers' National Federation: claim that... |
| Ministry of Labour and successors: Arbitration Tribunals, Registered Files | Award No. 618 Constructional Engineering Union v Broomhead Boiler Works Company Limited: dispute arising from... |
| Ministry of Labour and successors: Arbitration Tribunals, Registered Files | Constructional Engineering Union and Stothert and Pitt Limited: claim in connection with the wage rates... |

29 As above – this is also being discussed between LRAR, TNA and the BRA.

| Context Description | Title |
|---|---|
| Ministry of Labour and successors: Arbitration Tribunals, Registered Files | Award No. 1500 Constructional Engineering Union and Foster Wheeler Ltd: claim regarding payment of steel... |
| Ministry of Labour and successors: Arbitration Tribunals, Registered Files | Award No. 1145 Constructional Engineering Union and associations federated with the Engineering and Allied Employers'... |
| Ministry of Labour and successors: Arbitration Tribunals, Registered Files | Award No. 525 Constructional Engineering Union v Cozens and Sutcliff Ltd: claim for lodging allowance... |
| Ministry of Labour and successors: Arbitration Tribunals, Registered Files | Award No. 834 Constructional Engineering Union v Cozens and Sutcliffe Ltd: claim for the payment... |
| Ministry of Labour and successors: Arbitration Tribunals, Registered Files | Award No. 1425 and 1454Constructional Engineering Union and Dorman Long and Co Ltd: claim regarding ... |
| Ministry of Labour and successors: Arbitration Tribunals, Registered Files | No Award Constructional Engineering Union, Transport and General Workers' Union and National Union of General ... |
| LONDON COUNTY COUNCIL. Tramways Department: General. Arbitration proceedings | Joseph Westwood & Co Ltd – Arbitration concerning contract for construction of the superstructure of Greenwich Generating Station, 1908 – Proceedings and award |
| Department of the Environment: Directorate of Construction Industries, Building Regulations Administrative Division: Registered Files (BRA Series) | Future of building control in England and Wales: informal arbitration on disputes; comments on proposals ... |
| South Devon Railway Company. B V ELLIOT VERSUS THE SOUTH DEVON RAILWAY COMPANY ARBITRATION | Minutes of order on motion to dissolve injunction restraining company from constructing an embankment or ... |
| South Devon Railway Company. B V ELLIOT VERSUS THE SOUTH DEVON RAILWAY COMPANY ARBITRATION | Copy pleadings in action tried, at Devon Assizes, to determine right of defendants to construct ... |
| Union of Construction, Allied Trades & Technicians : Amalgamated Society of Woodworkers. London district management cttee | Minutes of an arbitration between Central Assoc. of Master Bldrs. and the London United Trades ... |
| Advisory, Conciliation and Arbitration Service: Recognition of Trade Unions: Reports and Case Files. Applications for Recognition | Report No. 55: R and T Howarth Ltd and Union of Construction, Allied Trades and ... |
| Haigh Estate Papers.THE EARL OF CRAWFORD & BALCARRES.RAILWAY COMPANIES & MISCELLANEOUS | Brief for Lord Crawford. Arbitration before Messrs. Thomas Statter & C.F.Cawley arbitrators and Gathorne Hardy,. |
| Ministry of Labour and successors: Arbitration Tribunals, Registered Files | Award No. 2073 National Union of Railwaymen v Southern Railway Company: claim that staff employed ... |
| Miscellaneous Papers and Records. Midland and South Western Junction Railway. Charles Braddock (Contractor) | Versus the Company. Arbitration proceedings regarding construction of line between Cirencester and Andoversford |
| Office of Works and successors: Miscellanea. WESTMINSTER BRIDGE. Miscellaneous Records | Lucey's Arbitration Claim for depreciation to Barges used during the construction of Westminster Bridge |
| Middlesbrough and Guisbrough Railway Company. DEEDS, AGREEMENTS, CONTRACTS, SPECIFICATIONS, ESTIMATES, PLANS | Agreements for land, construction, locomotive power, traffic working and arbitration etc |
| Ministry of Transport and successors, Railway Divisions: Correspondence and Papers | Regent's Canal & Dock Company v LCC: Arbitration re construction of Canal Bridge, City Road.... |
| Treasury Solicitor: Transcripts of Proceedings | Henry Kerswill v The Secretary of State for War in arbitration, over the construction of... |
| Ministry of Labour and Predecessors: Correspondence. Chief Industrial Commissioner's Department files and Wages and Arbitration Department files | Cable Workers: Arbitration Awards. Callenders Cable and Construction Company Limited Belvedere v Workers Union (Committee ... |
| Ministry of Labour and successors: Arbitration Tribunals, Registered Files | Award No. 254 National Federation of Building Trades Operatives, trade unions represented on the operatives... |
| Messrs. Hodding and Wordsworth, Potter Street, Worksop. 1. Worksop Estates. (ix) Administration – Railway Construction. a. Manchester, Sheffield and Lincoln Line | Arbitration in Dispute of Company with Duke of Newcastle relating to lands in Worksop awarding... |

| Context Description | Title |
|---|---|
| South Wales Railway Company: Records. COURT CASES AND ARBITRATIONS. South Wales Railway Company (Pembroke Branch), plaintiffs, vs Wythes and Tredwell, defendants, in Chancery | Copy memorandum of contract for construction of Pembroke Branch |
| Ministry of Labour and Predecessors: Correspondence. Chief Industrial Commissioner's Department files and Wages and Arbitration Department files | Cable Workers: Arbitration Awards. Callenders Cable and Construction Company Limited Belvedere v Workers Union (Committee ... |
| Office of Works and successors: Miscellanea. WESTMINSTER BRIDGE. Miscellaneous Records | Lucey's Arbitration Claim for depreciation to Barges used during the construction of Westminster Bridge |
| WHITWORTH URBAN DISTRICT COUNCIL. Miscellaneous | Minutes of first day's proceedings in arbitration concerning payment for construction of sewers between Whitworth... |
| Weymouth and Portland Railway Company: Records. DOCUMENTATION | Drafts of submissions of questions to arbitration between GWR, LSWR and W&PR for construction of... |
| Salisbury City Council. THE CORPORATE CITY. Legal Correspondence | Reed and Mallik Arbitration over construction of City Relief Road Stage II |
| LAND DRAINAGE AND COURTS OF SEWERS. Records of the Kent Rivers Catchment Board, the Kent River Board and the Kent... Legal | Papers relating to arbitration between the Demolition and Construction Co. Ltd. and the K.R.B |
| GREAT YARMOUTH BOROUGH COUNCIL, TOWN CLERK'S DEPARTMENT. INHERITED RECORDS: Yarmouth Local Board of Health | Papers in arbitration with Henry Margetson re construction of sewer near South Market Road, inc. plans |
| Weymouth and Portland Railway Company: Records. DOCUMENTATION | Drafts of submissions of questions to arbitration between GWR and LSWR for construction of W... |
| Transport Ministries: Contracts (CON Series) Files | Contracts let by North Western Road Construction Unit: North Cheshire Motorway M56, Stoak interchange; arbitration... |
| Ministry of Munitions, Munitions Council: Historical Records Branch. File sequence R. Files originally classified under the broad subject heading(s): Labour. (Described at item level) | Copy of arbitration award between employers and workmen engaged on construction of National Filling Factory, ... |
| Miscellaneous Papers and Records. Welshpool and Llanfair Light Railway. John Strachan v Cambrian Railways | Arbitration regarding contract of 6 August 1901 for construction of Welshpool and Llanfair Light Railway |
| PRESTON COUNTY BOROUGH. Ribble Navigation and Preston Dock. Arbitrations | Papers relating to estate of L. Rawstorne including agreement of tenancy of land in Howick... |
| Ministry of Labour and Predecessors: Correspondence. Industrial Relations Department files; Intelligence and Statistics Department files; Wages and Arbitration Department files ... | Intelligence and Statistics Department: Correspondence with civil engineering and constructional works labourers concerning an enquiry ... |
| Union of Construction, Allied Trades & Technicians: Manchester Unity Operative Bricklayers' Society. Printed Series | TPS: Nos. 294–309 [Lacks 304] ABS: Nos. 294–305 [Lacks 294–6, 303–4] Vol. incl. Report of Arbitration Board |
| Lord Chancellor's Office and Lord Chancellor's Department: Registered Files. Arbitrators, Chairmen and Referees, etc. other than those appointed by Lord Chancellor under statutory powers | National Insurance (Industrial Injuries) Act 1946 S.7: complaint by Trades Union Council about construction placed ... |
| Monmouthshire Railway and Canal Company. ARBITRATION CONCERNING ABERTILLERY OR CWMTILLERY BRANCH RAILWAY | Draft agreement between John Russell (of Wydlands, Monm) & Thomas Prothero Price (of Abertillery, Monm) ... |
| Ministry of Health and Department of Health and Social Security: Hospital Construction, Registered Files (File Office J Series). HOSPITAL BUILDING PROGRAMME. The National Hospital for Nervous Diseases, Queen Square, London | Development of the laboratory block: unofficial strike on the Phase 1 Site; arbitration hearing and ... |
| South Devon Railway Company. B V ELLIOT VERSUS THE SOUTH DEVON RAILWAY COMPANY ARBITRATION | Brief on motion for the defendants to dissolve the injunction obtained by Plaintiff to restrain ... |
| London Borough of Sutton and Predecessors. Local Government Records, 1862–1983. Worcester Park Sewage Works | Worcester Park Sewage Works: copy contract between S& C Borough and Alderton Construction Co Ltd re: construction of the works in Arbitration File |

| Context Description | Title |
|---|---|
| COUNTY OF BUCKINGHAMSHIRE QUARTER SESSIONS. COURT RECORDS. COUNTY GAOL. New county prison. Papers and correspondence relating to design, finance, construction, etc. Letters to... | Peirce: Giving the name of the arbitrator agreed with Locke & Nesham, the contractors. Please return the drawings |
| Ministry of Labour and Predecessors: Correspondence. Chief Industrial Commissioner's Department files; Trade Boards files; Industrial Relations Department files | Industrial Relations Division: Railway Industry. Bridgebuilding and Constructional Engineering Employers' Association v Constructional Engineering Union: ... |
| Edwards, Leslie (b 1945), engineer and arbitrator | Papers rel to the construction of Marsa shipyard at Malta |
| London Borough of Sutton and Predecessors. Local Government Records, 1862–1983. Worcester Park Sewage Works | Worcester Park Sewage Works: copies of documents to be produced in arbitration between S& C Borough and Alderton Construction |
| EGERTON FAMILY, EARLS OF WILTON, OF HEATON HALL. LEGAL DRAFTS AND CORRESPONDENCE | Papers relating to Heaton Reservoir construction |
| Transport Ministries: Contracts (CON Series) Files | Contracts let by North Western Road Construction Unit: North Cheshire Motorway, M56/5, Hapsford to Preston ... |
| The Stafford Family Collection. The Fitzherberts of Swynnerton. Title Deeds etc. Title Deeds. Norbury [co. Derbs.] estate | Presentments at Staffs. Assizes, arbitration bonds etc. re disputes on raising level of River Dove... |
| Miscellaneous Papers and Records. Llanelly and Mynydd Mawr Railway. Llanelly Harbour and Burry Navigation Commissioners | Correspondence, plans, arbitration reports, etc. as to Disputes over Harbour Works, Dredging and Scouring of ... |
| Miscellaneous Papers and Records. Llanelly and Mynydd Mawr Railway. Llanelly Harbour and Burry Navigation Commissioners | Correspondence, plans, arbitration reports, etc. as to Disputes over Harbour Works, Dredging and Scouring of ... |
| Ministry of Labour and Predecessors: Correspondence. Chief Industrial Commissioner's Department files and Wages and Arbitration Department files | Wages and Arbitration Department: Farriery. Val de Travers Paving Co. Ltd. (and other asphalt firms), ... |
| Miscellaneous Papers and Records. Port Talbot Railway and Docks | Construction of Railway and Dock works under Act of 1894 – contract with S. Pearson ... |
| Wycombe Railway Company. DOCUMENTATION | Agreement between GWR and WRC concerning payment for maintenance and cost of construction of junction ... |
| Ministry of Housing and Local Government and predecessors: Water Division and predecessors: Water and Sewerage, Registered Files. LOCAL AUTHORITY PAPERS. South Essex Waterworks Company (6026) | Construction of new reservoir – amount of compensation to be paid to owner of land... |
| Ministry of Labour and Predecessors: Correspondence. Chief Industrial Commissioner's Department files | Chief Industrial Commissioner's Department: Munitions Industries: Arbitration Awards. Ministry of Munitions v employees employed on ... |
| Miscellaneous Papers and Records. Llanelly and Mynydd Mawr Railway. Llanelly Harbour and Burry Navigation Commissioners | Correspondence, plans, arbitration reports, etc. as to Disputes over Harbour Works, Dredging and Scouring of ... |
| Miscellaneous Papers and Records. Llanelly and Mynydd Mawr Railway. Llanelly Harbour and Burry Navigation Commissioners | Correspondence, plans, arbitration reports, etc. as to Disputes over Harbour Works, Dredging and Scouring of ... |
| COUNTY OF BUCKINGHAMSHIRE QUARTER SESSIONS. COURT RECORDS. COUNTY GAOL. New county prison. Papers and correspondence relating to design, finance, construction, etc. Letters to... | Peirce: Thanks for sending the minute governing my appointment; inform me of the details of the proposed reference of my account to arbitration |
| Treasury: Treasury Board Papers and In-Letters. Papers registered in 1913. Papers registered in 1913. (Described at item level) | War Office. Arbitration of disputes arising on contracts. (Case of W. Hill, contractor for the... |
| Ministry of Labour and Predecessors: Correspondence. Chief Industrial Commissioner's Department files; Commercial Department files; Headquarters Department files; Industrial Relations Department... | Chief Industrial Commissioner's Department: Vehicle Building: Arbitration Awards. Ministry of Munitions Building Labour Committee Trollope ... |

| Context Description | Title |
|---|---|
| Ministry of Labour and Predecessors: Correspondence. Chief Industrial Commissioner's Department files; Commercial Department files; Headquarters Department files; Industrial Relations Department... | Chief Industrial Commissioner's Department: Vehicle Building: Arbitration Awards. Ministry of Munitions Building Labour Committee Trollope ... |
| Ministry of Labour and Predecessors: Correspondence. Chief Industrial Commissioner's Department files; Commercial Department files; Headquarters Department files; Industrial Relations Department... | Chief Industrial Commissioner's Department: Vehicle Building: Arbitration Awards. Ministry of Munitions Building Labour Committee Trollope ... |
| Ministry of Labour and Predecessors: Correspondence. Chief Industrial Commissioner's Department files; Commercial Department files; Headquarters Department files; Industrial Relations Department... | Chief Industrial Commissioner's Department: Vehicle Building: Arbitration Awards. Ministry of Munitions Building Labour Committee Trollope ... |
| Ministry of Labour and Predecessors: Correspondence. Chief Industrial Commissioner's Department files | Chief Industrial Commissioner's Department: Munitions Industries: Arbitration Awards. Ministry of Munitions v employees engaged on ... |
| Department of Employment and predecessors: Industrial Relations, Registered Files | Dispute between Christiani and Neilson Ltd (Construction Engineers) at Esso Oil Refinery, Fawley and Amalgamated ... |
| Ministry of Labour and Predecessors: Correspondence. Industrial Relations Department files and Trade Boards files | Industrial Relations Division: Iron and Steel Industry. Constructional Engineering Union v Messrs. James Allan Senior ... |
| COUNCIL SOLICITOR'S DEPARTMENT. BOLTON CORPORATION ACT, 1905: ARBITRATION BETWEEN EDWARD DEAKIN AND BOLTON CORPORATION CONCERNING COMPENSATION FOR... | File of Tables and Statistical Returns |
| Ministry of Labour and Predecessors: Correspondence. Chief Industrial Commissioner's Department files; Headquarters Department files; Industrial Relations Division files; Joint Industrial... | Wages and Arbitration Department: Electrical Power Engineers' Association's Award (No. 9281) Shipwrights' and Shipconstructors' Association, ... |
| Ballantine Dykes family of Dovenby Hall. Additional records. Estate | Cases for counsels' opinions, copy award and papers relating to arbitration between F L B... |
| Ministry of Labour and Predecessors: Correspondence. Industrial Relations Department files and Trade Boards files | Industrial Relations Department: Correspondence with the Industrial Court concerning the award given in arbitration by ... |
| Ministry of Labour and Predecessors: Correspondence. Chief Industrial Commissioner's Department files | Chief Industrial Commissioner's Department: Correspondence with W Addington Willis concerning the award given in arbitration ... |
| Ministry of Labour and Predecessors: Correspondence. Chief Industrial Commissioner's Department files | Chief Industrial Commissioner's Department: Arbitration Awards: Miscellaneous and General Labourers. Ministry of Munitions v Gretna ... |
| Ministry of Labour and Predecessors: Correspondence. Industrial Relations Department files and Trade Boards files | Industrial Relations Division: Iron and Steel Industry. Constructional Engineering Union v Messrs. James Allan Senior ... |
| Ministry of Labour and Predecessors: Correspondence. Chief Industrial Commissioner's Department files; Commercial Department files; Headquarters Department files; Industrial Relations Department... | Chief Industrial Commissioner's Department: Vehicle Building: Arbitration Awards. Ministry of Munitions Building Labour Committee Trollope ... |
| Ministry of Labour and Predecessors: Correspondence. Chief Industrial Commissioner's Department files; Headquarters Department files; Industrial Relations Division files; Joint Industrial... | Wages and Arbitration Department: Electrical Power Engineers' Association's Award (No. 9281) Shipwrights' and Shipconstructors' Association, ... |
| Ministry of Labour and Predecessors: Correspondence. Chief Industrial Commissioner's Department files; Commercial Department files; Headquarters Department files; Industrial Relations Department... | Chief Industrial Commissioner's Department: Vehicle Building: Arbitration Awards. Ministry of Munitions Building Labour Committee Trollope ... |
| Bridport Railway Company. MINUTES AND REPORTS. Board Reports and Papers | Papers relating to promotion of BRC, construction of line, dispute with K Matherson and subsequent ... |
| Treasury Solicitor: Transcripts of Proceedings | Thames Iron Works and Shipbuilding Company Limited v the Admiralty: construction of HM first class... |

| Context Description | Title |
|---|---|
| Ratcliffe and Henderson of Helston, solicitors. Records of the St. Aubyn family of Clowance, Crowan. ESTATE ADMINISTRATION. INDIVIDUAL PARISHES. Camborne | Brief, affidavits and award, Boswin Stream arbitration, Camborne Water Co. V. Rev. St. Aubyn Hender... |
| Ministry of Labour and Predecessors: Correspondence. Chief Industrial Commissioner's Department files | Chief Industrial Commissioner's Department: Arbitration Awards: Miscellaneous and General Labourers. Birmingham Building Trades Employers Association ... |
| BRADSHAW, GASS AND HOPE OF BOLTON, ARCHITECTS | St Annes on Sea Library: arbitration papers relating to the construction of a Carneige Library at St Annes on Sea, Lancashire, also correspondence, contracts, accounts, estimates, quantities |
| Papers and correspondence of Sir Frederick Edward Warner FRS, FREng. SOCIETIES AND ORGANISATIONS, C.1–C.584. INTERNATIONAL COURT OF ARBITRATION | Other printed material |
| South Wales Railway Company: Records. COURT CASES AND ARBITRATIONS. South Wales Railway Company (Pembroke Branch), plaintiffs, vs Wythes and Tredwell, defendants, in Chancery | Copy memorandum of agreement approved by George Wythes and Thomas Tredwell, between South Wales Railway ... |
| Ministry of Labour and Predecessors: Correspondence. Chief Industrial Commissioner's Department files | Chief Industrial Commissioner's Department: Arbitration Awards: Miscellaneous and General Labourers. Midland Employers Federation representing bridge ... |
| Union Of Construction, Allied Trades & Technicians : Operative Bricklayers' Society. Printed Series | Monthly Reports : Nos.56–103. Also incl. : Quarterly Rpts., Dec 1865 – Jun 1866; transcripts... |
| NELSON Municipal Borough. Town Clerk's Department. Municipal Borough Records. Judicial case papers | Arbitration in a contract dated 5 Dec. 1898 between Messrs. J. and M. Harley, builders... |
| Transport Ministries: Contracts (CON Series) Files | Contracts let by North Western Road Construction Unit: North Cheshire Motorway, contract M56/7, Preston Brook ... |
| Transport Ministries: Contracts (CON Series) Files | Contracts let by North Western Road Construction Unit: North Cheshire Motorway M56, Hapsford-Preston Brook section ... |
| Ministry of Labour and Predecessors: Correspondence. Industrial Relations Department files and Trade Boards files | Industrial Relations Department: Correspondence with the Bridge Building and Constructional Engineering Employer's Association, the Iron ... |
| Pearson Shaw and Son of Bingham, architects and surveyors | College of Estate Management, London, course notes and essay questions |
| NELSON Municipal Borough. Town Clerk's Department. Local Board Records. Contracts and Tenders. Miscellanea | James Thane and William Alfred Wilson, both of Maryport, Cumb., contractors Contract for the construction of... |
| Ministry of Labour and Predecessors: Correspondence. Industrial Relations Department files and Trade Boards files | Industrial Relations Division: Agriculture Industry. Bridge Building and Constructional Engineering Employers' Association, v the Iron ... |
| Great Northern Railway Company: Surveyor and Estate Agent: Correspondence Files | Tickhill Light Railway, purchase of land for construction from owners: Owston and Haxey, Lincolnshire; award ... |
| RAY OF HEANOR. Estate Papers. Heanor Hall estate. Legal papers | Award of arbitration in a dispute between John Ray and Messrs Smith and Frearson (trustees... |
| Transport Ministries: Contracts (CON Series) Files | Contracts let by South Eastern Road Construction Unit: South Coast Motorway M27, Ower to Chilworth ... |
| Transport Ministries: Contracts (CON Series) Files | Contracts let by North Western Road Construction Unit: North Cheshire Motorway M56, Hapsford-Preston Brook section ... |
| Transport Ministries: Contracts (CON Series) Files | Contracts let by North Western Road Construction Unit: North Cheshire Motorway, contract M56/7, Preston Brook ... |
| Transport Ministries: Contracts (CON Series) Files | Contracts let by North Western Road Construction Unit: North Cheshire Motorway M56, Hapsford-Preston Brook section... |
| Transport Ministries: Contracts (CON Series) Files | Contracts let by North Western Road Construction Unit: North Cheshire Motorway M56, Hapsford-Preston Brook section... |
| Catalogue of the records of Edmund Kirby & Sons architects and surveyors, Liverpool by... ENGLAND. LANCASHIRE: PARISHES. Widnes: other properties | Lunts Heath Road, Widnes: correspondence and papers concerning E B Kirby as arbitrator in dispute between Mrs Theresa O'Brien and F Smith, builder, relating to construction of house, Four Ways |

| Context Description | Title |
|---|---|
| Public Record Office: Maps and plans extracted to flat storage from various series of records held at the Public Record Office, Kew, from 1977 | 17 items (originally annexed to a document putting the Japanese government's case to the arbitration ... |
| Board of Trade Harbour Department: Correspondence and Papers. Board of Trade Harbour Department: correspondence and papers | Harbours. Particulars, etc. of dispute between Sir J. Aird and the Bristol Corporation on the ... |
| Foreign Office: Consulate and Legation, Greece (formerly Ottoman Empire): General Correspondence | Correspondence: F1. Contents of FO 286/1026–1027 include: Railway construction in Greece (18 April 1928); Settlement... |
| Nantes and Wilde (solicitors) MSS | UPHILL |
| Board of Trade Harbour Department: Correspondence and Papers. Board of Trade Harbour Department: correspondence and papers | Electric Lighting. Appeal against the refusal of the Battersea Borough Council to allow the laying ... |
| Foreign Office: Consulate and Legation, Greece (formerly Ottoman Empire): General Correspondence | Correspondence: F1. Contents of FO 286/1026–1027 include: Railway construction in Greece (18 April 1928); Settlement... |
| The Family and Estate Papers of the Willoughby Family, Lords Middleton, of Wollaton, Nottinghamshire,... Legal Papers of the Willoughby Family of Wollaton, Nottinghamshire, Middleton, Warwickshire and Birdsall, Yorkshire;... Estate Papers. Papers relating to Railway Development in the Nottinghamshire Estates | MS transcripts from shorthand writer's notes concerning Case in Chancery, Lord Middleton v The Midland Railway Company. Before R. J. Charlton esquire, arbitrator, 14, 15, 17, 24 July and 1 August 1871 |
| BRADSHAW, GASS AND HOPE OF BOLTON, ARCHITECTS | The Walker Institute, Southfield Estate, Bolton: construction of new football ground – quantities, 1933 K103661X 134... |
| Union of Construction, Allied Trades & Technicians : Amalgamated Society of Woodworkers. Miscellaneous files created at the ASW gen.office | Miscellaneous documents, including Engraving of Robert Applegarth, 1873 GUOCJ New Mills branch: pprs. re a disabled member,... |
| Great Northern Railway Company: Surveyor and Estate Agent: Correspondence Files | Mint Street property, London: agreement between London County Council and Great Northern Railway Company to ... |
| Brockbank and Tyson, solicitors of Whitehaven. Clients' records. Railway companies. London North Western Railway | Papers, including plans (3), relating to the dispute with Bain and Co., concerning land purchased... |
| IPSWICH DOCK COMMISSION. LEGAL PAPERS. Papers relating to dispute between David Thornbory of King's Lynn and Commissioners re his... | Articles of agreement (counterparts) |
| BOSWORTH (HIGHGATE HOUSE) COLLECTION. Teeton Hall estate | Alfred Andrew, solicitor, Northampton, to Thomas Jones Bosworth, Cadeby Compensation for the damage to Teeton... |
| Treasury: Treasury Board Papers and In-Letters. Papers registered in 1919. Papers registered in 1919. (Described at item level). | Foreign Office. Claim by the Rambla Co. of Montevideo Ltd., a British company, for compensation ... |
| Hornsey Local Board of Health, Urban District Council and Borough Council. Borough Officials. Engineer and Surveyor. Miscellaneous. Papers re. drainage and sewerage | Correspondence and other working papers re the construction of the Hornsey Outfall Sewer (Green Lanes to Manor Rd and Eade Rd Stoke Newington. Includes transcript of arbitration between Hornsey, Islington and LCC over drainage, 1905; reports by E and S over necessity to rebuild the sewer built 1871; complaints re damage to houses caused by building; photographs; costs of materials and wages; plans and drawings; copy 6'0s map 1920 rev. showing line of sewer |
| Montague Family. DEEDS. Midhurst. Easeborne | Agreement |
| General Board of Health and Home Office, Local Government Act Office: Correspondence. Urban Districts. Urban Districts: Upper Mill, 1867–1869; Upper Sedgley, 1867–1871; Upperthong, 1861–1869; Uxbridge, 1848–1871. Details given... | Folios 373–374. To: The General Board of Health. From: Charles Woodbridge, Clerk to the Uxbridge... |
| Shelly and Johns Solicitors | Papers relating to the case of Lang versus the Plymouth Devonport and South Western Junction Railway Company |

| Context Description | Title |
|---|---|
| RECORDS OF THE MOCCAS ESTATE. MISCELLANEOUS ESTATE CONCERNS | MOCCAS TOLL BRIDGE Papers relating to its building, (correspondence, statements of accounts etc.) Note: The bridge was... |
| General Board of Health and Home Office, Local Government Act Office: Correspondence. Urban Districts. Urban Districts: Upper Mill, 1867–1869; Upper Sedgley, 1867–1871; Upperthong, 1861–1869; Uxbridge, 1848–1871. Details given... | Folio 374. To: The General Board of Health. From: Charles Woodbridge, Clerk to the Uxbridge... |
| Public Record Office: Maps and plans extracted to flat storage from various series of records of the War Office. 10 items extracted from WO 44/23. Maps of land in Upper Canada (now Ontario)... | Upper Canada (now Ontario): Wolford (now part of Merrickville-Wolford). (8) 'Concession A. Lots 26 and ... |
| Department of Employment: Manpower and Productivity Service Division: Registered Files (MPS Series). | Department of Employment: Manpower and Productivity Service Division: Registered Files (MPS Series) |
| General Board of Health and Home Office, Local Government Act Office: Correspondence. Urban Districts. Urban Districts: Harrow, 1849–1869; Hartlepool, 1849–1870. Details are given at item level | Folios 171–173. To: The Local Government Act Office. From: A Montague Butler, Chairman of the ... |
| Trade Union Activity Within Gloucestershire. TRANSPORT AND GENERAL WORKERS UNION. EMPLOYERS | Industrial tribunal hearings |
| FYLDE WATER BOARD. Contracts | Correspondence and other papers |
| The Goodwood Estate Archives. ESTATE PAPERS. ESTATE ADMINISTRATION. GENERAL | Papers in a dispute between Caleb Rickman of Chichester and John Newman of Singleton regarding Cakeham Farm, West Wittering |
| War Cabinet and Cabinet: Minutes. Cabinet. Conclusions. 1(28) – 30(28). | Record Type: Conclusion. Former Reference: CC 1 (28). Attendees: S Baldwin; A Chamberlain; W Churchill;... |
| General Board of Health and Home Office, Local Government Act Office: Correspondence. Urban Districts. Urban Districts: Dartford, 1848–1867; Dartmouth, 1853–1871; Darton, 1864–1870; Dawdon, 1863–1869. Details are given at... | Folios 538–539. To: The Local Government Act Office. From: Percy Hockin, Clerk to the Local ... |
| General Board of Health and Home Office, Local Government Act Office: Correspondence. Urban Districts. Urban Districts: Exeter, 1848–1871; Exmouth, 1848–1870. Details are given at item level | Folios 29–31. To: The General Board of Health. From: J G Bidwell, Manager, The Landowners' ... |
| WINN PAPERS | Frodingham Ironstone Mines Ltd., Board of Trade |
| General Board of Health and Home Office, Local Government Act Office: Correspondence. Urban Districts. Urban Districts: Honley, 1864–1871; Hoole, 1863–1871; Horbury, 1863–1869; Horfield, 1865–1871; Horncastle, 1863–1871; Hornsea 1863–1871.... | Folios 319–320. To: Home Secretary. From: William Kent, Chairman of the Horfield Local Board, Horfield, ... |
| THE SCARISBRICK MUNIMENTS. Railway Correspondence and Papers | West Lancashire Branch of the Lancashire and Yorkshire Railway Company correspondence, plans and legal papers... |
| LAND DRAINAGE RECORDS OF WEST SUSSEX. RECORDS OF THE COMMISSIONERS OF SEWERS FOR THE WESTERN PART OF THE COUNTY OF... ADMINISTRATION. ORIGINAL BUNDLES. Documents relating to the reclamation of Pagham Harbour | Documents relating to an alleged breach of the Pagham Harbour Reclamation Act by the Pagham Harbour Reclamation Co |
| Deposit from Balderstone, Warren (solicitors), Biggleswade. Sandy and Edworth – watermains over LNWR property | Grant of right i) The London and North Western Railway Company Ltd ii) The Rural District of... |
| ARCHIVE OF THE DAVIES-GILBERT FAMILY OF EASTBOURNE, EAST SUSSEX, AND TRELISSICK, CORNWALL. ESTATE RECORDS. The estate as managed by F H Gell | Eastbourne Improvement Act |
| Cheltenham Borough Records. THE IMPROVEMENT COMMISSION, 1852–1876. Improvement Commissioners. Correspondence | Correspondence |

| Context Description | Title |
|---|---|
| General Board of Health and Home Office, Local Government Act Office: Correspondence. Urban Districts. Urban Districts: Bury St Edmunds, 1855–1871; Buxton, 1858–1871. Described at item level | Folios 96–99. To: The Local Government Act Office. From: James Sparke, [Clerk, The Paving Commissioners ... |
| General Board of Health and Home Office, Local Government Act Office: Correspondence. Urban Districts. Urban Districts: Margate. Details are given at item level | Folios 209–211. To: The General Board of Health. From: John Boys, Chairman of the Local... |
| John Fowler & Co., (Leeds) Ltd. LEGAL RECORDS OF COMPANIES AND BUSINESSES. PATENTING RECORDS | LICENCE |
| Records inherited and created by the Ministry of Transport and successors, Commissions, Tribunals and Inquiries | Records inherited and created by the Ministry of Transport and successors, Commissions, Tribunals and Inquiries |
| BROWN & MERRY (Leighton Buzzard). Sale Catalogues and agency papers – arranged by parish. TODDINGTON | (i) Bundle of correspondence, mainly between Hugh Millar (incoming tenant to Redhills Farm, Toddington), Ivan... |
| JOHNSON | Agreement, re conveyance and sale, for Â£711.7s.2d.: |
| DEAL BOROUGH. ECCLESIASTICAL AND CHARITY. Deal Chapel | Chapel wardens' accounts |
| WINN PAPERS | Frodingham Ironstone Mines Ltd., Frodingham Iron & Steel Co. Ltd |
| Additional Manuscripts, Catalogue F. Plans, diagrams and other memoranda concerning the Royal Military Canal between Hythe and Winchelsea... | Plans, diagrams and other memoranda concerning the Royal Military Canal between Hythe and Winchelsea |
| LONDON COUNTY COUNCIL | Tramways Department: General |
| Colonial Office and predecessors: British Guiana, formerly Berbice, Demerara, and Essequibo, Original Correspondence | Correspondence from 'offices' (Government departments and other organisations) and individuals on matters relating to British ... |
| HOOPER AND FLETCHER ARCHIVE. S.Wells & Co: Edmund Powers and E.Powers & Sons. Ham Brick Field, Faversham, Kent. Deeds etc | Copy of Lease for 10 Years from 11 October 1878 1) Reverend Henry John Rusk of... |
| Shackerley Collection. Jones Family Papers. George Jones | Deed of Copartnership – The Chillington Coal & Iron Co.' |
| WINN PAPERS | C Winn, Sir Robert Sheffield Bart |
| URBAN DISTRICT OF BARNOLDSWICK. Legal Papers | Legal papers relating to the Council's gas, water, sewage, education, health and private street works,... |
| | Business Papers of W.T.Nash |
| Miscellaneous Papers. Luton. Sworders' Brewery | Draft agreement |
| Employment Exchanges Reports on Employment and Unemployment | Employment Exchanges Reports on Employment and Unemployment |
| Manuscripts. Carew Manuscript | The EARL OF TYRONE and SIR TIRLAGH O'NELE |
| Records of the Salaries Branch and Burnham Committees | Records of the Salaries Branch and Burnham Committees |
| Colonial Office and predecessors: British Guiana, formerly Berbice, Demerara, and Essequibo, Original Correspondence | Correspondence from 'offices' (government departments) on matters relating to British Guiana. Correspondents and subjects are ... |
| SALTMARSHE FAMILY OF SALTMARSHE | |
| BEDFORDSHIRE COUNTY COUNCIL | |
| India Office Records.Records of the British Residency and Agencies in the Persian Gulf | Political Agency, Muscat |
| Papers and correspondence of Sir Frederick Edward Warner FRS, FREng | |
| FOLKESTONE BOROUGH | |
| Manuscripts. Shrewsbury Papers | Shrewsbury Papers |
| THE DANSON FAMILY ARCHIVE | |
| John Fowler & Co. (Leeds) Ltd | |
| THE GLYNDE PLACE ARCHIVES | |

## *Annex II: Construction arbitration records in London Metropolitan Archives*

Sunbury Urban District Council – ACC/2155

Records of Sunbury Urban District Council, 1895–1971, including presented reports; correspondence, memoranda and copies of bye-laws, relating to the adoption of certain provisions of the Public Health Acts Amendment Act 1907; deeds, agreements and other documents relating to The Cedars Estate, Sunbury; papers relating to a dispute between the owners of Sunbury Park Estate and the Council; agreements and contracts for various works to be carried out, particularly road maintenance works, sewer and drainage works, housing construction, civil defense structures and war damage repairs.

St Leonard, Streatham: Streatham High Road, Lambeth – P95/LEN

Records of the parish of Saint Leonard, Streatham High Road, Streatham, including papers relating to a legal dispute; financial accounts; registers of baptisms, marriages, burials and banns; papers relating to tithes; Parochial Church Council minutes; church services registers; papers relating to parish boundaries; papers relating to the construction and maintenance of the church including faculties and specifications; administrative papers; and papers relating to the parish schools. C 1439–1960 M 1538–1963 B 1538–1862.

Correspondence with William Haywood plus memoranda and press cuttings over proposed stations at Bank and St. Paul's, Feb. 1890 – June 1893 – COL/TSD/EG/03/02/001.

Subjects include:- statement as to proposed railway by Company Engineers – opposition to Central London Railway Bill, 1890 – negotiations between Company and W. Haywood over rate of railway beneath Holborn Viaduct – dispute over jurisdiction with London County Council – submitting Bank plans to Commissioners of Sewers for approval – future construction at Bank of stairs, subway, ventilation ducts.

Queen's Bench Division, Feb. 7. Faulkner and Others v. Chubb – CLC/B/002/10/01/018/016A

Dispute concerning the recovery of £30 for work and layout in construction of a working model of an apparatus for closing train doors, invented by Mr. Chubb. The jury found for Chubb, on the grounds that the contract had not been properly carried out. Unknown source.

## *Annex III: Records of arbitral organisations in archives*

**Source:** primarily TNA's *Discovery* portal. The list includes the records of both government arbitral organisations held by TNA and private or local authority sector bodies held in local authority or specialist archives. Records may vary from the complete written archive to miscellaneous papers or the archived website.

| Arbitral organisation | Archive repository (England & Wales) |
|---|---|
| Admiralty Transport Arbitration Board | The National Archives |
| Advisory Conciliation and Arbitration Service (ACAS) | The National Archives |
| Aircraft and Ship Building Industries Arbitration Tribunal | The National Archives |
| Anglo-American Pecuniary Claims Arbitration Tribunal | The National Archives |
| Anglo-Austrian Mixed Arbitral Tribunal | The National Archives |
| Anglo-Bulgarian Mixed Arbitral Tribunal | The National Archives |
| Anglo-German Mixed Arbitral Tribunal | The National Archives |
| Anglo-Hungarian Mixed Arbitral Tribunal | The National Archives |
| Board of Conciliation and Arbitration for the Boot and Shoe Trade of Leicester | Record Office for Leicestershire, Leicester and Rutland |
| Board of Conciliation and Arbitration for the Iron and Steel Trades of the North of England | Teesside Archives |
| Central Arbitration Committee | The National Archives |
| Civil Service Arbitration Tribunal | The National Archives |
| Epping Forest Arbitrator | The National Archives |
| Hinckley and District Boot and Shoe Arbitration Board | Record Office for Leicestershire, Leicester and Rutland |
| International Arbitration Commission | The National Archives |
| Lambeth Mediation Service | Lambeth Archives |

| **Arbitral organisation** | **Archive repository (England & Wales)** |
|---|---|
| Leicestershire and Rutland Board of Conciliation and Arbitration for the Boot and Shoe Trade | Record Office for Leicestershire, Leicester and Rutland |
| London Court of Arbitration | London Metropolitan Archives: City of London |
| London Passenger Transport Arbitration Tribunal | The National Archives |
| Mediation UK | LSE Library, Archives and Special Collections |
| Ministry of Labour, Wages and Arbitration Department | The National Archives |
| National Family Mediation | LSE Library, Archives and Special Collections |
| Official Arbitrator, Land Claims | The National Archives |
| Shoe Trade Board of Arbitration | Northamptonshire Record Office |
| Transport Arbitration Tribunal | The National Archives |

## *Annex IV: Papers of individual arbitrators held in archives*

**Source:** TNA's *Discovery* portal. This list should not in any way be seen as exhaustive, since many individuals undertaking arbitration work may have been not classified as such by the repositories with which their papers have been deposited. They should always be searched for by name.

| Individual | Records | **Archive repository (England & Wales)** |
|---|---|---|
| Edwards, Leslie (b 1945), engineer and arbitrator | 1975–1978: papers rel to the construction of Marsa shipyard at Malta | Institution of Civil Engineers |
| Fry, Sir Edward (1827–1918), Knight, judge, arbitrator and zoologist | 1834–1935 personal and family correspondence; diaries of prison visits | Cambridge University: King's College Archive Centre; Cambridge University Library: Department of Manuscripts and University Archives; Warwick University: Modern Records Centre |
| Guillebaud, Claude William (1890–1971), economist and arbitrator | 1927–1972: personal papers and corresp | Cambridge University: St John's College Library |
| Marsh, Arthur (1922–1999), academic and industrial arbitrator | c1960–1991: papers rel to work as industrial arbitrator | Warwick University: Modern Records Centre |

## *Annex V: Arbitral organisations contacted prior to this project*

The Arbitration Club

Centre for Effective Dispute Resolution

Civil Mediation Council

London Maritime Arbitrators Association (LMAA )

Society of Construction Arbitrators

UK Mediation

Worshipful Company of Arbitrators

# Appendix XI: Developing a national strategy to rescue legal records

docstockmedia/Shutterstock.com

The two papers in this Appendix represent attempts by LRAR to identify the need for a national strategy to rescue legal records in a co-ordinated way. This strategy would complement the work being done by professional bodies such as TNA and the BRA towards developing strategies to rescue private sector records in general and to recommend ways in which LRAR's work could feed into those strategies.

### *Paper 1: Legal Records at Risk: towards a national strategy to rescue private sector legal records*

Written in February 2017, this paper was circulated for comment to the LRAR Advisory Panel, TNA, LMA, the BAC and the BRA. It was intended to:

- Complement TNA's 2017 research survey into records at risk. TNA has since facilitated the creation of a Records at Risk steering group on which LRAR is represented.
- Suggest ways in which LRAR could work with the above groups to achieve our mutual strategic aims.
- Be a starting point for investigating the potential for creating a Legal Archives Trust.

### *Paper 2: Developing a working model to rescue legal records: a Legal Archives Trust*

This paper was written in May 2017 at the request of the LRAR Executive Committee. In December 2017 it was paraphrased in formal letters to selected individuals inviting them to join a steering group to determine the viability of setting up such a Trust.

..............................

## Paper 1: Legal Records at Risk: towards a national strategy to rescue legal records

### *What do we mean by legal records at risk (LRAR)?*

The LRAR project considers that private sector legal records in England and Wales are potentially at risk of becoming lost or inaccessible due to factors such as globalisation, digital obsolescence, physical neglect, lack of interest on the part of information owners or reduced archive resources to preserve and provide access to the records. All records in the private sector face similar challenges, but modern legal records are particularly vulnerable due to recent developments which are transforming the nature, organisation, regulation and economics of legal services and legal institutions.

The proposed outcomes of the LRAR project are:

- To broaden the concept of 'legal' records from the traditional definition of them as court records or formal documents such as deeds to records of institutions specialised to law (ISLs), including business records, mainly in the private sector.

- To identify legal records of potential research value.
- To identify records which may be at risk through neglect, digital obsolescence, lack of interest or lack of resources to preserve and provide access to the records.
- To provide generic recordkeeping advice and guidance to information owners.
- To identify potential repositories for legal records of research value.
- To facilitate the process by which information owners reach agreement to deposit with or donate records to those repositories.

There are few in-house collections of 'legal archives' in the UK. A small number of institutions specialised to law (ISLs) maintain in-house archives for their business records of historic value, which they may make available to the public[1]. These archives are not to be confused with the almost universal practice of depositing semi-current records en masse in a warehouse or a lower tier server for indefinite storage.

Some universities hold specialist collections of legal archives[2] and private sector legal records have for many years been collected by local county archives, but on an ad hoc and random basis. The principal category of 'legal' records held in archives still comprises deeds (probably as distributed by the BRA), not business records. Collection of legal material depends on a) the legal entity/individual information owner knowing about the archives b) the capacity of the archives to take the records c) how proactive the archives is in its collecting. Some archives, therefore, hold the business records of law firms or other legal entities or the papers of prominent individuals and some do not. Most archives LRAR has contacted can also no longer afford (and indeed should refuse in any case) to accept unlisted records, records in poor condition or records with unfeasibly lengthy closure periods. Many still don't have the facilities to collect born-digital records.

The main risk, therefore, lies in the fact that, other than by the archives mentioned above and the BRA, which has now discontinued the process, there has been no systematic collection of records of private sector ISLs, and even this has largely been limited to particular kinds of 'legal' document. So a strategy for a national, systematic collections policy for legal records – by which we mean all the business records of value of ISLs and prominent individual legal specialists – needs to be developed.

## *Is a strategy necessary if these records are of no historical interest?*

It is safe to say that the core strategic and operational records of any business have considerable value, not just for researchers but for the business itself – that is why all the big banks in the UK and many major businesses (e.g. Boots, Marks and Spencers, Diageo) maintain in-house archives.[3] Ingraining the understanding of information as an asset rather than as an overhead in ISLs is a major strategic aim of LRAR.

For legal entities such as regulatory bodies, pressure groups, membership organisations etc. it is hard to say without surveying the records, but any organisation which tries to influence government through consultations, which tries to formalise professional membership through examinations or accreditation or which regulates the legal profession will have material of long-term research value.

In relation to specifically legal entities, the huge changes in legal provision over the 20th–21st century, including breaking the solicitors' monopoly on services such as conveyancing, the rise in alternative dispute resolution and the development of alternative business structures providing legal services need to be documented and preserved or we will have an inaccurate/gap-filled picture of legal developments in this period. The same strategy is needed to save the records of other ISLs (regulators, membership bodies, pressure groups etc) and ancillary legal bodies (e.g. law stationers, law publishers).

Legal historians to date have been mainly concerned with studying pre-20th-century court and government records. This needs to change if we are to have a balanced historical viewpoint of legal service providers and their effect on/relationship with their local community and society in general. Researchers in other fields also need to grasp the potential use of legal records in, e.g., social, economic, political and family history, socio-legal research, local studies, gender and diversity studies. They additionally need to be aware that legal records will be found in unexpected and diverse locations, including within the business records of private organisations.[4]

1 See list at **Appendix III** (Source: TNA's *Discovery*). At the time of writing not one UK law firm has been identified which maintains an in-house archive routinely opened to the public.

2 Notably the archives of several educational bodies in the Records of Legal Education Archives at IALS, the archive of the British Institute of Human Rights at KCL Archives, the British Maritime Law Association archive at University College London Special Collections; London Court of International Arbitration records at London Metropolitan Archives; Mediation UK and National Family Mediation records at The London School of Economics Archives and Special Collections; the Howard League for Penal Reform archive at Warwick University Modern Records Centre.

3 At a recent LRAR seminar the Barclays Group Archivist gave a demonstration of how use of material in its in-house archives to win a court case saved Barclays upwards of £1 billion.

4 See, for example, the findings of the Legal Records at Risk Project – Case study: Alternative dispute resolution records held by Transport for London.

## *How is such a strategy to be developed?*

### *1. Engagement with stakeholders*

- *Archives*: TNA, the BRA, the BAC, the ARA and the IRMS are key stakeholders, representing the government and local archive sectors, business and other private archives and professional archivists and records managers. LRAR is in contact with all these bodies with the aim of jointly developing clear priorities and documented procedures for a) the identification and b) the collection of legal records of value.
- *Legal institutions and practitioners*: LRAR will continue to try to engage with legal entities and individuals by written and personal contact, publishing articles in legal journals and running seminars, emphasising the business benefits of managing records better and preserving archives, including cost and efficiency savings, use for branding and marketing, public relations, improved client confidence, community engagement and transparency and public protection. LRAR is also trying the 'don't be left out' factor – why are legal entities not doing what all the major banks and many businesses are doing (i.e. managing in-house archives or, in the case of small businesses, depositing records in archives)? Don't they want a balanced and accurate historical picture of their contribution towards legal services and other developments preserved? Do they want simply to be viewed historically through the prism of government records? Do they want to be seen as having something to hide?
- *Research institutions and researchers*: we are asking these stakeholders to tell us about barriers to research e.g. non-availability of records, confidentiality concerns on the part of information owners, poor cataloguing/indexing on the part of archives. We are also seeking to open a debate on whether the lack of accessibility to more recent records and to private sector legal records is a possible cause of the prevailing emphasis by legal historians on studying medieval legal history and records of the courts and the government sector.

### *2. Analysis of current, and drafting of new, best practice guidance and advice*

- There is considerable guidance on recordkeeping and disposal already available from regulatory and membership bodies.[5] This guidance, however, while giving excellent general advice on policies and procedures, does not extend to explaining exactly how and by whom this work should be carried out. There appears to be a general lack of understanding that records management is a job for professionals in just the same way as legal work, IT or finance. With some notable exceptions, the consequence is poor information management resulting in excess costs, inefficiency and compliance issues.
- In collaboration with the BRA and the LMA, we redrafted TLS's Practice Note *Depositing records and documents with public sector archives* and submitted it to TLS for consideration. LRAR has also, at the request of contacts in law firms and ISLs, drafted a number of model records retention and disposal schedules[6] for legal institutions and one for legal publishers plus some short guides to records management and intends to draft guidance on managing born-digital records and on resolving issues around confidentiality. All this guidance will be circulated to legal entities. The long-term strategy is to establish a community of best practice among legal practitioners, meaning records are more likely to survive to be archived (and of course resulting in cost and efficiency savings for legal entities themselves). LRAR will also lobby for information management to be included as a requirement in continuing professional education (CPD).

### *3. Developing a working model to rescue and preserve legal records*

- Redefining the definition of 'legal entities': LRAR will develop and publish a census of private sector law-related institutions and organisations in England and Wales, classified according to a) function and b) categories of records at risk. It is hoped that this census will help to inform strategic efforts to save private sector legal records.
- Providers of local legal services: the strategy is to continue – and expand – the work historically done by the BRA to rescue the records of local law firms. The emphasis will now be on saving the business records of the providers of legal services and, if appropriate, the papers of local legal practitioners. A clear set of requirements is to be drafted, including guidance to potential depositors on a) the categories of records which are of potential historical value b) how mutual

5 E.g. TLS, the SRA, the Bar Council, the Bar Standards Board, The CLC, the Institute of Barristers' Clerks, CIArb, CEDR etc.

6 See *LRAR Guideline 2: Advice to legal institutions on disposing of records.*

contact is to be made between legal bodies and archives c) advice on prior evaluation and listing of records and d) probable costs and benefits. In consultation with local record offices a standard set of forms and procedures to be used by archives when negotiating deposits with legal bodies could also be developed. This would be particularly valuable where ongoing deposit arrangements, especially of born-digital records, are to be agreed.

- London and England and Wales-wide based legal bodies and practitioners: LRAR intends to see if developing a model along the lines of the Pensions Archive Trust would work as a 'Legal Archives Trust'. Were such a Trust to be established, LMA would consider accepting records of value from London-based legal entities (associations etc.) identified by the Trust. Decisions on acceptance would be dependent on LRAR facilitating the process and obtaining full funding for deposits, for example from the depositor or through a Trust model. It is recommended that a working party comprising representatives from the stakeholders outlined above be set up to determine a) whether a Legal Archives Trust funded by donations from legal stakeholders is a viable proposition b) to decide how to persuade legal entities that such a Trust is in their interest and c) how to set up the Trust, appoint trustees and achieve charitable status.

### *4. Continuing records rescue work*

LRAR will of course continue to seek to save legal records of value on an ad hoc basis in consultation with TNA, the BRA, LMA and other stakeholders. This work will facilitate and inform the development of UK-wide procedures and processes for the systematic rescue and preservation of legal records.

.................................

## Paper 2: Developing a working model to rescue legal records: a Legal Archives Trust

### *Why is it important to rescue private sector legal records?*

While TNA, local authority record offices, HE and specialist repositories and stakeholders work tirelessly to preserve our heritage and some private sector bodies understand the value to themselves and the wider community of preserving key records, the legal sector (with some notable exceptions[7]) simply does not seem to be aware of – or is indifferent to – the risk of losing records documenting the developments in legal services over the past two centuries. This attitude needs to change if we are to have a balanced, accurate picture of the contribution of the legal profession to the history of the UK and if we wish to learn from past mistakes and achievements.

Legal records are the only major subject field left in the private sector which has not had some systematic collection policy applied to it; this leaves a big research gap. Unless, therefore, systematic efforts are made towards collecting private sector legal records, research into legal developments will continue to be weighted towards the study of government policy, legislation and the courts, producing a historical picture of the UK's legal framework and legal services which is skewed towards the policies and actions of central government. In short we are in danger of losing a significant proportion of our legal heritage.

There is a very real danger that this may happen: globalisation, mergers, apathy, concerns about confidentiality and data protection, digital obsolescence and resource issues are just some of the factors mitigating against the rescue of legal records.

### *Does this matter if the records are of no historical interest?*

It is safe to say that the core strategic and operational records of any business (and most legal institutions are businesses) have considerable value, not just for researchers but for the business itself – that is why all the big banks in the UK and many major businesses (such as Boots, Marks and Spencers, Diageo) maintain in-house archives.[8] Ingraining the understanding of information as an asset rather than as an overhead in legal institutions is a necessary part of the

7 Such as the Archives of the Inns of Court, the Law Society and the Records of Legal Education Archives (full list at **Appendix III**). These archives are not to be confused with the almost universal practice among providers of legal services of depositing non-current records en masse in a warehouse for indefinite storage.

8 At a recent LRAR seminar the Barclay's Group Archivist gave a demonstration of how use of material in its in-house archives to win a court case saved Barclays upwards of £1 billion.

records preservation process. Furthermore, any legal institution which tries to influence government and legislation through consultations, which formalises professional membership through examinations or accreditation or which regulates the legal profession will have material of long-term research value.

## *Developing a model for systematically rescuing legal records and raising awareness of their value*

LRAR and the BRA have talked with the Pensions Archive Trust, which has developed an excellent charitable model to facilitate the deposit of pensions records in the LMA, to see if a similar model could work for a 'Legal Archives Trust'. Such a Trust would work in partnership or collaboration with record repositories in the UK to ensure the permanent preservation of material documenting the history, management and development of legal services and of institutions (and individuals) connected with the law for the use and benefit of present and future generations.

LRAR therefore seeks to set up a working party be set up to determine:

a. Whether a Legal Archives Trust funded by donations from legal stakeholders is a viable proposition.

b. If so, to decide how to persuade legal institutions that such a Trust is in their interest.

c. Recommend individuals with influence to serve as patrons.

d. How to set up and run the Trust, appoint trustees and achieve charitable status.

The working party should include representatives from TNA, the BRA, the BAC, PAT, TLS, LMA, IRMS, the ARA and historical associations such as the Selden Society. LRAR is therefore asking that you consider nominating an individual from your organisation to join the working party. A draft Statement of Trust Objectives and notes on potential financing and administration for consideration by the working party follow.[9]

## *Legal Archives Trust: draft statement of objectives*

The Trust's principal objectives will be:

1. To rescue, by seeking archival provision for, legal records of historical value.
2. To promote the importance of preserving legal records amongst information owners and provide advice and guidance on how they can safeguard their archival material and reduce their own recordkeeping costs and risks through good records management.
3. To promote and develop the study of the history of the legal profession and legal change.
4. To advance the education of the public in the knowledge of all aspects of legal developments over the past two centuries.
5. To provide an easily accessible resource for researchers into the legal profession and legal change, whether that research is business-related, academic or personal.
6. To seek solutions to the obstacles to rescuing legal records.
7. Potentially, if resources allow, to establish a permanent archives for legal records which cannot be accommodated by an existing repository.

## *Funding*

1. Funding of the Trust's work will depend on the sponsorship of organisations and individuals connected with the law.
2. A network of Friends of the Trust will be established, whereby interested members of the legal, archives and research communities, past and present, can support the work with a small annual donation and in return be kept up to date with current developments.
3. Volunteers from among the archives profession will be encouraged to assist the work of the Trust by helping with the identification, surveying, listing and transfer of records to archives in much the same way as BRA volunteers have been doing for many years.

## *Administration and Governance*

9 LRAR initially sent this proposal and the draft objectives to a number of influential stakeholders from the legal, archives and research sectors, asking them to join the working party. The response was disappointing.

1. It is anticipated that the Trust will, at the appropriate time, apply for charitable status.
2. It will set up a Board of Directors and be managed by a President chosen from among its members.
3. It will establish committees to carry out specific tasks as required e.g. an archives liaison committee, a records management guidance committee.
4. It will appoint a secretary who will manage and maintain its records via a secure digital network.
5. The Trust will not require physical premises from which to work but will seek to use the facilities of stakeholder organisations as needed for meetings.

# Appendix XII: Legal records – horror stories

Noppadolsign/Shutterstock.com

The following blog was published on the LRAR website in May 2017. It gives examples of a) the reputational damage which may be sustained where legal institutions have failed to manage records properly and b) some of the issues faced by archives when seeking to rescue legal records.

## *Poor records management leading to the loss of our legal heritage: horror stories and other tales of woe...*

Clare Cowling, Director, Legal Records at Risk project, 5 May 2017

When it comes to managing their records, whether their own business records or client files and documents, we do not really know just how good or bad the legal profession in the UK is at records management in general, and at respecting privacy and data protection in particular, in comparison to the rest of the private sector. The main source of information on data breaches, the Information Commissioner's Annual Reports, does not include a specific 'legal sector' category; institutions specialised to law are presumably lumped in with 'general business' – the sector area generating the second highest rate of complaints and ICO investigations annually.

The fact that it is not singled out as a specific area of concern indicates that the legal profession can quite rightly congratulate itself on its record of handling confidential information appropriately. It should not, however, be too complacent about this, nor about its records management processes generally. The horror stories below are designed to alert institutions specialised to law and legal practitioners to situations where poor records management can adversely affect the reputation of the legal profession and may additionally mean that records documenting our legal heritage will be lost.

## *Fraud or just plain bad records management or both?*

http://www.wilson-nesbitt.com/news-updates/Wills/5854/Unregulated-will-writer-jailed-for-fraud:

> 'Walter Ventriglia of Berkshire, who operated the will-writing company under the name Tony Edwards....also ran a will storage business called UK Will Register which offered to store wills in a secure facility in London. The wills were actually found to be stored in the airing cupboard of his home'.

https://www.lawgazette.co.uk/law/shambolic-sra-criticised-by-tribunal/5057806.article:

> A case brought by the Solicitors Regulation Authority against a solicitor who used a client account as a banking facility has been described as at times 'verging on the shambolic'...the Solicitors Disciplinary Tribunal, in a judgment handed down on 13 September, said that 'at times the case had verged on the shambolic' due to late evidence that could have seen some of the charges not brought in the first place....Most of the allegations centred on a letter, referred to as 29(b) that set out the terms of a retainer between Lorrell and CEL. The SDT said it was 'exceedingly perturbed' that new materials kept emerging, including different versions of the letter. Barrister Thomas Buxton, who represented Lorrell, said he was very concerned that there was additional material from files initially prepared by the SRA's forensic investigation officer that came to light during the

trial he had not seen and that could be relevant. 'The tribunal considered that this situation should not have arisen. 'It was most unsatisfactory that relevant documents had not been identified and disclosed until this late stage' the SDT said. 'If their existence had been realised earlier this might have resulted in some of the allegations not being brought. This would have had an impact on the costs incurred.'

http://www.legalfutures.co.uk/latest-news/barristers-fined-data-protection-breaches-case-papers-end-bin-online:

A criminal law barrister whose case papers were found in bin bags has been fined by a Bar disciplinary tribunal, while the Information Commissioner's Office (ICO) has fined another barrister after a software update on her home computer placed hundreds of unencrypted client documents online. Maria Masselis of Linenhall Chambers in Chester was found to have breached the core duty to keep clients' matters confidential. The tribunal fined her £750 and said that she 'improperly handled documents containing confidential and sensitive information about cases she was instructed and failed to take adequate or appropriate security measures against the disposal of such documents resulting in their discovery in the household refuse bin bags'. It was explained at the tribunal that the bin bags were discovered by a local authority outside an unoccupied property for collection on bin day. When the contents were examined, the council was able to identify that the papers originated from Ms Masselis. The matter was then referred to the Bar Standards Board. A board spokeswoman said: 'Inappropriate disposal of client files breaches the core duty barristers have to treat client information confidentially. The tribunal's decision to fine Ms Masselis £750 serves as a warning to barristers to make sure that they dispose of client files in an appropriate way.'

The Information Commissioner's Office confirmed to Legal Futures that it did look at the case, but decided against formal enforcement action. More broadly, a spokeswoman said: 'If you are responsible for looking after personal data, you must keep it secure and that includes disposing of it securely too. Lawyers handle sensitive personal information, often belonging to people in vulnerable positions. They put their trust in lawyers to look after their data – that trust is hard won and easily lost.'

The ICO fined an unnamed female 'senior' barrister after information belonging to up to 250 people, including vulnerable adults and children, was uploaded to the internet when the barrister's husband updated software on the couple's home computer. It came to light after a local government solicitor informed her chambers that documents containing confidential and sensitive information could be accessed online. Some 725 unencrypted documents, which were created and stored on the computer, were temporarily uploaded to an internet directory as a backup during the software upgrade. They were visible to an internet search engine and some of the documents could be easily accessed through a simple search. Six of those files contained confidential and highly sensitive information relating to people who were involved in proceedings in the Court of Protection and the family court. Her husband quickly removed the files from the online directory and the internet service provider removed cached information from the internet the following day. Steve Eckersley, head of enforcement at the ICO said: 'This barrister, for no good reason, overlooked her responsibility to protect her clients' confidential and highly sensitive information. It is hard to imagine the distress this could have caused to the people involved – even if the worst never happened, this barrister exposed her clients to unnecessary worry and upset.'

http://www.legalsupportnetwork.co.uk/practice-management/news/72–legal-data-breaches-escalated-information-commissioner-s-office-2014:

Posted: 30 June 2015

A Freedom of Information request has revealed the number of data breaches reported to the Information Commissioner's Office (ICO) during 2014. A total of 72 incidents came to light in which private data was mistakenly made available to the public by legal firms. The incidents included flaws within internal systems, poor processes and human error. Some of the key stats are summarised below:

- The most common source of breaches was data being mailed, faxed or emailed to the wrong recipient in error. These simple human mistakes accounted for almost a third (23) of the incidents;

- Closely following this was the loss or theft of physical paperwork. These breaches accounted for 21 of the incidents;
- Devices passing out of the control of the legal firm with unencrypted information on them was another prominent cause of breaches (11);
- Interestingly, data being hacked maliciously only accounted for one incident all year.

Paul Doble, chief sales and marketing officer at DX, an independent secure mail operator for the legal industry, comments:

'With the exception of certain civil servants, there is arguably no other profession that has quite as much responsibility for handling confidential information than the legal sector; an issue compounded by the fact that the information often belongs to other companies and interests. As such, the pressure on the legal industry to become watertight where private data is concerned is mounting. Security is particularly hard to guarantee and track with information on physical documents, and is easily compromised as documents pass through the UK's mainstream mail networks. Whilst legal firms focus increasingly on cybersecurity, thought must also be spared for the secure transit of physical information. Sending documents through a secure postal network is a sure fire way to stop unencrypted information falling into the wrong hands.

Perhaps the biggest surprise revealed by the Freedom of Information request is not the quantity of breaches being reported, but the nature of the causes. Far outweighing hacking is the prevalence of human error, with accidental disclosures through mis-sent communications providing the leading cause. Email in particular is an undeniably necessary communication medium in today's working world, but firms need to ensure they are doing the minimum due diligence required to ensure that confidential information can't be shared with the wrong person or left vulnerable to attack.

In addition to providing this vital protection, email encryption can also provide the missing piece in the jigsaw that law firms need to satisfy industry regulators, as it will allow them to demonstrate that they are compliant with the latest data protection regulations.'

ICO guidance: https://ico.org.uk/about-the-ico/news-and-events/news-and-blogs/2014/08/information-commissioner-sounds-the-alarm-on-data-breaches-within-the-legal-profession/ (website link no longer available):

Information Commissioner 'sounds the alarm' on data breaches within the legal profession. Posted 05 August 2014.

The Information Commissioner's Office (ICO) is warning barristers and solicitors to keep personal information secure, especially paper files. This follows a number of data breaches reported to the ICO involving the legal profession.

The ICO can serve a monetary penalty of up to £500,000 for a serious breach of the Data Protection Act provided the incident had the potential to cause substantial damage or substantial distress to affected individuals. In most cases these penalties are issued to companies or public authorities, but barristers and solicitors are generally classed as data controllers in their own right and are therefore legally responsible for the personal information they process.

In the last three months, 15 incidents involving members of the legal profession have been reported to the ICO. The information handled by barristers and solicitors is often very sensitive. This means that the damage caused by a data breach could meet the statutory threshold for issuing a financial penalty. Legal professionals will also often carry around large quantities of information in folders or files when taking them to or from court and may store them at home. This can increase the risk of a data breach.

Information Commissioner, Christopher Graham, said: 'The number of breaches reported by barristers and solicitors may not seem that high, but given the sensitive information they handle, and the fact that it is often held in paper files rather than secured by any sort of encryption, that number is troubling. It is important that we sound the alarm at an early stage to make sure this problem is addressed before a barrister or solicitor is left counting the financial and reputational damage of a serious data breach. We have published some top tips to help barristers and solicitors look after the personal information they handle. These measures will set them on the road to compliance and help them get the basics right.'

## *Auctioning of legal records*

Not a horror story as such – this is as a rule a perfectly legal activity unless the material being auctioned does not belong to the institution offering it for sale or contains personal data. Isn't it sad, though, that some legal institutions would rather make money from selling off their history than making sure it is preserved in an archives for posterity?

Below is a sample of 'solicitors' papers' offered at public auction, courtesy of The National Archives' (TNA) manuscript Sales Monitoring Service. TNA keeps an eye on all auctions and notifies the relevant record office when something comes up in which the record office might be interested. The record office will then bid, but only if it has sufficient funds or time to apply for a grant before the auction. For an advertisement of a current sale see https://www.the-saleroom.com/en-gb/auction-catalogues/lloyd-cameron-and-partners/catalogue-id-srtheau10073/lot-b1afc31d-65ca-4b08-8389-a6be00e5deb1

| |
|---|
| 199: solicitors bill book, Chard, Somerset., 1802–1809 |
| 164: Cheltenham Solicitor Clerks day book, 1832–1834 |
| 116: Cheltenham solicitors: letter book, 1839–1846 |
| 134: Solicitor's bill book of John Reed Clarke, Chard area, 1802–1809 |
| 86: Cheltenham solicitor's bill book (prob TV Banner), 1827–1830 |
| 74: London lawyer's bill book, 1786–1809 |
| 74: Warwickshire solicitor's notebook, 1700–1800 |
| 457: Account book of Roberts & Carter, solicitors, Barnstaple, 1834–1837 |
| 131: Banner, Thomas Vaughan, solicitor, Cheltenham: bill book, 1827–1830 |
| 166: John Reed Clarke, solicitors, Chard: bill book and index of clients, 1802–1809 |
| 28: Hall, Robert, lawyer: ms legal commmonplace book, 1713 |
| 486: Legal case notebook, 1824 |
| 147: Solicitors ledgers for firm (Francillon and Willott?) in Dursley, Glos listing clients and cases, 1868–1915 |
| 109: Lewis & Lewis solicitors of Ely Place corresp including blackmail letters and details of payments relating to royal, noble and celebrity scandals (Quantity not given), 1800–1950 |
| 320463130450: Thorp & Dickson solicitors Alnwick legal papers (15 bundles), 1800–1850 |
| 320463132564: Legal papers of Robert Thorp, Nortumberland rel to Foster v Burrell, 1810–1820 |
| 128: Forster, solicitor of Aylsham, client corresp (several hundred items), 1883–1886 |
| 136: Wymondham legal corresp, files, lunatic asylum papers, court papers, 1800–1950 |
| 138: Bodenham & James, solicitors Hereford, letters received (100), 1860–1869 |

## *Depositing legal records in archives*

What happens when legal entities *do* decide to deposit records with a local authority archives? Here are some comments to LRAR on the legal profession's attitude to its records from five local authority record office archivists who accepted deposits of law firms' records in 2015–16. The examples below are verbatim quotes in emails sent to the IRAR Director by the archivists.

### Information not seen as an asset?

> We would actually find it impossible to take a large collection these days as we have no room and because they are generally a terrible mess; they take a huge amount of resources to make them usable…we do worry that many important documents are being destroyed particularly as land is registered and deeds are destroyed. Of course there are issues with preserving client files for historical purposes as I doubt any clients have given their consent to that and there are issues with solicitors not understanding the ownership of the material that they send us. The general attitude seems to be 'we don't want this you can have it if you want as a gift' without them understanding it is not their property and therefore we can only take it on deposit in case the owner turns up and claims it. It is increasingly difficult for us to keep track of who are the current firms responsible for our older deposits as firms merge and change and as far as I am aware no firm has contacted us about the material they have deposited with us since the moment it left their premises so I think

you can safely say that they do not consider them an asset to the firm and feel no link to them once they believe the file closed.

## Confidentiality issues?

There was one notable disaster in acquisition which was when a large collection was accepted unconditionally and was found to contain masses of rather uninteresting and fairly recent (e.g. still subject to DPA) records. It appears we can't give them back, we can't sample or destroy them, the firm has never requested anything back – and they've never been catalogued. I suspect the more general problem is just a simple lack of historical awareness by lawyers. I wonder how you could make reading that nice practice note[1] compulsory? I think you may also be right in believing there may be confidentiality issues – perhaps solicitors don't understand that archivists deal with data protection and other aspects of record security all the time. I suppose the most basic aspect of all this is that everyone is so busy – the preservation of [records] totally peripheral to the work of the lawyers. Other than by making an archival element to the CPD points system (perhaps it could be part of a wider recordkeeping agenda?) I'm not sure how best to go about changing the status quo.

## Problems with client files?

I was appointed in January 2015 to complete…..an 18 month National Cataloguing Grants funded project to catalogue the records of a historic law firm. This included a large accession (383 boxes) made in 1998 consisting mostly of client papers. Due to the time constraints, there was not time to catalogue in great detail (although this would not have been desirable in hindsight) and the project was designed to include a significant contribution from volunteers. The approach that was adopted was that it was not appropriate for volunteers to work with client papers so they were directed towards deeds and sale particulars while I catalogued the client papers. This work was completed with the Data Protection Act in mind but with a broad intention to make the records as accessible as possible….Because of how concerned the firm were about client confidentially, the partners were invited to look at the catalogue to agree access restrictions. The result is that on one of the catalogues, clients papers dated 1900 or later may only be accessed with permission of the firm…There were two separate concerns from the firm a) complaint to legal ombudsman for breach of confidentially from the descendent of a client and b) bad publicity from the impression that they would advise clients then make details public later on. We have since been offered additional deposits from the firm, but declined to collect additional client papers.

## Taking advantage of the taxpayer?

In my experience:

- Solicitors have extremely poor recordkeeping as far as older client records are concerned – the records can be kept in appalling conditions and in a state of disorder
- They don't recognise the ongoing historic value of what they hold and may therefore destroy records
- As an alternative to destruction, they are often happy to deposit with the local record office, but at no cost to themselves. This means that the financial burden falls to the record office (usually the local authority) to assess, transport, list, package and repair the documents – with the solicitors often imposing timescales for removal of the records at entirely their own convenience! As you cannot fail to be aware, local authority budgets are shrinking, and it is no longer appropriate to expect the taxpayer to cover the cost of solicitors' own neglect of their duty to their clients and their clients' records.

You can probably tell that I'm a bit fed up about all this. For example, we have a collection of over 600 boxes from one solicitor's firm, which has arrived in a disorganised state over several decades, which is unlisted and some of which has suffered terribly from damp and dirt. One of the clients of this firm (the owner of a landed estate) is trying to access his own legal documents from this collection and has been trying to do so for several years; the solicitor's firm themselves takes no responsibility and it falls to us to try and find, within these 600 boxes, the records that might relate

1 TLS Practice Note: *Depositing records and documents with public sector archives*, 15 December 2010 (no longer available on TLS's website).

to his estate. If I were him, I would be tempted to sue the solicitors for their neglect of his records. The problem we have is that when it comes to the crunch, much though we would like to refuse collections like this, we know that if we don't accept them, the firm will throw them into a skip.

## Lack of knowledge about how to manage records?

I was hired to organise the dreadful filing of one very busy solicitor, but also spent two solid months reorganising 800 boxes of closed files into a retention order. These boxes had been sent to external storage three years previously following a flood in the partner's basement where they had been kept. Many were flood damaged – little attempt had been made to conserve them. They weren't in any real order and there was no way, prior to my project, to know when files were ready to be destroyed. Whilst carrying out this project, I also looked into records management and archiving processes at the firm and found that it was a very confused situation. For example, they had two different retention schedules that no one really knew about and didn't seem to have a great understanding of how to use their external storage. All in all, this firm seemed to have a desire to improve their records management and archiving – for example, they had relatively recently appointed one of their receptionists to manage the closing of files and were pleased to be able to use me for the box reorganisation project. However, it appeared that records management was always going to take a back seat to their other activities, and while they may have liked things to be better, they didn't know how to go about it easily, especially since they were very busy. During my time there, I tried to find as much guidance as possible about managing legal records, but found that there was very little.

# Appendix XIII: Rescuing legal records – success stories

Guingm/Shutterstock.com

*This blog was published on the LRAR website in November 2017.*

In May [2017] I published a blog of horror stories about poor records management leading to the loss of our legal heritage. I'm glad to now be able to list some success stories about the rescue of private sector records documenting our legal heritage.

## *Who is rescuing our legal records?*

**The National Archives**, of course, is a massive collector of government and quasi-government legal records. Although its remit is not to collect private sector records, it does hold records of private legal bodies which have been nationalised, records of the courts and quasi-official papers of individuals who were prominent in the law and government (e.g. judges' notebooks).

**Local authority archives** are the true heroes. Despite drastically reduced resources they still manage to seek out and collect large quantities of private sector legal records of value relevant to their local area. They have saved many records of the following local institutions (as well as countless collections from individuals connected to the law):

- Citizens' advice bureaux
- Law centres
- Law societies
- Chartered accountants' societies
- Boards of conciliation and arbitration
- Law firms (some business records but primarily client documents such as deeds and wills).

**London Metropolitan Archives** (LMA). The LMA makes every effort to rescue not only valuable records of institutions relevant to Greater London, but the records of nationally or internationally focused institutions which have their headquarters there. Legal records already saved for posterity by LMA include those of a number of London-based:

- Legal associations, societies and institutes
- Law firms (including the business records of eight large London firms)
- Legal charities
- London Court of Arbitration

**Higher Education (HE) repositories**: most HE archives will keep records of their departments and faculties, including legal. Some HE archives also have specialist collections policies which may include certain categories of legal records. The London School of Economics in particular holds many collections of legal records relating to women's legal rights in its Women's Library, whilst its Archives and Special Collections section holds the records of mediation institutions and campaigns for social justice and human rights. The Records of Legal Education Archives at IALS has for many years collected the records of both local and national institutions specialised to legal education, as well as the papers of individual law teachers.

Other **specialist repositories** which collect legal records include Lambeth Palace Library, which holds records of notaries and the Bishopsgate Institute Library which has the records of some legal campaign groups relevant to radical, social, labour, feminist and gay history in London.

**Business and religious archives**: many have in-house archives or have deposited records in archives; nearly all will include some legal records. Diocesan archives in particular hold large quantities of property deeds and related material, including records of property disputes, while businesses will have a legal department and/or employ the services as required of legal practitioners or law firms. For examples of archived legal records see the LRAR case study of alternative dispute resolution records in the Transport for London Corporate Archives or the online catalogues of any diocesan archives.

**In-house archives of institutions connected to law**: these are not as numerous as should be expected, given the importance of the law to our national development, but do include some legal institutions holding records of incalculable value to researchers e.g. the institutional archives of the four Inns of Court, the Law Society and the Institute and Faculty of Actuaries. Some ancillary bodies such as Ede & Ravenscroft also have in-house archives. Astonishing no-shows appear to be barristers' chambers and large law firms; LRAR was unable to discover a single barristers' chambers or law firm, even in London with all its wealth, with an in-house professionally managed archives[1] accessible to the public in the same way as other archives.[2] We believe that it is frankly impossible that this should be the case and plead with the legal profession to let us know if their organisation does in fact maintain such a facility.

1 As opposed to a basement full of unmanaged boxes/files or use of a third-party bulk records storage facility. We have, however, spoken to many records managers of law firms asking for help in convincing partners of the need to manage records properly.

2 We were, however, contacted by the archivist/records manager of one firm, Chadwick Lawrence LLP, which maintains a well-managed archives for the use of the firm and will provide information to the public on request (for details see our case study of the firm's records). Surely there are more! If so, let us know.

# Appendix XIV: Institutions specialised to law: house histories

Sebastian Duda/Shutterstock.com

The websites of all legal institutions contacted by LRAR, plus a number of others representing different strands of the profession, were checked to see if they provided any historical information on the institution which could only have been provided by consulting at least some records. The information was located using the history search term in each institution's website or by browsing through the 'about us' section.

Those institutions with an * have, according to *Discovery*, an in-house archives or have deposited some of their institutional records in an archives (for details see **Appendix II**).

## Law firms

**Hard copy**: professional researchers were commissioned to write these house histories:

Jon Bauman: *Pioneering a Global Vision: The Story of Baker & McKenzie*, Harcourt Professional Education Group (Chicago), 1999

Laurie Dennett:

*Slaughter and May: A Short History*, Granta Editions, 1989

*Slaughter and May: A Century in the City*, Granta, 1989

A.G. Salmon, *The History of Wilde Sapte 1785–1985,* published by A G Salmon, 1985

Judy Slinn:

*A History of Freshfields** (Biddles Ltd, Guildford, Surrey, 1984)

*Linklaters and Paines: the first 150 years* (Longman, London, 1987)

*Clifford Chance: Its Origins and Development* (Granta Editions,1993)

*Ashurst Morris Crisp: A Radical Firm** (Granta Editions, 1997)

*The History Of Vizards: 1797–1997* (Granta Books, 1997)

**Online** house histories:

Baker McKenzie: https://www.bakermckenzie.com/-/media/files/about-us/firmfactsaug2017.pdf?la=en (1901 to date)

Blandy & Blandy Solicitors*: https://www.blandy.co.uk/about/our-history (1713 to date)

DLA Piper: https://www.dlapiper.com/history/ (2005 to date)

Farrer & Co*: https://www.farrer.co.uk/about-us/history/ (1701 to date)

Hempsons: http://www.hempsons.co.uk/about-us/our-history/ (1890 to date)

Irwin Mitchell: https://www.youtube.com/watch?v=GwdweRrTV8M&feature=youtube_gdata_player (1912 to date)

Linklaters: *Passing the Flame* (2013 e-book): https://issuu.com/linklaters/docs/linklaters_history_passing_the_flame?viewMode=singlePage&utm_source=about_us_section&utm_medium=download_link&utm_campaign=linklaters_175_years (1838 to 2013)

Simmons & Simmons: http://www.simmons-simmons.com/en/about-us/our-history (1896 to date)

## Patent and Trade Mark Attorneys

Bromhead Johnson Patent and Trade Mark Attorneys, http://www.intellectual-property.uk/about-us

Chartered Institute of Trade Mark Attorneys (CITMA): https://www.citma.org.uk/about_citma/about_us/our_history

Franks & Co, European Patent and Trade Mark Attorneys: https://www.franksco.com/about/history/

Marks & Clerk Intellectual Property, https://www.marks-clerk.com/Home/About-Us/Our-History.aspx?lang=en-GB#.WxEwV0gvyyI

Mewburn Ellis Intellectual Property, http://mewburn.com/about-us/our-history/

Wilson Gunn Patent & Trade Mark Attorneys: https://www.wilsongunn.com/history/timeline.html

## Alternative dispute resolution bodies:

Louise Barrington and Mirèze Philippe, 'A short history of *Arbitral Women*', *ArbitralWomen Newsletter* Issue 1, Jan 2010 http://www.arbitralwomen.org/DesktopModules/Bring2mind/DMX/Download.aspx?EntryId=147&Command=Core_Download&language=en-GB&PortalId=0&TabId=1117

Chartered Institute of Arbitrators (CIArb): http://www.ciarb.org/about/history

Family Mediators Association: https://thefma.co.uk/about-the-fma/history/

London Maritime Arbitrators Association (LMAA): http://www.lmaa.london/about-us-History.aspx

Sport Resolutions UK: https://www.sportresolutions.co.uk/about-us/our-history

UK Mediation: https://www.ukmediation.net/about-us/history/

## Solicitors' membership organisations:

Association of Costs Lawyers: http://www.associationofcostslawyers.co.uk/About-the-ACL

Association of Women Solicitors London: http://awslondon.co.uk/chronology/

City of London Law Society: http://www.citysolicitors.org.uk/index.php?option=com_content&view=category&id=102&Itemid=478

City of London Solicitors Company: https://www.citysolicitors.org/about-us/history-of-the-company

Commonwealth Lawyers Association: https://www.commonwealthlawyers.com/History

Immigration Law Practitioners Association: http://www.ilpa.org.uk/pages/sub-page.html

London Criminal Courts Solicitors Association*: https://www.lccsa.org.uk/

Society of Construction Law: https://www.scl.org.uk/about/history

Society of Trust and Estate Practitioners: https://www.step.org/history

The Law Society*, *A Short History – The Law Society: 1825 to today* (2016). Note that this is a history of the building at 113 Chancery Lane, not of TLS itself: http://www.lawsociety.org.uk/news/stories/a-short-history-of-the-law-society-published/

## Legal publishers:

H K Jones and W Gordon Graham, *Butterworths*: History of a Publishing House,* second edition (LexisNexis UK, 1997)

Wildy & Sons: https://www.wildy.com/our-history

## Chartered accountants:

Association of Certified Chartered Accountants (ACCA): http://www.accaglobal.com/uk/en/about-us/our-history.html

Worshipful Company of Chartered Accountants in England and Wales: https://accountantslivery.org/history/

## Other:

Joyce Arram, '50 years of CILEx', *CILEx Journal* (Jan 2013)

National Association of Licensed Paralegals: https://www.nationalparalegals.co.uk/about_nalp

# Bibliography

## Earlier work to identify and save legal records at risk at risk

**Commonwealth Legal Records Project** (Twining et al, supported by the Leverhulme Foundation and miscellaneous smaller grants. Book: W.Twining and E.Quick (eds) *Legal Records in the Commonwealth*, Dartmouth (1994) and various articles.

**Guide to Records of Legal Education and Law Schools**, 1998: report by Clare Cowling.

Establishment of the **Records of Legal Education Archives** (Institute of Advanced Legal Studies) in 1998 by Clare Cowling.

**LRAR pilot project** (2012–15) (Twining, Roebuck, D'Silva)

**Records of international commercial arbitration feasibility study**. Report (D'Silva, 2014) (short report to RICA; confidential report to University of Miami Arbitration Centre).

Gary Collins (Brass Paper Clip Consultancy) and Elizabeth Dawson (Archive Consultancy & Research) *Report on Archive & Record Repositories*, 20 April 2015 http://ials.sas.ac.uk/sites/default/files/files/Research/LRAR/LRAR_Repositories_report_April_2015.pdf

## International, national and sector policies, strategies and records reports

### International:


Digital Preservation Commission *The 'bit list' of digitally endangered species* (DPC, 2018) https://www.dpconline.org/our-work/bit-list

Douglas Hay, 'Archival Records in the History of Law: A User's Perspective', *Archivaria* vol. 24, 1987

International Council on Archives, *Universal Declaration on Archives* (Oslo, Dec 2010) https://www.ica.org/en/universal-declaration-archives

Melissa Webster, *International Data Corporation White Paper, Bridging the Information Worker Productivity Gap in Western Europe: New Challenges and Opportunities for IT* (sponsored by Adobe, Sept 2012) http://www.planetpdf.com/enterprise/article.asp?ContentID=Bridging_the_Information_Work_Productivity_Gap_New_Challenges_and_Opportunities_for_IT&gid=8420

W. Twining and Emma Varnden Quick (eds): *Legal Records in the Commonwealth* (Dartmouth Publishing Co Ltd, 1994)

UNESCO, *Recommendation concerning the Preservation of, Access to, Documentary Heritage in the Digital Era* (agreed at the 38th Session of the UNESCO General Conference in Paris in November 2015) https://en.unesco.org/programme/mow/recommendation-documentary-heritage


### United Kingdom:


British Standards Institution, *BS 10008:2014 Evidential weight and legal admissibility of electronic information: specification* (BSI, 2014)

Anna Guagnini, 'Patent Agents in Britain at the Turn of the Twentieth Century', *History of Technology* (2012)

Hawley Committee *Information as an Asset: the board agenda: checklist and explanatory notes* (developed on behalf of the KPMG IMPACT Programme by a committee under the chairmanship of Dr Robert Hawley, Chief Executive of Nuclear Electric plc, 1995)

Information Commissioner's Office, *Guide to the General Data Protection Regulation, 2018* https://ico.org.uk/for-organisations/guide-to-the-general-data-protection-regulation-gdpr/


### Legal sector:


Sir David Clementi, *Review Of The Regulatory Framework For Legal Services In England And Wales: Final Report* (Dec. 2004)

*Halsbury's Laws of England*, 5th ed., vol. 65 (LexisNexis, 2015)

Legal Services Board, *Lowering barriers to accessing services report* (LSB, 13 March 2016) http://www.

legalservicesboard.org.uk/news_publications/publications/pdf/2016/20160331_Lowering_Barriers_Final_Report.pdf

Reynolds, Michael, *An Overview of Arbitration in England* (CSLS, Dec 2014) https://www.law.ox.ac.uk/sites/files/oxlaw/a_report_by_dr_michael_reynolds_of_december_2014.pdf

Solicitors Regulation Authority, *Consultation paper: File retention following an intervention into a firm*, 14 October 2013 http://www.sra.org.uk/sra/consultations/file-retention-post-intervention.page

David Sugarman, 'Bourgeois collectivism, professional power and the boundaries of the State. The private and public life of The Law Society, 1825 to 1914', *International Journal of the Legal Profession*, Vol 3, Nos. 1–2 (1996)

William Twining, 'Legal Records at Risk' (unpublished funding proposal, 29 Apr 2014)

## *The National Archives:*

*Architecture, Building and Construction Records Survey 2011–2013*, a partnership project between The National Archives and the Business Archives Council (Apr 2013)

*Archives for the 21st Century in Action refreshed 2012–15* https://webarchive.nationalarchives.gov.uk/+/http://www.nationalarchives.gov.uk/documents/archives/archives21centuryrefreshed-final.pdf

*Archives Unlocked: releasing the potential of our archives* (2017) http://www.nationalarchives.gov.uk/documents/archives/Archives-Unlocked-Brochure.pdf

*Corporate memory: a guide to managing business archives* (2009 pamphlet)

*The National Collections Strategy* (May 2009) http://www.nationalarchives.gov.uk/documents/information-management/ncs-vision-strategy-and-principles.pdf

*Religious Archives survey & report* (Nov 2010) http://www.nationalarchives.gov.uk/documents/information-management/tna-ras-web-17-nov.pdf

Caroline Williams, 'Understanding Collections at Risk' (report prepared for TNA, March 2017), *Archives: The Journal of the British Records Association* Vol 53 Issue 36 (2018) https://online.liverpooluniversitypress.co.uk/loi/archives

## *Research reports and publications*

British Academy Research Project: *Digitising the Mixed Economy of Welfare in Britain* https://www.britac.ac.uk/digitising-mixed-economy-welfare-britain and the Charity Finance Group, *Records Management in Charities: A Toolkit for Improvement* (Charlotte Clements, June 2017) https://cfg.org.uk/resources.aspx

British Records Association:

*Records at Risk: A Report on the BRA Survey of Risks to Historical Records in the East of England and London Regions, Autumn 2010* (BRA, 2012) http://www.britishrecordsassociation.org.uk/publications/reports/

Nat Alcock and Penelope Baker, 'The original documents project undertaken by the British Records Association and the Solicitors Regulation Authority/Law Society', *Archives* Vol 1 no 130–1 (BRA, 2015)

Business Archives Council:

*National Strategy for Business Archives (England and Wales)* (July 2009) http://www.businessarchivescouncil.org.uk/materials/national_strategy_for_business_archives.pdf

*Managing Business Archives* (2018) http://www.managingbusinessarchives.co.uk/getting_started/

H.A.L. Cockerell and E. Green, *The British Insurance Business, 1547–1970* (2nd edition, Sheffield Academic Press, 1994)

Chris Cook and David Waller, *The Longman Guide to Sources in Contemporary British History 1: Organisations and Societies* (Longman, 1994).

Lesley Richmond & Bridget Stockford: *Company Archives – the survey of the records of 1000 of the first registered companies in England & Wales* (Business Archives Council, 1986)

## *Legislation and Regulations*

The acts and regulations below include a legal requirement or recommendation to create, maintain, keep or destroy records (see also Archives legislation guide: http://www.nationalarchives.gov.uk/information-management/legislation/).

Access to Health Records Act 1990 http://www.legislation.gov.uk/ukpga/1990/23/contents

Civil Evidence Act 1995 http://www.legislation.gov.uk/ukpga/1995/38/contents

Companies Act 2006 http://www.legislation.gov.uk/ukpga/2006/46/contents/2012-07-02

Computer Misuse Act 1990 http://www.legislation.gov.uk/ukpga/1990/18/contents

Constitutional Reform and Governance Act 2010 https://www.legislation.gov.uk/ukpga/2010/25/contents

Copyright, Designs and Patents Act 1988 http://www.legislation.gov.uk/ukpga/1988/48/contents

Criminal Procedure Rules 2015 http://www.legislation.gov.uk/uksi/2015/1490/contents/made

Data Protection Acts 1998 and 2018 http://www.legislation.gov.uk/ukpga/1998/29/contents and http://www.legislation.gov.uk/ukpga/2018/12/contents/enacted

Electronic Communications Act 2000 http://www.legislation.gov.uk/ukpga/2000/7/contents/enacted

Electronic Signatures Regulations 2002 http://www.legislation.gov.uk/uksi/2002/318/made

Employers' Liability (Compulsory Insurance) Act 1969 http://www.legislation.gov.uk/ukpga/1969/57/contents

Environmental Information Regulations 2004 http://www.legislation.gov.uk/uksi/2004/3391/contents/made

Equality Act 2010 http://www.legislation.gov.uk/ukpga/2010/15/contents

Family Procedure Rules 2010 https://www.legislation.gov.uk/uksi/2010/2955/contents/made

Finance Act 1998 http://www.legislation.gov.uk/ukpga/1998/36/contents

Freedom of Information Act 2000 http://www.legislation.gov.uk/ukpga/2000/36/contents

General Data Protection Regulation (GDPR) https://www.eugdpr.org/eugdpr.org.html

Health & Safety at Work etc Act 1994 http://www.legislation.gov.uk/ukpga/1974/37

Human Rights Act 1998 https://www.legislation.gov.uk/ukpga/1998/42/contents

Income Tax (Pay as You Earn) Regulations 2003 https://www.legislation.gov.uk/uksi/2003/2682/contents/made

Land Registration Act 2002 https://www.legislation.gov.uk/ukpga/2002/9/contents

Latent Damage Act 1986 http://www.legislation.gov.uk/ukpga/1986/37/contents

Legal Services Act 2007 https://www.legislation.gov.uk/ukpga/2007/29/contents

Limitation Act 1980 http://www.legislation.gov.uk/ukpga/1980/58

Limited Liability Partnerships Act 2000 http://www.legislation.gov.uk/ukpga/2000/12/pdfs/ukpga_20000012_en.pdf

Local Government Act 2000 https://www.legislation.gov.uk/ukpga/2000/22/contents

Money Laundering Regulations 2007 http://www.legislation.gov.uk/uksi/2007/2157/contents/made

Openness of Local Government Bodies Regulations 2014 http://www.legislation.gov.uk/ukdsi/2014/9780111113554

Payment Card Industry Data Security Standards https://www.pcisecuritystandards.org/pci_security/maintaining_payment_security

Pensions Act 2008 http://www.legislation.gov.uk/ukpga/2008/30/contents

Public Contracts Regulations 2015 http://www.legislation.gov.uk/uksi/2015/102/contents/made

Public Records Act 1958 http://www.legislation.gov.uk/ukpga/Eliz2/6-7/51

Regulation of Investigative Powers Act 2000 http://www.legislation.gov.uk/ukpga/2000/23/contents

Rehabilitation of Offenders Act 1974 http://www.legislation.gov.uk/ukpga/1974/53

Reporting of Injuries, Diseases and Dangerous Occurrences Regulations 1995 http://www.legislation.gov.uk/uksi/1995/3163/contents/made#mdiv7

Social Security (Contributions) Regulations 2001 http://www.legislation.gov.uk/uksi/2001/1004/contents/made

Statutory Maternity Pay (General) Regulations 1986

http://www.legislation.gov.uk/uksi/1986/1960/contents/made

Statutory Sick Pay (General) Regulations 1982 http://www.legislation.gov.uk/uksi/1982/894/contents/made

Taxes Management Act 1970 http://www.legislation.gov.uk/ukpga/1970/9/contents/enacted

Value Added Tax Act 1994 http://www.legislation.gov.uk/ukpga/1994/23/contents

## *Archive catalogues and online resources*

AIM25 (Archives in London and the M25 area): http://www.aim25.ac.uk/

The Archives Hub: http://www.archiveshub.ac.uk/index.html

ARCHON directory of archives: http://discovery.nationalarchives.gov.uk/find-an-archive

Bishopsgate Institute Library Special Collections and Archives catalogue: http://www.bishopsgate.org.uk/content.aspx?CategoryID=1519

British Library catalogue: https://sussex-primo.hosted.exlibrisgroup.com/primo-explore/search?sortby=rank&vid=44SUS_BLDS&lang=en_US

DANGO (Database of Non-Governmental Organisations): http://www.dango.bham.ac.uk/index.htm

*Discovery*: online catalogue of records relating to Britain and British history held at The National Archives, archives and institutions across the UK and some archives and institutions abroad, incorporating the National Register of Archives): http://discovery.nationalarchives.gov.uk/

Essex Record Office catalogue: http://seax.essexcc.gov.uk/

Hull History Centre catalogue: http://catalogue.hullhistorycentre.org.uk/

Inns of Court Archives:

Grays Inn: https://www.graysinn.org.uk/history/archives

Inner Temple: http://www.innertemple.org.uk/history/the-archives

Lincolns Inn: http://www.lincolnsinn.org.uk/index.php/library/the-inns-archives

Middle Temple: https://www.middletemple.org.uk/library-and-archive/

Institute and Faculty of Actuaries catalogue: https://www.actuaries.org.uk/learn-and-develop/research-and-knowledge/library-services/historical-collections

Institute of Chartered Accountants (England and Wales) catalogue: https://www.icaew.com/en/library/historical-resources/archives

King's College London Archives catalogue: https://www.kcl.ac.uk/library/archivespec/index.aspx

London Metropolitan Archives catalogue: https://www.cityoflondon.gov.uk/things-to-do/london-metropolitan-archives/Pages/search.aspx

London School of Economics Archives and Special Collections catalogue: http://www.lse.ac.uk/library/collections/collection-highlights/collections-highlights

Oxfordshire History Centre catalogue: https://www2.oxfordshire.gov.uk/cms/content/catalogues-oxfordshire-history-centre

The Peoples' History Museum catalogue: http://www.phm.org.uk/our-collection/

Political Parties and Parliamentary Archives Group, UK, Guide to Political Records: http://www.bodley.ox.ac.uk/pppag/pppag-records.htm

Political Parties and Parliamentary Archives Group, UK, Guide to Repositories holding Political Records: http://www.bodley.ox.ac.uk/pppag/pppag-repositories.htm

Records of Legal Education Archives catalogue: https://ials.sas.ac.uk/library/archives/ials-archives-collections/records-legal-education-archives-ials

Southwest Heritage Trust (Devon and Somerset) catalogues: https://www.swheritage.org.uk/online-catalogues

The National Archives' Accessions to Repositories: http://www.nationalarchives.gov.uk/accessions/

Transport for London Corporate Archives catalogue: https://tfl.gov.uk/corporate/about-tfl/culture-and-heritage/corporate-archives/the-collections

UK Web Archive: https://www.webarchive.org.uk/ukwa/

University College London Special Collections catalogue: http://www.ucl.ac.uk/library/special-collections/catalogues

Warwick University Library Modern Records Centre catalogue: http://mrc-catalogue.warwick.ac.uk

## *Codes of Conduct and Codes of Practice relevant to archives and managing records*

### *Archival*

The National Archives: *Code of Practice for Archivists and Records Managers under Section 51(4) of the Data Protection Act 1998*: http://www.nationalarchives.gov.uk/documents/information-management/dp-code-of-practice.pdf

Information Commissioner's Office: *Section 46 Code of Practice – Records Management, 2016*: https://ico.org.uk/media/for-organisations/documents/1624142/section-46-code-of-practice-records-management-foia-and-eir.pdf

UK Government Cabinet Office: *Freedom of Information Code of Practice*, 2018: https://www.gov.uk/government/publications/freedom-of-information-code-of-practice

### *Legal*

European Commission: *European Code of Conduct for Mediators*, 2004: http://ec.europa.eu/civiljustice/adr/adr_ec_code_conduct_en.pdf

Council for Licensed Conveyancers: *Code of Conduct*: https://www.clc-uk.org/wp-content/uploads/2017/12/Code-of-Conduct.pdf

Faculty Office: *Code of Practice for Notaries Rules for Recordkeeping and File Storage* (Chapter 17): http://www.facultyoffice.org.uk/notary/code-of-practice/ http://www.facultyoffice.org.uk/chapter/recordkeeping-and-file-storage/

The Law Society: *Solicitors' Code of Conduct 2011*: https://www.lawsociety.org.uk/support-services/advice/articles/solicitors--code-of-conduct-2011/

Institute of Barristers' Clerks: *Code of Conduct*: https://www.ibc.org.uk/wp-content/uploads/IBC_Code_of_Conduct.doc

Institute of Professional Willwriters: *Code of Practice*: https://www.ipw.org.uk/professional/code-of-practice

Society of Will Writers and Estate Planning Practitioners: *Code of Practice*: https://www.willwriters.com/code-of-practice/

## *Guidance on archives and managing records*

### *General:*

The National Archives: *Information management guidance and standards* (2018) http://www.nationalarchives.gov.uk/information-management/browse-guidance-standards/

Andrew C. Hamer, *The ICSA Guide to Document Retention, 3rd edition* (ICSA Publishing Ltd, 2011)

### Personal data:

TNA: *Archives and data protection law in the UK* (2018) https://webarchive.nationalarchives.gov.uk/+/https://www.nationalarchives.gov.uk/archives-sector/advice-and-guidance/managing-your-collection/archives-data-protection-law-uk/

TNA: *Guide to archiving personal data* (August 2018) http://www.nationalarchives.gov.uk/documents/information-management/guide-to-archiving-personal-data.pdf

Information Commissioner's Office: *Guide to the General Data Protection Regulation (2018)* https://ico.org.uk/for-organisations/guide-to-the-general-data-protection-regulation-gdpr/

### *Legal-specific:*

Barristers: *BSB Handbook* v 3.2 (1 Feb 2018), recommends (p. 268) that a record keeping policy be drawn up to identify compliance and records retention requirements. https://www.barstandardsboard.org.uk/regulatory-requirements/bsb-handbook/

Licensed Conveyancers: the Council for Licensed Conveyancers' *Handbook* advises on maintenance of proper records, compliance and retention of financial records. https://www.clc-uk.org/handbook/

Patent Attorneys and Trade Mark Attorneys: the Chartered Institutes of Patent Attorneys and Trade Mark Attorneys have produced joint *Business practice guidance* on ownership, storage and confidentiality of files: https://www.citma.org.uk/search/results?query=business+practice+guidance&Submit=Submit

## *Solicitors:*

The Law Society: Practice Notes:

- *Business continuity* https://www.lawsociety.org.uk/support-services/advice/practice-notes/business-continuity/
- *Closing down your practice: regulatory requirements* https://www.lawsociety.org.uk/support-services/advice/practice-notes/closing-down-your-practice/
- *Depositing records and documents with public sector archives* (currently not available from TLS; copies may be obtained from the BRA)
- *File closure management* https://www.lawsociety.org.uk/support-services/advice/practice-notes/file-closure-management/
- *File retention: trusts* https://www.lawsociety.org.uk/support-services/advice/practice-notes/file-retention-trusts/
- *File retention: wills and probate* https://www.lawsociety.org.uk/support-services/advice/practice-notes/file-retention-wills-and-probate/
- *Who owns the file?* https://www.lawsociety.org.uk/support-services/advice/practice-notes/who-owns-the-file/

The Solicitors Regulation Authority:

- Records retention schedule: https://www.sra.org.uk/sra/how-we-work/records-management.page
- SRA *Handbook* v 19 (1 Oct 2017) https://www.sra.org.uk/solicitors/handbook/welcome.page
- The new Statement of solicitor competence also includes a section (Section D) on the need to 'keep, use and maintain accurate, complete and clear records, including:
  - (a) Making effective use of information management systems (whether electronic or hard copy), including storing and retrieving information
  - (b) Complying with confidentiality, security, data protection and file retention and destruction requirements'.

LexisNexis guidance: http://www.lexisnexis.com/applieddiscovery/lawlibrary/whitePapers/ADI_WP_DocRetentionDestruction.pdf and https://www.lexisnexis.com/applieddiscovery/lawlibrary/whitePapers/ADI_WP_ElementsOfAGoodDocRetentionPolicy.pdf

Lexcel: *England and Wales Standard v.6 for legal practices* (downloadable from The Law Society website: https://www.lawsociety.org.uk/search/?q=Lexcel+standard)

Law firms' advice:

Bristows LLP in conjunction with Iron Mountain, *Document Retention Guide*, United Kingdom 2013

Herbert Smith, *Document Retention in England and Wales: law, practice and cross-border issues*, UK, 2011

Herbert Smith Freehills, *Document Retention: an International Review*, Legal Guide, Second Edition, 2013 https://www.herbertsmithfreehills.com/latest-thinking/document-retention-an-international-review

Will writers:

Society of Will Writers: *Practitioner's Guide to file retention* (http://will_writers.com/blog/practitioners-guide-file-retention/)

## *Stakeholder organisations' websites*

Archives and Artefacts Study Group (A2SN): http://www.a2sn.org.uk

Archives and Records Association: http://www.archives.org.uk

Bar Council: http://www.barcouncil.org.uk

The British Records Association: http://www.britishrecordsassociation.org.uk

The Business Archives Council http://www.businessarchivescouncil.org.uk and http://www.managingbusinessarchives.co.uk

Centre for Socio-Legal Studies: https://www.law.ox.ac.uk/centres-institutes/centre-socio-legal-studies

Charity Finance Group: http://cfg.org.uk

Chief Archivists in Local Government Group: http://www.archives.org.uk/about/community/groups/viewgroup/39–chief-archivists-in-local-government-group.html

Information and Records Management Society: http://irms.org.uk

Institute of Advanced Legal Studies: http://ials.sas.ac.uk

London Metropolitan Archives: https://www.cityoflondon.gov.uk/things-to-do/london-etropolitan-archives/Pages/default.aspx

Selden Society: http://www.selden-society.qmw.ac.uk

The Law Society: https://www.lawsociety.org.uk

The National Archives: http://www.nationalarchives.gov.uk

# Index

Lightning Source UK Ltd.
Milton Keynes UK
UKHW050453280819
348720UK00004B/45/P

9 781911 507147